PRAISE FOR *INSIDE MONEY*

"Powerful . . . There is something quietly stirring in the tale of Alexander Brown, a Belfast linen merchant who emigrated to Baltimore in 1800, and together with his four sons became, first, a major linen importer, then a dealer in cotton, coffee, copper, iron, and sugar, then a financier. Karabell, the author of several books on business and history, uses Brown Brothers as a lens into the nation's growth. . . . His narrative of a firm that remained private and true to its credo is engaging and new."
—*The New York Times Book Review*

"An engaging history . . . Karabell, who has worked in banking himself, tells a brisk and muscular story." —Robert Armstrong, *Financial Times*

"[*Inside Money* is] a book worth reading for anyone interested in the history of Wall Street, a well-told tale of how American finance evolved from a relative backwater into the collateralized colossus it is today." —*Forbes*

"Karabell weaves a fascinating tale of the East Coast WASP establishment."
—*Bloomberg*

"*Inside Money* can be read as a rather convincing declension narrative of the twentieth-century U.S. establishment, financiers, and foreign-policy mavens alike."
—*Foreign Policy*

"Karabell provides as good a discussion of the 'dollar diplomacy' and corporatism that defined that era as any I have read. These are complex ideas and a deeply challenging part of U.S. history. The blending of corporate and national interests in the late nineteenth and early twentieth centuries—a blending that led U.S. soldiers to literally die to protect the financial interests of the Brown family of bankers—is a valuable perspective through which we can view our present foreign entanglements."
—*American Banker*

"Karabell tells the tale with vigor, bringing the leading characters to life while locating their exploits in America's broader economic and political history. He does not shy away from darker episodes, acknowledging the cotton traders' dependence on the labor of slaves and exposing the casual anti-Semitism of some partners."
—*Reuters*

"Historian Karabell examines the long history of a financial services firm that exercised outsize power in the political sphere. . . . Karabell digs deep into the history of the intertwined firm, sometimes revealing uncomfortable truths, such as Brown Brothers' deep involvement in the Southern cotton economy and thus implication in the institution of slavery. In the balance, however, the more important story is the wedding of American money to global power. . . . A readable, unfailingly interesting study in the making of the American century." —*Kirkus Reviews*

"Extensively well researched . . . The history of American capitalism is intricately intertwined with the evolution of the private investment firm Brown Brothers Harriman. . . . Karabell had full access to the company's archives and has produced the first comprehensive inside story of Brown Brothers Harriman and the people behind it. A long overdue history." —*Library Journal* (starred review)

"Brown Brothers Harriman has weathered wars, banking panics, and stock market crashes by following Alexander Brown's advice to his sons, including 'avoid unnecessary risks,' don't trade with 'unvetted partners,' and 'be known as someone whom others could trust.' . . . Karabell draws an illuminating contrast between Brown Brothers Harriman and behemoths such as Chase and Goldman Sachs. Fans of business history will be rapt." —*Publishers Weekly*

"Author, columnist, and podcast host Karabell clarifies the record, revealing this bank's outsize influence in U.S. life, both in finance and in politics. . . . Karabell writes financial history compellingly, transcending dull accountancy with the drama of humans creating and managing wealth." —*Booklist*

"With judicious insight and a flair for storytelling, Zachary Karabell has made an immense contribution to understanding money and power in America, and globally. In this history of Brown Brothers Harriman we can chart the often-porous relationship between governance and capital at a time when both are under renewed stress and strain. Karabell's achievement is to give us the human story of seemingly abstract forces—and anyone who aspires to understand what Henry Luce called 'the American Century' and beyond will find Karabell's lucid and compelling book to be essential reading." —Jon Meacham

"*Inside Money* is a history of American capitalism with an unusual and welcome slant. Suppose the gospel of wealth included the idea of 'enough'? That partners in a firm could choose relationships over ever more riches? That greed could be subordinated to trust and integrity? Brown Brothers Harriman still has much to answer for, but its story tells us a great deal about the emergence of the winner-take-all world."
—Anne-Marie Slaughter, CEO of New America

"*Inside Money* is the sweeping and storied history of Brown Brothers Harriman, one of the great Wall Street firms, which came to embody that distinctive marriage of money and power that marked 'the American Century.' With his unique talents as a historian and one of our liveliest writers on finance, Zachary Karabell has crafted a wonderfully engrossing narrative, full of fascinating historical insights about the American elite at the height of its global influence."
—Liaquat Ahamed, Pulitzer Prize–winning author of *Lords of Finance*

"Zachary Karabell understands both money and American history. Here he weaves them together in a fascinating story that reads like a good multigenerational novel."
—Joseph S. Nye Jr., professor at Harvard and author of *Do Morals Matter?*

"A captivating secret history of the rise of the American way of capitalism through the story of one powerful and insular family firm, *Inside Money* reminds us that a dominant caste's sense of noblesse oblige conceals many ironies and much self-interest, but they knew when enough was enough and when private interest needed to give way to the public good." —Dambisa Moyo, economist and author of *Edge of Chaos*

"Zachary Karabell's *Inside Money* is a monumental history of behemoth investment firm Brown Brothers Harriman. Whether dealing with Wall Street intrigue or Big Railroad power or financial booms and busts, Karabell proves to be a master of his trade. It's impossible to understand how America became such a global power without reading this superb book. Highly recommended!"
—Douglas Brinkley, Katherine Tsanoff Brown Chair in Humanities and professor of history at Rice University and author of *American Moonshot*

"With his customary elegance and acuity, Karabell tells the engrossing story of one of America's most storied private banks, whose quiet influence did much to define the international system that took shape after World War II and endures, if perilously, to this day. A luminous work of history."
—Fredrik Logevall, professor at Harvard University and author of *JFK*

PENGUIN BOOKS

INSIDE MONEY

Zachary Karabell was educated at Columbia, Oxford and Harvard, where he received his PhD. He is a prolific commentator, both in print and on television, and the author of a dozen previous books, including *The Last Campaign*, which won the Chicago Tribune's Heartland Prize, and *The Leading Indicators*. He is also a longtime investor, former financial services executive and the founder of the Progress Network.

ALSO BY ZACHARY KARABELL

INSIDE MONEY

BROWN BROTHERS

HARRIMAN

and the

AMERICAN WAY

OF POWER

ZACHARY KARABELL

PENGUIN BOOKS

PENGUIN BOOKS
An imprint of Penguin Random House LLC
penguinrandomhouse.com

First published in the United States of America by Penguin Press,
an imprint of Penguin Random House LLC, 2021
Published in Penguin Books 2022

Illustration credits: Insert p. 1 (top) and p. 8 (bottom): courtesy of BBH; p. 1 (middle): Granger;
p. 1 (bottom) and p. 3 (bottom): Library of Congress, Prints and Photographs Division; p. 2 (top): Gift of
David Edward Finley and Margaret Eustis Finley, Courtesy National Gallery of Art, Washington;
p. 2 (bottom left): © The Trustees of the British Museum; p. 2 (bottom right) and p. 5 (right):
Brown Brothers Harriman Records, MS 78, Collection of the New York Historical Society; p. 4 (bottom)
and p. 6 (bottom): courtesy of the author; p. 4 (top): Rykoff Collection/CORBIS/Corbis via Getty Images;
p. 5 (left): From The New York Times. © 1930 The New York Times Company. All rights reserved.
Used under license; p. 6 (top right): from TIME. © 1948 TIME USA LLC. All rights reserved.
Used under license; p. 6 (top left), Everett Collection/Bridgeman Images; p. 7 (top): National Museum of
the U.S. Navy; p. 7 (bottom), Dmitri Kessel/The LIFE Picture Collection via Getty Images; p. 8 (top),
Herbert Gehr/The LIFE Picture Collection via Getty Images.

Picture Research by Toby Greenberg

ISBN 9780143110842 (paperback)

Printed in the United States of America
1st Printing

BOOK DESIGN BY LUCIA BERNARD

Contents

INTRODUCTION

In the cold dark of a premarket December morning in 1930, four clerks emerged from the service entrance of the office building at 39 Broadway, each with a cart loaded with documents. They hauled those carts for only a few blocks, to the newly refurbished and expanded offices at 59 Wall Street, the marbled site of one of the most storied firms on Wall Street, Brown Brothers. The carts contained stock and bond certificates that the Harriman family, whose fortune had been born in the railroad boom, had accumulated from Europe and the United States, tens of millions of dollars of notes that were themselves precious assets. The street was barely stirring, but each trip of several hundred yards was escorted by a security guard, armed and alert.

The day before, a small innocuous headline had explained why those clerks were transferring millions of dollars from one office to another: BIG BANKING HOUSES DECIDE ON MERGER. Though meriting a front-page mention in *The New York Times*, the announcement was dwarfed by the two major stories of that day in 1930: the collapse of the mammoth Bank of United States and the demand by President Herbert Hoover that Congress pass an emergency employment bill to stem the bleeding in the U.S. labor market. In the weeks and months ahead, stories of collapse and chaos would proliferate, but the new banking house survived and thrived. That was surprising, though it shouldn't have been. Brown Brothers had always survived, through crisis after crisis, as it still does today.

What we now call the Great Depression was in full force on December 12, 1930, the day of the announcement. More than 1,200 banks had already closed their doors, their deposits lost forever as vaults were drained by panicked customers who had watched the stock market collapse at the end of 1929 and who had then seen a brief false dawn followed by much worse. No federal deposit insurance covered those losses, and no safety net existed to cushion the fall. The panic infected every segment of society, from farming to banking, from manufacturing to retail, and then spread throughout the world.

Yet no outward sign of distress would have been noticed one fall day in 1930 when a group of nattily dressed young men chartered a railcar on the New Haven line to take them from Grand Central Station to their college reunion at Yale. They were a self-confident lot, in their midthirties, ambitious, all of them born to wealth, none of them having known a day of want. Among them was a tall and lanky man named Prescott Bush. He had married well, wedding the daughter of George Herbert Walker of St. Louis, who had started his own investment firm before becoming president of W. A. Harriman & Co., founded by Averell Harriman, the debonair yet tight-lipped eldest son of the pugnacious railroad baron E. H. Harriman. Prescott had gone from selling rubber flooring to working as a vice president at Harriman with his college friend Roland "Bunny" Harriman, Averell's younger and more easygoing brother. Roland wasn't on the train that day, but Ellery James and Knight Woolley were. Ellery was a partner at Brown Brothers, and Knight, who was rarely without a bespoke double-breasted suit, was managing partner of another one of the Harriman firms. These young men were entwined by professional and personal bonds, each having been sworn into Yale's exclusive Skull and Bones society before enlisting in the military for America's brief and bloody participation in World War I. Their tight circle included not only the Harriman brothers but also the wiry, intense Robert A. Lovett, whose father, Robert S. Lovett, had served as the elder Harriman's general counsel.

But while they had reveled in the prosperity of the 1920s, they were not immune to the storms outside in 1930. As they headed to their reunion, cosseted in their private car, playing poker for stakes well in excess of the average weekly wage for millions of Americans, they knew that all was not well in the world. Both Harriman and Brown Brothers were teetering under the weight of credit they had extended to businesses that could no longer repay. Given the deep personal connections between the partners of the firms, it must have seemed organic when the idea of a merger was broached over poker and scotch. Other firms weren't merging; they were collapsing, and both Harriman and Brown Brothers needed to shore up their business and preserve their capital.

Brown Brothers had more than a century on Harriman's firm. It was a titan of Wall Street, but in reputation and standing rather than size. It was not particularly large in assets, but its influence and reach were as extensive as the flashier J.P. Morgan & Co. or the much larger Chase National Bank, which was infused with Rockefeller money. Because Brown Brothers was a partnership without one figurehead, it attracted neither notoriety nor much public attention, and it did not have the benefit of one man's fortune ever at the ready. The partners of Brown Brothers shunned the public spotlight and cultivated a sterling reputation within the close-knit world of finance and banking. To become a partner, each man had to be invited and then was required to contribute his share to the firm's working capital. Like all partnerships, Brown Brothers lent and invested the partners' money. Each deal had to be assessed in terms of how much of their own personal fortune they were willing to risk. In sharp contrast to the investment banks and venture firms and private equity groups of today, the partners at Brown Brothers were not agents acting on behalf of anonymous shareholders or mammoth institutions. Every Brown Brothers partner was *personally* exposed. They could gain immensely or lose painfully from each deal.

But by the end of 1930, as the economic collapse accelerated not just in the United States but around the world, transactions and deals that had looked sound and wise a year earlier turned sour. Even after each of the Brown Brothers partners had ponied up more money to cover losses, they were skirting peril. The firm had been in business for more than 120 years, since Alexander Brown set up shop, aided by his four sons, in Baltimore. It was unclear whether it could last into 1931. Thatcher Brown, great-grandson of Alexander and managing partner of his firm, saw that drastic action was necessary. Though nearly a generation separated him from those young bucks on the train, Thatcher, a product of the same schools and the same upbringing, was essentially an older version of them. The cohort of younger Yale grads saw the opportunity, but it was Thatcher and his older cousin James who understood the need. So did Averell Harriman, who was flush with the millions provided by his father's fortune. He had money, but his business was struggling as well. Brown Brothers had the history and the standing. And so, following that genial conversation over cards and drinks in a first-class railcar, it was agreed that the two firms would merge to save both, with the fortune of Harriman attached to the reputation of Brown Brothers.

For Wall Street, that innocuous December *New York Times* headline wasn't so innocuous. It signaled to the financial world that two of the major players of Wall Street would, at least for the moment, be fine. In a time of rampant bank closures and widespread panic, the announcement of the formation of Brown Brothers Harriman was a respite, a message that said, "It will be all right; there is shelter in the storm."

The Great Depression would get considerably worse before it got better, but Brown Brothers Harriman remained standing and became a pillar of what would soon be called the American Establishment. Its partners would play a central role in the creation of what *Time*'s founding editor and fellow Yale alum Henry Luce dubbed "the American century," a mid-twentieth-century imperium that saw a marriage of American money and American power that spanned the globe. It didn't last a century, but at its apex, the American century was staffed by Brown Brothers. Prescott Bush served as a U.S. senator for Connecticut and progenitor of two presidents. Lovett became assistant secretary of war, assistant secretary of state, and finally secretary of defense during the height of the Korean War. Averell Harriman would have a long career as a diplomat and statesman, serving as Franklin

Roosevelt's envoy to Stalin, secretary of commerce under Truman and then governor of New York and finally as the most senior diplomat in the Kennedy and Johnson State Department, though not, to his unspoken chagrin, as secretary of state. These men were, as Dean Acheson (who to his everlasting pride *was* secretary of state) would later remark, present at the creation. They defined the Cold War political and economic system that governed the world after World War II, a system that remains largely, if shakily, in place. Directly or indirectly, this cohort created every major institution that shapes the international system today, from the World Trade Organization to NATO to the United Nations to the World Bank. They established the primacy of the almighty dollar. And they built the apparatus of the American national security state, including the Defense Department, the National Security Council and the CIA.

The influence of the firm, however, is even deeper than that, spanning nearly the entire history of the United States. The firm started, as most ventures do, innocuously enough, founded at the turn of the nineteenth century by an immigrant with modest dreams, an Irish refugee fleeing the sectarian violence of his homeland. He set up a linen importing business in Baltimore, which morphed into a merchant bank, and as it grew and evolved under his sons, Brown Brothers helped turn the United States into a country where money had an outsized role. The American economic system was messy, chaotic and often hugely destructive even as it unlocked unprecedented potential. The House of Brown, straddling the Atlantic with branches in Liverpool, Baltimore, Philadelphia and New York, was at the center of the alchemy, managed by a family of upright, God-loving bankers, fathers and sons and then grandsons, steeped in rectitude and service, at times dull, always—more or less—honorable. In a world where money was plentiful, and promiscuously so, it helped to have stolid bankers at the choke point, regulating the flow, steering through crises, keeping the excesses of greed and panic at bay.

In the United States, the pursuit of profit was woven into the founding fabric, not as explicitly as the pursuit of happiness but there all the same. The Jeffersonian ideal was a nation of yeoman farmers guarding their freedoms and independence, but it was Alexander Hamilton's financial system that ultimately defined the economy. Following the Revolutionary War and then the War of 1812, which sealed American independence, the United States began its ascent to become the world's largest economy within little more than a century. How that happened has been a source of constant debate. Perhaps it was a function of a vastly fruitful continent, the lack of regional competition, the protection afforded by two oceans, the influx of immigrants who brought their own dreams and ambitions and then inscribed those on a new nation, or none of those or all of them. But perhaps the key lies in one of Alexis de Tocqueville's many piercing observations: "I know of no other country where love of money has such a grip on men's hearts."

One of the prerequisites for rapid economic growth is capital. Land, property and labor are all vital, but none are liquid. For much of human history, wealth locked up in land and property was rarely turned into productive capital to fund businesses or ideas. That began to change in the nineteenth century, and the United States was ground zero for the shift. Money, especially in the form of paper promises, was a fuel. In the United States, making money and putting it in motion came easily, often too easily. Money flooded markets, and then receded. It unlocked potential, and then unleashed havoc. Unburdened by an entrenched aristocracy of land or church, and with the Jeffersonian ideal of yeoman farmers shunted aside in favor of a Hamiltonian economy, nineteenth-century America became a land of money.

Until the Civil War, it wasn't federal money. There were coins minted by the federal government, but those floated in a sea of paper promises issued by different banks and merchant firms such as Brown Brothers. Coins mattered, but paper was everywhere. It was a bewildering mix, kaleidoscopic and constantly changing. There is always a tension between order and chaos, and it is hard to find the right balance between just enough chaos to nurture innovation and enough order to keep everything from unwinding. Hence the sharp and constant economic crises of the nineteenth century. But that roiling, unsettling and harmful though it could be, was outweighed by the advantages. If you had a good idea in America, you had a better chance than anywhere in the world of finding money to fund it. Capital rarely flowed evenly; the 1870s and 1880s were flush with capital for the railroads but not so much for the working class or the farmers. Throughout the nineteenth century, there was paper money and credit, but there was also gold and silver, land and labor. The United States was fluid compared with the Old World, but it was easier to lose a fortune or never make one than to ascend the heights.

Brown Brothers acted as a conduit. From early in the nineteenth century, it became one of the primary channels through which money flowed. And flow it did, to merchants and their ships, to cotton plantations and to railroads and new farms and new towns and new businesses in the sprawling vastness of the continent. Brown Brothers facilitated that trade, first between Liverpool and Baltimore, and then once off-loaded by stevedores onto wagons, from Baltimore to the Ohio Valley. It funded, with offices in England and the Americas, successive generations of ocean-crossing vessels, some of which it owned outright, and for a brief moment, the house had a monopoly on the shipment of the Royal Mail from England to the United States. The Browns spurred the birth of transatlantic steamships and underwrote the Collins Line, which might have surpassed Cunard had it not been for a tragic accident. They created the first railroad, the one we all know from games of Monopoly, the Baltimore & Ohio line, the B&O. They expanded to Philadelphia and to New York, and their reach grew. They were financial innovators and one of the largest cotton merchants in the world. So influential was Brown Brothers by the mid-nineteenth century that when the thunderous celebrity preacher Henry Ward Beecher wanted to make a point from his pulpit in Brooklyn, he constructed an entire sermon lambasting his congregants for placing more faith in letters of credit issued by Brown Brothers than they did in God.

Brown Brothers was, in short, woven into the economic fabric of nineteenth-century America, its transportation network and its trade, with the cotton South and the agrarian West, with England and by extension with the rest of the world. It provided the credit that was more trusted than the notes issued by governments or the promises printed with abandon by the wildcat banks that dotted the American frontier. Paper issued by the House of Brown was essential to commerce, and without trusted paper, trade at the scale and scope required would have been impossible. The Browns determined exchange rates, and they provided travelers with letters to use abroad, which was a necessary prerequisite to a more interconnected world. Wherever American commerce flowed, Brown Brothers was there to keep it flowing. It didn't just make money for itself; it made money for America. And without money, there would be no rise of the United States as a global power.

In the nineteenth century, the economic ambitions of the United States focused primarily on conquering the continent. But the conservative qualities that allowed Brown Brothers to thrive and survive in the first half of the century kept them largely on the sidelines of the investment craze of the second half of the nineteenth century: the railroads. Alexander Brown and his sons had helped create the first American railroad in the 1830s, but they largely eschewed the railroad boom in the decades after the 1860s. Fortunes were there to be made, but most of the railroads went bust, leaving their investors with worthless stocks. The innate caution of Brown Brothers prevented them from reaching the heights of J.P. Morgan, but it almost certainly protected them from being deluged by waves of bankruptcies and failures. Then the Great Depression hit.

The merger of Brown Brothers and Harriman blended two distinct cultures born of different paths to success. In the late nineteenth century, the lasting money was usually made by those who picked up the pieces after the initial railroad investors had lost everything, which was how E. H. Harriman built his empire. He was, in the 1890s, the nouveau riche, crass and aggressive, a rough and tough bundle of intensity. He courted attention where the partners of Brown Brothers avoided it. But while Edward Harriman and Alexander Brown could hardly have been more unlike, by the time Harriman's fortune merged with the House of Brown in the 1930s, the world of his sons and of the next generations of Browns was more similar than not, nurtured by a small set of boarding schools and colleges that distilled the values of their fathers into a coherent, rigid web of money, duty and service that became the backbone of "the Establishment."

The world this elite created after 1945 was not by design or intent. After the ravages of the Depression and a harrowing war, the United States found itself with immense relative power confronted by an adversary in the Soviet Union that was championing a system antithetical to its own. Whether the conflict of the Cold War was inevitable, Brown Brothers and the Establishment saw no other path. To meet the challenge, they distilled a formula to defend the world they knew and that they believed would serve everyone just as it had served them. The framework they erected unleashed the productive capital of the world, and established the foundation for the globalization of commerce and capital that so defined the rest of the twentieth century and the beginning of the twenty-first.

Having reached the apex of its influence in the years immediately following World War II, Brown Brothers, by the end of the twentieth century, had faded in relevance. Its competitors, the firms of Goldman Sachs, J.P. Morgan, Morgan Stanley, and so many others, elected to go public in the 1980s, turning what had been skin-in-the-game partnerships into publicly traded entities relying on shareholder capital instead of their own. Those firms used that money. They accumulated almost unprecedented wealth, and they courted attention. That allowed them to outstrip Brown Brothers in size and scope, and, perhaps most critically, in greed and ambition. And then, in 2008, they almost destroyed the system they had made and that had made them.

Brown Brothers Harriman stayed out of that fray. Today the firm remains a large global financial institution with more than five thousand employees across the world. Its business has changed radically. It now acts as a custodian for trillions of dollars of global assets, a large amount of money that earns the firm relatively small but steady fees. Its culture revolves around service. In cleaving to the idea of a partnership, the company didn't join the drunken capital party of the 1990s and 2000s and never rose so high that it could jeopardize the entire financial system. In that crucial sense, it stands as a reminder of what once was, and perhaps what all these banks should have remained. Mention the firm today, and many wonder if it still exists, if they wonder at all; others shake their heads and sigh as if to say, "How sad." It is not at all. Given how close the global financial system came to the abyss in 2008–9, and given that it was caused by the detachment of personal gain from public risk, the quiet continuance of Brown Brothers Harriman is a lesson for what capitalism can be. It provided the fuel, and it also set boundaries.

For sure, its particular ethos of service could mask a multitude of sins. Without question, it was self-serving and self-enriching, but more often than not it also served the needs of society at large. That was not without its own excesses. The firm was crucial to the cotton trade, and cotton depended on the labor of enslaved men and women. At the beginning of the twentieth century, Brown Brothers plunged into financing businesses and banks in Central America, indifferent to the disruptions that ensued, and then worked closely with the U.S. government to overthrow a government that threatened its investments. That was the darker side of how money made the world.

We live in a time when we have all become acutely aware of the role of capital as the glue binding our economy and as tinder that can cause it to implode. Spread widely, it can be a ballast; spread too unevenly, it can open fissures. Money can create a nation; it can energize technology revolutions, from the steamships and the railroads to the internet and the smartphone. But it can also unleash greed and deluge industries and countries, causing shocks that can shake society to its core. It can spread wealth but also concentrate it. It is indifferent to inequality. Nonetheless, the American formula, a capitalism distilled in the mid-twentieth century composed of rules and laws designed by Americans and cemented by the dollar, has been the formula for the world, from a China governed by the Communist Party whose economy is capitalist to the core, to a Nigeria whose government may be corrupt but whose society is market driven, from Scandinavian countries whose social contract flirts with socialism to authoritarian regimes in the Middle East that suppress expression but court investment.

Fiat money and the dollar are the bedrock of the global system, and Brown Brothers is part of the underwritten history of how that world came to be. Money is the power contained in the atom, which is why having people who believe their role is to serve the greater good and consider themselves stewards is a necessary prerequisite for a stable society. The Hippocratic oath does not guarantee that doctors will do good, but it tries to ensure that they knowingly do no harm. And in an age of pandemics and economic crises, Brown Brothers also demonstrates that being ever prepared for a storm is not just prudent; it is imperative.

The story of the Brown Brothers is the secret history of Wall Street. It is a story of sustainable capitalism. You might not like it if you object to capitalism, but you might want to emulate it to guard against capitalism's inevitable excesses and imbalances. After the 1980s, their model of capitalism was superseded by more avaricious and ultimately more toxic variants, which is all the more reason to remember that other paths are possible. The partners of Brown Brothers have never wanted to be *the story*, and that reticence has made the firm's centrality easy to overlook. But it is an underground river that flows through the American past, and its saga is a window into the crucial nexus of money, power and influence that made America. It is at times a heroic tale, sometimes prosaic and beneath the veneer of gentility, occasionally brutal and rapacious. But such is the history of America, of global capitalism and of any rise to power. Celebrated or reviled, it is necessary history, and in the case of Brown Brothers, one that has never been adequately understood. This is their story, and ours.

CHAPTER 1

COMING TO AMERICA

Like most things American, the Establishment had immigrant roots. Brown Brothers started life not in New York and not in the United States but in Ireland. The business that eventually morphed into a pillar of Wall Street began with the ambitions and tribulations of a middle-class Irishman named Alexander Brown, born in 1764 near the town of Ballymena, in County Antrim, some twenty-five miles north of Belfast. Alexander was destined at birth for a modest life, a destiny he defied.

By the age of twenty, he was married to Grace Davison, forever known thereafter as Mrs. Alexander Brown, and in short order they had seven children. Four survived infancy: William (born in 1784), George (1787), John (1788), and James (1791). The deaths of the other three were painful but in that era and in that place hardly unusual. By the early 1790s, Alexander had moved his business to Belfast to become a linen merchant, and by all accounts proved more than adept. He was better than decent looking, with fine, defined features, high cheekbones, sharp but not unkind eyes seen behind a pair of scholarly spectacles, a slight hook in his nose, and a mess of wavy curls that stayed tight even as they turned gray.

Linen was the primary industry of Ireland. The flax was grown on local farms, and in the words of one observer at the time, "There is scarcely a cottage without a loom." Once spun, in modest batches at farm after farm, the linen cloth was bleached to make it attractive for sale, dried out on the local grass, and then sent on to Belfast, where it was auctioned at Linen Hall by men such as Alexander Brown. Dublin was also a vibrant linen trading center, but Belfast had the advantage—or disadvantage, depending on your denomination and allegiance—of closer links to England. Unlike the predominantly Catholic south, Belfast and its surroundings had a considerable population of Protestants, many of whom were Presbyterian, descended either from Scottish settlers or from the Huguenots who fled France at the end of the seventeenth century.[1]

Like most Ulstermen, Brown was from a Presbyterian family. Creed mattered, but Alexander focused his passion on business and family, not doctrine and politics. As in most families, there were struggles. All of the four sons who survived infancy performed poorly at the local classroom, no matter how much their parents implored, and no matter how much their teachers cajoled or punished them. The reasons for their academic woes were hard to fathom. Alexander and Grace did not think that their sons were especially slow; quite the opposite. The boys were curious and animated, in varying degrees, and by all rights they should have been doing well at school. They had loving, supportive parents and a stable home. Something was clearly off. After a few exasperating years, the family discovered the problem: the boys were all extremely nearsighted. Once they had each been fitted with glasses, their academic performance improved and the disciplinary issues vanished. But the genetics remained. Poor eyesight was passed down over the generations and became known in the family as Brown sight.

Wanting to make the most of their sons' nascent talents, the Browns looked to better schooling. Alexander was by then successful enough that he was able to send each of the sons to a boarding school in England, in Yorkshire, run by a local Anglican minister. Family lore held that the boys received a stellar education in typically drab, dull and austere conditions. The budget-conscious headmaster skimped on food costs but promised the hungry students a second helping of pudding (hardly a treat but rather a mushy starch flavored with the fat drippings of the roast) provided that they didn't eat too much of the meat itself. Whatever lesson that imparted, the boys learned the classics by rote, along with a steady diet of bland pudding, staid liturgy and arbitrary discipline.

And there things might have stayed, with Alexander primed for the life of a prosperous linen merchant and broker, had it not been for the Irish rebellion of 1798. Not for the first time and not for the last, Ireland was rent by conflict triggered by resistance to English rule. The United Irishmen—a movement that included both Catholics and Protestants and was inspired by the American and French revolutions—rebelled after years of trying peacefully to carve out more autonomy from the British Crown. They looked to the French, embroiled again in war with the British, for aid. The French were willing but not able. The rebellion ended badly for the Irish, who were not only slaughtered at the battle of Vinegar Hill but who also then fragmented violently into Protestant versus Catholic and Protestant versus Protestant factions. Much of the fighting took place in the counties surrounding Belfast and sharply disrupted the linen business. Apolitical though he was, Alexander could not escape the collateral damage of the rebellion and its violent defeat.

For reasons that remain obscure, Alexander went into hiding and then rather suddenly left the country in 1800 and sailed for Baltimore, along with Grace and his eldest son, William, leaving his three younger sons still in school in Yorkshire. The rebellion and its bloody suppression had taken a toll on his business, and like many, he almost certainly confronted pressure to choose a side. Alexander managed to stay alive and preserve his considerable wealth, and he decided that a sectarian Ireland riven by strife and ruled by an increasingly repressive British army was not where he wanted to be, economically or politically. He left no record of how he engineered the move, but even if he had, it is unlikely he would have waxed maudlin or bemoaned the sudden shift. Life was life. Crises were inevitable. How one managed those was what mattered.

At the turn of the nineteenth century, Baltimore was a major port and the commercial gateway for Virginia and the states to the south. Fine Irish linens were much in demand among the plantation barons and for those who strove for the finer things. Linen was supple and durable, especially valuable in the humid climate of the American South. The American cotton industry was still in its infancy; most of the southern plantations produced tobacco. Soon enough, cotton production would explode and cotton textiles would supplant the linen trade, causing severe economic disruption in Ireland, for which Alexander bears some indirect responsibility. As Brown Brothers became the major facilitator of the southern cotton trade after 1820, which ran through Liverpool and not Belfast, Alexander helped undercut the very business that had made him in the first place.

The choice of Baltimore was not only economic, however. Alexander had family there; a distant in-law of Grace's had immigrated in the 1780s, followed by Alexander's younger brother Stewart, whose son by the same name would later become an integral part of the firm. Stewart settled in Baltimore to facilitate the family's linen trade, and that smoothed the way for Alexander to abandon his business in Ireland, book passage to the United States and establish himself as a linen importer in the New World.

There is some irony in the fact that Alexander left an Ireland bitterly divided between Catholic and Protestant to move to the one community in the United States that had a substantial Catholic populace. Maryland was founded by George Calvert, Lord Baltimore, and then overseen by his son Cecil as a haven for Catholics trying to avoid persecution in the fractious England of the mid-seventeenth century. For more than a century, the colony (much like most of the early settlements outside of a few towns that barely could be called cities) was almost entirely agrarian. The city of Baltimore wasn't developed until the early eighteenth century, and it fast became the most important mid-Atlantic port in the colonies. By the time Alexander arrived in 1800, it had more than 20,000 inhabitants and was firmly established as one of the commercial centers of the new country, along with Philadelphia, New York and Boston to the north, and French New Orleans to the south.

As promising as the city was, however, its grandees understood that New York was likely to be the commercial capital of the new nation unless

Baltimore took extraordinary measures. New York had a bigger, more navigable harbor as well as the Hudson River, and its population and its commercial activity were increasing more quickly. Even so, at the turn of the century, New York's advantages had not yet made it a clear winner. Its inhabitants were packed into Lower Manhattan. Most everything north of Canal Street was patchy farmland, and visitors could be forgiven for thinking that New York had not yet made the most of its natural advantages. If Alexander considered settling in New York, there is no record. He had connections in Baltimore, which was dynamic and rapidly growing in a dynamic and rapidly expanding America. New York was the future of Brown Brothers and of American trade and finance; in 1800, Baltimore was its present.

While the new world of the United States had immense potential, it was far less developed than England or even Ireland. Dublin alone had a population of close to 200,000 in 1800, and that was in turn dwarfed by London. With barely 5 million people spread out from Georgia to Massachusetts, from Maryland to the Ohio River valley, the United States was almost entirely rural, with some basic industry in the Northeast, but most commerce concentrated in agricultural exports and the import of finished goods. The bulk of trade was with Great Britain, and though American merchants ventured far, including into the Mediterranean Sea, the American economy was still tightly bound with the country that it had so recently been a part of. Cities such as Baltimore, Philadelphia and New York were the locus of economic growth and offered opportunity because they had established themselves as marketplaces in a country that was still finding its way as an independent nation. They were the parts of the United States most closely tied, economically, to England, Europe and the Caribbean.[2] They also were crucial to the finances of the federal government—state governments depended on property taxes, while the federal government relied on whatever duties it could collect from the export trade and tariffs on imported goods.

Outside of these centers of commerce, people were largely self-sufficient. Almost 90 percent of the population eked out a living from the land. Basic necessities were made by each family in their homes, barns and workshops, rather than purchased from a small factory, let alone imported from abroad. Rural Americans in 1800 rarely used coin money and even more rarely paper in their daily lives. They had their own land, and their farms were microeconomies. The yeoman farmers so admired by Thomas Jefferson grew their own food and made what they needed.

In the small towns and burgeoning cities, however, it was a different story, with merchants thriving or surviving on commissions and craftsmen and laborers living on wages, often precariously. While most Americans were tied to the land, already by 1800 the new United States had developed a reputation in Europe as a nation of commerce populated by a people ambitious for more. Said one French observer, "Everywhere, everything is for sale, provided the owner is offered a tempting price. He will part with his house, his carriage, his horse, his dog—anything at all."[3] The rapid growth of the country after 1800 created endless possibilities. Settlers poured by the hundreds of thousands over the Allegheny Mountains and into the new territories and states stretching west toward the Mississippi River. Even though most economic activity was local, with largely self-sufficient homes and farms, more people streaming into the country and more settlements meant more trade and more industry, especially for the ports of the mid-Atlantic.

Cloth was a ubiquitous human necessity, and while anyone with some sheep, a spinning wheel and some needles or a small loom could—and often did—make woolen clothes, if those could be bought already made for a reasonable price, that would save considerable time and energy. Wool was adequate, linen was useful, but cotton was far more malleable, comfortable and scalable. The basic, universal need for more cloth—along with the innovation of the industrial cotton gin, which made cotton production at a much larger scale possible—drove the transition of the South after 1800 into a cotton economy. That system was erected on the backs of enslaved men and women, and enabled by merchants and bankers, Brown Brothers among them. But even before the rise of cotton, the cloth economy was a prime factor in the evolution of the northern coastal cities. Linen made it possible for Alexander Brown and his family to leave Ireland on short notice and quickly establish themselves as significant players in transatlantic commerce. Merchants had been facilitating the trade between England, America, the Caribbean and beyond for more than a century. But with the United States newly independent, with tens of thousands of loyalists having fled the coastal cities during the Revolution in the 1780s to relocate in Canada and with a postwar surge in immigration to the former colonies, Alexander arrived at a propitious time and as an importer of linen filled an ongoing need.

Linen was only the start. With so much trade flooding into Baltimore, and with the city a prime hub for the export of Virginia plantation-grown tobacco, Alexander added exporting to his business. Then he arranged for the rest of his family to relocate. Each of the other three sons left school in Yorkshire and joined their father and mother in America. Finally, Alexander dispatched his eldest son, William, to Liverpool to become the family's local point person. After shuttling back and forth, William married and settled permanently in Liverpool, where he anchored the House of Brown for the next forty years and became a man of some influence, not just in that burgeoning port but in national politics as a representative in Parliament.

The wide and shallow River Mersey made Liverpool a perfectly protected harbor off the Irish Sea. In the early eighteenth century, Liverpool was a sleepy village. A century later, after a stratospheric rise, it was one of the busiest ports in the world, with tentacles reaching not just North America and the Caribbean but India and beyond. Liverpool became the primary port for the industries of Lancashire, proximate to Birmingham and Manchester. Its natural advantages were necessary but not sufficient. Without human ingenuity engineering an elaborate dock system and then decades of work building those docks and dredging the shallows of the Mersey estuary, the city would never have become the principle gateway into England and then out to the world.[4]

The House of Brown thrived in its first years. Alexander deployed his sons, mentoring them and using them as trusted lieutenants, William most of all. He intended to create a lasting family business, and training his sons was imperative. While William soon became the point person in Liverpool, Alexander insisted he spend time in Baltimore to ensure that he understood both sides of the equation; in turn, he sent his other sons to Liverpool to learn that side of the business, which involved building close relationships with the competitive English merchant community and learning the rhythms of how prices moved.

The primary threat to his growing business in these years wasn't competition, however, but rather the volatile and tense relationship between the United States and Great Britain, and the unpredictable power and reach of Napoleonic France. As Britain and France continued their interminable war, now between a Napoleon poised to rule over Europe and a British imperial state determined not to allow that, the United States was buffeted by the attempts of each to cut the other off from vital trade. The French passed laws outlawing trade by neutral countries with England; Parliament passed laws forbidding all trade with France. Eventually, unable to protect American ships from boarding and seizure by the British navy and helpless to prevent American seamen from being pressed into involuntary service, the United States under Thomas Jefferson passed the Embargo Act in 1807, banning American trade with both countries.

That was not good for Alexander Brown, but he was able to muddle through. The end of Jefferson's administration in 1809 ended the embargo, but the relief was short-lived. Spurred by yet another punitive attempt by Great Britain to restrict American trade, the government of James Madison inched toward a conflict that had been brewing for years, even though the commercial community and the northern states were vigorously opposed to further tension and lobbied aggressively for peaceful relations with their main trading partner. Alexander had built a new business based entirely on commerce between the United States and Great Britain and had navigated years of unpredictable and arbitrary restrictions. He had close connections with the English merchant community in Liverpool, and William had astutely cultivated good relations with royal and parliamentary officials in London. By 1812, Alexander was enjoying a stable franchise even with the embargoes, but a full-out war would place a much greater and unwelcome burden on his fledging business.

In the spring of 1812, William was in Baltimore while his younger brothers George and John were temporarily managing the business in Liverpool. The Browns—and many other merchants—erroneously thought that the intense opposition to war in New York, New England and the central states would keep Madison from plunging into a conflict whose outcome was hardly clear. That proved to be wishful thinking. Until the actual declaration of war, Alexander continued to believe that it would be avoided, not just because his business would be harmed but because he honestly believed that armed conflict would be a terrible mistake for the United States. "I still think it impossible our Executive can have any serious intention of going to war with England, in the unprepared state of this country," he wrote to George in Liverpool in April. Not for the only time, a belief that deep economic ties would prevent war proved to be sadly wrong.

Alexander was hardly the only one surprised by the war, but he was not unprepared. While he was gravely wrong in his expectations, he was not one to assume the best. He instructed his sons to plan for various contingencies, ranging from continued embargoes to war. The family under Alexander's direction also wisely stocked up on cargoes such as tobacco that were likely to go up significantly in price if war was declared. That proved to be a lucrative call. George, however, did not heed that directive and sold large amounts of tobacco in Liverpool as the drums of war beat louder. Though Alexander didn't think war would actually be declared, he wanted to be able to sell at higher prices if it happened. He berated George for precipitous selling that cost the family lost profits: "A moment's reflection should have told you that war would double and treble the price of tobacco. I am greatly disturbed and distressed over your action in selling." Alexander insisted that in the face of uncertainty, it is always better to hedge and take fewer risks. That also guided his decision to relocate the ship he had recently commissioned, the *Armata*, an investment that had consumed considerable capital, away from the North Atlantic shipping lanes to the neutral port of Lisbon, in Portugal. That would put it out of commission, but it would also ensure that it was not seized.

In addition to advising William and George to refrain from selling goods should demand for them spike with the outbreak of hostilities, Alexander told his sons to reduce any outstanding paper obligations. Like all merchants, the Browns used paper in lieu of holding large amounts of gold and silver to settle trades. Soon enough, Brown Brothers would become a leader in issuing paper promissory notes and profit handily as bankers, but in 1812, the family operated as typical merchants. Most of its notes involved promises of future payments on a certain date; if, for instance, the firm had taken tobacco on consignment from a Virginia plantation, it might have issued the planter a note saying that it would pay X dollars by Y date once it had sold the tobacco in Liverpool. Already by 1812, there was a vigorous market for buying and selling those notes, just as there is today for all sorts of financial instruments. The House of Brown was by then doing some modest business not just as a merchant buying and selling goods but as a banker buying and selling paper notes. Alexander understood that any paper instruments promising future payments were immensely vulnerable should war prevent ships from sailing or unloading goods in enemy ports. Whatever his expectations, he knew he had no control over what London and Washington might do. He instructed his sons to curtail the family's paper holdings as quickly as possible, before it was too late and they were left with worthless promises of payment for goods that could not be delivered.

Alexander had no aversion to using paper credits to facilitate trade. His wariness in 1812 was purely tactical. If anything, the War of 1812 made him less enamored of trading goods on his own account. A ship full of stuff that his house had bought and not yet sold was always vulnerable, to war, weather or sudden market gluts. Even selling goods on consignment carried those risks, especially if he had advanced considerable sums that could only be recouped once the goods were sold. Those were challenges that have bedeviled merchants from time immemorial. Already in these early years, Alexander had grasped intuitively that he stood to make more by servicing trade than by taking on the significant burdens of physically acquiring, shipping and then off-loading the goods themselves. By 1812, his firm was already diversifying, both in the range of goods it imported and exported and by charging fees on advancing credit to select clients. For Alexander, the lessons of the war were that you can never trust any government to make the right financial decision and that there was more money to be made with less exposure if you earned that money on the trade of others.

William, who was said to be most like his father—ambitious, stubborn, headstrong but also meticulous—echoed Alexander's determination to reduce risk during the chaos of war. "The primary object is safety," he wrote to George, who had already tried the confidence of both his father and his elder brother. But safety alone would not yield returns. As hostilities intensified, another imperative was information. A successful merchant was one who could get reliable information about prices on both sides of the Atlantic, about economic conditions in multiple countries and multiple markets, and about supply and demand. There was no consistent clearinghouse for economic data in the early nineteenth century, which was why it was critical to have trusted intermediaries at each node where goods were bought and sold. Alexander used his sons and cousins to gather information and then used that intelligence to assess what to buy, what to sell and at what price. He also used it to determine what paper to issue to settle trades that started in dollars and ended in British pounds and vice versa. There was no agreed upon or published exchange rate, and it was up to each merchant to estimate what the right rate would be. Merchants who had the best and most-up-to-date information tended to be the ones who thrived, and none were better informed than Alexander Brown and his sons. Constant flow of information from Liverpool to Baltimore and back again was key.

Though Baltimore faced competition from Philadelphia and New York in these years, one of its advantages was that much of its commerce relied on paper promises, whether in the form of bank notes or notes issued by merchants for future payment. As the gateway for southern commodities sold to England, Baltimore's economy relied heavily on paper that converted dollars into pounds and pounds into dollars. At any given time, there could be dozens upon dozens of notes with different rates issued by different houses. That was confusing enough, but adding to the muddle were the paper notes issued by the government and by chartered banks. The result was a sea of paper money, each note with its own value, and each susceptible to dizzying fluctuations.

The backdrop was an immature economy that had only recently started using paper to fund commitments. The United States had come a long way from its seventeenth-century days when wampum (seashells) and whatever country's coin one could find were the only forms of currency. Colonial state governments had tried to aid economic activity by issuing paper notes backed by land, and then the Continental Congress in the 1770s issued passels of paper to fund the Revolution against Great Britain. That proved insufficient to meet the needs of war, and so states issued more paper money, often with no tax revenue to ensure its value. By the 1780s, the new nation was awash in paper, much of it worthless. It was an untenable system. Hence the reason that the Constitution gave the U.S. federal government the sole power to mint coins and print money.[5]

Vesting the federal government with that monopoly created some order, but merchants still faced significant challenges exchanging currencies. U.S. dollars were useless for foreign trade, given their questionable reputation and unproved status. An American planter would want to be paid in dollars, but his goods would be bought by pounds in Liverpool. Merchants bridged that gap, and foreign exchange was an informal process controlled by a handful of traders. A merchant such as Alexander Brown would offer that planter dollars up front, but not for the total amount. He would take the tobacco or cotton or whatever on consignment, write the seller a note promising payment at a future date, ship it across the Atlantic and sell it for pounds in England. The merchant would then provide the rest of the payment in dollars some months later. The challenge for anyone involved was knowing whether the promises written on that paper would be honored. Wariness of paper was prudent, given how often it ended up worthless. In a world without published, centralized information, what set one house apart from another—and what separated good paper from bad—was *trust*.

Baltimore stood out because it had a decent financial infrastructure, with three reputable banks. One was the Bank of the United States, which was a legacy of Alexander Hamilton, the nation's first treasury secretary. Hamilton had focused on binding together the states of the new republic by having the federal government assume responsibility for the crushing debts incurred by a number of states during and after the Revolutionary War. While the bank was a vital part of the nascent federal financial system, however, its charter limited how much money it could print. Baltimore also was home to the Bank of Maryland and the Bank of Baltimore. Both issued paper money, which helped fund the physical infrastructure needed for a harbor and transit and established a precedent for an economic system that rested on paper.

One English visitor to the city soon after Alexander immigrated observed that in Baltimore, "As for gold, it is very scarce. I hardly ever met with it during the two months that I remained there."[6] The town was inundated with paper notes, not so many that inflation was rampant but enough to make it relatively easy to get capital when it was desired and needed. That was in contrast to Europe. There, governments resorted to paper money only when absolutely necessary, during times of war or upheaval, when they were strapped for gold and silver (hard money) and needed to bridge the gap between what their treasuries held, what they could collect in taxes, and what they needed to spend on men and machines to raise armies and build navies.

But in the United States, paper money was not seen as a temporary tool. The Old World was defined by concentrations of wealth and power defined primarily by land and people and coins minted by the government. In Europe, wealth tended to be locked up in physical things, which made it illiquid. The result was that wealth was scarce, and therefore so was power. If wealth was bound up in physical things, there was a clear limit on how much there was to go around, and those who had more therefore had absolutely more. It was a zero-sum world, a nonexpanding pie. If you had land, someone else did not; if you had men at your service, then they could serve no other lord or state; and if coins filled your treasury or vaults, they did not fill those of someone else.

Alexander Brown began as a merchant like any other, but the rise of his house above the rest began when he started to see paper notes themselves as a path to prosperity. Paper money was supposed to be a derivative of hard money, but paper often made promises that went beyond what hard money could fulfill if all the demands happened at once. The gap between the finite supply of hard money and the potentially limitless supply of paper has been a fundamental fissure in modern history. The economic struggles and disruptions as well as the incredible growth of the United States and then the rest of the world over the past two centuries are rooted in promises made by paper money.

These questions are hardly unique to American history. What was unusual about the United States was how easy it was to get capital compared with how difficult it was in the Old World. Money was an act of American promiscuity, and yet it was the paragons of virtue, men like Alexander Brown and his sons and their sons, who stood at the epicenter of money creation. Easy money and paper were often seen as a mark of a decadent culture, as many would decry throughout the nineteenth and twentieth centuries, but holding back the tide of greed and chaos were families like the Browns, whose deep conservativism, ramrod rectitude and innate propriety stood in stark contrast to the culture of gain and speculation they helped fuel.

The tension between the perceived vices of easy money versus the virtues of hard, between those who inherently distrusted the issuance of credit and paper and those who understood those as vital instruments to unlock capital, has never dissipated. It began before America became independent, had roots in Europe extending back to the ancient tension between money lenders and debtors, and would become more intense in the nineteenth and twentieth centuries with each financial crisis. Money may have made America but not without heated debate over its morality, its centrality and its issuers.

Early on, Alexander understood that what distinguished valuable paper from worthless was reputation and trust. Anyone could buy and sell stuff, but not just anyone could develop a trusted reputation. The only thing that would elevate the Browns above the competitive fray was whether their paper was backed by a sterling reputation, whether the notes that bore their name were seen as reliable. If the House of Brown promised payment on a certain date at a set rate, then that promise would be honored.

That is why Alexander's letters to his sons constantly hammered home the message of trust and reputation. With businesses in multiple cities already by 1812, his letters were the primary family form of communication. While Alexander must have lectured his children in person, across the dinner table, in the modest sitting room of his Baltimore home or in the counting rooms of his offices by the docks, letters were the conduit of knowledge and instruction. They maintained family relationships and built a family ethos. Many of his letters contained homilies not dissimilar to the finger-wagging advice that Polonius gives his son, Laertes, in Shakespeare's *Hamlet*:

> Neither a borrower nor a lender be,
> For loan oft loses both itself and friend,
> And borrowing dulls the edge of husbandry.
> This above all: to thine own self be true,
> And it must follow, as the night the day,
> Thou canst not then be false to any man.

Alexander would have done Polonius proud. He wrote to William, "Don't deal with people about whose character there is question. It keeps your mind uneasy. It is far better to lose the business." He cautioned against being spread too thin and trading with unvetted partners. "Where the risks are too great," he warned, "one loss may wipe out a hundred safe arrivals. . . . You cannot make a mistake by being sure." Again to William, he wrote, "Look around you and see those Merchants who have so many concerns which they cannot superintend themselves—how sooner or later it does them injury if it does not ruin them altogether. Having too many things to attend to, it distracts your attention and draws it off from regular pursuits." And then there was the maxim that he repeated endlessly to his sons: "Shoemaker, stick to thy last!" Better to cleave to what you know, and be known as someone whom others could trust, than to speculate, to be carried along by the fickle winds of ambition, and to get so caught in the passions of the moment that caution is thrown to the proverbial winds.[7]

Alexander's attitudes formed an adamantine foundation for the firm that bore his name. Family businesses rarely survive more than a few generations, let alone hundreds of years, and no matter how disciplined and focused Alexander may have been, luck and fortune played a role in his family's rise and persistence. But it would be hard to overstate the import of the culture he created, with his four sons adopting his worldview, and they in turn passing it down to their children, who in turn passed it down to theirs. It was, remarkably, a family devoid of black sheep, a multigenerational business that made no significant missteps in whom they made partner. Not all decisions went perfectly, of course; mistakes were made. But the template established by Alexander—stick to your last, stay focused, guard your reputation zealously as your most precious asset, be always prepared for hard times, and avoid unnecessary risk—formed the lasting core of the firm.

Another secret of the family's success, one harder to discern in the haze of the past, was the influence of Grace Brown, the matriarch who stood with Alexander and raised their sons. Women are largely absent from the history of men, money and power. In Europe, there had been queens who ruled, but in America in these years, women were almost completely invisible in politics and business. That doesn't mean they were without influence at home, but they were without public voice. Grace's grandson John Crosby Brown later wrote of his grandmother that she was "a silent partner in the firm, one whose name nowhere appears among its members but who kept thoroughly informed of its business, and whose sound judgment in every grave crisis was always acknowledged by husband and sons. . . . Father and sons used to talk over their business ventures in the evening with the wife and mother, and on many a knotty question an appeal was often taken to the mother's shrewd common sense."

In family lore, Grace was very much aligned with Alexander on the core family values. She may not have left a written record of her ethos, but at least one anecdote passed down suggests that she was every bit as determined that her progeny reflect the values of work, reputation and thrift, along with staying the course in times of duress. During a particularly unsettled week in these early years in Baltimore, one of the sons (almost certainly not William but which one of the other three is unclear) became agitated and panicked about impending ruin. Hearing his complaints, Grace did not comfort him, and she did not offer consolation. Instead, she exclaimed, with "withering scorn," according to John Crosby Brown writing decades later, "I should be ashamed if any son of mine were not man enough to bear misfortune, when it comes."

That story, passed down over the generations, was not told by her children and descendants with an iota of reproach. It was seen as emblematic of the strong woman she was, and of the iron will she hoped to instill in her children. This was not a sentimental family, nor one prone to introspection. They just got on with it.

In 1812, as the conflict escalated between the United States and Great Britain, Alexander showed no signs of panic. His letters were measured and sure, as were his directives. He knew that it was a delicate time, and that his family needed to conserve resources, be positioned for a rough few years and contemplate what might work best in the interim. Not holding paper promises was one imperative; making sure his ship, the *Armata*, wasn't seized was another, as was trying to figure out who would live where while the war lasted. Alexander, from his office in Baltimore, deployed his sons between Lisbon (to protect the *Armata*), Liverpool and New York. He knew his strengths—caution, meticulous planning, loyal and competent progeny as his lieutenants. He also knew his vulnerabilities—two countries fighting a war, privateers trawling the trade lanes like sharks and the British navy eager to seize and impound. If there was incidental profit to be made, he would make it, but his first priority was to preserve and conserve. Better less upside than lose it all. As he wrote to George, "Circumstanced as we now are, it would be wrong for us to run the risk of commencing any establishment or trade that could not be carried out without hazard."

As a businessman, Alexander was alert to the financial challenges, but as a father, he was also worried about the safety of his children. A steady stream of letters were dispatched from his home in Baltimore, duplicate copies on different ships in case the mail was seized or the ships lost, an added expense that he gladly bore, and his sons did the same. Better to know that everyone was safe than be consumed by the anxiety of the unknown. In a December 1812 letter to John, Alexander acknowledged that there might be some profit to be made if the *Armata* attempted to sail for Charleston and thereby evade British ships trolling to the north and unload its cargo for a nice gain. But that was hardly a sure thing. He concluded that it was better for the ship to remain docked in Lisbon for the duration, and he wanted John to find some way home to Baltimore. Lisbon was safer, but not exactly safe. "Having learned some Algerine cruisers are outside the straits . . . we shall feel uneasy until we hear of your arrival." The pirates of Algeria were a formidable problem in the western Mediterranean and around the straits of Gibraltar, so much so that Thomas Jefferson had only a few years earlier dispatched the U.S. Marines to subdue their leader, Yusuf Karamanli, and force Algerian corsairs to stop raiding American merchant ships. The Marines won that battle, which is why the Marine Corps anthem contains the words "To the shores of Tripoli." But once the Marines had left, the Algerians went back to their raids and took advantage of the war to redouble their efforts.

It is no small irony, then, that one of the most successful American techniques in its war with the sea-faring British Empire and its formidable fleet was the use of private vessels licensed by the federal government to raid and burn English ships. Alexander would have none of it. He understood the hypocrisy of being outraged at the corsairs while simultaneously licensing American merchants as an unofficial navy, unbound by any rules of war. His son William shared that indignation; the very idea offended him. Giving added voice to his father's stance, he excoriated privateering as "a degrading and demoralizing pursuit, and there is not a member of my family who ever did or ever would embark in it directly or indirectly, in any shape or form."[8] Had they been alive two centuries earlier, they would have denounced Sir Walter Raleigh and the English embrace of privateers during the long struggle with Spain spanning the sixteenth-century reign of Queen Elizabeth I. It didn't matter to Alexander or his oldest son that many others enthusiastically supported these tactics.

And yet their scruples did not extend to human bondage. The Browns were for many decades until the Civil War complicit in the slave system, especially as their business shifted ever more toward cotton. So too, of course, were millions of other nonslaveholders in the United States, the United Kingdom and Europe who benefited from the tobacco, sugar and, above all, cotton that was produced by enslaved laborers. In any event, the Browns' animus toward privateers was cast in moral tones, but it also had a more self-interested angle: for a burgeoning business dependent on reputation, and with reputation dependent on actions, serving as privateers might have ended the House of Brown as a merchant family. All might be fair in war, but Alexander was wisely attuned to the longer arc. Sooner or later, the war would end; trade with Great Britain would still be essential for the United States; and there was a nonnegligible chance that English merchants and shippers would be loath to entrust the Browns with letters or cargo if they had used their own ships as weapons of war against their English trading partners.

Throughout 1813, the family continued to hope that the conflict, derisively called Mr. Madison's War by its opponents, might soon be ended. But the situation took a more dire and even life-threatening turn in 1814. Until then, Alexander had elected to keep his stores of linen in his warehouses within the Baltimore city confines, though he did make plans to relocate temporarily to the countryside in case the city was attacked. Other businesses weren't so sanguine. Toward the end of 1813, anticipating that the fighting, which had been largely confined to Canada and the North, might shift to the mid-Atlantic, Baltimore's banks moved their specie out of the city. Merchants then moved their nonperishable items, those that could be stored and sold later, to hastily built warehouses in the countryside. Alexander considered his options. He wrote to John in 1813 that "there was not the smallest chance of any kind of business" being done in Baltimore while the war lasted, but he also did not believe that the English "will ever be able to destroy Baltimore."[9] He was right, but just barely.

It was an odd war, with the British mostly distracted by the final challenge of Napoleon in Europe. Until Napoleon's first defeat in the spring of 1814, Great Britain was able to devote only limited resources to North America. The United States, however, was barely up to the task of confronting even a British fleet at skeletal capacity. In the brief period between Napoleon's surrender in 1814 and his escape from the isle of Elba and the Hundred Days War a year later, culminating in his defeat at Waterloo in June 1815, the British were able to dispatch more ships and soldiers to fight the Americans. Flush with resources, the British shifted attention to the main ports of the United States and launched the campaign against the mid-Atlantic states that Alexander and the other merchants of Baltimore had hoped would never happen.

First, the British occupied Washington in August 1814 and destroyed what little was there. The city had minimal strategic value, but it had symbolic importance as the young nation's capital. The new but not all that impressive White House was left in flames. The British then turned their attention to the north, planning to capture Fort McHenry, which guarded the sea lanes to Baltimore. Though British forces were better armed and more experienced, after several days of intense fighting in September, culminating in an overnight bombardment of the fort, they were unable to overcome the Americans and withdrew. Watching the fireworks of the failed assault, a young man held prisoner on one of the English ships was moved to compose a poem about "the rocket's red glare, the bombs bursting in air." Within weeks, copies of the poem were being reprinted in paper after paper, and so was born the fame of "The Star-Spangled Banner" and Francis Scott Key.[10]

As many had anticipated, the war ended with little to show for it except lost time and lost lives. Yes, the conflict ended any dreams the British might have harbored of winning back their wayward colonies, and the conflict did lead to a mostly stable boundary between Canada and the United States with British troops and their Native American allies no longer an intractable obstacle to American westward expansion. Andrew Jackson's capture of the city of New Orleans, which made him a celebrity and later propelled him to the presidency, was perhaps the most dramatic military victory, but because of the snail's pace of communications in that era, it had no effect on how the war concluded. He took the city two weeks *after* the peace treaty had already been signed in the town of Ghent in late 1814.

The legacy of the war for the United States was ambiguous at the time but ultimately consequential. Internationally, trade relations with Great Britain and France largely reverted to the status quo antebellum. Domestically, 1815 marked the rise of the new territories to the west of the Appalachians. With the British threat gone, the West was unequivocally open for American settlement and American business. The war's end was also a factor in the explosive growth of the southern cotton economy, with the port of New Orleans now firmly under American control aiding the sale of cotton to Europe. The rise of cotton likely would have occurred regardless of the war, but the immediate aftermath saw the rapid transformation of the Deep South into the land of cotton and the solidification of the mid-Atlantic cities of Baltimore, Philadelphia and New York as the dominant financial and trading hubs.

For the House of Brown, the end of the war was an unmitigated boon. It had weathered a few rough years, and Alexander's meticulous deliberation set a precedent—and provided a model—for the many financial and political upheavals to come. Again and again, Brown Brothers survived because it was able to navigate crises that brought others low. It is often said that crisis presents opportunity. Alexander would have cocked an eye at that and snapped that sometimes a crisis is just a crisis and the point is to get through intact. He spent much of the two years weighing what to buy and what to sell, and at times, the answer was to do nothing. He ultimately concluded that if an opportunity did not pose an existential risk, then, yes, the right choice was to pursue it, but modestly rather than avariciously. During the war, Alexander honed his core messages and basic sensibilities, which, judging from later history, his sons absorbed.

The postwar years saw the family branch out beyond Baltimore and Liverpool. Though more of the business was morphing into financing the trade of others in addition to importing goods from Ireland and England,

Alexander still saw himself as primarily a linen merchant. In 1818, in order to expand his reach, he sent John, barely thirty years old, to head a new outpost of Alex. Brown & Sons in Philadelphia. The office was initially on Market Street before moving to a more permanent home on Chestnut Street. Chestnut was also the headquarters of the Second Bank of the United States, and of the First Bank of the United States before that. Philadelphia was the de facto center of American finance, and any firm that hoped to compete nationally needed a presence there. Under the moniker "Importers of Irish Linens," the October 10 announcement read, "John A. Brown & Co. take this opportunity of informing those who have been in the habit of purchasing linens imported by Alexander Brown & Sons of Baltimore, that the above firm is a branch of that concern, and that both houses will import a constant supply of cheap linens." There was little fanfare with the opening of the Philadelphia house, but the date—1818— became the symbolic founding year of what would later be known as Brown Brothers.

The timing wasn't auspicious. In 1819, the United States was plunged into an economic crisis. These crises would come to be called "panics," and they became regular features of the nineteenth century, occurring with startling consistency almost exactly every twenty years: 1819, 1837, 1857, 1873, 1893. Each was slightly different, but all shared a sudden drop in prices, a sharp contraction of economic activity, and a slew of merchants and banks left with too many commitments and not enough capital. Very few firms made it through all of them. Brown Brothers did. Luck and contingency certainly played a role, but the operating principles about risk and reward developed by Alexander were a key reason for the firm's endurance where so many others foundered.

The crash of 1819 was precipitated by the end of the transatlantic boom that followed the Napoleonic Wars and the cessation of hostilities between the United States and Great Britain. It was the culmination of years of explosive economic growth. Waves of new settlement and the eradication of Native American tribes transformed the Ohio Valley, and steamboat navigation made more inland trade possible. With that growth came hunger for capital, so that settlers could buy land and build homes and create farms and so that traders and merchants could cater to them. In 1819, the United States, with too much paper money in circulation, too much speculation in land, and not enough oversight of local banks and transactions, suffered a sudden sharp contraction when bank failures triggered a domino effect.

Alexander was dismayed—he took no joy in seeing colleagues and competitors flail and fold even if their own imprudence was a cause. He reminded his sons in multiple letters that almost no one is a hero during a financial panic. He wrote that in "times that require caution, it is not worthwhile to run any unnecessary risk. A man is a fool to do so under these circumstances, unless his need is great. Ours is not."[11] The family buckled down, reduced its exposure, and emerged from the economic storm largely unscathed. By surviving when so many other merchants and traders were drowning, the House of Brown thrived.

That then led to what in retrospect seems an inevitable expansion. In 1825, in the continuing rotation of his sons, Alexander sent James Brown (who had headed the Philadelphia branch for a few years when John returned to Baltimore) to set up a New York branch of the house. In time, that branch would become *the* branch. Unlike in Philadelphia only a few years before, there was no mention of linen. The circular announcing the New York opening stated only that the office would be dedicated to facilitating trade with both the Liverpool house headed by William and with the American South. "For that purpose," the circular read, "our James Brown has established himself in New York, to conduct a Commission Business, under the firm Brown Brothers, & Co." For the first time, there was also specific reference not just to the financing and commission business, but also to cotton. "Should you send us Cotton, or other produce, we will either dispose of it in this market, or re-ship it to our Liverpool House, as you may direct." And if the clients were so disposed, the firm would be "willing, at all times, to make reasonable advances, on property consigned to us, or our Liverpool house."[12]

The opening of the New York office meant two things: one was that the House of Brown, once a proud importer of Irish linen, had morphed into a merchant bank, earning fees off the business of others and crafting a new financial system that would spur the immense growth of the United States in the years to come. Given the need for credit standards and a trusted source of paper promises, it's likely that some bank or merchant house would have filled that role if Brown Brothers had not, but it was Brown Brothers that did.

The expansion to New York also coincided with the rise of cotton as the primary focus of the House of Brown. The family bought southern cotton on consignment, advancing a planter or his agent half to two-thirds of the final sale price and then charging a fee of 6 percent of the total sale. The Browns also charged fees of one-half a percent for storing the cotton or other goods in warehouses before shipping, and then if needed, warehousing in Liverpool if there was some lag between arrival and selling at auction. The Browns arranged financing for shipments, and they earned fees on foreign exchange, harmonizing the dollars that plantations and their agents received for the cotton with the pounds that the cotton was sold for in Liverpool and then converting those pounds back into dollars. Because the House of Brown advanced money to those planters and their agents, it began to act as a de facto bank. The business of financing was lucrative and more scalable than buying and selling physical shipments. Managed well, guided by mantras of taking measured bets and exercising caution at all times, a business that revolved around paper and financing offered far more upside. Managed badly, it could mean ruination, but so could the loss of a ship full of cargo.

The complicity in the cotton trade, however, meant a tacit support for the southern slave system. That was true for Alexander and his sons, and true as well for most of the mid-Atlantic merchant community, for the textile industry of New England, for the economy of Liverpool and for the mills of Manchester. As we shall see, the Browns ultimately opposed slavery and supported the rise of the Republican Party in the 1850s and the Union cause in the Civil War. But not before they had garnered immense wealth from the cotton empire.

The Browns' new focus on New York coincided with the shifting fortunes of Baltimore and Philadelphia, both of which sustained lasting economic damage after the harsh contraction of 1819. The Philadelphia-based
Second Bank of the United States was supposed to have reined in the excesses that led to panic, but its measures came too late to halt the sharp recession. By the time it moved to tighten credit, it was too late to prevent the
spiral but not too late to make it worse. The bank may have acted prudently,
but its stinginess at the very moment many were clamoring for help made
the bank deeply unpopular, especially in the hard-hit western states and
territories. Farms were seized, local banks were shuttered and businesses collapsed. The Second Bank came to be seen as a fortress of privilege, and its
moves reignited the late-eighteenth-century tension after the Revolution
over hard money and paper, over easy credit and tight credit. As a result, the
United States emerged from 1819 with a new and permanent fissure between
the interior of the country and the coastal cities.

The intense animus to the bank weighed on the economy of Philadelphia, and it was now faced with the rise of New York as an additional challenge. New York had natural advantages with the broad and navigable
Hudson River and the opening of the Erie Canal. It also had a larger population and had seized the lead in transatlantic trade with the 1817 launch
of the Black Ball Line of regularly scheduled trips to and from Liverpool.
Until then, ships came and went erratically depending on the weather and
only sailing once their holds were full of cargo. The Black Ball Line, with
its printed timetables and schedules set months in advance, changed the
dynamics of trade from erratic to routine. That made it easier for merchants
to plan, knowing that at a specific time, a ship would leave New York and
reach Liverpool twenty-five days later, and would depart Liverpool at a set
time and arrive in New York after battling winds for the longer westward
journey of seven weeks. The regularity was especially appealing to cotton
traders and to the owners of the mills in Manchester, a scant thirty miles
from Liverpool, who could now precisely plan production.

The regular shipping lines were known as "packets." With them, trade volume increased, and then increased more as the Erie Canal channeled trade to and from the American West, as the American South underwent its rapid transformation into a cotton economy and as the newly independent and ambitious countries of Latin America that had emulated the United States and rebelled against imperial Spain hungered for goods. More trade brought more workers to the docks of New York. Those workers needed food and clothes and housing, which meant more shopkeepers and wholesalers, which led to yet more shops. As ships carried an ever wider array of finished goods, specialty stores proliferated. More people meant more entertainment and more construction as the city expanded north from the tip of Manhattan and extended to the New Jersey side of the Hudson and across the East River into Brooklyn. And with all that trade, the city developed a new industry: shipbuilding, especially steamships for navigating the rivers of the American interior but also high-seas vessels for the oceans beyond.

All of these factors combined to spur an economic takeoff in New York. The dizzying growth of trade and business demanded financing, and that led to New York's transformation into a money center. The New York Stock Exchange, though its founding myth held that it was created by an agreement between a few traders under a buttonwood tree in 1792, was formally incorporated in 1817. Foreign firms, such as London's Baring Brothers (which had arranged loans to the U.S. government to pay for the War of 1812), used their New York presence to became more deeply involved in American trade finance. By the time Alexander sent James to open a New York office in 1825, the city had started to acquire the qualities of a real metropolis, from high culture to low, replete with theaters and gambling dens, salons and pubs, with poor laborers in cramped, filthy shanties and the rich surging north and east in Manhattan to build ever grander homes.[13]

By 1825, the House of Brown had offices in four cities and agents in several others. Alexander had cultivated a family business that had survived more than twenty years. Three major events—the Irish Rebellion of the 1790s, the War of 1812 and the Panic of 1819—had tested Alexander Brown and his sons and had propelled their way forward. The family, graced by a patriarch with an unshakable code of prudence, thrift and hard work combined with a deep streak of conservatism and a vein of opportunism, weathered these political, military and economic tsunamis. But Alexander was not ready to abandon Baltimore. The office in New York ultimately became the most consequential, but not before the patriarch made one last attempt to catapult Baltimore to the forefront. He did not succeed, but the attempt changed America.

CHAPTER 2

THE B&O

The United States had vast potential, with unparalleled natural resources, a fluid political system, and chaotic and creative emerging financial markets, but it was stunningly difficult to get around. It is hard to overstate the paucity of transportation infrastructure in the United States at the turn of the nineteenth century. Unless goods and people could more efficiently get from point A to point B, only a fraction of the country's potential could be unleashed. Paved roads with adequate drainage were a start; using the bounty of navigable waterways was better; carving canals was a major step; but finding a way to harness machines and engines to go anywhere would trump all of those. The United States was blessed with bountiful fertile land, forests, rivers and ample varieties of stone, but it lacked the man-made connective tissue that was essential to use those resources fully.

The past was a slower time. Distances that in later years could be traversed in hours took days and weeks. To go from New York to Baltimore in 1820 took the better part of four days for a distance of less than two hundred miles, and that was only if weather was good and the road was in decent shape. It took about twenty-four hours between Philadelphia and Baltimore, by water for the first leg and then on wagons overland the rest of the way, assuming it wasn't the dead of winter and that the Delaware River wasn't clogged with ice. Once on the other side of the mountain barrier that the Appalachian chain presented, there were even fewer roads or reliable routes. Travel became even harder, and crossing those mountains was arduous and time-consuming if you were hauling goods.

The Louisiana Purchase, the end of the War of 1812 and the resulting dispersal of Native American tribes triggered a new wave of settlement to the West between the Appalachians and the Mississippi. Settlers needed to sell their crops and pelts. The eastern and southern states bought some of what the West produced, but even more was sold abroad, transported from the interior to the coastal ports and then shipped across the Atlantic to Europe. Those ports in turn received manufactured imports from England and Europe. Everyone was in search of faster and cheaper ways to transport those finished goods to the settlers and then to get the raw goods to clamoring customers in the East and across the ocean. That amplification of trade spurred a transportation infrastructure boom. The major mid-Atlantic cities invested so that they could get products more quickly and more cheaply to the West and so that the West could get its crops and pelts more quickly to the ports of the East. The western states—Tennessee and Ohio especially—clamored in Washington for funding of roads and canals. Henry Clay, the young, ambitious leader of the new crop of western congressional representatives, championed an "American system" of federal infrastructure plans. That met strong pushback from the settled Northeast, which objected both constitutionally and selfishly. The states of New England didn't want to pay for roads in Kentucky and argued that the Constitution made no allowance for national spending of that sort. The result was that while intermittent federal funding could be wrangled, it was largely up to each state and city to pay for its own initiatives, which led to a patchwork of overlapping projects and a flurry of activity.

In the early 1820s, Ohio was the most coveted market and the fastest growing region, with multiple rivers feeding its fertile lands. The only obstacle to even faster growth was the line of mountains separating it from the Atlantic. Baltimore enjoyed closer proximity to the Ohio Valley than its northern rivals. It also had the Cumberland Road—called the National

Road due to its partial funding by Congress—which in 1811 began to connect Baltimore to the Ohio Valley, and gave the city a distinct commercial advantage. The road was a marvel of early nineteenth-century frontier engineering, with macadamized gravel and drainage ditches to make it passable by multiple horse coaches over hundreds of miles.

Baltimore's advantage, however, proved fleeting. New York City had a burgeoning steamship industry trolling the Hudson along with the new regular ship lines to England. More crucially, its leading citizens had a plan for dominance and the money to execute it, aided by a government in Albany that saw the city as the engine of the state's economic might. In 1817, the New York State legislature approved an audacious project to dig the 350-mile-long Erie Canal between Albany and Lake Erie at Buffalo. By 1821, the first segments had opened; by 1825, the canal was complete. Suddenly, transporting goods from the bustling ports of New York City to the Great Lakes and from there into the Ohio Valley was both cheaper and faster than it was from the more proximate cities of Baltimore and Philadelphia. New York—already the fastest growing and most populous American city—was poised to become the economic heart of the entire country.

The Erie Canal was the most significant public works project of the new United States, yet it received no support from the federal government. Congress did agree to back its construction, but the aid bill was vetoed by President James Madison, who did not think that it was the role of the federal government to support state public works and believed that the Constitution's interstate commerce powers did not extend to improving transportation. That left the canal to the New York government, which turned to its own citizens for loans. At first, the wealthiest shunned the venture, unsure whether it could or would be completed. But the middle class cottoned to the project, in part because of the ill effects of the Panic of 1819. The sharp economic downturn wiped out many small investors and debt holders. The preceding years had seen a proliferation of paper money issued by private banks, which then became largely worthless. The Erie Canal benefited from the crash because it was seen as a legitimate investment and a tangible asset that would retain value. After 1819, wealthier citizens also started to buy the bonds, as did the English. The result was that the project never lacked for funds and was completed relatively quickly. It vindicated its backers immediately, sharply reducing costs of shipping and fulfilling the promise of an increased trade and tighter links between New York and the lands to the west.[1]

Philadelphia, which feared being surpassed both by Baltimore and New York, responded in kind. In 1826, the Commonwealth of Pennsylvania passed the Main Line of Public Works Act that authorized the construction of a network of canals and roads to link the city to the interior of the country via the Susquehanna River. The Mainline Canal would eventually surpass the Erie Canal in scale, but not until the 1830s, which proved to be too late to close the economic gap with New York. Even so, Philadelphia still had some advantages over Baltimore, including an easier route to Britain, which meant some imported goods could be had more cheaply in Philadelphia. Baltimore had a superb port, but its wealthy and ambitious merchants couldn't alter the reality of time and distance.

Or could they? Faced with these immediate and dramatic threats to the city's position as a major trading and shipping center, the city fathers responded with a bold initiative. They decided to invest millions on a new and untested technology, hoping to leapfrog ahead of their rivals, knowing that if they failed, they would be forever behind. They decided to build a railroad.

That was more than risky and costly. It was terra incognita. In the early 1820s, there were only a handful of very short railroads, none more than a few dozen miles in length, used only for hauling granite from quarries. They were all horse drawn. There was no railroad anywhere in the world on the scale imagined by the leaders of Baltimore. To reach the Ohio Valley, the proposed railroad would extend for hundreds of miles and cross difficult terrain that had yet to be surveyed. Every part, from the rails to the ties to the cars, would have to be custom designed and then manufactured. There were no preexisting parts or plans.

And yet they decided to do it anyway. The city would build a railroad over the mountains to the West. The planners knew at the time that they were embarking on something momentous. They couldn't have known that railroads would transform the United States in later years, though they might have had an inkling. Their railroad, winding through the few passes over the mountains, would not just carry freight. It would be the first passenger line in the United States, and one of the first anywhere. It was an audacious plan. After less than two years of study and debate beginning in 1826, the leaders of the city of Baltimore decided that a railroad was the best way their city could remain a commercial center to rival New York and Philadelphia.

By the mid-1820s, Alexander Brown wasn't just one of the city's leading merchants. He was arguably *the* leading merchant, in terms of the volume and variety of his business and its increasing complexity involving not just goods but letters of credit and assorted paper. While he had already recognized that his franchise could thrive only with a strong presence in New York and Philadelphia and Liverpool, he remained committed to his adopted city and determined not to see it slip. He and the other elites of Baltimore, after careful study and debate, concluded that the Erie Canal would create an insurmountable advantage for New York and that Philadelphia was likely to jump ahead with its planned Mainline project, not yet funded but whose outlines were clear. Believing that they would be unable to compete with the canal builders to their north, the city fathers turned instead to the idea of a road made of iron carrying wheeled cars pulled by horses.

Without question, they would have preferred a canal. A Chesapeake & Ohio Canal was tentatively approved by the Maryland legislature, but initial cost estimates were stratospheric because of the challenges of the terrain across the mountains to the west. An expensive canal may have been better than no canal, but the Baltimore city fathers rightly feared that construction would take too long and cost too much to allow Baltimore to maintain its position relative to the cities to the north. It was also likely that Washington, DC, would wrangle federal funding and get the jump on access to the canal, which would set Baltimore back even further, and that is precisely what happened in early 1825 when outgoing president James Monroe, reversing his earlier opposition to national public works, signed a federal bill chartering the Chesapeake & Ohio Canal.

That left Baltimore with few palatable options, which was why its leaders gambled everything on the unknown. It wasn't quite the 1820s equivalent of a moonshot, but it was close.

At the end of 1826, the final report on the engineering of an alternate canal to compete with the Chesapeake & Ohio was submitted to the city leaders. The report confirmed what was already suspected: that the work would take years and cost millions. The elevation over the mountains would require multiple locks and massive digging and earth moving. That left the leaders with two choices: Baltimore could join the canal craze, accepting its lot as an also-ran, or they could turn to a scheme that Alexander Brown, working with his sons George and William, had been concocting for the better part of a year with the aid of Philip Thomas, the Quaker president of the Mechanics Bank, which Alexander Brown had helped set up. They had already concluded that the canal plan would be too little, too late, and once that final report was submitted in late 1826, the Browns and Thomas knew what had to be done: "The people of Baltimore had but one course left; and they adopted a railroad system."[2]

The only precedent at the time was not in America but in England. The Stockton & Darlington Railway was up and running between . . . the English towns of Stockton and Darlington. It was a twenty-five-mile track powered by a rudimentary locomotive steam engine invented by George Stephenson in collaboration with his son Robert, who had made names for themselves as coalfield engineers. For the short line, they designed flatbed cars to carry coal and covered cars with seats for passengers. Their steam engine was anchored on top of a flatbed that was designed to haul the rest of the train, forming a very rudimentary locomotive. The engine did not perform as well as horses. It was slow and had a tendency to break down and occasionally explode. Even so, its promise was immense, and it attracted the attention of Liverpool and Manchester, both of which were looking for better ways to connect the booming port with the booming manufacturing center.

The debate in Liverpool over the pros and cons of a railroad piqued the attention of William Brown, who informed his father. Aware of the challenges facing Baltimore and Alexander's interest in solving them, William suggested that the Stockton railroad might be the solution to Baltimore's plight and the key to a glorious future. Alex concurred. "If this railroad be accomplished," Alexander wrote to William, "it will resuscitate Baltimore . . . and will make her in short time second to no city in the union."[3] His vision was both right and wrong: the railroad did not catapult Baltimore ahead of other cities, but it did ultimately catapult the United States ahead of the rest of the world.

Alexander had relentlessly focused on trade, but over the course of thirty years, he had gradually allowed the business to evolve. He had diversified beyond linen; he had commissioned the *Armata* to carry the firm's goods and then cotton consignments; he had then built a few additional ships. And after the crisis of 1819, he had invested more of the firm's energy in the buying and selling of credit notes. Alexander Brown's risk aversion did not preclude experimenting with something new, provided that the new did not distract too much time and money or entail a dramatic shift away from the core business.

Yet there is no small irony in Alexander's embrace of an untested speculative railroad and his stern refusal to allow his son William a similar venture into the unknown. Walking the almost indiscernible line between controlling and hypocritical, Alex plunged his family into a multimillion-dollar capital project but had only a few years before firmly rejected a much smaller venture into a related business. Granted, the Baltimore railroad would be financed by many players, and the Browns' exposure would be modest. Even so, in 1819, William had presented his father and brothers with a new investment opportunity. He had suggested that they buy and run a cotton mill in England, and thereby diversify the business. If the house and its various branches were going to trade cotton using the firm's capital on the firm's ships, then why not take the integration one step further and use the firm's looms to make thread and cloth?

Alexander Brown was guided by opportunity, and the only lodestar for his decisions was whether or not the family could achieve maximum profit for minimal risk. That, at least, was his rationale for rejecting William's idea. Invoking the family "we," which was in truth more like a royal "we," Alexander wrote, "We all agree that it would be wrong and imprudent to embark on any other pursuit than that we are engaged in. . . . However profitable the business may be now, we know of none more subject to reverses than the Cotton spinning trade. . . . Your capital, credit & resources would be called into action for the use of that establishment whenever it would be required. . . . Having too many things to attend to, it distracts your attention & draws it off from your regular pursuit." For those reasons, Alexander opposed William's suggestion to open a Brown family cotton mill. In case his views were not already crystal clear, he ended his rather dismissive letter with a parting homily, "We find that persons who have kept steadily to one pursuit are far the richest men, & those who are interested with one & another different pursuits, no matter how profitable they may be or appear to be at first, are always ruined sooner or later. . . . In the management of one's business, it's not only necessary to be correct but not to be suspected of incorrectness."[4]

There is no record of William's response. He kept his disappointment either to himself or off the printed page. It was not the first time he and his father had clashed. William, the eldest Brown brother, had come with his father to Baltimore in 1800 at the age of sixteen. By the time his brothers joined them, William was in questionable health and in an increasingly troubled relationship with Alexander. As the oldest son, he not only looked like his father but had the same flinty, strong-willed temperament. As a young man in his twenties, he frequently came into conflict with a patriarch who may have settled in a democracy but had no intention of running his business like one. Rather than engage in perpetual conflict with his father, William decided—and Alexander agreed—that it was best for him to relocate to Liverpool and set up that vital branch of the family business.

He married, bought a fine house near the waterfront and just steps from what was then a smallish cotton exchange, and opened up William Brown & Co.[5]

Free to run his own branch in Liverpool, William became one of the most important of the city's businessmen, known for his astute judgment of other merchants and their creditworthiness and for his tight relationships with the largest manufacturers of Lancashire. He had offices right off the docks, and a fine house a short walk away. He enjoyed the easy banter not just with other traders but with all who worked, from stevedores who unloaded the ships to the captains who sailed them. He led a rich social life, entertaining guests at his home frequently, and he used that web as a source not just of enjoyment but of information. He listened and watched, and by the early 1820s, he had developed a keen sense of how cotton would trade in Liverpool and hence what price the American branches should pay for it. Alexander managed the profitable but waning linen trade, but it was William who built the Browns' cotton trading empire in Liverpool and it was William who was instrumental in the new business of making money in foreign exchange, conveying what was happening in the English economy that would determine the price of pounds so that Alexander and the other brothers could make the right purchases in dollars. William also developed with his father a system of ranking competitors and potential partners numerically from one to three, with those ranking a one considered to be almost risk-free and of sterling character, while those at the other end were of "doubtful character and considerable risk." That ranking was kept private and secret. The point was to marshal the information, not to call anyone out or cause embarrassment. That mix of deep engagement with the community and systematic use of data and discretion would become a hallmark of the firm over the decades.[6]

Being rebuffed by his father did not discourage William. If anything, it acted as fuel to his ambition to build a name and leave a lasting legacy. He saw the potential of the railroad and urged his father to consider it even though some of his earlier ideas had not been met with a warm reception. Instead of nursing wounded pride, William pushed on. Without that, the railroad would have come to America sooner or later, but because of it, the first major line was born in Baltimore, care of Brown Brothers.

In February 1827, a few dozen men gathered at the home of George Brown to mull "the best means of restoring the City of Baltimore, that portion of Western Trade, which has lately been diverted from it by the Introduction of Steam navigation, and by other causes." George had arranged at the meeting for a presentation by Philip Thomas and his brother, who had recently returned from a trip to England where they had seen the Stockton line in person. They made the case that Baltimore was too late to the canal game and that a railroad would be cheaper to build and would convey men and materials faster. Judging from the speeds of the Erie Canal, it would take ten days to ship goods using a canal that stretched from Baltimore to central Ohio. A railroad, they promised, would take only three. While the capital required was significant, faster would eventually mean cheaper, and that would lower the cost of transporting goods, which would then make Baltimore that much more attractive.[7]

So was the promise and the hope. In that era, promise and hope were their own form of currency. The men who gathered at George Brown's house shared a particular sensibility of their time, prevalent in England, France, Germany and the new United States. It was a sensibility that progress was the inevitable outcome of technology, and that mankind, led by a few select nations, was on the cusp of solving the essential problems of human existence from time immemorial. With the revolutions and upheavals of the late eighteenth and early nineteenth century receding into the past, there was a widespread belief that a new era had dawned and that the age-old challenges of transport, food and the sheer obstacles of the physical world were soon to be conquered. That sense was still nascent in the 1820s, but it was palpable in that room in Baltimore.

Canal building and railroads were emblems of that spirit. In France, the utopian followers of Henri de Saint-Simon avidly pursued canal building and railroad schemes in the belief that those would not only make it possible to supply everyone with the food and clothing and materials needed to be prosperous and secure but also would heal the divisions between nations. They believed that the separation of bodies of water had kept societies from realizing their full potential. In addition to this airy metaphysical belief, they were also convinced that by connecting sundered waters and distant lands, canals and railroads would unleash a new wave of progress. Canals were a relatively straightforward feat of engineering and had been made since antiquity. Railroads, however, were entirely new, a pure manifestation of human ingenuity and creativity. In the words of Thomas Gray, one of the earliest apostles of building the lines that would crisscross England, railroads "would revolutionize the whole face of the material world and society." Canals and rails epitomized the era's heady fervor that the peoples of Europe and North America were on the verge of something great, of technological and industrial revolutions that would transform everything. Not all went as planned, but canals were dug and railroads soon covered continents.

It was an intoxicating vision, one that lured Alexander and his sons and captivated the age. Progress meant that not only would the Brown family get rich, but their city, their state, their country and the world would all be better for it. Progress meant that the growth of their fortunes could be inextricably linked to the growth of the fortunes of their adopted countries, England and the United States. While many of Baltimore's great families feared that the success of New York and Philadelphia would leave Baltimore lessened, they also hoped that it would not be a zero-sum game. The West was vast, and, in theory, there were more than enough opportunities for everyone to prosper.

The attendees that February night had been debating what to do for several months, which may explain how they were able to commit so quickly and emphatically to constructing a railroad that would far surpass in scope and length anything like it at the time. In fact, they committed to building a railroad with the hopes that it would eventually connect Baltimore to the Ohio Valley and traverse the mountains without any actual evidence that a railroad was either financially or technically feasible. And they committed without knowing whether steam-powered locomotives would work, and planned on horse-drawn trains as a fallback option. Other than the experiments in England over short distances and flat ground that were prone to blowing up and maiming or killing their operators, there were no railroads whose cars were pulled by engines.[8]

The leaders of Baltimore, however, were undeterred. They were galvanized by a potent mix of ambition, vision, naivete and desperation. They agreed that evening in 1827 to form a smaller committee to report back to the larger group by the end of the month, and Alexander Brown wrote to his son William in Liverpool requesting a copy of the Liverpool and Manchester Railway charter that had recently been granted. The elder Brown was particularly interested in any advances being made in "the application of Steam to land Navigation." A few days later, the same group reconvened and decided to form the Baltimore & Ohio Railroad Company. That company would be responsible for building a double-track railroad over hundreds of miles on a route to be determined.

Within weeks, the group had obtained a charter from the Maryland legislature for a company capitalized at about $3 million, which was much less than the estimates for a canal. Philip Thomas was elected president, George Brown treasurer, and Alexander one of the directors. The stature of the men involved made obtaining that charter an easy affair. No one questioned the urgency of doing something when every other major municipality appeared to be ahead. The vision for a revolutionary form of transportation connecting the coast to the West was praised fulsomely in the press as "a plan for making a railroad from the city of Baltimore to some point on the Ohio River . . . considered and adopted by certain of our most intelligent, public spirited and wealthy citizens."[9] Local newspapers maintained no pretense of objectivity on matters so significant: the owner of one of the city's primary papers, Hezekiah Niles of *Niles' Weekly Register*, was an unabashed booster of the city's fortunes.

The favorable press also aided the novel means of funding. Given that the project was meant to benefit the city as a whole, the Browns and the other founders decided to finance it through a public offering. What is commonplace now—turning to the community for funds to build needed public works—was novel then. Yet asking the public to invest proved to be wildly popular. When the books were opened by the Mechanics Bank (whose president and trustees included most of the directors of the newly formed B&O) in late April, the offering was massively oversubscribed. Nearly twenty thousand people (a quarter of the city's population) bought shares valued at $100 each. Parents bought shares for their children; the city itself took five thousand shares, as did the State of Maryland. Alexander Brown bought five hundred. All told, forty thousand shares were bought, raising $4 million.

Construction would prove to be more difficult, costly and time-consuming than anyone planned or foresaw. But astonishingly little time elapsed between conceiving of the idea, chartering a corporation and raising the initial capital. Fueled by a heady combination of foolish optimism and urgency, the town leaders acted within the space of months. And not only acted but managed to raise millions (about the equivalent of $75 million in today's dollars) in what would later be called a public-private partnership bringing together state and local government along with the city's wealthy, led by the Browns, and then thousands of ordinary citizens who were willing to put a considerable portion of whatever meager savings they had toward a dream that promised a brighter future for their city and might make a good investment as well. The charter made it clear that the company could charge tolls and intended to pay dividends to shareholders once the road was complete.

The euphoria for the endeavor extended well beyond Baltimore. One local paper in the Massachusetts Berkshires editorialized about the Baltimore & Ohio, "Pyramids . . . palaces and all the mere pride and pomp of man sink to insignificance before a work such as this. . . . A single city has set on foot an enterprise . . . worthy of an empire." The crescendo only continued to build over the next year. First, the B&O directors began to assess the feasibility of a steam-powered engine rather than horse-drawn cars. George Brown ventured north with several of the directors to view the one functional rail line in the United States, in Quincy, Massachusetts, where horses pulled a few coal trains back and forth from a mine. Horses could pull thousands of pounds on railcars, which meant that a horse-drawn railroad could compete with canals. But steam power, largely untested as a locomotive force, could be a step change. The directors also evaluated the relative merits and costs of stone bridges versus wooden (stone was costlier but more durable). And, most important, they hired engineers to map and survey prospective routes. Without adept surveying and route laying, the whole endeavor would founder, regardless of how well designed the cars, tracks and engines. Alex Brown, consistent with his meticulous, conservative approach, urged that no corners be cut in hiring engineers and surveyors to check and double-check one another's work. "It is a work of immense magnitude," he wrote to William in Liverpool with typical understatement, "and if not begun on the proper route, and conducted on the best plan, it would be unfortunate."[10]

The initial route was mapped out by early 1828. The line would begin at Pratt Street and head west. Soon enough, a spur branch would be built south to Washington, but it would be five years before the line extended from Baltimore to Harpers Ferry on the Potomac in Virginia, seventy miles away, the meeting point of the Shenandoah and Potomac rivers and home of the primary federal armory. It would be years more before the line extended to Cumberland and then Wheeling, in present-day West Virginia. Had they known how long construction would actually take, they might have been less euphoric.

With endless hope about the future, and not cursed with a crystal ball, the company and the City of Baltimore planned a ceremony to lay the first stone on July 4, 1828. Baltimore was not the first city to link the day's celebrations to the inauguration of an ambitious project: on July 4, 1817, crowds had cheered in Rome, New York, as work began on the Erie Canal. Rome, however, was a small town. Baltimore was one of the largest and most cosmopolitan cities in the United States, and its festivities on Independence Day 1828 were of another order.

Nearly the entire city participated in the parades and preparations. Forty-seven different groups marched in a procession, representing every guild, trade and profession in the city: bakers, blacksmiths, whitesmiths (metalworkers), tanners, printers and bookbinders, and of course masons, who would lay the first stone. The procession began early in the morning of a sweltering summer day with the temperature in the mid-90s save for a brief few temperate hours in the morning. The parade started near the famed Merchants Exchange, designed by Benjamin Latrobe. The elegant domed building, which defined commercial Baltimore, would be demolished at the turn of the twentieth century. The parade then snaked through the downtown and emptied out onto an open field to the south, where a viewing pavilion had been built and where the guest of honor, the last living signer of the Declaration of Independence and the only man there wealthier than Alexander Brown, Charles Carroll, waited.

Toward the end of the procession strode Alexander Brown, whom one paper called "the royal merchant of America," likening him to one of the Medicis, the grand Renaissance rulers of Florence famous for their lavish public works. He beamed and waved and was in no rush as the parade meandered along the route for hours. Arriving at the pavilion, the parade dispersed; hands were shaken, backs were clapped, drinks were drunk. Then the band started up and played a commemorative song, the first railroad ballad, a genre that would become immensely popular over the coming decades. The song was dubbed "The Carrollton March," in honor of the esteemed Charles Carroll. Its lyrics aptly summed up the euphoria of the day:

> O we're hopping skipping jumping, O we're all crazy here in
>   Baltimore
> Here's a road to be made, with the Pick and the Spade
> Tis to reach the Ohio for the benefit of trade.
> Here are mountains to be leveled, here are vallies to be fill'd
> Here are rocks to be blown, and Bridges to build.
> And we're all digging, blowing, blasting, And we're all crazy in
>   Baltimore

At the end of the procession, the ancient Carroll was presented with item after item: reports from the B&O engineers bound in leather by the city's bookbinders; a sealed glass container with the corporate charter; and a silver shovel made by the city's blacksmiths for the sole purpose of the ceremonial groundbreaking. After speeches heralding a new era of commerce linking the settled East of the new nation with the West, Carroll, ninety years old and spry, was led to the pavilion erected to shield him and the grandees from the summer heat that was already oppressive by ten in the morning. John Morris, one of the directors, lauded Carroll as a hero of the Revolution and announced that only a few generations separated the visionaries who made the republic from those assembled in Baltimore that Independence Day fifty-two years later. They were all, Founding Fathers and the citizens of 1828, made of the same stuff, and the people of Baltimore were simply continuing what the founders had started. Morris handed Carroll a ceremonial shovel, which Carroll then gingerly tapped into the ground, digging up a few scoops of token dirt while the crowd cheered. Masons anointed the cornerstone with oil and wine, and Carroll proclaimed, "I consider what I have just done to be among the most important acts in my life, second only to the signing of the Declaration of Independence, if even it be second to that." The next day, *Niles' Weekly Register* published a gushing editorial, praising the courage of the city leaders and its citizens and offering a paean to the emerging "American System" of massive projects aimed at "internal improvements."[11]

All were not smiling. The president of the United States, John Quincy Adams, had declined an invitation to attend and instead presided over a groundbreaking ceremony of the rival Chesapeake & Ohio Canal in Georgetown, where he played the same role as Carroll and stuck a ceremonial spade into the ground. Adams made what seemed the prudent choice. The railroad struck many as a ridiculous scheme, doomed to failure. Canals were a known entity. Adams wanted to be on the right side of history. Time would prove him wrong.

Within a year, twenty-five miles of track had been laid. Costs predictably exceeded initial estimates of $20,000 per mile, especially with the decision to use stone for bridges rather than wood. The directors decided within the first year that the initial surveyors and engineers they had hired were not up to the task, and Alexander made the hard call to replace them, the right choice but one that set the company back months and many dollars. Another reason for the cost overruns, however, was the momentous decision to use, for the first time, a steam-driven engine to pull the cars. In order to make locomotives powered by steam feasible, however, the route required wider turns, which meant more engineering and new surveying.

In the months after the July groundbreaking, the Browns were key to each critical decision. One challenge was how to offset the massive weight of the cars so that they could be pulled effectively either by horses or by an engine. The publicity the project had received drew not just attention but also anyone with an invention. At the end of 1828, a thirty-two-year-old New Jersey farmer named Ross Winans presented the directors of the B&O with his patented friction-saving wheel. An inveterate tinkerer, he had created a system for hanging a wheel on an axle that substantially reduced the friction and made it possible for a horse to draw a car on a metal track carrying tons of cargo at four to five miles an hour. Hearing of the grand plans for the new Baltimore railroad, Winans decided to just show up with his invention, believing that he could persuade the directors to give him, and his wheel, a chance.

They did.

In December 1828, Winans brought his small test car to Baltimore, and Alexander Brown rode the flatbed as a horse easily pulled it. It felt frictionless and moved swiftly. Alexander was ecstatic. He wrote to William in Liverpool in January 1829, "We have tried Mr. Winans' wagons on a large scale and it answers our most sanguine expectations. A man can easily push along 5 or 6 tons on a level road, and we really believe a horse will draw 30 to 40 with ease. . . . There is no doubt that this discovery will revolutionize the carrying trade of the world, and be the means of multiplying rail roads everywhere with prodigious rapidity." Winans got the contract and eventually became extremely rich. On the eve of the Civil War, he would be arrested on the B&O Railroad for fomenting secession as a vehemently anti-Northern representative of the Maryland legislature. Before that, however, he helped launch the United States into the railroad age.[12]

By May 1830, there was enough track to start charging tolls all the way to Ellicott's Mills, some thirteen miles from the downtown terminus. Even before then, a few miles had been in operation as a sort of amusement park ride for the many curious visitors who were willing to pay a tad to see what the fuss was about. The cars were rudimentary at best, no more than wooden platforms with a few benches, drawn at a leisurely pace by teams of horses. The Browns spent considerable time and energy that year arguing with the first set of engineers who had been hired, and then firing them and replacing them with a new cohort. At the same time, another inventor, named Peter Cooper, who had made his money operating a glue factory in New York, had set up an ironworks in Baltimore. Along with Winans, he began experimenting with a steam engine that could pull the carriages. These efforts were similar to what was then happening in England, where George Stephenson, who had been working to get the most optimal combination of wheels, tracks and steam for more than a decade, was trying out models on the Liverpool and Manchester Railway. Stephenson believed that his engine could attain speeds in excess of thirty miles per hour. But for the B&O and its particular track and route, with sharper curves than those on English rails, the ambitions were more modest, and no one knew what was ultimately going to work best.

Like Winans, Cooper would have been at home in a Mark Twain novel. He was the prototypical American tinkerer, with experiments strewn about his property and a new idea constantly on deck. Unlike thousands of others like him, who in later years might have applied for patents and then waited passively, hoping that their revolutionary inventions would be noticed, Cooper was a hustler who had the right idea at the right time. He presented the B&O engineers with a novel design: a lead car with a steam engine placed vertically. That image of the smokestack belching fumes would later become iconic and ubiquitous, but other engines at the time had horizontal boilers and a lower profile. As they had been with Winans and the new wheel design, Alexander, his son George and the rest of the directors were open to experimentation. They commissioned Cooper to build a prototype and arrange a test, which was held on a perfect late summer day in August

1830. At first, they were underwhelmed by what they saw. Cooper presented them with a normal car supporting a modest engine, "a very small and insignificant affair." It weighed less than a ton and was no more than thirteen feet wide. It was affectionately called the Tom Thumb, and it carried the directors a few miles at about twelve miles an hour. Not bad, but hardly awe inspiring. To make the most of the day, the directors decided to have the little engine race against a horse-drawn train.

In the engine-drawn carriage were Philip Thomas, Alexander Brown and his son George. If they were concerned about the possibility of an explosion, that was more than outweighed by the excitement of the new. Soon the car was racing along smoothly and, at eighteen miles an hour, at a faster clip than the more cautious first run. At the turn, the race with the horse-pulled carriage began. That would be the test, to see if Cooper's steam-powered carriage could outpace the horse. At first, the horse raced ahead; after making the turn, the engine needed to heat up, idling it for precious minutes. Soon, however, the engine car gathered speed, and with Thomas and the Browns cheering, they pulled ahead of the horse. Victory was brief. Suddenly, there was a loud snapping sound, and the band that powered the wheels slipped out of place. Despite the valiant efforts of Peter Cooper to reattach the band, all he got were lacerated hands, and the engine lost to the horse. Still, its promise was clear.[13]

By 1830, the Baltimore & Ohio had mapped out its first one hundred miles of track, and the directors had committed to using steam engines. The B&O spurred the first major wave of railroad construction in the United States. Year by year, the line grew, and it would eventually stretch for thousands of miles along multiple spider routes. The track to Washington was completed in 1835, and then formed the same route as the first telegraph lines, culminating with Samuel Morse in the U.S. Capitol building in 1844 tapping his code to his assistant in the B&O station in Baltimore with the message, "What hath God wrought!" Financed in part by the state of Maryland, the railroad spur to Washington was then used as collateral for the company to borrow $1 million, half of which was then deposited in the Liverpool branch of Alex. Brown & Sons, marking the first time American railroad securities were ever sent and sold in Europe, a trade that would reach massive proportions in the second half of the nineteenth century.

Alexander Brown and his sons, however, saw minimal return on their investment of tens of thousands of dollars. The Baltimore & Ohio began to pay modest dividends in the 1830s, but the income was negligible compared with the rest of the family's business. The railroad was not a moneymaker for them, not directly. They had, however, and not for the last time, been present at the creation of the next phase of American growth. Without expending too much of their capital, they had helped finance what would become the engine of American economic progress. The railroads eventually made possible the settlement of the West on the other side of the Mississippi and unleashed a scale of economic activity greater than the world had ever seen. Later in the nineteenth century, as railroad mania seized the investing world, Brown Brothers didn't join the party, unwilling to commit capital that could so easily be lost and usually was. They invested in the B&O because it was the right thing for their community and their country, not because they stood to make outsized gains. They did it because it had to be done. As it turned out, the railroad did not succeed in catapulting Baltimore ahead; it succeeded instead in catapulting the growth of the nation.

The firm's mounting success was shaken in 1834 with the sudden death of the patriarch. Alexander died more or less in the line of duty. In March 1834, the Bank of Maryland, one of the earliest iterations of a state bank, collapsed. Brown led a coalition of business leaders and used the resources of his firm to guarantee that no "merchant in Baltimore who could show that he was solvent would be allowed to fail." A week of intense meetings followed, and Brown, seventy years old, caught a cold that morphed into pneumonia. He died on April 4. The *Baltimore American* eulogized him the next day: "Few men occupy so large a space in the esteem of the whole country as the deceased. As a merchant he stood in the first rank for ample means and the skill and enterprise with which his large concerns were managed. His energy was not more remarkable than the liberality of spirit which marked all his undertakings. . . . As a citizen he was eminently valuable, and his loss is a subject of universal regret. Not less estimable in his private relations, to his family and personal friends this bereavement is an afflicting disposition."[14] He left a personal estate valued at more than $2 million, which would likely be close to $100 million today. Even that understates his relative wealth, because in that era in the United States, there were few fortunes to rival those of the Robber Barons later in the century or the very wealthy today. His personal wealth also did not include the substantial capital now owned by his sons.

The suddenness of his death was a shock. George wrote to his brothers, "The head that thought for us is gone."[15] As the grief settled, the sons began to look to the future, from a position of financial strength that few could rival. Having trained his sons and bound them together in a web of houses in four cities, Alexander Brown left his business empire in more than solid shape. Just as he was not one for emotional reflections and introspection in print, his sons greeted his passing with the same stoicism that had come to define their burgeoning merchant bank. George in Baltimore, William in Liverpool, John in Philadelphia and James in New York were left with a franchise that was only growing, and whatever emotion they may have felt at their formidable father's passing remains lost to us, if it was even known to them.

Theirs was the language of commerce, trust, integrity and propriety, as Alexander had preached and demanded. There was not a renegade among them, nor would there be among their children and grandchildren. They were, as their portraits suggested, men of affairs and of the world. And it was a world they were shaping with paper and plans. By the time the first phase of the railroad was operational in the early 1830s, Brown Brothers had extended its own business beyond cotton, linen and assorted other goods and ever more into buying and selling letters of credit to other merchants. In Liverpool, William Brown emerged as the dominant cotton trader, aided by a capable staff. In New York, James Brown built the house into a hub of information about prices, of cotton for sure but also of the relative rates of dollars versus pounds. As we shall see, the firm eventually turned that information into revenue. Everyone involved in transatlantic commerce needed clarity about rates, and the Browns became the most trusted source.

They collected fees on every aspect of transatlantic trade, starting with the linens imported by Alexander Brown from Ireland and then extending into dozens of other goods, cotton most important among them but including coffee, copper ore, guano, iron and sugar. They also started to act as a money center and a source of investment funds and capital raising. They slowly became what we would now think of as an investment bank, a merchant bank, and a lending bank all rolled into one. And their letters of credit were so respected and honored that they became a de facto issuer of currency, literally making the money that others used just as they used a dollar or a piece of gold in an era when both sovereign currency and metals were susceptible to massive and unpredictable swings in value.

Alexander's death, however, did clarify which sons were more deeply devoted to the business. Within a few months, on July 12, 1834, George resigned from the job as treasurer of the railroad and from the board of the Mechanics Bank. He explained his decision in a letter to William, "I observe you still take a good deal of interest in Railroads. It is to be hoped they will pay better with you than here."[16]

With the passing of Alexander, the locus of the firm moved to New York and Liverpool. George remained head of the Baltimore office, now named Alex. Brown & Sons. He was the official Baltimore agent of the New York house. His office was profitable, vital to the economic and urban life of Baltimore, but nonetheless eclipsed nationally by Brown Brothers & Co. It may have been inevitable that New York would surpass the Baltimore branch, but George's temperament hastened it. He was an adept businessman, but he had less hunger. Making New York even more central was the decision of another of the brothers, John A. Brown, to retire from the Philadelphia house in 1837, which he did on the heels of an experience so traumatic that it nearly ended Brown Brothers. It wasn't the first financial crisis to hit the United States, but it was the most formative. The collapse of 1819 was severe, but the Panic of 1837 was much worse. It was America's economic baptism by fire. Brown Brothers nearly succumbed, and by surviving, it ended up saving the entire system.

CHAPTER 3

EVERYBODY IS SPECULATING

*Everybody is speculating, and everything has become an object
of speculation. The most daring enterprises find encouragement;
all projects find subscribers. . . . Thus far everyone has made
money, as is always the case when speculation is in the ascendant.[1]*

The beginning of the 1830s saw the fortunes of the House of Brown
expand rapidly. Some of that can be attributed to the wise management of Alexander and the discipline he had instilled in his sons.
But the firm also benefited from the rising tide of American wealth. There
were no national economic statistics in those years, no calculating of GDP,
and at best a rudimentary census taken every ten years. But there was careful accounting of trade by merchants and planters, by shopkeepers and
shippers, and by state governments and the federal government in Washington, whose primary source of revenue was tariffs on that trade. The
government kept careful records of shipments of goods and above all of
cotton, which was by the 1830s the most lucrative and important of all
American products.

From the various records, historians have guesstimated that the economy of the United States grew by nearly 40 percent during the 1820s and
by another 35 percent in the first part of the 1830s.[2] The Browns were a
direct beneficiary, and then some. That portion of their business tied to

physical goods and the ships they owned likely grew in step with overall economic growth. But the portion of their business that was tied to paper, to letters of credit and earning fees on foreign exchange, grew even more quickly as they became one of the most trusted issuers of credit and paper. The house could ship only a finite amount of cotton, but they could handle vast quantities of paper.

The evolution of Brown Brothers from being merchants to becoming a merchant bank wasn't linear, nor was there any one sharp break or dramatic decision. As we've seen, Alexander Brown inculcated an ethos that his heirs embraced. Sometime after the War of 1812, Alexander realized that in a world where the value of paper money and hard metal money were constantly and chaotically in flux, meeting financial obligations fairly and on time had incalculable worth. Business acumen, timing and luck helped, but reputation was nonnegotiable. Cultivating an image of steadfastness, calm and sound judgment; being perceived as simple servants of their clients; earning a decent fee but not demanding an excessive one; measuring risks and steering clear of too many obligations—all of those ingredients were needed to build a house that could stand and survive the inevitable setbacks.

Brown Brothers was not uniquely structured. Family was almost always the foundation of durable trading houses. Trade for centuries had been a family affair because in most societies, blood was thicker than law and more reliable. A merchant invested considerable capital in each shipment, hoping that on the other side a promise to buy would be met. Having a family member on the receiving end was a guarantee against being defrauded. As merchant banks evolved in the United States and in Europe in the nineteenth century, they were almost always run as close-knit family partnerships: the Rothschilds; the Baring Brothers; the Warburgs; and later on J. & W. Seligman & Co.; Kuhn, Loeb & Co.; George Peabody & Co.; and the various houses of Morgan. All were partnerships that involved multiple generations of fathers, sons, uncles and cousins.[3] Family dynamics of centuries past were no less complicated than in our day, but in a world without robust and global financial institutions, family ties ensured a degree of trust: a stranger could abscond, disappear, default; a son, a brother, even a cousin were tied more closely into clan and tribe.

There was a prevalence of Jewish families in these foundational merchant banks, none grander or more famous than the Rothschilds. That house began in the eighteenth century when Frankfurt banker Amschel Rothschild dispatched his sons as his agents in London and Paris much as Alexander Brown had sent his progeny to New York, Philadelphia and Liverpool.[4] For centuries in Europe, Jewish merchants acted as bankers and moneylenders to noble families, providing the liquidity for princes and barons to fight whatever war for whatever reason and to build churches and palaces. With the early and medieval Christian world viewing money lending and the charging of interest as inherently immoral and biblically forbidden, it often fell to Jewish families, barely tolerated and living precariously under Christian rule, to provide the capital that was always in short supply. That led to a love-hate relationship between power and money. Rulers and aristocrats frequently needed loans in excess of whatever tax receipts they could collect and hence needed bankers who were a source of funds. But they also hated the dependency, distrusted the suppliers of capital and turned on them periodically.

Many of the colonists who settled America shared these ambivalent and usually hostile attitudes toward credit and money. The New England and mid-Atlantic colonies of eighteenth-century America valued thrift and embraced commerce, but as much as they needed credit and money in order to conduct trade, they remained wary of too much of either. Money was a necessary lubricant for trade, but outside the merchant class, it was not valued as an end unto itself. The aristocrats of the south were even less comfortable with money as a source of wealth, preferring instead tangible assets—land and slaves above all. Credit and paper money were seen as a dilution of real value, and while most recognized a need for a public institution to issue national coin and paper, private control of credit stirred unease. Thomas Jefferson frequently inveighed against private banks lending money and issuing their own notes as a threat to public order and stability. His attitudes hardened with the years. As he wrote to his friend John

Taylor in 1816, "Banking establishments are more dangerous than standing armies; & . . . the principle of spending money to be paid by posterity, under the name of funding, is but swindling futurity on a large scale."

Jefferson's hostility toward private money lending echoed ancient attitudes toward moneylenders, stemming from the biblical stories of Jesus overturning the lending tables outside the temple in Jerusalem and winding from there through the centuries. And while Jefferson was explicit about his contempt and discomfort, it's equally telling that numerous false quotations have been ascribed to Jefferson that make his distaste of banking and money seem even more intense than it actually was. The letter to Taylor became the basis for even more vituperative—and false—words attributed to Jefferson railing against moneylenders and bankers as the central threat to the yeoman democracy that he believed to be at the heart of the union.

The upshot was that money and credit and the bankers and merchants who provided them were viewed with distrust. An urban commercial world was at odds with the Jeffersonian ideal of landowners controlling their own economic destiny. Even in mid-Atlantic and New England towns that produced finished goods from the raw materials that the South provided, money was tolerated as necessary evil but not trusted as a store of value. The initial rise of merchant banking families like the Browns was largely beneath the radar of public consciousness, but as these families grew richer and as their reach began to extend, the tensions surrounding money, credit and democracy moved to the foreground. Mild at first, those anxieties morphed into something much darker in the 1830s, triggered by the acrimonious debates about the fate of the Second Bank of the United States and by the first great financial crisis of the early republic, which would subsequently be called the Panic of 1837.

As it turned out, the Panic of 1837 was only prevented from becoming a full-blown transatlantic economic collapse because of Brown Brothers—not because the Browns rescued the financial system, but because they were rescued by the Bank of England. By 1837, Brown Brothers, a financial linchpin on both sides of the Atlantic, had become too big to fail.

Alexander Brown's conservative, and occasionally sanctimonious, philosophy did not prevent the House of Brown from expanding into other businesses. The family bought and built its own ships to transport goods across the Atlantic, and the patriarch's injunction to focus on "one pursuit" did not prevent the family from developing a lucrative business in issuing paper credits. Brown Brothers was not a state-chartered bank; it could not issue legal tender, print sovereign dollars, nor stamp official coins. But at a time when money itself was not quite the fixed thing it would later become, Brown Brothers became a de facto creator of money. It was not the only house to issue letters of credit, but it was by far the most reliable.

In a world without global banks, letters of credit were vital to international trade. The reason was simple: without an accepted global currency (other than gold, which was illiquid and limited in supply, and the British pound sterling, which was hardly a neutral vehicle), the most precious currency was trust that payments would be made. Merchants, especially those sending goods across an ocean, took considerable risk. Storms were a chronic threat to cargo, and even with smooth waters, it could take months before the merchant knew whether or not the cargo had arrived and had been paid for. That meant that all the money tied up in a shipment was in doubt and unusable until the trade settled. Importers were wary of committing money to goods that hadn't yet arrived or might never. They certainly wouldn't send gold across an ocean or overland for months of travel in the hope that the sellers on the other side would then faithfully dispatch the goods. And what if the ship sank or the caravan was robbed? Hence the evolution of letters of credit, which had existed in one form or another for centuries but which merchant bankers such as the Browns began to formalize.

Here's how it worked: the seller, let's say a cotton plantation owner with a shipment from New Orleans bound for Liverpool, would contract with an agent of a Liverpool buyer. The buyer, however, would not advance full payment until the shipment was actually received safely in Liverpool, while the seller would be loath to send the cotton without assurances of payment.

Hence the need for a trusted intermediary. Brown Brothers would issue a letter of credit to the seller redeemable even if the buyer couldn't meet his obligations. In return, Brown Brothers received a fee, on every letter.

Of course, issuing such a letter put the firm issuing it at risk for having to make a payment in case the buyer defaulted. Brown Brothers spent considerable time doing due diligence on their clients, creating that rating system grading potential customers on a scale from one to three. The family issued letters only for those whom it deemed trustworthy and financially sound, much as banks would later develop credit scores and credit-worthiness for potential borrowers.

Letters of credit were a central aspect of the trading system, but given multiple ports and products, it soon became considerably more complicated than just letters of credit. A host of other paper promises underpinned transatlantic and global trade, especially bills of exchange and bankers' acceptances. Each fulfilled distinct functions, some guaranteeing payment to a seller, others indicating that a bank had "accepted" a note as valid, and others promising specific payment at a set date in the future. Depending on who had accepted them and what the underlying product was, these various pieces of paper were then treated as having their own intrinsic worth, just as a bond today can be bought and sold by numerous intermediaries, none of whom will actually pay the interest or principal on the full amount or hold it for very long. Often the letters were accepted by other banks "at a discount," which meant that the bank would discount their face value and advance the holder partial payment until the entire commercial transaction on which they were based was complete. These bills and letters of the early nineteenth century, which made trade between the United States and Great Britain possible, thus became a form of currency and were bought and sold many times over, exchanged and discounted along the way. They also became the primary means of harmonizing dollars and pounds because all trade between America and Britain involved payments to Americans in dollars that were then sold in Liverpool for pounds, and vice versa.

Trading bills and letters became its own submarket. Bills were not only bought and sold; they were also bundled and packaged. Those bundled financial instruments were priced according to perceived risk and creditworthiness, ranging from individual assessments of whether the person writing the bills was overextended to whether the underlying assumptions about the price of the cotton crop were reasonable and whether the exchange rate had been estimated wisely. Financial centers such as New York, Liverpool and London teemed with notes issued, discounted and repackaged. The bill might begin with a promise of party A to pay party B at a set date based on goods being shipped, but in the interim it would be traded back and forth by third parties with no connection to the actual deal. If that sounds vaguely familiar, it's because the same process run amok and fueled by twenty-first-century computing technology was one reason for the financial upheaval of 2008–9, when mortgages—which began as a promise of a homeowner to repay a bank loan by a certain date—were also diced, sliced and packaged by individuals and groups who had no connection to the original transaction. What distinguished then from now was that these nineteenth-century notes were not just physical paper but paper whose worth was partly determined by the reputation of the issuer. And in that world, the House of Brown had built a reputation unblemished by the War of 1812, undented by the crisis of 1819 and undimmed by mounting competition. Notes issued by Brown Brothers were more than just words on a paper. They were as good as gold, and in some ways better, easier to carry and convey, promising that the holder would get paid in currency he could use.

These instruments could be complicated. All professions have their jargon, and finance is no exception. Letters of credit, bills of exchange, discounts and bankers' acceptance are just a handful of a multitude of trade finance tools, much as a snake, a pipe wrench and a hole saw are the stock-in-trade for a plumber. Unless you use them on a regular basis, they are a bit of a mystery, which is why people pay other people to do things they neither understand nor want to take the time to figure out. A cotton seller in New Orleans in 1835 knew that he wanted to get a good price from Liverpool, and he paid intermediaries such as shippers and brokers and merchants to make that happen even if he didn't fully understand how the whole system worked.

By the 1820s, transatlantic trade was dominated by cotton. American production of cotton went from 80 million pounds and 16 percent of all production globally before 1820 to 385 million pounds and 49 percent in 1830 to 654 million pounds and 62 percent in 1840.[5] Nothing else compared with cotton as a source of income from abroad, and the cotton trade was a boom not just to southern ports such as Mobile, Savannah, Charleston and New Orleans but also to the northern cities that facilitated it. Every bale of cotton shipped to Liverpool made possible the import of finished goods from England, and those bales in turn fueled the textile boom of Lancashire. As the cotton trade blossomed, so did Brown Brothers, and while Alexander may have run the overall business, it was William who propelled the cotton franchise from Liverpool. His offices were adjacent not just to the docks but to the cotton exchange, and having cultivated so many connections, he became one of the leading cotton merchants of the city. He also nurtured capable lieutenants, none more adept than Joseph Shipley, an American Quaker who eventually became a partner of the firm and whose name was added when the Liverpool house later spun off independently to become the storied London bank of Brown Shipley.

Alexander managed the purchase of shipments in the American cotton ports and arranged the advances to the planters, working with a network of agents. But it was William who was responsible for selling the cotton in Liverpool, and at the right price. It was William who informed his father and brothers what the market would bear, what quantities the merchants of Liverpool and the factories of Manchester and Birmingham demanded and what price they would pay for which strain. English factory owners knew William would deliver what he promised, and that his supply was guaranteed by Alexander in Baltimore and then by James in New York. It was a potent triad. By the late 1830s, William handled nearly 10 percent of all cotton imports into Liverpool, while James managed as much as 15 percent of all American cotton exports, mostly on consignment, some outright. And those numbers understate the family's influence, because what was unmeasured—and in those years largely unmeasurable—was the amount of paper that the house managed and the commissions and fees that they earned not from physical cotton but from financing the entire cotton trade.

Out of an estimated total of about $100 million in trade between the United States and Great Britain in 1835, Brown Brothers alone accounted for $11 million. Only some of that was finished goods and cotton that they bought and sold directly; a larger portion was cotton they bought and sold on consignment; but the largest segment was paper that they issued or underwrote on behalf of other merchants and banks. So substantial was their business that the Bank of England began to monitor Brown Brothers as a possible source of instability should something go wrong. "They act as agents for some of the American banks," said one report, "so that a considerable portion of the Exchange business between the two Countries is effected through this House . . . and they give credits to approved agents of American Houses who travel through the manufacturing districts and order goods at Manchester, Birmingham, Sheffield and other places and who pay for such goods by bills drawn upon this House, on which they receive a commission for which they are repaid by consignments of American produce." In other words, the House of Brown made money coming and going, on goods they exported and imported and then on goods that others exported and imported.[6]

As the Bank of England recognized, even as the Browns' influence as cotton merchants grew, the family was diversifying away from consignments and the physical sale of goods. That shift was under way before Alexander's death and accelerated under the joint efforts of James in New York and William in Liverpool. The brothers began as well to offer financing to other agents, advancing money not just to planters directly but to agents and factors (as buyers of cotton in the South were called) who dealt directly with planters. William also developed a robust business providing paper promises of pound sterling payments in advance, taking fees each time, always in coordination with his brother James in New York, always backed by the knowledge of what James was about to buy or underwrite. It was all meticulously managed and choreographed, and there was no question that with Alexander's passing, it was William, as the eldest son, who directed the ballet.

Through all of this, there is no way to sugarcoat the fact that the Browns, because of their prominence in the cotton trade—whether physical or financial—profited greatly from slavery. In the broadest sense, *no one* who traded and profited from cotton could claim to be free of slavery's stain. Brown Brothers in the 1830s was an integral part of a financial ecosystem that depended on enslaved people producing cotton. Liverpool had been a center of the Atlantic slave trade in the 1700s, and as the new international center of cotton trading, it remained tethered to an economy that had slave labor at its center. William both benefited from that system and objected to it morally. He was an outspoken advocate of abolition and strongly supported Parliament's Slavery Abolition Act of 1833, which ended slavery in the British Empire. Like many in the northern states and in England, the Browns found slavery distasteful. They would never have purchased slaves themselves. And yet they nonetheless wholeheartedly embraced the cotton trade. Even with their moral objections, the Browns did not opt out. Perhaps that is not a fair burden to place on them retroactively; they could hardly have unilaterally changed the slave system; they did not directly deal in human chattel; and far more people were complicit in the slave-fueled cotton economy than were actively opposed to it. Anyone who bought cotton cloth and wore cotton clothes benefited from slave labor, and even the most ardent abolitionists used cotton. William, in Liverpool, would rarely have encountered enslaved men or women. Slavery had been banned in England for decades. But James and John and George had each been sent at various times by their father to meet with their partners in New Orleans, Mobile and Savannah, all of which were southern cities where slavery was legal and prevalent. More than millions of other people in the north, the Browns would actually have interacted with slave owners, and been served meals by enslaved men and women. Slavery was also legal in Maryland, though the vast majority of African Americans living in Baltimore were free. The Brown family later took a stance against slavery and were strong

Unionists and Republicans, but slavery was not an abstraction for them. It was part of their business.[7]

And business in the 1830s, fueled by cotton, was very good. In boom times, most people ride the wave. More cotton meant more trade, more trade meant more money, more money meant more trade. Prices started to rise, and sudden fortunes were made. And as is often the case, with increased prosperity came increased risk and speculation. That rarely ends well, and in 1837, it ended quite badly.

Like most major crises, the one in 1837 had multiple causes. It was, in truth, many crises that overlapped and fed on one another, and only after the denouement in the spring of 1837 did all of those get lumped together as the Panic of 1837. The most immediate trigger was the expiration of the controversial but systemically vital Second Bank of the United States in 1836. The idea of a national bank had always been divisive. The First Bank of the United States had confronted powerful opposition, and the 1816 federal chartering of the Second Bank of the United States hardened the fault lines between those who believed democracy rested on land and property and saw in money and finance the sins and weaknesses of man and those who thought that trading and credit backstopped by a national monetary authority were the essential lubricants of a strong and prosperous country. The Second Bank may have been necessary, but it widened the fissure between the Jeffersonian vision of a democracy based on landowners and the Hamiltonian one of a republic fueled by commerce and capital.

Almost from the moment the Second Bank received its federal charter, it generated a backlash that helped propel a new political movement, based in the western states and animated by an angry conviction that the elites of the coasts were using the bank to enrich themselves and take from the settlers and the farmers. Their champion was Andrew Jackson, himself a son of that frontier, the general who captured New Orleans in 1815 and who was carried to political prominence and the presidency in 1828 on waves of that anger. Jackson was determined to give more power to those who had yet to enjoy the rewards of the new republic. His presidency unleashed a populist fervor and produced a series of democratic reforms that expanded voting rights and enfranchised those who had felt, with good reason, that their voices had been ignored. The bank became a symbol of elite power, and Jackson and his followers vowed to end it. The contest was personalized by the clash between the patrician head of the bank, Nicholas Biddle, ensconced in his neoclassical offices on Chestnut Street in Philadelphia, and the rough, blunt Jackson. Jackson asserted that he stood for the common man. He said the bank was "a monster," and he denounced it as a relic of "nobility systems that enabled a few and rich intelligent men to live upon the labor of many." He singled out Biddle as a leading perpetrator of that injustice. The battle between Jackson and Biddle was dubbed "the Bank War," a war that Jackson won conclusively when he campaigned for reelection in 1832 vowing not to renew the bank's charter in 1836. True to his campaign promises, Jackson undermined the bank, vetoed its renewal, and happily danced on its grave.[8]

It proved to be a pyrrhic victory. By the early 1830s, the bank was more than doing its job. It was one of the few stable financial institutions in a country where speculation was rampant. The bank under Biddle had brought order to the issuance of money and paper and kept a partial rein on local banks. Those banks, chartered by state governments who wanted them to boost activity, happily took deposits and lent out liberally, with little in the way of risk controls or assessment of what we would now call deposit ratios. They were nicknamed "wildcat banks," and they saw their business as lending as much as possible and charging high interest rates. They printed their own paper, which was honored when times were good. The wildcats were immensely profitable, until the music stopped.

Jackson was less a champion of the wildcats than of the rugged individuals whom they served. He didn't much like paper money, seeing it ultimately as a tool of the elite, even though he conveniently ignored how much his own supporters relied on the paper money of the wildcats. He cast the Second Bank as an antidemocratic institution guarded by an unelected elite who controlled the supply of paper money in order to monopolize power and wealth. His message played well politically, but it was economically flawed at best. In practice, the Second Bank used its limited powers to facilitate the burgeoning wealth of the growing middle class by tamping down the economic wildness of earlier years. The unruly armature of American banking and finance was unlike that of anywhere in the world. There were far more banks and quasi banks. State legislatures gave out charters like aunts giving out candy to nephews whose cavities they didn't have to worry about. The early United States had more banks, more money in circulation, more income and more growth than anywhere in the world. As the U.S. economy boomed, the Second Bank of the United States checked some of the excesses of American capitalism. It was damned for what it did and for what it didn't do. After 1819, it was condemned for restricting the supply of money, and then a decade later, under Jackson, it was assailed for printing too much and creating inflation that ate into the income of the working classes and the farmers. But its paper was also sound, and there was no repeat of what had happened in 1819. Then the bank died (or rather was executed by the president and his party), and the system started to unravel.[9]

Jackson himself pulled the string. One of his final acts as president was to insist that government lands be paid for only in gold and silver coins, not paper. His Specie Circular act wasn't a law but rather an executive order that wouldn't have been able to pass in Congress but which had as much impact as any piece of legislation. The act was Jackson's farewell revenge on the bank and its control of paper currency. As he said in his farewell address, "The paper-money system of this country may be used as an engine to undermine your free institutions, and that those who desire to engross all power in the hands of the few and to govern by corruption or force are aware of its power and prepared to employ it."[10]

Conflating paper money with elite privilege, Jackson hoped his Specie Circular would kneecap the eastern elites by cutting off their supply of paper. Instead, he helped trigger a financial meltdown, one that ultimately did imperil those elites but also decimated the economy of his supporters. The result of the circular was that specie—the term for "hard money"—shifted out of banks, mostly New York ones, and into the U.S. Treasury as people paid for land. As more gold poured into the U.S. Treasury, less was in circulation, and where gold went, silver followed. There was such a demand for specie that American banks began redeeming whatever notes they held against British pounds by demanding specie from English counterparts in lieu of the normal flow of paper, which meant that gold began draining from the Bank of England. Given that all paper money ultimately rested on a foundation of hard money, the scarcity of gold and silver triggered a disastrous chain reaction.

The sudden contraction of activity caused by the Specie Circular set off the first wave of what would become the Panic of 1837. But that wasn't the sole cause. There was enough blame to go around: blame for Jackson for not renewing the charter of the Second Bank and for demanding hard money; blame for the speculators who had been using easy credit to buy up land in the West; blame for the merchants who gorged on letters of credit and ignored the value of the underlying goods; blame for English banks for letting standards lapse in the face of the immense profits to be gained from trade with the United States. Most people at the time, however, were united in the belief that banks and bankers had made a bad situation worse. Wrote one ardent Jacksonian, "The moment a spirit of speculation can be excited, the banks increase the flame by pouring oil upon it; the instant a reaction takes place, they add to the distress a thousand fold."[11]

Starting in late 1836, a series of small crises erupted, extending from the French Quarter in New Orleans to the halls of the Bank of England in London. The long distances and slow communications meant that just as one crisis subsided in the cotton-trading hub of New Orleans, another intensified in the merchant cities of Baltimore, Philadelphia and New York; and just as it began to wane there, another flared in Liverpool and London. Sailing from Liverpool to the East Coast could take anywhere from thirty to seventy days, depending on winds and weather. On the one hand, the snail's pace of information prevented a rapid chain reaction. On the other hand, that same pace meant that even when New York took measures to prevent an escalation, by the time information reached Liverpool and London, it was often too late to halt the contagion.

At the end of 1836, the price of cotton started to sag. Combined with the upheaval of Jackson's policies, the ingredients were in place for serious tumult. The Bank of England, already reeling from the Specie Circular, took the preemptive step of tightening its requirements for accepting discounted American letters of credit based on the price of cotton. That in turn put pressure on merchants and middlemen to sell their cotton before credit became scarcer and prices declined further, which in turn pressured the many who had bought and sold paper at a bull-market premium based on future sales.[12] If a similar set of stars had aligned in later years, when travel was faster and the cities and continents were linked by telegraph and telephone, there would have been a rapid credit crunch as information spread nearly instantly, leaving a horde of people holding worthless paper and unsold goods. But in the 1830s, it took longer for things to unravel. Only after months of worsening news and problematic price action did multiple financial centers panic at about the same time, shortly after the inauguration of Martin Van Buren in March 1837, who could hardly have assumed the mantle of the presidency at an unluckier moment.

Even before then, London merchants and financiers were feeling a sense of dread. By refusing to honor letters of credit trading at discounts, the Bank of England threw the whole system of paper and credit into turmoil. William Brown traveled to the bank's headquarters to urge the directors not to make decisions reactively in haste and fear. He knew that if the bank acted purely in its narrow and short-term self-interest, it could set off a cascade of unintended consequences. In an age where there was no central clearinghouse and no public accounting of credit, no one knew exactly who was holding what, including the sovereign Bank of England. Brown pleaded for the directors to let events unfold a while longer. They ignored his advice.

As banks on both sides of the Atlantic began to horde specie, rumors and whispers then began to take on inordinate weight. Shortly after Van Buren's inauguration, the main New York agent of the powerful House of Baring collapsed because it had advanced too much credit to cotton sellers in New Orleans. News reports captured the drama in breathless prose. *The New York Spectator* reported first: "Early in the forenoon, the word was passed from street to street, and from counting room to counting room, that the firm of J.L. & S. Josephs had stopped in consequence of failures in New Orleans." Then the *New York Herald* added to the fire: "As soon as it was known, the news flew like lightening—people rubbed their eyes, and would scarcely believe the reality of the fact. Crowds collected in Wall Street—and that busy avenue was filled with anxious faces through the live-long day. . . . The street is full of rumors, every one more frightful than another."[13]

Distances may have been great between the various centers, but within each, the business community was packed together in a few square blocks, whether in New York, New Orleans, Baltimore, London or Liverpool. Wall Street then wasn't just a thoroughfare in Lower Manhattan; Lower Manhattan *was* Manhattan, and Wall Street was one of its fulcrums. The French Quarter wasn't then a haunted bacchanalian tourist district; it was the commercial center of the fifth-largest city in the United States, with 50,000 people densely packed. In such cramped spaces, the cliché that rumors traveled like wildfire was only a tad hyperbolic.

As concern and uncertainty blossomed, the press of the day did what the press have always done: it stoked hot emotions. If there were reports of merchants seeking news from Liverpool, the papers would describe them as "frantic for some bit of information." But hot stories alone would have burned themselves out without kindling. Credit, which depended then and now on the faith that borrowers would make good and creditors would not pull the plug, stopped flowing. Wages went unpaid. In New York, hungry workers rioted outside of flour mills. Established players such as the Browns, the Barings and the Rothschilds remained solvent, but even they were unsure about whose shoes would drop next.

For the first time, the word *panic* was used as a label for a major financial crisis. In 1837, a new lexicon was created to describe a spiral of financial institutions collapsing, credit drying up, businesses shuttering. The Panic of 1837 also established a template for how these times would be depicted in the media over the subsequent decades. Until the twentieth century, *media* meant newspapers, and the newspaper business was highly competitive, with multiple papers clamoring for readers and ads in any given city or town. Then as now, panic wasn't good for business in general, but it was certainly good for the news business. Writers and editors sought language to stir up passions, gin up readers and juice circulation. What was true in news held in politics as well. Political factions saw opportunity in calling the evolving events a *panic*. Nicholas Biddle, who had lost the bank war to Jackson but was not about to go gently, seized on the crisis as an opening to embarrass Van Buren and establish himself as the manqué defender of the business class so despised by the Jacksonians.

By April, Biddle, now the head of the Pennsylvania-chartered Bank of the United States, helped organize the merchants of New York. They petitioned him in Philadelphia asking that he use the prestige of the bank's name—no longer a federal institution but still symbolic—to provide a backstop. He then came to New York and went from home to home and business to business, commiserating with those in danger of losing their franchise and engaging in multiple head-shaking sessions that something had to be done. Having known John Brown socially and worked with him professionally in Philadelphia, Biddle met with James Brown in New York. They shared the conviction that the whole thing was a sorry mess that could have been avoided were it not for the hot-tempered ex-president. But while blaming Jackson released some tension, it solved nothing.

Energized though Biddle's group may have been, they were unsure of what to do. They drew up a list of grievances saying that they were being unfairly maligned in popular imagination and by politicians eager to ride the wave of populist animosity. That list was duly printed, and quickly rebutted. But by mid-May, Biddle's impromptu faction was able—in the absence of any state or federal intervention—to suspend the requirement that New York banks redeem paper with specie. This one move nullified the Specie Circular. That then prevented a complete run on the banks that would have drained them entirely of metal money, which would have precipitated an even greater implosion.

Even as some calm returned to Lower Manhattan, panic was accelerating in Liverpool and London and rippling outward. New Orleans was also roiling. In the age of cotton, each of these nodes needed to be stable for each one to be functional. Whatever calm had settled over New York would be short-lived if panic accelerated across the ocean or down the river. Just as New York was settling down, Liverpool was melting down, with Brown Brothers at the epicenter. Though William had discerned signs of froth in 1836, having watched his competitors loosen their standards, take on more questionable paper and accrue liabilities that far exceeded what they had on hand, he was helpless in the spring of 1837. He had been trained by his father to sniff out any scent of speculative bubbles, and he had. He had made sure that the Browns stayed conservative, and they did. He had instructed the New York house to conserve capital and curtail its commitments. He had made modest assumptions about the price of cotton. And by the end of May, none of it mattered. Big and vital though the House of Brown was, it was at the mercy of forces the brothers could not control. In London, the Bank of England demanded more and more specie, and William's branch in Liverpool, through little fault of its own, found that it was about to face a time crunch that threatened its existence.

Like all merchant bankers, the Browns took on obligations based on the arrival and sale of cargo. The whole reason for the existence of letters of credit and the various other financial instruments was the chronic mismatch between when people required payment and when goods actually arrived and were sold. If all banks and creditors started to demand full payment immediately, irrespective of whether the underlying cargo had been delivered and sold, *anyone* holding paper or issuing it was vulnerable. When banks on both sides of the Atlantic simultaneously called in specie in 1837, the Browns could not find a safe haven. They had multiple obligations in pounds and in dollars, all due at different times. In normal circumstances, their obligations could be delayed or deferred by a matter of weeks if need be, and given how careful and systematic they were, delays were rarely necessary. But the late spring of 1837 was not a normal time.

One reason that the family may have been most imperiled was the same reason it was less exposed subsequently: having franchises on both sides of the Atlantic was a strength when there was a purely American economic crisis or a purely English one, but the risk was magnified in the rare case of a crisis on both sides at the same time, which is what happened in 1837. The crash of 1819 had been almost entirely American. Then, in 1825, there was a sharp panic-like contraction in England. Both had done many merchants and banks great harm, but the Browns had sailed through. The Panic of 1837, however, metastasized and spread from America to Liverpool. By June, William Brown and his house were facing a wave of demands that they could not possibly meet. It was as if every piece of paper bearing their name was suddenly presented for payment, some at a discount for sure, but no house or bank ever had enough specie on hand to meet all of its outstanding obligations simultaneously. William Brown could not just write more notes promising payment. Or rather he could, but not ones he could honor, which would have meant ruination for sure. The New York house was well capitalized, but it needed every bit of capital it had on hand to manage the problems in New York. It had little to spare for William in Liverpool.

As a result, the Liverpool branch was in dire straits. It needed ships full of cotton or other goods to arrive from New York and Baltimore. It needed to sell that stuff in Liverpool, and then it could redeem its paper and letters. It needed then for the exports it had arranged—clothes, furniture, metalwork, lace, and any number of products that emerged from the factories of Britain—to be shipped to America and sold there. Otherwise, the Liverpool branch would be asked to remit money it simply didn't have.

William Brown was not just financially helpless; his body was also betraying him. Having suffered from various ailments as a young man, he had periods throughout his life when he was bedridden and unable to work. Fortunately, he excelled at bringing in nonfamily deputies, and Joseph Shipley proved an able steward in these months. Shipley observed about the House of Brown, "We do not suffer from speculations of our own, as we enter into none. We are suffering from the imprudence and misfortune of others to whom we have given credit. . . . No human precaution could have guarded us against heavy losses from widespread convulsion in both countries." William Brown's house could be prudent and careful, but it couldn't speed up shipping times or loading times, and it couldn't redeem paper with other paper in a time when nobody wanted *any* paper. William held out hope that the crunch had subsided somewhat in April, but when the mail packet arrived in Liverpool in late May, it showed that New York had worsened, and more houses there had failed. What a difference a few weeks would have made: a letter in mid-June would have showed New York stabilizing. Instead, Brown wrote to Shipley, "The packet is in and nothing can be worse than the news. It is quite certain we cannot sustain ourselves." Ill and confined to bed, he dispatched Shipley to London to plead with the Bank of England for more time and for a lifeline.[14]

Shipley arrived, with proverbial cap in hand and with a detailed financial statement showing that the firm's liabilities were more than covered by its capital in the United States, but that if it was forced to cover its outstanding obligations in full and immediately, it would collapse and with it a considerable portion of the transatlantic trade system. In its official letter to the bank, the firm concluded, "We regret the necessity of pressing this upon your attention at this moment, but as our payments must be met tomorrow, without your aid we have no alternative . . . and as about two-thirds of all of our engagements arise out of exports of British manufacturers, you can readily judge what disastrous consequences would follow our stoppage at this time . . . and as no doubt a very large proportion of our acceptances is held by the Bank, we hope that you will feel an interest and find an advantage in supporting us."[15] The Browns were holding paper with dates certain; those dates were approaching fast, and they would be unable to meet the demands.

It was, in essence, a plea to the bank suggesting that William Brown & Co. was too big to fail. The governors of the Bank of England, who had refused multiple pleas from other firms, understood that whatever the moral hazards of Shipley's argument, the collapse of Brown at that juncture would have jeopardized far more than the money of a few merchant houses. If Brown went down, there was a sizable chance the system would buckle. The House of Brown was simply too systemically important, and so the bank decided to bail them out.

It was not a generous bailout, just a loan to cover possible losses, and a short-term one at that. But it was enough to keep the Liverpool house afloat as more bad news poured in from New York. Shipley wrote to Brown, still bedridden in Liverpool, "The Bank views our position as altogether different from most of the others, as it really is. . . . We have gained some triumph amid the general wreck." Shipley returned to Liverpool and was greeted by the clerks at Brown with cheers, and those cheers spread from street to street. Backs were clapped and drafts were downed. William emerged from his bed and stumbled to the office a few hundred yards away. His firm had just had a near-death experience, and he wasn't going to have one as well. His house had lived to see another day, and he would live almost thirty more years. The crisis wasn't quite over, but there was a palpable sense that it had at least crested.[16] Several weeks later, the bank agreed to cover Brown through the end of the year. That ended up being unnecessary, and the house paid off its entire debt well before December. It would not have made it till the end of the year, however, without the bailout.

In the United States, the crisis also subsided, because of the joint actions of multiple private firms rather than any central response, which would have been impossible now that there was no federal Bank of the United States. That collective of banks in New York continued to freeze specie payments into early summer, halting the run. Historically, sometimes that works; often not. Halting can often aggravate matters, as people who otherwise had taken a wait-and-see approach respond to the freeze by assuming that things are much worse. Fortunately, in the summer of 1837, the de facto bank holiday ended the panic. Banks in other cities followed suit, with the result that the entire banking system, decentralized and unorganized though it was, just stopped. Word spread from place to place that banks wouldn't honor demands that they could not meet and would shutter until they could. Rather than intensifying anxieties, that was enough to bring the crisis to an end. The financial system, primitive compared with later years, stabilized. The "real" economy remained depressed, however, and it was years before economic activity fully recovered in the United States.

As recognition for his vital role in saving the firm, Shipley was made a partner of the Liverpool house, which was soon renamed Brown Shipley & Co. Just as the locus in America shifted from Baltimore to New York, so too did it shift from Liverpool to London. William Brown remained a powerful presence in Liverpool but opened an office in Founder's Court in London. Brown Shipley would later supply the Bank of England with several of its directors and governors. Bolstered by the emergency loan, Brown Brothers had emerged in more than decent shape. Hundreds of firms had failed, but the Browns suffered losses of maybe a third of their holdings. It was a humbling experience. Writing to his older brother William, George Brown reflected on the summer's trauma, "I feel mortified at the way in which we are placed with the Bank of England."

The crisis also marked a new chapter for the family. The tumult of 1837 was too much for John in Philadelphia. It was more of a final straw than a sudden rupture. John was already being marginalized by the sheer weight of business in New York and Liverpool and by the force of personality of William and James. And he was, according to his nephew, "less fitted by temperament than his brothers for the competition and hurry of modern business life." He decided to cash out and bow out. He maintained an interest in the Chestnut Street branch and turned his focus to various Presbyterian charities in Philadelphia, including churches, schools and hospitals. As for George, who had already partly exited, he took the logical next step and cashed out his share of the partnership. "I would not have so much anxiety if I were to withdraw and do a limited business," he wrote to William. Having already reduced his role after his father's death, George redeemed the remainder of his shares. Alex. Brown & Sons in Baltimore continued, a separate and smaller business, albeit one that survived as an independent entity until nearly the end of the twentieth century.[17]

The panic clarified but did nothing to resolve the divide between those who saw an American future propelled by capital and those who believed that this path was the road to ruin. The Jacksonian animus toward the merchants of capital did not fade with Jackson's passing. His belief that corporations and wealthy individuals sought "to engross all power in the hands of the few" remained deeply engrained in popular consciousness, and it resonates just as much in the twenty-first century as it did in the nineteenth. On the other side, that view was contested by the Whigs in the 1830s and 1840s, who saw paper money and credit as a way to help "the poor industrious man become a rich man," because it liberated economic activity from the tyranny of inert gold and silver, whose finite supply meant that the world was forever in a zero-sum game of winners and losers. The Panic of 1837 was one battle in a long war that paper money would eventually win. In 1837, it was at best a stalemate.[18]

The Browns were central players in the drama of 1837, but they were as yet hardly a household name. Almost no merchant house was, outside of Lower Manhattan or the Liverpool waterfront or the riverbanks of New Orleans. Within the tight community of traders and merchants, however, the Browns were a brand name, burnished and trusted. That aided their business, but soon enough it also became a public liability. Jackson and his heirs believed that these men hid in obscurity because it served their dark plot. The opacity of financial transactions, the arcana of all of those confusing pieces of paper many times removed from actual specie, carrying different maturities and different prices, all controlled by faceless bankers whose names were unknown, added to the sense that levers were being pulled by a shadowy cabal that thrived in secrecy and anonymity. Over the coming decades, wave after wave of populist movements took aim at the financial elite as the source of all economic ills. That strain had, of course, been around since the original split between Thomas Jefferson and Alexander Hamilton, but it deepened as the nineteenth century progressed. The House of Brown became a perfect example of a pernicious banking cabal. Alexander Brown had spent decades crafting a firm that purposely did not draw attention to itself; how ironic that staying out of the public eye had the effect of drawing even more attention.

Negative attitudes, however, sat side by side with the yearning American hunger for more, for more land in the West, more new industries, more power. That hunger couldn't be sated. There was never enough. It sent settlers into the West, it built railroads stretching across the continent, and it demanded ever more trade across the ocean. Many people may have hated banks and distrusted bankers, but almost everyone wanted money and needed credit. And unlike Europe, which was still shaking off the sclerotic hold of aristocracy, the United States did not look down on the creation of new business and new industries. Credit and capital were the fuel for American growth, and how ironic as well that the archetypal American populist Andrew Jackson, in his zealous opposition to bankers and those pulling the levers of money, would by ending the life of the central bank lay the foundation for waves of boom and bust that would cause such pain to the farmers and workers and settlers whom he purported to defend.

And as for the Brown brothers, even as their houses began to drift into separate businesses, they saw no diminution of their activity. Quite the opposite. After 1837, they grew faster and became ever more profitable. By the end of the 1830s, even after spending millions to redeem John and George, Brown Brothers still had a value in excess of $3 million, and that was increasing rapidly. In addition to cotton and finance, they began to build another empire, this time of ships to carry not just goods but people. The House of Brown never stopped being a financial house, but had things gone differently in the 1840s and 1850s, it might have become not the longest-lived merchant bank but the most powerful shipping company in the world. It almost happened, but for the rise of the company that would later launch the *Titanic* and a disaster at sea that forever altered the lives of the brothers Brown.

CHAPTER 4

DREAMS OF THE *ARCTIC*

T he fog over the ocean, miles away from Newfoundland, was thick, though that wasn't rare for a late September day. Aboard the transatlantic steamship *Arctic*, pride of the Collins Line, seven days out from Liverpool and making its usual swift passage to New York, all was well. It was like no other passenger ship before it. Crossings had been necessary but rarely comfortable. Chilly spartan quarters and mediocre provisions were the order of the day. Not for the *Arctic*. The passengers were treated to luxurious service, attentive staff, ample food (regular and elaborate four-course meals), ampler liquor. The decks were outfitted with lush, steam-heated cabins, a barbershop and baths, and a one-hundred-foot-long stateroom clad in rosewood, lit by windows of stained glass and cushioned with fine carpets.

The ship had made multiple crossings in its nearly four years of operation, but on that September voyage in 1854, it carried an unusual number of VIPs, among them the son of the captain; the wife and son of the eponymous founder of the line, Edward Knight Collins; and the son, two daughters and a grandchild of James Brown, head of the New York house and the prime backer of the Collins Line as well as the company president. The *Arctic* was the largest steamship to traverse the Atlantic Ocean, and the fastest, having cut the travel time from New York to Liverpool from three or more weeks to a mere nine days, seventeen hours, and fifteen minutes. Commanding the ship on that September crossing was the same man who held the speed record, James Luce. The Brown and Collins families knew that their progeny were in good hands on such a sturdy, speedy ship. Disasters happened at sea, but this ship was not supposed to sink. And then, that night, in the middle of the Atlantic Ocean, it did. So many lives were lost, and the Brown family was forever scarred. Yet the sacrifice of those children was not entirely in vain. James Brown never fully recovered from the loss of his family in the wreckage of the *Arctic*, but Brown Brothers may never have survived until the twenty-first century had the ship made a safe passage.[1]

James Brown and Edward Collins were strange bedfellows. In the years since his father's death, James had gradually emerged from the shadows and asserted himself. He was scrupulous and focused. His son later told of how as a young man, James had terrible writing and quietly engaged a tutor so that his penmanship would be legible instead of a burden to the many young clerks who worked at the firm. He was known for excessive courtesy even to those who worked for him, asking a junior clerk to mail a letter as if it were a Herculean task and apologizing for the inconvenience. He was the antithesis of Ebenezer Scrooge; he fit more the mold of Mr. Fezziwig, the kind, caring boss who treated all as family. James did prove to be more of a risk-taker than his father, which surely would have earned him Alexander's disapproval. It would soon earn him William's. Even so, a daring Brown brother was still more conservative than a character such as Edward Knight Collins, who would be recognizable in any era as a hustler who spun grand tales, made unfulfilled promises and through force of will and ambition did things that few others could. James and Edward even contrasted physically: the stolid, somber Brown was bespectacled, black suited like the prototypical banker he was, and meticulously well kempt. His homes were decorated in high Victorian fashion befitting his image and place in society. Collins, roly-poly and ruddy cheeked, his home a nouveau riche mansion, always appeared to have just rushed from a hearty meal without having fully wiped off the crumbs.

Raised by a widowed father who began his career as a seaman and then became a successful merchant, Collins followed the same path, learning the trade by watching his father in New York City. Barely a teenager, he signed on to a ship in the West Indies, and experienced the gritty reality of seafaring. After a few years as a seaman, he returned to New York and launched a small line of packet ships to service the cotton boom out of New Orleans. Success there led to a bolder venture: launching a new mail packet service from New York to Liverpool in the 1830s. Collins, with an early flair for showmanship, named it the Dramatic Line. Packet ships carried the mail, and while you could make a living transporting goods and people, mail contracts were the most coveted. Generous federal mail contracts granted by Washington carried the promise of regular income. With a guaranteed and predictable income, an aggressive businessman could branch out. Collins was hungry and ambitious and wanted it all. It should come as no surprise that Collins and P. T. Barnum—not yet famous as a circus impresario but striving in New York to make his mark—were friends.

Collins was every bit the dramatist. He understood the value of making a splash and drawing attention. He named his first ships after Roman and Shakespearean protagonists and designed the cabins and the public spaces of his vessels to appeal to moneyed passengers—"the cane and glove crowd"—who, he believed rightly, would pay extra for an experience. That was in sharp contrast to his main competition, the Black Ball Line. Founded by a group of Quaker businessmen in 1817, Black Ball was reliable, consistent, drab and slow. Collins offered flash, style and speed. The Dramatic Line had only four ships, but by the late 1830s, they were all making the crossing in lightning time, smashing one record after another.

The rage for speed wasn't just vanity. Yes, the press of the day reported giddily about the latest and greatest with the ardor of latter-day sports reporters. With each new record, Collins and the Dramatic Line earned favorable press, which was free advertising for the business. But faster also served real needs. Faster meant that buyers and sellers had that much less time to wait before getting paid in full, or that much less time for financial brokers such as the Browns to hold assets that in the best of times carried some risk of being written down or completely worthless should a cargo ship sink. Fast also meant more trips back and forth, and more trips with full hulls and occupied berths translated into more profit.

The Dramatic Line made Collins wealthy enough to acquire a new house on Houston Street and then to purchase a mansion in Mamaroneck, in Westchester County, overlooking the Long Island Sound. The Westchester manse had been the home of the son of John Jay, the first Supreme Court chief justice and diplomat. It was a marginally marquee address. Collins then spent a small fortune on renovations, so that it had better views and more room for his four children and three unmarried half-sisters who preferred to live under the roof of their garrulous brother than with their anxious mother.[2]

But as wealthy as he was by the 1840s, Collins lusted for more. In 1838, the British ship *Sirius* made the slower westward Atlantic crossing from the Irish port of Cork in just over seventeen days, fewer than half the forty days that passage usually required. And the *Sirius* was no fluke; another steamship was only a day behind. The New York papers gushed, "Suddenly there was seen over Governor's Island, a dense black cloud of smoke, spreading itself upwards and betokening another arrival. On it came with great rapidity, and its cause was made fully manifest to the multitudes. It was the steamship *Great Western*, this immense moving mass propelled at a rapid rate through the waters of the bay. . . . If the public mind was stimulated by the arrival of the *Sirius,* it became intoxicated with delight upon view of the superb *Great Western*."[3]

Steam had already transformed inland river transport. River magnates such as Cornelius Vanderbilt had invested heavily in flat-bottomed steamers chugging up the Hudson and to the Erie Canal, and steamships had vastly enhanced the volume of trade on the Mississippi down to New Orleans. But oceans were a greater technical challenge. Throughout the 1820s, the steam magnates were less quick to launch ships on the ocean, given the expense and risks. But then the B&O marked the birth of railroads pulled by steam-powered engines, and the success of a few solitary steamships flying across the Atlantic in the 1830s signaled the dawn of a new maritime age. Collins saw an opportunity. "There is no longer any chance for enterprise with sails," he observed. "It is steam that must win the day." He envisioned a fleet of steamships commissioned and owned by him that would make Collins the line of choice from New York to Liverpool. The only catch? The type of steamships he needed would cost far more money than they could ever hope to recoup in passenger and freight fees alone. The ships would require massive amounts of coal and larger crews, which would make each voyage a certain money loser. In order to bridge that gap, Collins turned to both public and private sources of capital, to the deep-pocketed House of Brown on the one hand and to the even deeper pockets of the government of the United States on the other.

Collins's endeavor gained an added sense of urgency when, in 1840, the British-Canadian shipper Samuel Cunard unveiled the first in a line of steamships designed to ply the route between Liverpool and Boston with a stop in his native Halifax, Nova Scotia. Cunard himself then relocated his headquarters to Liverpool, and the Cunard Line was granted a subsidy by the British Post Office as the official Royal Mail packet to Boston. That contract gave him cash on hand to build more ships and expand operations to New York. Collins tried to use Cunard's emergence to persuade potential backers. Not only did he spin dreams of fortunes to be made, but he appealed to American investors on patriotic grounds. American mail should be carried on American ships, he argued, and the new nation should not cede transatlantic shipping to the British.

He did not find a ready audience. He met with the wealthy of New York and made his pitch. He went to Washington to lobby senators and congressmen. They didn't bite. Meanwhile, a number of other marine entrepreneurs attempted to launch a steam line. But ocean steamships proved trickier to operate than riverboats. Too often the ships foundered and the engines broke. Even so, Collins, with his boundless energy, had no doubt that he was onto something. He was certain that someone would launch an American transatlantic steam line, and he would be damned if that someone wasn't him. He hammered away, undeterred and raking in money from the Dramatic Line, unable to fund his dream.

In May 1846, the United States declared war on Mexico, using the dubious claim that Mexican cavalry had attacked American troops on the U.S. side of the Rio Grande in Texas. Ardently believing that it was the manifest destiny of the United States to bestride the North American continent, President James Polk had been in search of a casus belli. He claimed in his war message to Congress that "the cup of forbearance had been exhausted," charged Mexico with invading the United States and demanded that Congress declare war, which it did. With that came a rush of appropriations in Congress to fund the military.

Already there had been rumblings in Congress that other nations—above all England—were powering ahead with ocean steamships that would give them a significant edge over the United States not just in commerce but in any potential future war. John Tyler, the outgoing president in 1845, had warned as much. Polk was not just eager for war; he wanted to turn the United States into a world power. Fissures in Congress over how much the government should subsidize private companies had stalled appropriations for ocean ships. The same debates that had clouded government funding for roads, canals and railroads, and that had spurred the private investment in the B&O that the Browns had led, erupted again over whether and to what extent the federal government should underwrite the cost of ocean steamships.

Collins argued that it was impossible to raise enough private capital to fund the construction of more than a handful of the large and expensive ships that steam required. And even if the start-up money could be raised, there was also no way that a new company with heavy expenses could cover the cost of each journey, especially because the British government via the Admiralty and the Royal Mail had already committed to subsidizing a British company. Cunard had secured the support of Her Majesty's government to close the gap between what he could charge and how much steam travel cost. Collins argued that unless the federal government stepped up and subsidized an American line, the British would own the Atlantic.

It was a sound case, but many in Washington had other priorities. Southerners were no fans of federal money aiding New York private ventures. Of course, most southern plantation owners (who were overrepresented in politics) depended on northern finance and the Atlantic trade even as they opposed federal funds to bolster them. The southern bloc in Congress tended to reject the idea that the federal government should support private industry, even to augment American maritime strength that would directly benefit the southern economy. They preferred to see the energies of Washington go toward humbling and potentially occupying northern Mexico along with expanding slavery into the territories west of Texas. The Mexican War offered that chance.

The Mexican War tested but did not yet end the tenuous truce between the North and South over the question of slavery's future. As the lines continued to harden, the complicity of the Browns with a slave system became harder for them to reconcile with their self-image. Like most northern Presbyterians, they would have thought of themselves as opposed to slavery. In 1844, the firm signed a petition opposing the annexation of Texas out of concern that it would lead to the spread of slavery. That opposition may have been moral, but it was also pragmatic. More slave states would upset the delicate political and economic balance of a system that, however flawed, was serving the Brown family.

And they were not just indirectly complicit. After the Panic of 1837, the firm began to reconsider its involvement with the direct consignment trade. Jockeying for position as a cotton trader remained volatile, and too many of their competitors were willing to take excessive chances in order to make a profit. Said William Bowen, the Brown deputy who took charge of the Philadelphia house after John stepped down, "It seems as if the Cotton trade was never to be governed by the same commonsense rules that prevail in other commercial transactions, and there seems to be a charm in the great southern staple that leads people out of their sober senses." But well until the mid-1840s, the firm remained a major trader of physical cotton, handling between 10 and 15 percent of American cotton exports to Liverpool. After 1837, the Browns opened offices in New Orleans and Mobile to manage the volume of both consignments and financing the exchange between dollars and sterling. By the mid-1840s, William and James had nearly $1.5 million in southern assets. Much of that was in bonds and bank accounts.

Several hundred thousand dollars of the total, however, were in sugar and cotton plantations owned by the Browns.

William and James had not wanted to own plantations. They had acquired them in the early 1840s after the owners defaulted on debts owed to Brown Brothers. And almost as soon as they took possession, they looked to exit. But selling those assets at anything other than large losses in the 1840s was not possible, and so the Browns held on to those plantations and hired managers who by definition oversaw an operation based on slave labor. William Brown wanted to get rid of those assets. They were, by his lights, bad investments. "The more I think about it the more I see that it is desirable to get every shilling we can unlocked from fixed property."[4] But until prices recovered enough for them to sell the plantations, they ran them as absentee landlords.

Like many northern businesses, the Browns preferred the status quo of a slave South and a free North. They were strong supporters of the Compromise of 1850, for instance, which admitted California as a free state in return for a draconian Fugitive Slave Act that gave wide latitude to slave owners to recapture escapees by whatever means necessary. The firm might have taken clear stands in favor of its commercial interests, but its members were uninterested in upending a system that sustained them, nor were millions of others in the North who profited directly and indirectly from the cotton economy. Year by year, however, the robust Northern economy became much more variegated and diversified. The Southern economy revolved almost entirely around cotton. Much like companies reducing exposure to fossil fuels today, the Browns became less dependent on cotton and slavery because they perceived that those were dwindling assets. That had little to do with opposition to slavery per se. But weaning the dependence on cotton and by extension on slave labor was a necessary ingredient in eroding the system. Changing economics were one reason why the morality of slavery came to the foreground and enabled the rise of the antislavery Republican Party, which the Browns staunchly supported.[5]

The messiness of the entanglement with the slave system was not the only ambiguity of their business. As much as they saw a future of finance without the burden of physical assets, all around them were fortunes made by men building empires of goods and things. Cornelius Vanderbilt in New York was a more prominent public force than James, and Edward Collins generated more attention. The family creed may have dictated that none of that mattered, but just as William was tempted by the prospect of owning a cotton mill decades earlier, James would now have his moment. And without an Alexander to say no, James did what William had been unable to and entwined the firm in one of the most capital-intensive businesses imaginable.

The Mexican War was the proximate cause. The wave of bellicosity revved up American restiveness with British dominance of the Atlantic trade and acted as a tailwind for Collins and his grandiose plans. He had been declaiming for years that a strong United States needed ships to compete with the British and with the Cunard Line. Many listened, yet no one had acted. With nationalism surging as troops were mustered and sent south, members of Congress seized on the rivalry with Great Britain to argue that no subsidy for steamships would be too big. Senator James Asheton Bayard of Delaware proclaimed, "I suggest cost must not be considered. I suggest too that Congress grant a carefully selected American shipping expert a completely free hand to proceed with the absolute conquest of this man Cunard."[6] After months of wrangling, Collins secured a subsidy of $385,000 along with a promise of the federal contract as the exclusive carrier of U.S. mail, but there was a catch. The subsidy was contingent on actually building steamships that could make the crossing reliably. Without ships, there would be no subsidy. In order to build the ships, Collins needed a financial backer with deep pockets, one who could provide him with at least $1 million.

James Brown and Collins had been in discussions for years. Collins was hard to ignore and impossible to miss in the small social and business worlds of New York, and he had early on approached James as an investor. Like William, James looked to expand and diversify the family portfolio beyond the cotton trade. Yes, the Browns acted as brokers for millions of dollars of British manufactured goods exported from Liverpool to the United States, but much of that was linked to incoming cotton. And yes, the firm had an active business in finance and foreign exchange as an agent for other merchants and other banks, especially since the demise of the Second Bank. But James hankered for variety, now that the firm was just him and his elder brother across the ocean.

By the 1840s, James and William controlled 90 percent of the firm's capital.[7] The branches had able nonfamily partners and a few Brown cousins in the mix, but the partnership was dominated by the two brothers. James had dutifully accepted his role first as the youngest son and then as younger brother for decades. Now, at the age of fifty-five, he had had enough. Barely seven years older than James, William had adopted his father's more conservative approach, while James started to act more like a restless and rebellious son than the not-much-younger and independently wealthy brother that he was. Just as Alexander had quashed William's ambition to own a mill, William tried to curb James's ambition to become a shipping tycoon. Such is the way of families and their businesses.

The Browns had owned ships on and off for decades, but they had always steered away from major stakes in companies and businesses not in their core area of expertise. Alexander had demanded that, and his sons had complied. But in the 1840s, a fissure opened between James and William. At heart, the dispute was simple: James wanted the Browns to be the main backer of Collins and his new line of steamships; William did not. James wanted to tie up more than a million dollars of the Browns' partnership capital to build Collins's steamships, arguing that the investment would be repaid multiple times over in a few short years once Collins received the promised federal subsidy. William and his partners in Liverpool scoffed at the plan.

With two strong-willed brothers, the dispute quickly became fraught. William was no longer minding the day-to-day affairs of the firm. He was focused instead on politics and began to speak for the Liverpool business community on issues such as free trade. He also used his considerable fortune to embellish Liverpool with grand buildings. His younger partner, Joseph Shipley, who had been so key in persuading the Bank of England in

1837 to save the business, took on most of the day-to-day management responsibilities, especially after William was elected to Parliament in 1846. Whether it was Shipley or William who took the initiative, the Liverpool house never spoke without William's assent. In repeated letters, it was made clear that Brown Shipley did not like the idea of putting millions at stake in a partnership with a man like Collins.

The problem with Collins for the English house was not just the business model but also the business person. Collins just wasn't their kind of man. It's tempting to mark that down to English disdain for brash Americans, but Shipley hailed from a Quaker family from Delaware, while William was Irish born and American raised and had only moved to Liverpool in his late twenties. And Liverpool merchants were just as focused on profit and gain.

For all the tension between William and James, the firm's risk spectrum remained narrow. James Brown may have been worth millions, but he didn't show it. He was, in fact, less ostentatious than his elder brother. William lived in an unremarkable house near the docks in Liverpool, but he spent lavishly to underwrite the public library and other buildings in his adopted city. James was more modest. His home on University Place, a quiet upper-class enclave north of the teeming commercial streets of Lower Manhattan, struck no one as gaudy. He lived in the right neighborhood, but given his character, his house was, at least according to his son and successor John Crosby, "plain and rather ugly," albeit nicely furnished and spacious on the inside. Like most men of his class, James also had a summer residence, but his country estate in Weehawken, New Jersey, site of the duel between Alexander Hamilton and Aaron Burr and later the scenic overlook for the Lincoln Tunnel, hardly screamed wealth.

And it was not as if James was deploying capital that he didn't have or that wasn't his own. He had already made direct investments, albeit modest in size, in industries removed from his core competency, including a stake in the shipbuilding Novelty Iron Works on the far east side of Manhattan at Twelfth Street, and another in a new rail line in upstate New York called the Canandaigua & Niagara Falls Railroad. The early backing of the B&O had already established a precedent for some railroad investing. But the B&O had been graced by Alexander, who as the founder of the house was freer to break his own rules, and in any event, it was his own capital, the actual size of the investment was de minimis, and it was, according to Alexander, in the public good.

The core issue was that James was willing to put the firm's liquid capital at stake, and to bet on a hustler as nakedly ambitious as Collins. That sounded exactly the wrong notes to his partners in Liverpool. On the first point, the Liverpool cohort objected to capital being locked into ventures that would render it unusable and would require significant time and effort to liquidate the holding. The capital locked up in plantations was an added weight and additional pressure on the balance sheet. William Brown's junior partners were if anything more concerned than he was. They noted in an internal memo, "The House cannot extend its business unless it can fall back on investments in the case of emergency." But with James investing in Collins combined with the plantations they had yet to sell, they feared that too much capital would be tied up and unavailable in case of an emergency. Having faced near ruin because of the lack of a capital cushion during the Panic of 1837, the Liverpool house was understandably anxious that if some new financial storm hit and James had used the remaining cushion for investments that could not be easily liquidated, the firm would face extinction.

The two brothers and their respective branches were playing out an age-old debate in finance land: Is it better to invest in financial instruments such as stocks, bonds and letters of credit or in hard assets such as land and shares of a private business? No doubt, James was pursuing a potentially more lucrative strategy. The firm could and did make considerable money from commissions on letters of credit and consignments, but a new business with an immense potential market had, if not infinite possible growth, many times the multiple. It also demanded more capital, all of which could be lost if the venture went sour.

Agitated by James's decisions, William wrote a stream of passionate letters expressing his annoyance and dismay: "The more I think of it . . . the more desirable to get every shilling unlocked from fixed property. . . . When you think in our extensive Bill Business the very large amount of disappointments we must have even when we ultimately recover a large amount, it must be guarded against." He believed that it was best to maintain a "defensive position; that is, the purchase of low risk securities with appropriately low yields." There were reasons it was easier to find money for a great idea or a crazy scheme in America: Americans tended to focus more on the upside, whereas investors in Great Britain and the continent were more prone to view money as too serious to gamble and not something to be wagered. In the 1840s and into the 1850s until the *Arctic* went to its watery grave, the Liverpool house mirrored the mores of Alexander Brown, while New York became more American and more willing to roll the dice. Said one of William's juniors, "We look upon the advancement of the United States as certain, but the Americans are an extravagant & wasteful people."[8]

The aversion to Collins was more than the instant dislike of a prospective new in-law; it was an immune system reaction to a dangerous virus. James Brown's investment caused the agitation, but Collins got the brunt of the explicit criticism. His sheer outlandishness made him an easy scapegoat. Stewart Brown, James's younger cousin who had become increasingly involved in the business in New York in the 1840s, wrote of Collins that "he is certainly a strange being . . . he has a low unrefined mind with an overbearing disposition & I think that a situation under him would be anything but agreeable especially to one of any sensibility." As James refused to waver from his faith in Collins, William became more explicitly opposed. "I do not know when I was more surprised, astonished and mortified . . . to find that you had become principals in the Collins Boat Scheme," William wrote to his brother in early 1848. James was not dissuaded. "If you take $200,000 [of your own money] you will never regret," he told William. "It will pay you better than any investment you have two or three times over."[9]

If anything, the opposition coming from his brother and the Liverpool house made James want to double down. He explained his reasons for believing in Collins and the proposed new line of steamships: "I have no more doubt of his line of ships getting the preference over any British Line, in the same way our sailing packet ships got the preference, and the more I look into it the more assured I am to take a good interest in it." James believed, and with good reason, that Americans wanted an American-owned company to control the mail routes and to prevent the British from dominating the Atlantic crossings.

This back-and-forth—between one brother and his cohort advocating slow and steady investments safely placed, and another willing to lock up capital to yield higher returns—neatly epitomized the contest between the Old World and the New, between a culture that placed a premium on safety and managing risk and one that celebrated the maverick who was willing to lose anything to gain everything. The divide between James and William was, of course, minor compared with the cultural gap between America and the Old World. Both brothers were at heart more conservative than the teeming mass of Americans who speculated in the 1830s or mortgaged everything for equipment during the gold rushes or who took a loan from a wildcat bank in paper whose value fluctuated daily and might soon be worthless. James went ahead with his investment, but the tragic fate of the *Arctic* would settle the argument—for the House of Brown at least—conclusively in favor of William.

With more than $1 million from James and Stewart (in direct investments and loans) along with the promise of an annual federal subsidy of $385,000 and a contract to carry the U.S. mail to Liverpool, Collins was ready to go. He commissioned the building of four immense ships, with massive paddles and engines to turn them. They were built quickly. The first ship, the *Atlantic*, was launched in the spring of 1850, and its mixture of speed and comfort was an immediate draw that directly cut into Cunard's business. Even so, each single voyage lost tens of thousands of dollars, hence the need for that subsidy. The competition from Collins had ripple effects. It meant that Cunard had to lower its prices, so it was now losing money as well. Even if Cunard was more secure in its financial backing from the British government, bleeding money is never a good business proposition. The emergence of Cunard and the Collins Line was a boon for passengers and for transatlantic travel, but the competition undermined both companies. Cunard now needed more operating capital, while Collins depended on a federal subsidy that had been authorized for only a few years and with the end of the Mexican War faced opposition from a Congress that was sharply divided over the question of renewal.

Recognizing that the competition might not be in either company's best interests, the two lines entered into secret negotiations. The broker was William Brown, whose dislike of the Collins venture paled in comparison with his determination not to let his brother's substantial stake harm the firm's standing. William had himself made a modest investment in the Cunard Line, though his was a pittance compared with how much James committed to Collins. William was on good terms with Cunard's directors and wrote them in 1849 about "how unpleasant it would be for your vessels and those coming to us to be carrying on a war of mutual injuries. . . . I have written my Brother James . . . to see Mr. Cunard and if possible make such arrangement as would prevent injury to either concerns." To keep the two lines from driving each other out of business, the directors of Collins and Cunard agreed in May 1850 to pool revenues, fix minimum rates and then divide them, two-thirds to Cunard and a third to Collins. Cunard was more established and had multiple routes and would have been better able to weather a zero-sum contest, which was why it received a larger share. But the agreement was to the advantage of both parties. It created one of the first global cartels, complete with price fixing.[10]

William Brown, who had in private so strongly opposed his family's investment, agreed to use the resources and connections of the Liverpool house to help market the Collins Line in England. What was done was done, and with his family already committed, it was in his best interest for Collins to succeed. Brown Shipley paid for an expensive display of the novel design of the Collins ships to be installed at the Crystal Palace Exhibition in London in 1851, and William acted as the perfect host, throwing dinners for bookers and wooing the press and the business community.

The Collins ships shattered time records. The line attracted passengers willing to pay a premium. And the secret arrangement with Cunard prevented a deadly price war. Even so, each time a Collins steamship crossed the Atlantic, no matter how full the berths and how much cargo packed its holds, it operated at a loss. In 1852, therefore, Collins had to persuade Congress not only to renew its subsidy but to increase it substantially to more than $800,000 per year. That meant petitioning a new administration and new factions in Congress.

With James's financial backing, Collins began to woo Congress with the subtlety of a K Street lobbyist unconstrained by ethics rules. While there is no evidence of outright bribery, there was certainly outright extravagance. In later years, it would become common for members of Congress and the executive branch to be taken on lavish junkets in order to secure their backing. That was a novel idea in the 1850s. Knowing that few in the halls of influence in Washington had been aboard an ocean steamship, Collins arranged for the *Baltic* to voyage from New York down to Washington with a gaggle of press, who would be well fed and well soused by the time they arrived in the Chesapeake Bay to pick up the president of the United States, Millard Fillmore, along with a posse of "Cabinet Ministers, Senators, members of the House of Representatives" and hundreds of others who had clamored for a coveted ticket. The ship then ambled for a leisurely day cruise. There was wine, and harder stuff, and the guests were duly impressed by the "extravagant finish and furniture" on a ship whose size and technical sophistication was greater than any other vessel then afloat.[11]

The excursion made an impression, but the subsidy still hung in the balance. Nervous that the vote could go against them, Brown and Collins dispatched William Bowen, one of the key nonfamily members of the firm in Philadelphia, to Washington with suitcases full of cash. Bowen called on various representatives and offered to make donations to their campaigns, to their staffs, or to whatever causes they asked for. Today these would be called bribes, but at the time they were legal. No campaign finance laws stood in the way. Bowen's handouts pushed the appropriations bill over the top, and Collins and Brown won an even larger subsidy.

The new subsidy provided the funds needed to keep the *Arctic* sailing. It was the jewel of the Collins Line, nearly three hundred feet long, forty-five feet wide, with twenty-five-foot paddle wheels on either side. It had cost more than half a million dollars to construct. It was lauded for its decorations, its passenger comforts, and its speed. And that was why it was the ship of choice on that September 1854 trip from Liverpool. That was why James Brown's son William Benedict, his two daughters, Maria Miller and Grace, his infant granddaughter and his daughter-in-law were on board, and why it carried Edward Knight Collins's wife, daughter and youngest son as well. What other ship should they have taken? It was fast. It was spacious. It was comfortable. It was captained by the best and owned by their family. Aside from some dense fog, the weather was normal for that time of year, and as busy as the sea routes were, most of the ocean was an expanse of untouched emptiness.

It was, in every way, a fluke accident. The *Arctic* was not felled by a severe storm. It was struck in the fog by another vessel, a compact French iron steamer named the *Vesta*. The odds of two ships in the middle of the ocean colliding were infinitesimally small. And yet it happened, off the coast of Newfoundland, in normal shipping lanes where ships occasionally passed one another, but usually at a great distance. The lookouts of the *Arctic* spotted the other vessel just as it disappeared, enveloped in a fog bank, but even then, no one was particularly alarmed. As the captain steered away from where the other vessel was last seen, the two ships collided, quietly and, according to later testimony, almost gently.

Initially, the captain and the passengers of the *Arctic* were concerned about the smaller ship. As the two ships detached, it appeared as if the *Vesta* was the one mortally wounded, but as the *Arctic* pulled away, the rip in its hull from the collision caused it to list. It began to take on water. As the captain tried to steer away from the scene of the collision, the crew of the *Arctic* realized that it was their ship that had been fatally damaged and that it was going to sink. Panic ensued, and in the chaos, there were no codes of honor. The crew were not military men, trained and disciplined. They were for hire, there for the money, and as water poured in, they looked out for themselves. Contrary to the norms of the sea, it was not women and children first. The crew piled into the lifeboats, which had room for only half the people on board, and left the passengers to drown. Of the 233 passengers, only 22 lived; of the 150 crew, 64 survived. James Luce, the captain, also survived, but he lived the remainder of his life as a wounded shell, never captaining again and never free from the whispers that he had allowed the disaster to happen.

When news hit New York, the tight-knit business community of the city was crushed. Wrote editor James Gordon Bennett in the *Herald*, "The public mind was altogether unprepared for the shock. . . . No one thought that so stout and good a ship had met with disaster. . . . When we announced the terrible news, the metropolis assumed the appearance of one great funeral. The feeling spread through all the classes of the community. The business streets, usually so gay and bustling, were filled with little groups of men whose solemn countenances showed that they were fully impressed with the belief that no common disaster had befallen the city. . . . It appeared that a great pall had been lowered upon us and that everything was overshadowed by its gloom."[12]

The news devastated the Browns. James's son and grandson later kept detailed records of the family, and both published books that discussed the episode. Diaries and family lore recall that when James was told by his pastor that the ship had sunk and that his offspring had been lost, he fell to the floor crying, "My children, my children," and said sobbing to his wife, "I shall never see them more in the world, but thank God, you are left to me yet." She was not. Eliza Brown was so shaken by the disaster that she was unable to speak for nearly two years, and rarely left her house, communicating only through written notes.[13]

In a chronicle of a death foretold, a family friend recalled that a few months before the disaster, William Benedict Brown, the eldest son of James and heir apparent of the New York firm, went to visit the museum of

Collins's friend P. T. Barnum in Manhattan. There he sat down with a fortune-teller, and according to several witnesses, she gasped and said, "I see an awful wreck in your hand, Sir." Brown did not appear too disturbed and asked what she meant specifically. "I can only say that I see an awful ship-wreck in your hand."[14]

The loss of the *Arctic* was the most famous passenger ship disaster to that point in history and would remain so for sixty years until the Cunard–White Star Line lost its great ship the *Titanic*. Had it not been for the sinking of the *Arctic*, the history of transatlantic shipping might have been quite different. The Collins Line, flush with Brown Brothers financing and the underwriting of the U.S. government, might have become the preeminent shipping company connecting America and the United Kingdom. Even with the *Arctic* sinking, the Collins Line initially survived, in part because the outbreak of the Crimean War in 1854 meant that Cunard's ships were called into service by the British government, temporarily ceding the Atlantic to Collins. But then another of the four steamers sank in 1855, with less loss of life but leaving Collins with only two vessels and an unfinished one stuck in the boatyard and mired in cost overruns and delays. James Brown, who was forever changed by his loss, refused to offer Collins any more cash. He had no appetite for further investments in shipping.

Sensing weakness, rivals began to circle the Collins Line. Commodore Vanderbilt, who had made a fortune in river steamships, had largely steered clear of the transatlantic trade, given the logistical challenges and the much larger sums required. But the congressional subsidy for Collins grated on him. Vanderbilt had created his shipping empire without any "handouts," and he detested the idea of private enterprise turning to government for aid. He had built his franchise meticulously, controlling costs and using his hard-earned profits to expand. He had thrived on his own money, and he had little but disdain for anyone who couldn't do the same. By the mid-1850s, he had had enough, and in 1855, he underbid Collins for the U.S. mail contract. He then sat for a slew of interviews to explain his aversion to government subsidies. The journal *Scientific American* summed up Vander-bilt's view: "He considers the large sums now paid by the American and

British governments for carrying the mail as a blight on individual enterprise." The Commodore stated that while he had nothing against Collins personally, he had stayed quiet long enough in the face of the excessive government interference in the market. Vanderbilt set a tone for the years ahead, and his attitude epitomized a blend of laissez-faire capitalism and Jacksonian disdain for government funding that would become a hallmark of big businesses.[15]

With Vanderbilt entering the fray and Cunard resuming its Atlantic routes after the Crimean War wound down in 1856, the Collins Line was squeezed. The fact that two of its expensive steamers had sunk, one with considerable loss of life, did not help Collins in his quest for additional capital and continued government contracts. Outwardly he projected an air of confidence and appealed to patriotism. "Every nation has acknowledged what we have done, and I am sorry to say that the only opposition we have met has been from home." He touted that he and James Brown had invested millions on ships that strengthened the United States both commercially and militarily, and he challenged Congress with the question of who else could be found to do the same. Congress was not swayed. In 1856, it made the decision to cut back on a flailing venture, reducing the annual Collins grant but not yet wholly eliminating it. In 1858, Collins defaulted. Presented with a writ for more than $600,000 from the sheriff of New York County, Collins was forced to sell his two last ships at a bankruptcy auction. They were purchased for $50,000 by an agent of James Brown and his lawyer and in-law Clarkson Potter. Kept in dry dock for more than a year, the two steamers were sold, stripped of all their finery, and crammed with bunks for nine hundred passengers. They then plied the heavily trafficked route between Panama and San Francisco for years—steady, unspectacular and profitable. Writing the obituary for the company, *Harper's Weekly* concluded, "An odor of corruption and roguery hung round the line to the day of its death. It was badly managed, badly officered and badly engineered in every way."[16]

That was perhaps too harsh, and written with the full benefit of hindsight. Collins had, however, exposed a fault line, one that would only deepen

over time: on the one side, the brash investor, the self-promoter, the quin-
tessential American cliché, hustling, without shame, brimming with confidence earned or not, with a bold dream, promising a glorious future and
untold riches. On the other, the upright man of affairs, proper, reserved,
unimpeachable in reputation, investing and not speculating, steering clear
of ideas too bold and erring on caution's side when faced with something
that seemed too good to be true and likely was. Collins exposed other fault
lines as well, which Vanderbilt underscored, between those who believed
that national greatness was best served by private industry and capital un-
encumbered by government, and those who argued that in the contest of
nations, government needed to spend and to encourage private capital to be
deployed in order to unlock potential that might otherwise have remained
dormant. In the United States, the ideologies were pure, but the reality rarely
was. Canals and those early rail lines such as the B&O benefited from direct government investment and favorable grants of corporate status. Later
railroad construction would largely be underwritten by the federal government, with a combination of land grants and loans. Private capital was, of
course, essential, but it was rarely sufficient for the most capital-intensive
industries.

The sinking of the *Arctic* and the collapse of the Collins Line ended
James Brown's flirtation with risk. The combination of tragedy and bad
management left a bitter taste. William had been tamed by Alexander;
James was reined in by fate. The culture of the firm was reinforced by
testing the boundaries. In subsequent years, the Browns would rarely be
exposed to any one investment to the degree that they were with the Collins
Line. Of course, even that investment, while tying up more of the firm's
liquid capital than the Liverpool partners would have preferred, was hardly
the stuff of the epic speculations of robber barons in later years. The Browns
never took on substantial leverage; at times, they lent more than they should
have, but they did not borrow; and as always, it was their money, their earn-
ings, their accounts, and no one else's, that they exposed to loss. Their near
misses taught them the perils of striving for too much.

That private reality, however, was not the public impression. By the

1850s, Brown Brothers came to represent the unequal rewards that went to the world of finance. For those concerned about the growing materialism of American society, who believed that the moral fiber of the country was imperiled by the lure of money detached from labor, the success of the House of Brown and their brethren was not to be celebrated but resisted. Southern planters, echoing Thomas Jefferson, never fully embraced money detached from the property of plantations and slaves, even as they depended on northern commerce and on financial intermediaries such as Brown Brothers. The farmers of the Ohio Valley and the Midwest needed credit but distrusted those who supplied it. Even in the Northeast there was ambivalence. The yeoman and the Yankees trusted the value of hard assets and property. Money was necessary but also a temptation.

In New York City, the sinking of the *Arctic* in September 1854 was a collective loss. The funerals and the mourning brought people together in doleful communion. Yet the tragedy was also held up as a symbol of God's displeasure. Sorrowful sermons poured from the pulpits of the city's many churches, none more prominent than Plymouth Church in Brooklyn. Its pastor was one of the celebrities of the age, Henry Ward Beecher, and his Sunday sermons attracted listeners from Manhattan, which meant waking early to catch a ferry to get to morning mass, as hundreds regularly did.[17] In October, at an evening memorial service packed with parishioners and visitors, he did not soothe the wounds of the *Arctic* but instead took the opportunity to preach against the perils of money. Quoting from the Book of Psalms, he began mildly, "God is our hope and strength, a very present help in trouble." But he did not intend to be mild. "It was an ocean grave," he intoned, and if there was any solace in that, there should not be, because it was not just another accident. It was a warning. "In the morning the waiters served the titled and the rich. . . . It is not to be disguised that all the monstrous and infidel legislation of our country . . . has had its root and sap in the supposed interests of moneyed circles. . . . God is striking thundering strokes at the wealth of the whole community."[18]

Not exactly words to comfort, but wholly in sync with Beecher's character. He did not see his role as applying a soothing balm to the culture, let alone to his bourgeois congregants. He instead played Jeremiah, though he himself failed to listen to his own warnings of the seductions of the flesh and the wayward path of a culture following the call of money. His later life was mired in scandal, brought on by lurid affairs and the excesses of celebrity. His fame was propelled by picking the right targets, and in the 1850s, the target was Brown Brothers. Beecher inveighed against the proliferation of letters of credit issued by the House of Brown, and he railed at the ease with which people trusted those and yet doubted the power and mercy of the Lord. "Suppose I were to set out on a pilgrimage to Jerusalem," began one sermon,

> And before I started were to go to Brown Brothers & Co., and obtain letters of credit for the cities of London, Jericho, etc. Then, with these papers which a child might destroy, which would be but ashes in the teeth of a flame . . . I should go on with confidence and cheer, saying to myself, "As soon as I come to London I shall be in funds. I have a letter in my pocket from Brown Brothers." . . . But suppose that instead of this confidence I were to sit down on shipboard, and go to tormenting myself in this fashion: "Now what am I to do when I get to London? I have no money, and how do I know these bits of paper which I have with me mean anything or will amount to anything?" . . . I should be a fool, you say; but I should be *half* the fool that that man is who, bearing the letters of the Eternal God, yet goes fearing all his way, cast down and doubting whether he shall ever get safe through his journey. No fire, no violence, nor any chance, can destroy the checks of the Lord. When he says: "I will never leave thee, forsake thee," believe it; and no longer dishonor your God by withholding from him the confidence which you freely accord Brown Brothers & Co.[19]

Beecher may have had particular animus toward Brown Brothers, or perhaps it was simply a perfect foil. In another sermon, he scorned those who sought power, political and financial, and assured his listeners that he would never be vulnerable to such temptations. "Do you suppose I could be bribed out of the pulpit if Brown Brothers offered me a full half-partnership of their business? Never. There is not enough money in all the Rothschilds' coffers to bring me the happiness that I have in your confidence and generous support, and the liberty which I have in discharging my conscience by free speech in your midst."[20]

As America entered the second part of the nineteenth century, it was ever more defined by money and wealth, and that wealth increasingly went to the few who controlled it, to capital over labor. Beecher's sermons showed a growing tension between money and spirit, between an America that honored its Puritan roots and one that worshipped instead at the altar of Mammon. Beecher's warnings of the moral dangers of paper and money echoed down the years, from the later thundering of William Jennings Bryan in his futile pursuit of the presidency at the end of the nineteenth century to the early twenty-first-century distrust of the merger of money and power. Like most jeremiads, however, those warnings were heard but not heeded.

For the House of Brown, the *Arctic* tragedy also marked the transition to the next generation of family partners and the broadening of the partnership. That would have happened regardless, though the death of James's oldest son certainly hastened it. Joseph Shipley and William Bowen were just two of those outside of the family to be granted partnership over the next decades, though the firm remained at heart a family affair. The houses also started to become more separate, in their businesses and cultures, with the passing of the four brothers after the 1860s. Already by then, a new generation was assuming control.

The tragedy had a deep and lasting effect on James. He actively and forcefully managed the New York office until his death in 1877, but scarred by the loss of so many of his dearest ones in the wreck, he also turned inward to focus on his faith and philanthropy. Philanthropy was itself a new idea for the wealthy in America. As in everything they did, the Browns did not seek attention or public acclaim for their philanthropy. There was no Brown Foundation equivalent to what Andrew Carnegie or the Rockefellers bequeathed. Given the inherent reticence of the family, that shouldn't be surprising, but they nonetheless spent considerable sums, especially in New York but also in Liverpool and Baltimore, on libraries, museums, schools and churches.

After the Collins affair, James Brown did not want his name in the papers. He did not wish his house to be a subject of contention, debated in the halls of Congress or assailed from the pulpits. He had tasted celebrity, and it had left him only bitterness. In the subsequent decades, the Browns assumed an ever lower public profile but became vastly richer, which would have pleased Alexander. That combination of substantial wealth and low profile became one of the defining features of the American WASP elite, but that ethos was not organic. It had to be invented. In the second part of the nineteenth century, Brown Brothers created a mold, born of an acute sensitivity to the perils of being too identified with wealth and privilege. Better to work behind the scenes than be the constant subject of Beecher-like attacks; better to stay quiet in public than provoke the backlash of millions who would come to resent the privileges of capital. If that made them boring, that was a small price to pay, and one that the family paid willingly. First, however, the business had to survive another financial panic and then the turmoil of the Civil War and the disruption of the cotton trade. The Panic of 1837 nearly ended the firm; the Civil War nearly ended the country.

CHAPTER 5

A VERY CIVIL WAR

By the 1850s, the ascendency of New York as the economic capital of the United States was complete. Having surpassed Baltimore and Philadelphia, the city began to grow even more rapidly. Half of all U.S. trade was now handled by its docks, and nearly three-quarters of all immigrants passed through the Narrows and ended up in Lower Manhattan. The city's population boomed, to more than half a million people, plus another quarter of a million in Brooklyn (a separate city until 1898), making the metropolitan area larger than the combined populations of Baltimore, Boston, Philadelphia and New Orleans.

With that explosive population growth came unprecedented wealth creation. Brown Brothers was at the center of a robust and expanding merchant and banking community that numbered in the thousands. The city, however, was much more than an atoll of banking. It was a manufacturing center, with ironworks and shipyards and garment factories. The city became more stratified by class, with immigrants and workers, some itinerant and seasonal and others there more permanently, packed densely into Lower Manhattan. The more well-to-do, such as James Brown and his cousin Stewart Brown and his nephew James Muncaster Brown (both junior partners by the 1850s), lived to the north of Bleecker Street, James in that "rather ugly" town house on University Place and the other two off Waverly Place.

With wealth came striving and with striving came gossip. By the 1850s, New York was home to its own cottage industry of papers feeding the popular thirst to see into those drawings rooms of the elite. News of the lives of the rich and famous sold briskly, ranging from Charles Astor Bristed's *The Upper Ten Thousand*, a compendium of sketches on the upper crust, to the city's multiple papers with their daily tidbits and weekly obituaries that listed the net worth of the deceased.[1]

While the Browns were of society, they were not ones to make a show. The firm's headquarters at 59 Wall Street was grand and imposing, and Brown Brothers would remain in the same location for more than a century. A stately office was necessary to assure clients that they could entrust their business to the Browns, who understood that an office made an impression. The Browns were no less nouveau in their richeness than most others; almost all of New York society in the mid-nineteenth century was by definition nouveau. But already the Browns—in New York, in Philadelphia, in Baltimore and in Liverpool—seemed like old money. They not only shunned publicity, but they found outward displays distasteful except when it would help them raise capital or shape local or national policy to their advantage. They reacted to gossip the way most of us react to milk that has turned.

While the *Arctic* tragedy led James to focus more on his Presbyterian faith and to take up duties as an elder at the church just steps from his home, he remained firmly in control of the New York office. As he aged, he evolved into a more polished and refined version of his father. He was seen by friends in society and by members of his church as "punctual in all business appointments; a keen and self-poised man; of ardent temperament always under complete control; modest and retiring in disposition; sound in judgement of men and affairs; slow in giving his confidence, but thereafter rarely withdrawing it in spite of faults and mistakes; of very genial nature but finding most of his social pleasures in his own home and his own family circle; courteous in his intercourse with his employees but expecting every man to do his best."[2] Another contemporary marveled that both he and his cousin Stewart "were the most modest and unassuming of our citizens. There is no show or parade with them. James never rides except in a one-horse coup." Not for him was a fancy carriage or the flash of high society, and that DNA was embedded in the business as well.

As the Collins imbroglio demonstrated, the House of Brown was forever steering a course between caution and too much caution. The dispute between the houses over the Collins investment cast William as the cautious one and James as the profligate, but both houses recognized that there was such a thing as being too suspicious and too risk adverse. And attitudes were not always consistent. William fumed at James for getting too cozy with Collins, yet he himself invested in Cunard and then in other ventures, the most notable being a transatlantic cable company bankrolled and organized by New York entrepreneur Cyrus Field. The Atlantic Telegraph Company was formed in 1856, and William was appointed chairman of the board. Its first efforts at deep sea cables failed, and the project was a sinkhole for investors for many years. Not until after William's death did it succeed in laying a workable—and profitable—cable across the ocean.[3]

James was acutely attuned to these questions and sought the right balance. He wrote to William in the mid-1850s that there was "such a thing in business as being over-careful and over suspicious of the integrity of parties with whom we are dealing. It makes the house highly unpopular. Better to be taken in and lose a little occasionally than to be so rigid as to make parties afraid to approach you."[4] Better at times to step outside one's comfort zone than become mired in the same groove. The House of Brown valued and nurtured tradition and continuity, but Alexander's own life had hardly been static. He may have loved the slogan "Shoemaker, stick to thy last," but in practice, he understood that any lasting business must evolve with the times. The trick, of course, was to be exposed but not too exposed, to risk some but not too much, to entertain uncertainty without putting everything on the line and to test the new without relinquishing the old. The House of Brown didn't stumble its way to success. Alexander and his heirs consciously grappled with the right formula and were rigorous in thinking through the ramifications of their actions and of their inactions. The firm cultivated a culture that encouraged "the fullest liberty of discussion . . .

and the full expression of opinion."[5] It wasn't just financial discipline that set them apart. It was continual self-assessment and internal debate.

The failure of the Collins Line, the flood of competitors into consignments and the cotton trade along with the unhappy and morally unsustainable experience of owning plantations led William and James to focus the firm on finance and wind down its business in the physical trade of cotton. The younger partners in Liverpool (one of whom, Mark Collet, would later become governor of the Bank of England) had been adamant during the Collins debates that the firm focus on liquid capital and investments, and their views eventually won out. There was no sudden dramatic decision, but by the late 1850s, the locus of the business had decisively shifted toward finance and paper, without veering into speculation.

Brown Brothers navigated the next major economic storm to hit the United States, the Panic of 1857, with only minimal damage. The meltdown had a similar cadence to the previous crises of 1819 and 1837. It began slowly and then accelerated rapidly. More than the prior two, it was a pure financial crisis, triggered over the summer by the peak in railroad stocks followed by rapid declines, the collapse of the Ohio Life Insurance and Trust Company, and the rush on banks by fearful investors and exposed speculators who tried to exchange their bills for gold and silver before the banks halted specie payments and left them with paper worth nothing.

While stock trading was a tiny fraction of overall economic activity in this period, sudden sharp losses could and did begin a chain reaction that quickly spread to more vital sectors such as letters of credit, foreign exchange, insurance, and then manufacturing. When the Ohio company collapsed, it was some days before the contagion spread. The anticipation was excruciating, and on those swampy late-August days, "People's faces in Wall Street look fearfully gaunt and desperate," wrote one observer. From their offices at 59 Wall Street, James and his younger partners looked on and wondered, with some trepidation, if they were about to witness a replay of 1837.[6] The partners in Liverpool were much more sanguine than they had been twenty years earlier, and for good reason: they were barely exposed to the New York railroads and to the American insurance companies that set off the panic, and they had also learned from the past to be more conservative. Writing from Liverpool, one of Brown Shipley's younger partners wrote to Shipley, "I believe few houses are entitled to a higher position, and looking at the difficulties that now embarrass American affairs with a calm mind, I see nothing to create the alarm that seems to have pressed on Mr. James Brown."[7]

In New York, things looked grimmer, especially as the crisis metastasized in late September and October, leading to the failure of the Bank of Pennsylvania and the suspension of much of that state's banking system to prevent complete collapse. That set off a cascade of failures elsewhere. Liverpool was not spared, even as Brown Shipley was. In England, the government of Lord Palmerston (Henry John Temple) suspended its own banking laws regulating the levels of specie versus paper so that the Bank of England could issue more currency. The crisis affected large parts of Western Europe before subsiding in December.

As it turned out, the Browns emerged not only unscathed but in a stronger relative position because of the carnage all around them. During the worst of it in September, the public was hungry for villains. Stock speculators were singled out for opprobrium, even though the insurance companies and banks that failed were brought down by the overextension of their businesses rather than by the stock market. But that was a more complicated story, whereas the evils of speculation was a simpler narrative with a ready audience. Countless accounts held paper money and its purveyors as responsible for a meltdown that tossed tens of thousands of laborers out of work. Said *Harper's Weekly*, "Stock gambling is certainly the most ruinous of pursuits; for it not only leads to pecuniary loss, but it unfits a man for any work, and in nine cases out of ten saps his moral principles. . . . The miserable, idle good-for-nothing creatures who hang about the Stock Exchange . . . are really the most pitiable wretches in the city; for they could not, if they would, work at any honest labor."

Brown Brothers was not a broker, and its business had little to do with stock trading. That inoculated it, somewhat. But the firm also anticipated crises. That was not a question of forecasting. It was a matter of culture. None of the partners believed that the firm was uniquely qualified to predict the future, but they knew from experience that there would be sharp and unexpected reversals and that the time to be ready was before, not during. As James wrote to Shipley, "Seeing merchants, corporations and banks going by the board and of the former those generally of the first standing, it was enough to alarm us. . . . Fortunately for us, we had very few credits, not being confined to any one branch of business, and as all business interests were not equally in trouble, our collections have on the whole resulted better than we feared."[8] In essence, because the firm and its affiliated branches had both a wide range of financing operations and tight credit standards, it was less exposed than many other institutions.

James and William had not just moved the firm away from the direct trade of cotton but also developed new business lines that were organic offshoots of their credit business. The most important of those was providing letters of credit to travelers going between the United States and England, and to Europe. In a world without published or fixed exchange rates, it was always a challenge for travelers to obtain currency in foreign countries without the vulnerability of carrying too much money in coins that could be lost or stolen. These travelers' letters were early versions of travelers' checks, and the ones issued by Brown Brothers were widely accepted. They were also widely decried by those distrustful of the evolving system of paper money, such as the Reverend Henry Ward Beecher. Loved and hated, these travelers' letters of credit not only became a steady source of revenue for Brown Brothers but also spurred the rise of American tourism abroad in the second part of the nineteenth century.[9]

The House of Brown's combination of diversification along with constant attention to how much of the firm's capital was exposed allowed it to sail through 1857. Yet the very survival of Brown Brothers was taken by some as a sign that the captains of finance would always find a way to float while others drowned. Even something as seemingly benign as travelers' letters, which for the Browns was an act of financial innovation making it possible for more people to travel on business and pleasure and more businesses to expand across the oceans, was for others a symbol of the pernicious role of finance. The Browns were deeply averse to losing their own capital and were rarely speculators, but popular culture saw all finance as inherently suspect. Financial panics fueled that impression, and in those times, the benefits of paper and credit appeared minor in comparison with the harm that too much easy money appeared to do.

Observing the 1857 panic and its global dimensions, a twenty-eight-year-old reporter and writer for the *New-York Tribune* named Karl Marx greeted the crisis with the enthusiasm of one whose theories were being vindicated. "The American Crash is beautiful . . . and it's far from over," he wrote to his friend and collaborator Friedrich Engels. Having carefully observed the events of 1857, Marx would then refine his theory of capitalism as a system whose reliance on the proliferation of paper money would inevitably produce crises, destroying value and decimating workers, with only the institutions and elites in charge of printing more paper coming out ahead. Financiers and governments emerged from each crisis stronger, while workers suffered and bore the losses. Marx reacted to the panic by feverishly revising his theory of capital and its deficiencies, which eventually led to the publication of *Das Kapital.* By then he was revolutionary (though not quite as outside the mainstream as later perceived), but in the 1850s, his critique of the excesses of capitalism was hardly radical.[10]

Increasingly, William and James and their junior partners, at the epicenter of trade finance as they were, leading a firm that issued letters that were as trusted as any paper currency issued by the U.S. government, the Bank of England or any regional bank, saw themselves as guardians of a system constantly threatened by greed and speculation. They were at once part of a problem—too much finance—and part of the bulwark that kept the edifice from collapsing. They helped fuel the growth of trade, shipping, cotton and railroads while simultaneously disdaining rampant speculation and greed. They helped unleash the wild ambitions of mid-nineteenth-century

Americans, and they then kept those forces from spinning utterly out of control. Money, including their money, helped build America, but without guardrails, money kept threatening to bring the country crashing down.

These questions became more acute later in the nineteenth century and into the twentieth. But first the United States had to survive its greatest challenge: the Civil War. The struggle between North and South was at its heart about slavery, proving Abraham Lincoln's warning in 1858 that a house divided could not stand and that the country could not stay half slave and half free. In addition to the moral imperative of ending the slave system, the war was also a contest between the dueling economic systems of North and South, one based on industry, wage earners, commerce and money; the other on the labor of enslaved people and cotton. The 1850s had seen a more dramatic gap open between the cotton economy of the South and the increasingly industrialized and diversified economy of the North, along with the rapidly growing states of what is now the Midwest. The North, therefore, was in a stronger relative position to force the South to accede to a different system.

That was the big picture, one more apparent in retrospect. At the time, for the Browns and all merchants, traders and financiers, the war looked like a potentially fatal threat. They had built up a business facilitating Southern exports whose sale in England funded American imports. By 1860, Brown Brothers was less dependent on the actual trade of cotton, but the outbreak of hostilities in the spring of 1861 immediately severed relationships that had been built over decades, between Northern businesses and Southern, between English merchants and their trading partners, between families with relatives on both sides of the divide. Within days of the attack on South Carolina's Fort Sumter in April, Lincoln declared a naval blockade on the Confederate States in order to disrupt the cotton trade and destroy the Southern economy. Maryland was a slave state, but it did not secede from the Union and join the Confederacy. Baltimore's trade with England was thus not immediately imperiled to the degree that English trade with the Confederacy was. In Liverpool and in Lancashire, the war and the blockade were greeted with intense apprehension. Cotton from the

South was *the* vital input for the English textile industry, supplying Lancashire with almost 80 percent of its raw material. Though England would find new sources of cotton in Egypt and India as the war progressed, in 1861 there were more than a few in Parliament who wanted to recognize the Confederacy as an independent nation and thereby assert the right to trade directly with the Southern states.

The war also opened yet another fissure between Liverpool and the American branches of the House of Brown. The New York house, and James especially, was adamantly pro-Union, supported the Republican Party, and expected the other houses to follow suit. Philadelphia was aligned with New York, which was not surprising given the powerful antislavery sentiment in the Quaker city. The Republican and pro-Union stance of James and New York presented a political problem for the Browns in Baltimore and a business problem for Brown Shipley in Liverpool.

George William Brown, cousin to the brothers, had been elected mayor of Baltimore in 1860. The city was bitterly divided and economically stagnant, and by the late 1850s had developed a well-earned reputation for civil unrest, unruly mobs, and disturbingly high numbers of melees and murders. Lincoln needed to go through Baltimore on the way to his inauguration in March, and receiving intelligence of a plot to assassinate him, passed through the city in the dead of night and unannounced. In April, after the assault on Fort Sumter, Lincoln called for the mustering of state militias. That pushed Virginia, North Carolina, Tennessee and Arkansas, which had been wavering, to secede and join the Confederacy. Many in Baltimore wanted Maryland to secede as well. As the mayor described it, "The situation in Maryland was most critical. This State was especially important, because the capital of the nation lay within her borders. . . . Immediately after the call of the president for troops . . . a marked division among the people manifested itself." The most immediate tinderbox was the contest of whose flag would fly where. Union flags were put up and then torn down in various parts of the city; the Palmetto flag of South Carolina, the symbol of the Confederacy and secession, suffered the same fate. Rival groups tearing down flags was only a prelude to much worse.

As Northern regiments began arriving in the city, some carried by the very Baltimore & Ohio Railroad that the Browns had been instrumental in creating, deadly riots broke out. Fearful that the city itself was descending into civil war, Mayor Brown ordered that no flags were to be displayed. The Alex. Brown & Sons building on Calvert Street had been proudly flying the Stars and Stripes at the directive of the New York office. Alex. Brown was technically a separate business by then, but George Brown had died in 1859, and the Baltimore office was now led by his son, also named George Brown, who normally tended to defer to his uncle James. James, however, completely misread the intensity of the moment in Baltimore. He had been out of the country for months traveling in Europe after attending festivities honoring William, now Sir William, as the primary benefactor of the Liverpool Library, which was named the William Brown Library and Museum in his honor. Attending the ceremony, the American novelist Nathaniel Hawthorne said that in a sea of grandees, William "was the plainest and simplest man of all: an exceedingly unpretending old gentleman in black, small, withered, white hair, pale, quiet and respectable."

By the time the war had begun, William and James had long moved beyond whatever tension had once disturbed their relationship. Even so, New York, Baltimore and Liverpool were bound to have different views of the war. James was unequivocally supportive of the Union efforts, and he instructed George in Baltimore to disregard the mayor's proclamation and fly the Stars and Stripes. George Brown ignored James, heeded his patronymic cousin the mayor and took down the flag.[11] The city was soon occupied by Northern troops, though only after one of the Browns' partners in the early years of the B&O, the engineer Ross Winans, tried to raise an informal militia to ambush the Massachusetts regiment in the city and force Maryland into the arms of the Confederacy.

The divisions in Baltimore, however, paled in importance compared with the question of whether the government of Lord Palmerston in London would recognize the Confederacy as an independent nation. The English reliance on Southern cotton and Northern merchants made the prospect of a protracted war deeply alarming, although the moves of the government of Jefferson Davis to confiscate property held by Northerners in the South did not help the Southern cause in Parliament. While targeting Northerners, a fair amount of British property was seized or frozen in the chaos of these early months. On the flip side, Lincoln's Southern trade embargo enraged the politicians of London, the merchants of Liverpool and the industrialists of Lancashire.

For the Browns, and for all merchants and financiers, the most pressing issue was whether goods could be safely transported across the Atlantic without being seized either by the Union navy or by Confederate privateers. Like many, the Browns miscalculated in 1861, thinking that the conflict would last no more than a year and would end with the Confederacy as an independent nation. In their view, the split between the states was irreconcilable, it would be take too long and cost the North too much in lives and money to subdue the South. As always, the Browns took a cautious view. James wrote that "there is no knowing what ruin will overtake the North and the South, hence B. B. & Co. cannot be too prudent and cautious, for in the end we may be embroiled with European powers and our property at sea have a poor chance of escape, capture and loss."[12] Internationally, so long as the South was considered to be part of the sovereign United States and in a state of rebellion, no one contested the legal right of the Lincoln administration to take military action, including a blockade. If the Confederacy persuaded England to recognize its independence, however, the blockade could be taken as an act of aggression against the Crown. The economic damage caused by the sudden cessation of the American cotton trade made the British at best ambivalent and at worst hostile to the North, and the Palmerston government maintained a regular dialogue with the Confederacy as the South desperately tried to obtain British recognition.

On November 8, 1861, the U.S. Navy seized a British ship called the *Trent*, which was carrying two Southern envoys bound for Britain and France. The move was greeted enthusiastically in the North, and by Lincoln himself, but it caused outrage in Britain, where public opinion viewed the seizure as an arrogant and unlawful violation of British sovereignty.

The coming weeks were the closest that the British government came to recognizing the South and then supporting the Confederacy against the Union. Palmerston's government drew up plans for a British blockade of Union ports, and an invasion of the Union from Canada. There was open talk of a British declaration of war on the North. The irony of Great Britain, an intensely antislavery nation, contemplating an alliance with the Confederacy was not much remarked on, perhaps because Liverpool and Lancashire had been relying on Southern cotton for decades untroubled by how that cotton was actually produced. The Browns, who had cultivated a climate of asking hard questions about their business models, were similarly silent about the inherent tension between their staunch Unionism and the fact that they had made millions on the cotton trade. Better late than never, perhaps, but those were questions they preferred to avoid.

At the time of the *Trent* affair, James was with William in Liverpool, and both brothers worked strenuously to prevent a rupture in Anglo-American relations. William had faced opposition from his Liverpool partners, who were shocked that James seemed insensitive to the damage that Lincoln's policies were causing them. Both brothers recognized the peril of the *Trent* hysteria. They reached out to the U.S. ambassador in London, Charles Francis Adams, whom they both knew. They had already met repeatedly with Adams to urge him to assure the English business community that the Lincoln administration would honor the laws of neutrality and that trade would be protected from seizure and confiscation. In addition to impressing on Adams the gravity of the moment, they wrote to Secretary of State William Seward, whom they had dined with several times in the 1840s when Seward was practicing law in New York after having served two terms as governor of the state. William Brown forwarded a letter that Seward had written him in those years opposing on principle the confiscation of property in wartime. He hoped that the past correspondence might persuade Seward to make assurances that British property wouldn't be seized. Seward didn't respond till January 1862, and then only perfunctorily with homilies about how much he valued the input of the Browns and wished only for comity between the two countries. By then the worst of the

Trent crisis had passed. James was deeply unimpressed. "I have no confidence in Seward . . . considering him a reckless politician, and it's said sometimes in his Cups, so that it seems very important that the Bankers and the Merchants make themselves heard." Whether their messages were indeed heard, Lincoln understood that the priority was defeating the Confederacy, not fighting with London, and that it was best not to court two major conflicts at once. He ordered the envoys released and said that the *Trent* had been seized by a navy captain acting on his own accord, not on instructions from the White House.[13]

Had the British government recognized the Confederacy and then gone to war with the North, the history of the world would have been very different. But even though diplomatic tensions subsided after the *Trent* affair, the economic dislocations intensified. Those do not receive the same attention as the bloody battles—Antietam, Shiloh, Gettysburg—or the arduous campaigns down the Mississippi and across the South, or the amount of focus given to the political machinations and the struggles between Lincoln and his generals, or to the emancipation of American slaves. Perhaps that is as it should be. But the war disrupted a rich and interdependent ecosystem of goods, money and people, and that had permanent effects.

Not only did cotton cease to be the central U.S. export, but the nature of trade changed, and with it the Browns' business. Some of that had less to do with the Civil War than with the emerging technology of the telegraph. When the transatlantic cable was finally up and running, information about crop yields and the value of other goods being shipped could be transmitted nearly instantly, which made some of the services provided by houses such as Brown Brothers no longer necessary. The war itself, however, damaged the delicate web of letters of credit and financing that had underpinned trade. The *Trent* affair triggered a brief financial panic in December 1861, which drained banks in the North of their specie reserves. That could be problematic at any time, but the Lincoln administration had been funding the war in conjunction with local banks in the Northeast, and in those weeks when war with Great Britain seemed possible, their financial position deteriorated to the point that federal funding of the war was jeopardized.

As a result, Congress and the Lincoln administration passed a bill suspending specie payments, thinking it would be a temporary measure. As it turned out, that began a revolutionary new phase in American history, an age of federal paper.[14]

With specie payments suspended, by early 1862, the Union was in sore need of immediate funds. War has always been a spur to innovation, both technological and financial. To solve its funding needs, Congress passed the Legal Tender Act in February 1862. That law stands as one of the least appreciated and most consequential moves of the government during the war. It authorized the federal government to print paper money—called greenbacks for the color that the U.S. dollar still bears—not directly backed by gold or other specie. The Legal Tender Act was the beginning of the end for hard money and the start of the fiat currency world we now inhabit. It inaugurated the idea that paper printed by the government has value because the government promises that the paper will be honored as "legal tender." The notion that a sovereign government could literally manufacture money detached from some underlying store of value like gold was not totally new, but it was, and in some quarters remains, deeply controversial. The untethering of paper from what it is supposed to represent was a revolutionary step in the evolution of money, one that the House of Brown had inadvertently helped create. Issuing bills of exchange, letters of credit and travelers' credits was a private version of creating money treated as legal tender because of the unimpeachable reputation of Alexander and his sons. Their paper made it easier to fund businesses, easier for people to travel, for goods to be shipped, for dreams to be funded, railroads to be built, ships to be launched and cable to be laid under the Atlantic Ocean.

The Legal Tender Bill was not passed without debate. Democrat George Pendleton of Ohio warned that the proliferation of government paper would be a disaster. "Prices will be inflated . . . incomes will depreciate; the savings of the poor will vanish; the hoardings of the widow will melt away." Another congressman thundered that "gold and silver are the only true measure of value. These metals were prepared by the Almighty for this very purpose." These qualms, however, paled in comparison to the fact that the government was about to run out of money. It had been borrowing from banks, and Lincoln's secretary of the treasury Salmon Chase had been creatively shifting funds. By the end of 1861, however, the government had exhausted its fiscal options.

As a result of the act, the U.S. government printed $150 million of paper money in 1862. These so-called greenbacks supplanted state-bank currencies. Rather than generating inflation as feared, the proliferation of greenbacks provided a needed sense of economic order and stability. The notes were guaranteed by a government that, at least during wartime, was given the benefit of the doubt by most people—its promises were taken at face value, literally. The financial innovations did not stop there. To generate more income, Congress passed the Internal Revenue Act, which authorized higher excise taxes and, for the first time, an income tax, meant to be temporary. To ensure that those were collected, it created another agency, the Internal Revenue Service.

Not only was there no debilitating inflation, but the industrial output of the North surged with the war effort. Having undertaken one radical innovation with little public outcry, the Lincoln administration and Congress went one step further the following year and passed the National Banking Act in February 1863. Sponsored by Senator John Sherman of Ohio, who would later give his name to the nation's first major antitrust law in the 1890s, the bill was designed to strengthen faith in greenbacks and to make the Union stronger. "We cannot maintain our nationality unless we establish a sound and stable financial system; and as the basis of it we must have a uniform national currency," Sherman said. To govern the 1,600 state-chartered banks then operating, the act created national oversight along with reserve requirements and limitations on how much state banks could lend. While it did not quite re-create an official "Bank of the United States," it established the framework for the American financial system that lasted for fifty years until the establishment of the Federal Reserve in 1913. It was justified as a necessary wartime measure, and it was that. But it rectified the deficiencies of the chaotic muddle of banks and currencies that had proliferated since Andrew Jackson's successful bank war. The act also empowered the federal government to issue bonds, along with more greenbacks, and hence use deficit spending for the war. There was nothing particularly unusual about governments borrowing to pay for wars, but it was nonetheless a signature moment for the United States.

As we will see, the act did not solve all American financial ills or magically establish stability. The new national system was essentially an overlay on top of a decentralized local jumble, and the statutory authority to regulate local banks proved largely meaningless absent a bureaucracy to enforce it. But there can be no mistaking what the war wrought in terms of a permanent shift in American economic history that marked the beginning of the financialization of the United States. These bills were passed under the cloak of wartime exigency, and even in Congress, debates over their passage did not receive the same intense scrutiny that funding the army and navy did. Public focus remained on Union army setbacks and the carnage of battles such as Fredericksburg and the Second Battle of Bull Run in the latter half of 1862. And why should greenbacks and banks have garnered much attention when the fate of the nation hung in the balance and tens of thousands were being killed? And yet the Civil War marked a transformation of the American economic system that, even beyond the destruction of the slave system of the South, reshaped the arc of the country forever.[15]

The House of Brown was a microcosm of these shifts. The war pushed the house almost entirely out of its business in trading actual goods and more rapidly toward what it was already becoming: a merchant bank whose profits were a function of the paper it created and the paper it provided to others. As James wrote in 1863, "Our business is now entirely buying & selling Exchange." The house also profited from the war. Wars not only make nations; they make bankers. The Browns' ascendency as a paper merchant continued as the war ended, and the firm expanded its business in foreign exchange, in facilitating foreign travel through letters and credits, and in financing the trade of others. For the Browns, the Civil War marked the final end of their consignment business and the beginning of the next phase of their history. Alexander had started as a merchant. His heirs became bankers.

The war also marked a generational transition and the next step in the gradual separation between the English and American branches. In 1864, William Brown, now a baronet, died peacefully in his sleep just shy of his eightieth birthday. He was lauded by Palmerston as a man "of eminent commercial position" enhanced by his "generous conduct towards the people of Liverpool." His last surviving son had died decades before, and his sole grandson eschewed the business. That meant operational control of Brown Shipley, now relocated to London, passed to Mark Collet, while financial control resided with James Brown in New York. Though James was ably supported by younger partners such as Howard Potter, he wanted the firm to remain a family business, which meant grooming his only surviving son who had shown any aptitude, John Crosby Brown. James would live until 1877, but John Crosby led the firm for the last three decades of the nineteenth century. He proved a more than capable steward.

His Civil War story was typical of his class but not without controversy. Born in 1838, John Crosby was of age during the Civil War, but he did not serve. He was in Liverpool when the war began, learning the business, and stayed there throughout 1861. His younger brother, Clarence Stewart, did serve, and survived, as did several of the firm's young men. But the paucity of upper-class New Yorkers in the Union army was a source of deep tensions in New York City. Those erupted in the summer of 1863 in a three-day orgy of violence later dubbed "the Draft Riots." One of the main grievances was a provision of the congressional Enrollment Act instituting the draft that made it possible for wealthy white citizens to pay $300 for others to take their place in the army. The Draft Riots pitted poor Irish immigrants against free African Americans, but class resentment was the underlying cause.[16] Though the violence raged near them, the Browns, like most well-to-do New Yorkers, were largely unscathed. The rioters destroyed mostly their own neighborhoods, and of the more than one hundred people who died, almost all were from the very groups doing the rioting.

John Crosby Brown, the next leader of the clan and the firm, was the embodiment of the best of the family—modest, hardworking, deeply committed to his role first as a son and then as a father, dedicated to charity and the church. He was also, more passively, the embodiment of what was most myopic about the moneyed class—insensitive to the deep divisions that opened in American society in the decades after the Civil War, almost to the point of being unaware, and seemingly unconcerned about the many injustices birthed by the massive economic and industrial expansion of the country. His sense of noblesse oblige was sated by his commitment to the church and his devotion to the Union Theological Seminary in New York, which also became the home of his son William Adams Brown. But he was not overly troubled by the woes that this new era of capitalism unleashed.

It's not that the House of Brown was indifferent to the tumult swirling around them. After all, James Brown, in addition to his business and philanthropic endeavors, was one of the first investors in a new weekly journal focused almost entirely on the pressing questions of what constituted a good society. In 1865, he, along with a number of others, backed the launch of *The Nation* and its founding editor, the Irish-born E. L. Godkin. The magazine's early brief was to support the abolitionist cause and supply the intellectual foundations for a postwar America based on racial equality and the enfranchisement of African Americans. Godkin himself wasn't so keen about the more radical stances of some of his backers in Boston and New York, and he soon steered the publication toward a moderate and at times milquetoast liberalism. The eschewing of radicalism likely had the support of James Brown, who always preferred a gradualist approach to social reform. Under Godkin, at least until the surge of American imperialism in the Caribbean and the Philippines at the end of the nineteenth century, *The Nation* was not a fire-breathing journal demanding social change. It embraced the market and profit and democracy and incremental moves toward a more equitable society and shunned the "change it now at all costs" fervor of reformers. James Brown was only one of a coterie of financial backers, but the journal in those years perfectly reflected his temperament.

As the war ended, Brown Brothers was now essentially two houses, Brown Shipley in London and Brown Brothers in New York. James was positioning John Crosby to lead the next generation, but the other younger partners were not pleased. The firm's capital was in excess of $10 million, and while James controlled a little more than 20 percent of the shares of the partnership, he had almost three-quarters of all the money. The English partners after William's death attempted to change the balance of power, in effect arguing that because they had been managing the English business, they were entitled to a much larger share of the firm. Other resentments spilled over. Stewart Brown, the often-overlooked cousin of the brothers who had been a partner in New York and who had the largest number of shares after James, complained bitterly in 1865, "I have felt very much hurt at the cool way in which I am treated. I am not avaricious and do not care for additional shares as a matter of dollars and cents, but I have with great annoyance thought over the thing & been pained to see that out of sight is out of mind."[17]

It was left to John Crosby to solve the problem, which took years of careful negotiation. At critical moments, it seemed as if the partnership might dissolve. The Brown Shipley partners had a legitimate gripe and some leverage. They were running the business, so why should they not have more control and James and his heirs less? John Crosby, however, pointed out that when his father, James, did eventually die, all the firm's partners would receive his shares proportionally. Why then not wait? he asked. James himself wrote to the London group stating that if he retired and cashed out his shares, "the prestige of the house in the point of credit would be seriously affected. . . . My death would not so effect it as it would be known that three-fifths of my property would remain in the house." Even so, John Crosby then reminded Brown Shipley and the dissenting New York partners that his father's "private fortune as well as his active capital is essential to the continuance of the concern on its current footing." He also crystallized what had not needed saying as long as the firm was Alexander and his sons: the firm had been founded as a family business and it was imperative that it remain a family business. If that was altered by a different partnership structure, then the essential nature of the firm would be destroyed. "Our interest and pride in the house as a family institution [would] cease and our connection with it would become simply a question of dollars and cents."[18]

With James's backing, John Crosby eventually persuaded the London and New York partners to accept a new governing agreement that enshrined family control while allowing "everyone connected with us to get rich as fast as possible." The junior and nonfamily partners would have every opportunity to act autonomously in London and collegially in New York. They would be able to build their own fortunes, but subsumed to the larger entity. Brown Brothers would remain a family firm, controlled by family members. That was more than a matter of corporate governance. It meant that the firm would cleave to a set of values that Alexander had defined, that his sons had refined, and that his grandson and great-grandson would uphold.

John Crosby didn't know it, but the end of the war and the settling of the partnership was part of a larger evolution: the emergence of the WASP elite and what became known as the Establishment. The second half of the nineteenth century was the chrysalis. The characteristics of this new class were still slowly coalescing, but Brown Brothers checked all the main boxes. The idea that the firm existed for reasons other than "dollars and cents" was essential to its character, to its continuance and to the world that its partners and their class would shape in the middle of the twentieth century. It was, as John Crosby said, fine and well to get rich, but there was a larger purpose, one that channeled wealth for the greater good of the family, the firm and then all of society. It was a vision at once self-serving and in service. And it proved remarkably potent.

CHAPTER 6

A NICE SENSE OF
COMMERCIAL HONOR

Well groomed to take over from his father, John Crosby Brown was ready when James passed away in November 1877. James worked almost to the end of his eighty-six years, and he was eulogized with nothing but kind words. They were more than the usual pro forma platitudes; they spoke to a man whose inner and outer character were more or less the same, where the line between text and subtext was thin, who was largely as he appeared. He wore till nearly the end of his life "the old-fashioned costume of a New York merchant—black trousers, swallow-tail coat, wide black stock, low open waistcoat and thick linen shirt bosom always exposed to the air in the coldest weather." As attentive as he was to the business, he did what many men of wealth and status do toward the end of their lives and devoted more time and effort to giving back to his community. He donated hundreds of thousands of dollars to the Union Theological Seminary next to Columbia University in Morningside Heights. He endowed Presbyterian churches and a parsonage near his Weehawken home. And he turned his attention to the political cesspool that was New York politics in the hope of making the city's government more accountable to its citizens.

For all the advances of the first part of the nineteenth century, public health and hygiene, nutrition, education and violent crime remained acute problems. So, relatedly, did political corruption. New York City in the 1860s had the highest death rate in the Western world,[1] in part because of the dense nexus of tenements and settlements housing the thousands of immigrants who arrived each year in conditions that can only be described as squalid. The rapid changes of new technologies—the railroad, the telegraph, electricity and then, starting in the 1880s, the telephone—not only brought people closer together but exposed the glaring issues to a wider public and with more immediacy than ever before. Improving the human condition was seen by the emerging new elite as both imperative and feasible. It was, in short, a class that believed in progress, and believed as well that they—and increasingly the United States—could and must be in its vanguard.

In New York, that meant political as well as social reform. Post–Civil War urban politics in the city were controlled by one of the earliest political "machines" centered around Tammany Hall, the party headquarters of the St. Tammany Society founded in the late eighteenth century. By the mid-nineteenth century, Tammany had morphed into a potent Democratic political organization commanding the loyalty of Irish immigrants and local businesses, who voted as one bloc dictated by the society's leaders. The Tammany machine in the 1860s was captained by the powerful William "Boss" Tweed. The financial elite of the city found Tweed personally distasteful and politically abhorrent. Tweed did, at times, provide law and order, but he preferred muscle, music, booze and enforcers, preferably burly and not averse to bullying and bloodying. To James Brown and his clan—his cousin Stewart, his sons and in-laws—Tweed and his ilk were anathema.

That was why James was a founder and chairman of the Committee of Seventy, established at a meeting at the Cooper Union—a bastion of genteel liberalism—in 1871. The goal of the committee was to break up the Tweed ring. Tweed was in part brought down because he had allowed the city to borrow money for public works projects that never got done, and likely never were intended to. The money instead ended up in the pockets of the machine, helping its grandees furnish homes, buy carriages and dine lavishly. Tweed made for good fodder, both in the pages of Godkin's *Nation* and at the hand of the premier caricaturist of the day, Thomas Nast, whose drawings of Tweed in *Harper's Weekly* as the epitome of corruption, fat and dripping with excess, forever demonized the "Boss" as a symbol of urban political decadence.[2] The tipping point for Tammany came after a riot between Protestant and Catholic Irish in the city led to the deaths of more than sixty people, which Tweed and his handpicked mayor failed to prevent. As in most things, James remained behind the scenes, lending office space at 59 Wall Street to the legal team that helped bring down Tweed. At the end of 1871, Tweed and his cronies were swept from office, and Tweed himself was then tried and convicted of fraud and embezzlement. Politics in the city didn't suddenly become transparent, and Tammany Hall remained a powerful force. But after the fall of Tweed, City Hall was, at least, less dominated by an organization that resembled the mafia.

Tammany was hardly the only obstacle to good governance. In New York and in the nation at large after the war, a new world of money was flourishing along with a new class of men of questionable character. On September 24, 1869, on "Black Friday," a garrulous stockman turned financier named Jim Fisk, a rotund dandy who enjoyed flaunting his wealth, partnered with the dour and brilliant Jay Gould in an attempt to corner the gold market. Their plot failed, but not before fortunes were lost as Fisk and Gould bid the price of gold higher and higher. "The agony depicted on the faces of men who crowded the street made one feel as if Gettysburg had been lost and the rebels were marching down Broadway," noted one account.[3] Gould and Fisk were not just any pair of New York speculators. They were disturbingly close to the inner circle of President Ulysses S. Grant, whose administration would soon be embroiled in scandals revolving around cozy access to a president who seemed easily duped by acquaintances whom he should not have trusted. What's more, while Gould and Fisk may have sought personal gain at the expense of everyone, they were also creatures of a new era when the paper money printed in the bushels to pay for the war developed its own life detached from gold and from any underlying hard, physical asset. The attempt to corner the gold market depended on bids for gold using greenbacks to pay for it. The two men may have failed, but the forces they unleashed remained unleashed.[4]

That fact was not lost on one of the day's leading intellectuals and critics who would soon move to the center of American culture as a writer and gadfly, Henry Adams. Grandson of one president, John Quincy Adams, great-grandson of another, John Adams, and son of an ambassador, Henry Adams came from the country's first political dynasty. His relationship to power was intimate and fraught, and he evolved into a powerful critic of a system that his family had helped construct. His writings on the gold crisis emphasized not just the role of speculation and corruption in Washington and especially in the Grant White House (Adams was one of Grant's most astringent critics), but the power of speculators to upend American democracy. Reflecting on Gould and Fisk's plot, Adams concluded that speculators and their ephemeral paper money were only in the early stages of their ascendency. Cornering the gold market may have failed, but it still demonstrated that moneymen were acquiring the power "to override and trample on law, custom, decency and every restraint known to society, without scruple and as yet without check. The belief is common in America that the day is at hand when corporations . . . after creating a system of quiet but irresistible corruption will ultimately succeed in directing government itself."[5]

The themes that had percolated earlier in the century—the tension between the integrity of hard money and hard work and the promiscuous hunger for wealth and profit, between a society grounded in the simple virtues of faith and land and one driven by the chaotic energies of ambition and dreams—were briefly subsumed by the struggle over slavery and the Union. With the Civil War settling those issues, however, the tensions reemerged with renewed intensity. The vast western lands beyond the Mississippi became the focus of American hunger for more. The financial system of paper money and greenbacks created in 1862 fueled westward expansion, industrial growth and the great postwar railroad boom.

The explosive growth not just of railroads but of commerce in general demanded capital. There was not enough gold to meet those needs, but there was essentially no limit to paper. Brown Brothers was an integral part of the burgeoning private financial industry that provided that paper. For much of the 1870s and 1880s, the firm focused on what it did best, issuing letters of credit for international trade and acting as the premier foreign exchange broker. The result was that these decades were ones of immense and quiet profitability for the firm, even as they were a time of deep tumult for the United States. Brown Brothers in New York and Brown Shipley in Liverpool and London did not receive the same scrutiny and public fascination that J. P. Morgan, J. D. Rockefeller, Andrew Carnegie and other leading robber barons did. Having been stung by the attacks from the likes of Henry Ward Beecher in the 1850s, the firm preferred a less public profile combined with a strong balance sheet and expanding influence and wealth. The result was that the firm was rarely in the news, much to the relief and satisfaction of the partner who led the firm after the death of James Brown in 1877.

John Crosby Brown had none of the verve of Carnegie, nor the arrogance of Morgan, the snobbery of Astor or the obsessive intensity of Rockefeller. The Brown family had dealt with the tragedy of too many premature deaths, but they were fortunate and in fact extraordinary not to have any wayward heirs. The children of James Brown who survived did not all go into the business, but John Crosby Brown perfectly embodied the spirit of his grandfather Alexander and his father, James. Multigenerational family businesses strive to find the right stewards generation after generation; rarely do they find one as perfectly suited for the role as John Crosby Brown to carry on his family's legacy.

Having settled the partnership crisis, John Crosby turned to the business itself. The main challenge, as he saw it, was that the firm was "afflicted with too much prosperity" and needed to remain disciplined and tightly run by family and a few outside partners lest that prosperity become a liability. That prosperity meant more cash for the partners, which in Brown fashion was reinvested as working capital back into the firm.[6] Without question, there was wealth to be had and money to be made, and John Crosby slid comfortably into the life of an upper-class New Yorker, with an ease and unquestioned acceptance of his milieu that his parents and grand-parents could never have. Uninterested in keeping up with the Astors and the Villards and the Flaglers, the Morgans and the Fricks, he lived in a new forty-foot town house on East Thirty-seventh Street that had been part of a multimansion development begun by James. He also built a country home in West Orange, New Jersey, called Brighthurst, where the family could escape the summer heat and oppressive smell of summertime New York, its streets clogged with mounds of horse manure and the overflow of human sewage. The summer house, a Victorian fantasy of towers and steep vaulted roofs, was also home to an increasingly large assortment of musical instru-ments that the family had started collecting and that John Crosby's wife, Mary Elizabeth Brown, eventually donated to the new Metropolitan Mu-seum of Art in 1889, where John Crosby was treasurer and one of the first trustees. Their initial gift of more than 270 pieces from around the world—African drums, Scottish pipes, assorted reeds and other musicals devices from "Oriental Nations & Savage Tribes" became the founding collection of the museum's musical instruments department.[7]

With the epic struggle over slavery conclusively settled, the next great cleavage in the United States was over what would constitute money and who could access it, over the nature of currency and the yawning gulf be-tween the very rich and everyone else. The battle to define money in the last decades of the nineteenth century shaped political parties, gave rise to labor movements, and birthed economic theories. The battle was, at heart, a con-test over who would profit from the explosive growth of the American econ-omy in the decades after the war. Arguments over gold, silver and paper defined the fault lines of American politics. The Greenback Party, formed in the 1870s, was founded on the premise that a monetary system based on federally issued paper notes, not backed by gold or silver, would benefit both farmers and laborers, whereas a gold system, by constricting the supply of money, inevitably helped bankers and financial elites at the expense of the rest. Whether the economics were correct, the sentiment was powerful. The Greenback Party then morphed into the Populist Party, which in turn became one of the largest voices in the Democratic Party. It was largely true that farmers and workers were chronically unable to come up with enough money to meet their needs. The United States may have been flush with capital, but it did not flow evenly and it did not end up in the pockets of the working classes or the farmers.[8] It was during these years that the Republican Party became identified with the party of the elite and powerful, from the crony capitalism and scandals of the Grant administration through the presidencies of Rutherford Hayes, Chester Arthur and Benjamin Harrison, punctuated by two Democratic Grover Cleveland administrations that for the most part (the Sherman Antitrust Act being a notable exception) spurned populism in favor of the same strain of elite capitalism that had also defined the Republicans.

These brawls over what constituted money were not abstract or arcane. They were the struggles of the day, felt and argued passionately and acutely by large swaths of the population. The main camps—paper versus gold, gold versus silver, national banks versus a federal system—became metaphors for labor versus capital, Jefferson versus Hamilton, good versus evil, God versus the Devil, farmers versus the coast, and North versus South redux. This is not hyperbole, or if it is, it is the hyperbole of the people at the time, expressed in speeches and pamphlets brimming with apocalyptic language.

At its core, the question was what constituted value and what type of currency could benefit not just a privileged few but the bulk of society. It's not as if any country in the world at that point, or before, or for that matter since, has answered that question to the full satisfaction of most citizens. The idea, however, that paper money issued by a government, detached from gold or silver, could in and of itself be the primary source of value was both controversial and relatively new. In the early seventeenth century, the Scotsman John Law explored the idea of paper money backed only by government and not by specie, but that remained mostly theoretical. The idea of paper money as *the* money persisted as a minor note and not one in especially good repute until the exigencies of the Civil War turned the U.S. federal government into a reluctant issuer of greenbacks.

Others began to justify the new paper system. Prominent nineteenth-century intellects such as Walter Bagehot, the editor of England's newspaper

The Economist, emphasized what the Browns already knew: that the system of trade, commerce and financing had long depended on paper, letters of credit, bankers' acceptances, and notes backed not by silver or gold or even the government but by trust in the issuer and belief that the paper was backed by real assets. For merchant bankers such as the Browns, the assets were the goods being exported or imported; for government, it was the tax revenue and the overall economic activity of the country. Paper credit was, for Bagehot as well as for the Browns and others, about trust, trust that the person or entity issuing the note was good for the promise. These moderate men inherently made a radical argument that paper money was in and of itself worth something.[9]

As John Crosby steered the firm through the end of the nineteenth century, the firm largely avoided the railroad boom. That spoke volumes. Railroads were the defining feature of the age. Railroads were to the economy of the 1870s through the 1890s what the internet and information technology and smartphones were to the 1990s through to the 2020s. It's estimated that nearly two hundred thousand miles of track were laid in the thirty years after the Civil War and that this amounted to a fifth of all capital invested during that time. It was the path to wealth for new players on Wall Street. The boom and bust and boom of the railroads made a few financial houses immensely powerful and ruined many others. The construction of those hundreds of thousands of miles of tracks across the United States was by far the single greatest source of wealth creation and the most frequent cause of wealth destruction. Brown Brothers stayed largely on the sidelines, avoiding the high highs as well as the lows but also becoming less central to the dramas of the era. Because they sidestepped the railroads, Brown Brothers became relatively less influential and relatively smaller in the final decades of the century, but by sidestepping the railroads, they almost certainly raised the odds of their long-term survival. Railroads were the ultimate financial crapshoot.

Brown Brothers did piggyback on railroad bonds issued by others, and they bought tranches of refinancing issues and participated, modestly, in capital raises. They did not take the lead. That suited their DNA and their general disinclination to occupy center stage. Instead, under John Crosby's stewardship, they focused on more arcane areas of finance that were nonetheless essential to domestic and international commerce and earned the firm steady and mounting income.

First, they consolidated their leading position in the lucrative arena of foreign exchange. The scale of British, French and German investment in the United States in the latter part of the nineteenth century was many multiples of what it had been before the Civil War, and involved a much broader range of investments. As the American economy mushroomed in size, the scope of American imports of European goods also grew exponentially, as did exports of American commodities and cheap manufactured goods to Europe. Someone had to reconcile the multiple currencies and arrange for exporters to be paid in one currency while importers settled the transaction in another. Brown Brothers earned fees and commissions by harmonizing the prices of goods shipped in pounds sterling and then sold in dollars, or shipped by New England manufacturers who were paid in dollars to customers who bought in francs, pesos or guilders. And it didn't just do that directly with its own trading clients; it began to do a substantial business for other banks. A bank in Illinois might advance a local manufacturer or farm collective a portion of the eventual sale of their goods to England; rather than try to find counterparties to settle the transaction in London, the bank paid Brown Brothers to take the letters of credit. Brown Brothers was one of the few firms to specialize in this profitable niche, which further propelled it into the business of finance and only finance.

The firm also took the lead with financial innovations such as futures contracts, which were used by buyers and sellers on both sides of the Atlantic to plan more effectively and manage their cash flow and margins by locking in prices in advance. That wasn't risk free, and there was always the possibility that a futures contract would either overprice or underprice what would be realized in the final sale. But unlike the hydra-headed derivatives markets of later years, the Browns kept tight control on the contracts they issued and at what price they were guaranteed. More crucially, they focused on earning fees and commissions rather than on aggressively trading their own contracts. In other words, they did not become addicted to their own product.

These businesses were vital. They made possible the vast flow of goods, but intermediaries taking small fees on every transaction was not the stuff of breathless news stories or the cause of much drama. So much of what is imperative to the smooth functioning of a system happens beneath the surface. Swaths of modern business and government would be impossible without double-entry bookkeeping and insurance actuarial tables. Those do not make for vivid stories or heroic tales. Charging 4.2 percent interest rather than 3.9 percent might have entailed a celebratory dinner, but it was no Pickett's Charge. The business of Brown Brothers in these decades lubricated international commerce and domestic finance, but without drama. And that was intentional.

Brown Brothers, despite its purposely low profile, could not escape entirely the escalating class war. The next in that metronomic series of financial crises, the Panic of 1873, was once again laid at the feet of Wall Street and the captains of finance who underwrote the railroads on the backs of labor and farmers. Implicated in the causes of the collapse was the Coinage Act, enacted by Congress in January 1873, which discouraged silver-backed money and made gold the standard. The combination of speculation on railroad construction combined with a huge supply of questionable bonds raised on unrealistic expectations of railroad profits was the kindling. Anytime there is a huge debt bubble and the supply of money is suddenly restricted, as it was by the Coinage Act, you get problems.

Beginning on another Black Friday, the proximate cause of the panic was the collapse of Jay Cooke & Company, one of the leading financial houses that blossomed with the postwar railroad boom. That then triggered a wave of bank failures followed by a rapid contraction of economic activity and then a national wave of job losses. There were then no figures measuring unemployment, though the crisis did spur the state government of Massachusetts to begin the arduous task of trying to measure who was employed and who was not. Even without specific numbers, no one was under any illusions about the severity of the downturn, with breadlines standard in multiple cities, idle and vacant-looking working men milling around with no work, and the commentariat ever shriller in their assessments. In New York City, according to one account, the "midwinter of 1873–1874 found tens of thousands of people on the verge of starvation, suffering for food, for the need of proper clothing, and for medical attendance." A large group assembling in Tompkins Square Park was routed by police mounted on horses, who beat the protesters—unarmed, weak, children included—until they fled. The panic added to the stain of the scandal-prone Grant administration and ignited intense anti-immigration sentiment as well as demands that Washington issue more greenbacks in order to bail out bondholders bankrupted by the collapse of banks and railroads.[10]

The Republican Party was hardly heedless to the suffering, but its leaders were adamant that more paper was not the answer. In 1876, Representative James Garfield of Ohio wrote a long defense in *The Atlantic Monthly* of "hard money" and the gold standard, which formed the basis of the economic platform that helped propel him to the White House in 1880 and soon thereafter to a fatal date with an assassin's bullet. Garfield vehemently rejected paper money, not just as an economic sin but a moral one. He quoted Lincoln's secretary of treasury Salmon Chase, who grudgingly accepted that the exigencies of war demanded paper notes but believed that "legal-tender notes must be the devil made manifest in paper; for no man can foresee what mischief they may do when they are once let loose." By the 1870s, Garfield was confronting a society where multiple voices were clamoring for paper money, and for an abundance of it, arguing that all stores of value are human creations and that gold, silver and paper are just abstract substances that people agree have value that government then supports. Said one defender of paper money, "The government can make money of any material and of any shape and value as it pleases."

Garfield made the counterargument that gold and silver had been, as Edmund Burke said, "the two great, recognized species that represent the lasting, conventional credit of mankind." Paper and letters of credit had a role in the ecosystem of trade and commerce so long as they were underpinned by gold and silver. The heresy of "soft money" would lead not, as its proponents claimed, to liberation from wage slavery and from subservience to a moneyed elite but to the loss of reliable value and then social chaos. The idea that printing money was the answer was for Garfield "a delusion and a snare." Only a nation whose currency was based on "the standard of gold" could thrive and survive over the long term; all else were empty promises made by false prophets.[11]

The Browns and many other barons of finance kept out of the public debate. The battles between hard money and soft, between paper and metal, always cast the financiers of New York and Wall Street as the villains, so taking a strong public stance was never in their interest. In the narrow and confined circles that the Browns and their peers inhabited, there was a general consensus that credit and paper were essential components to the system, provided that the right people and institutions were in charge of their issuance. There was also a general consensus that advocates of pure paper money were, on the whole, uneducated and ill informed and would lead the country to economic ruin if their ideas were widely adopted. Only a system led by sound men backing sound money would work, and they saw themselves as the men supporting that system.

The formation of a group identity is, of course, a slow and mysterious process, clearer in retrospect than in the moment. The coalescing of a financial elite with a certain set of values took decades, but at some point by the 1880s, New York City saw the formation of a class that may not have felt unified but that nonetheless shared a view of the world and a certain sensibility. The downfall of Tweed and Tammany, the pushback against the cornering of the gold market, the defense of a gold system in the face of populist opposition even during a severe economic crisis—all helped that cohort define themselves in contrast to what they were not. They were not speculators; they were not willing to upend decades of tradition about what constituted money; and they believed that only a system guarded by a select few men, disciplined, of integrity and rectitude, would preserve the hard-won and ever tenuous prosperity that was America's destiny.

These years were later named the Gilded Age, keying off the satirical Mark Twain novel that portrayed Washington in the 1870s as a den of moneycrats and charlatans, where greed and ambition were the coin of the realm. The story of these decades includes a colorful cast of robber barons, outsized titans such as Andrew Carnegie, August Belmont, Leland Stanford, Collis Huntington and John Pierpont Morgan. Many were already wealthy and established before the 1870s and 1880s, but in the years after the Panic of 1873 and with the rise of populism, they became symbols of the worst excesses of American capitalism, seen by many as fundamentally immoral and as having enriched themselves at the expense of the masses of laborers who worked in wage slavery to build empires with little to show except broken bodies and lives. Like all cultural brushstrokes, that image was an exaggeration and lumped together not only people of different ilk and morals but also multiple layers of experience that varied from the dingy, long and deadly workdays of workers in mines and mills to a new middle class, urban and now educated, enjoying a life of their dreams.

Meanwhile, the moneyed class was defining itself. People who ascend into the ranks of an elite often rewrite their own past. Legions of British merchants and yeoman grew richer over the years and were eventually granted titles, and then assumed the identity of aristocrats. Gone were the rough edges of the past, replaced by an easy myth of "so it is, so it ever was." Self-reflection had no place, especially because it might muss up an otherwise clean story. In the final decades of the nineteenth century, the families that grew wealthy from trade and railroads and finance coalesced into a social set that emulated the British aristocracy and elided a messy past to create a simpler present. New York at the height of this Gilded Age, with a population fast approaching one million people, saw the rapid formation of social and economic circles that were new then, yet quickly established roots that made it seem as if it were always thus. Clubs proliferated: the Knickerbocker, the Metropolitan, the Union League and the Union. Cultural institutions, such as the Metropolitan Museum of Art, the New York Public Library and Carnegie Hall, took root and expanded through philanthropic donations. New York was said to be led by four hundred families of repute, with the Astors on the apex, who populated those clubs and funded those institutions. John Crosby and his partners were card-carrying members of this class. The differences between them and their flashier, greedier compadres may have been significant within that fold, but their similarities compared with Iowa farmers or Irish laborers were even more pronounced.

As he looked back on a hundred years of the firm in the memoir he published just before his death in 1909, John Crosby offered one sweeping lesson: "a nice sense of commercial honor, an absolute fairness in all dealings, a willingness to suffer pecuniary loss, if need be, rather than tarnish by one unworthy act the good name of the firm. I have known instances where unfair losses have been quietly assumed rather than that there should be any appearance of repudiating an obligation. . . . Character was prized more than wealth, and it brought its great reward in happy, useful lives."[12] He lived his life by an inner code, and he was deeply devoted to his faith, and to the Union Theological Seminary. James had been an early benefactor, and John Crosby later served as president of the board and helped finance the building of the massive campus adjacent to Columbia University. So central was he to the school's funding and growth that the centerpiece of the new campus was named in his honor, the John Crosby Brown Memorial Tower. His wife, Mary, was the daughter of a theologian who had founded and was later president of the seminary, and one of their children, William Adams, became a minister and professor of Systemic Theology at the school. The seminary in the 1890s was racked by a near schism with the Presbyterian Church General Assembly that ultimately led the seminary to break with the assembly and become independent. The major fissure was liberal versus conservative theology, whether God's love and forgiveness extended beyond just the faithful and whether the church should place more emphasis on original sin. Brown led the board to emphatically reject the harsh dogma of the conservatives.[13]

The understated religiosity of John Crosby and his family was common to this new class. In contrast to the ecstatic outward fervor of the Second Great Awakening and the Baptists of the Great Plains, the Protestantism of wealthy New York and the Northeast was private and sedate. That did not make it less intense. The governing creed emphasized humbleness in the face of God's power and love, and constantly reminded the faithful that this life was but an ephemera, a fleeting moment during which you had one opportunity to do good. And if you happened to be fortunate enough to be graced with wealth and status, it was your responsibility to give back, to make the world around you a better place and not just luxuriate in a warm bath of privilege.

The business of Brown Brothers in these years was simultaneously lucrative and uneventful compared with the passion play of railroad construction and the growth of heavy industries in the United States. Brown Brothers did have modest dealings in railroad bonds, but as a trader, not as an issuer. Its most significant dip into the railroad world was Maine's Bangor and Aroostook; the firm ultimately owned a majority interest and managed the company. The line consisted of a few hundred miles, mostly in northern Maine. John Crosby was attentive to the needs of the railroad and served on the board. Brown Brothers was not, however, at heart an operating company, nor did John Crosby and his partners lust for bigger, better and faster. They were not primarily railroad men, nor entrepreneurs, nor aspiring business titans. The family had had its experience of launching a major rail line, the B&O, and of nearly capturing the transatlantic passenger trade. The B&O had gone adequately; the Collins Line ended badly. Neither led the family to embrace those enterprises as their next new thing. The Bangor and Aroostook was a junior league version of the Union Pacific and the Northern Pacific and a dozen other lines spanning thousands of miles and untold millions of dollars that transformed America and made the career of E. H. Harriman, who would later become so important to the history of the firm.

The business of Brown Brothers, separate from its direct involvement with the Bangor line, began to modernize under John Crosby's leadership. As he wrote, "If the firm was to hold its own, new lines of business must be sought and cultivated." With the rise of trusts in the 1890s, which were a new form of corporate organization that owned the assets of multiple businesses without actually managing them, larger and larger companies were forming. That made the highly profitable and carefully managed Brown Brothers seem smaller and less significant by comparison. Those who directly financed and managed the larger rail lines, and especially those who refinanced them after the initial wave started going bankrupt after 1873, also ballooned in size, especially the financial empire of Junius Morgan and his even more illustrious son J.P. In addition, insurance companies entered the arena as a source of investment capital. Insurance companies rarely risked their primary capital on industrial financing such as building steel mills or railroads, but they did invest in trust companies, and those trust companies then invested directly. Facing these multiple prongs of competition, John Crosby Brown sought out new investment opportunities. Brown Brothers became a source of secondary financing for smaller railroad companies that were being restructured. The firm almost never took the lead, but it provided capital for distressed assets, and many of those generated considerable returns. Among its other ventures, it financed trolley companies in San Francisco that had gone bankrupt. The need for trolleys didn't go away just because the initial operators folded. Brown Brothers entered the second wave, and made money.

As an outgrowth of the foreign exchange business, John Crosby also propelled the firm more into travelers' letters of credit and the buying and selling of stocks and bonds on behalf of clients. The travel business remained substantial well into the 1920s, as did the commissions earned on buying and selling securities. To facilitate its brokerage business, Brown Brothers purchased a seat on the New York Stock Exchange. Years later, its experience as a securities broker for high-end clients would become the foundation of a new investment management business after the Great Depression.[14]

An undercurrent of the Brown franchise was careful attention to systems. Alexander had trained his sons to be meticulous in their assessment of potential clients, and ranking of risk had been only one manifestation. James was a rigorous and almost obsessive record keeper, and the junior partners in Liverpool had been trained to collate multiple streams of information in order to determine the correct exchange rate and then expand or contract their outstanding business accordingly. John Crosby built on that foundation, and one unexpected outgrowth was to charge fees to handle travelers' mail. Starting in the 1870s, the volume of tourism and business travel between England and the United States increased exponentially.

Americans had more money to travel, and the British began investing heavily in American railroads. Not only did these travelers need cash to spend but they needed somewhere to get their mail. There was no international postal service, but there was a need for one. With its offices in New York and London and thousands of people using its travelers' checks, the House of Brown was perfectly positioned to become a private post office. By the end of the century, according to John Crosby, the London branch alone was handling as much as twenty thousand letters a day, along with hundreds of cables and dozens of packages. Managing that service demanded a complicated cataloging system and a staff of dozens of clerks. The firm didn't earn much money on each letter, but its reliability and the sheer number of people who depended on what amounted to the Brown Brothers post office cemented its reputation more than any advertising ever could.

During John Crosby's long life and nearly forty years at the helm of the firm, he was at the heart of New York finance but not at the forefront of society. Like his father, James, John Crosby was content to be intimately known and respected by the close-knit circle of fellow bankers. And he *was* respected, and included. In 1889, J. P. Morgan convened a meeting at his Madison Avenue home to organize the banking community in support of the newly minted Interstate Commerce Act. He wanted to ensure that the group avoided railroad rate wars that could erase the already thin profit margins of the struggling lines. In later years, such a meeting would have been in violation of antitrust statutes, but at the time it was just business as usual. The cabal included John Crosby along with Jay Gould, who had picked up where he'd left off after the failed gold corner. Gould got the press, but John Crosby still got the invite.[15]

In addition to shunning the limelight, Brown Brothers also had a distinct aversion to getting too big. In 1896, Andrew Carnegie invited one of John Crosby's junior partners to lunch. Carnegie personified big, with his vast steel empire and fortune, as well as a forceful personality that drew the oxygen from any room. Crosby told the junior partner to be careful. "Carnegie & the concerns he represents are very rich & his business is very ably managed. At the same time they are large borrowers & somewhat difficult to deal with. When I know what he has in mind, I will see if BB & Co & BS & Co can serve him. We are good friends & I can usually get on well with him."[16] That was as close to braggadocio as Brown got.

Business frequently took John Crosby on travels for months at a time, and in the 1880s, he was in the habit of writing long letters to his daughter Amy and shorter notes to his son Thatcher, who was several years younger. The man who emerges from these letters is a patient, solicitous father, with a penchant for homilies much like his grandfather's. Inspecting the midwestern Rock Island rail system, a small rail line that the firm had arranged financing for, he wrote to Amy, "If Thatcher were here with me he would see miles and miles of freight cars and hundreds and hundreds of locomotives of all kinds of shapes, big and little, some numbered and some named, but all of them hard at work, puffing and dragging heavy trains. No room or place for idlers or lazy bodies. Last night I slept in a nice room on the car with a big bed and everything comfortable. I hope you are trying to be a good girl and to mind Momma. . . . I am getting very lonely without my little children and Momma and wonder when the time will come for me to return. Good night my darling." In later letters, he urged Amy to keep studying Scripture, and to learn one of the great lessons of life, "we grow by failures."

Nowhere is Brown's code more evident than in his long and detailed correspondence to his son Thatcher over the years. Born in 1876, Thatcher would eventually become one of the managing partners of the firm, and a key figure in the 1920s. Much like his father, he was groomed for the position beginning when he was a teen. John Crosby's letters to him are a veritable compendium of diligent, dry, and genial advice, a trove that combined the sensibility of Ben Franklin's Poor Richard with that hectoring of Polonius. The only major parenting impasse was amusingly benign. Young Thatcher, owlish, gangly and studious looking, was at Yale in the early 1890s and facing temptation: he was considering taking up smoking. He asked his father for advice. John Crosby wrote a long letter in response. "Let me say first of all, it is your question, not mine, the decision with all its consequences is your own and not mine; except of what there is of moral element involved in the act of deciding, it is a question which does not involve any-thing morally wrong." He went on to weigh the pros and cons. "Now your position is simply this: that if you smoke in moderation, say one or two pipes a day, not as a luxury and occasionally . . . it will not do you any seri-ous harm & will give you a great deal of pleasure. Let us admit in this you are absolutely correct, but let us also face the facts. One or two pipes a day is not occasional smoking but regular smoking, moderate I admit, but reg-ular notwithstanding and must in time become a habit from which it will be hard to break off."

Moreover, he continued, it was his experience that stopping at will would be no easy task, nor would Thatcher find it easy to keep his habit to just a few a day. On that basis alone, he counseled waiting to smoke till at least after college. And what's more, there was the expense to think of. "It will of course make a decided hole in your income, for it will be necessary for you to reckon for not only the tobacco you smoke yourself but what you will need for your friends." John Crosby then reflected on the whole busi-ness of sending a son off to college, and the wisdom he hoped to impart to Thatcher. "It is true that I never had any desire to smoke and could not therefore sympathize fully with anyone who did. . . . Like a true manly fellow, you have told me, and you find my advice hard to follow. . . . I take no exception to that. You have done the right thing, and it is quite possible that I may be mistaken." But given that Thatcher had asked the question, perhaps that was itself an indication that he was not so sure of the right course. "You have come to one of the crises of your life my son. I cannot settle this question for you. . . . The good book says apropos of such ques-tions as these: Let every man be fully persuaded in his own mind. If you can, follow that clear persuasion, whether it be to smoke or not to smoke. If you cannot, better wait as you are till you have more eyes." A week later, Thatcher replied, "Thank you for your helpful letter. I have at last decided not to smoke until I am twenty-one."[17]

You know you are privileged if one of the crises of your life is whether or not to smoke. By the end of the nineteenth century, the Browns had become ensconced in a world of security and status and wealth that contrasted sharply with the rising anguish and anger of millions of Americans who were at the whim of large corporations, indifferent banks and forces of change they could not control that were taking place at disquieting speed. Another panic, in 1893, had been a tipping point for populist anger, whose culmination was the selection of William Jennings Bryan as both the Democratic Party and Populist Party nominee in 1896.

Giving voice to the grievances of his supporters, Bryan delivered a thundering convention acceptance speech. Only thirty-six years old at the time, Bryan was a son of the Midwest, a devoted Christian and a brilliant orator with a powerful sense that the changes sweeping over the country were not benign. Comparing the acolytes of silver and paper money to the zealous crusade led by Peter the Hermit in the thirteenth century that assembled the poor to march on Jerusalem, Bryan declared that the Democratic Party was the only one in favor of the working man, the farmer, the denizens not of the Atlantic Coast but of the heartland. In words that will seem eerily modern, he announced that, "the sympathies of the Democratic party are on the side of the struggling masses who have ever been the foundation of the Democratic party. There are two ideas of government. There are those who believe that if you will only legislate to make the well-to-do prosperous, their prosperity will leak through on those below. The Democratic idea, however, has been that if you legislate to make the masses prosperous, their prosperity will find its way up through every class which rests upon them." He concluded by donning the mantle of faith, positioning himself as a messiah who would lead his people away from the oppression of the Republicans: "You shall not press down upon the brow of labor this crown of thorns, you shall not crucify mankind upon a cross of gold." He lost the election, but the battle continued to rage.[18]

You wouldn't have known that, however, reading the correspondence between John Crosby and Thatcher. Nor is it evident in John Crosby's long and detailed history-cum-memoir of the first hundred years of Brown Brothers. In his written legacy, the world of Pullman strikes and labor unrest, of miners thrown out of work and riots in Chicago, of crime in New

York City and the surge of immigration is invisible. The cries of anger and outrage barely left an echo in the muffled rooms of the Knickerbocker Club.

The relationship between Thatcher and his father was unusually close. John Crosby not only dispensed advice but also shared his own experiences. In a letter that can be seen as a portent of the firm's later course, he counseled Thatcher in 1903, "I was brought up in my early business career under the prevailing influence and a practice to do everything one's self and not to trust anybody, and hence in my life I have concerned myself too much with detail." The trade-off was that he had been diligent about the business but not as good at cultivating relationships. He was, in short, a good business operator but not such a good schmoozer. He advised Thatcher to delegate the details to subordinates and focus on "planning, thinking and keeping up with men, broaden your circle of friends, friends of your own age. They will be the business men of the future and in days of active competition you will need all your friends." Even so, he reminded his son that he was just a man with an opinion and an experience. "Just because I advise a course do not follow until you have tested and tried it in your own experience. There are many ways of reaching a goal, some longer and some shorter. The important matter is to keep a high ideal and work towards it with God's help."[19]

As it turned out, friendship and connections were precisely what saved Brown Brothers in the dark days after October 1929, when the firm faced an extinction moment and was saved by its fortuitous merger with Harriman and Co. That would never have happened had it not been for the friendships cultivated by the next generation of the firm's leaders, whose college bonds and social connections turned into professional ties that propelled both firms forward.

The quiet profitability of Brown Brothers in these years was matched by the success of Brown Shipley, now transplanted to London and Founders Court. William's grandson Alexander Hargreaves Brown was a capable leader, but it was the energies of Mark Collet and then Montagu Collet Norman (who was Collet's grandson and would himself later helm the

Bank of England at the height of the Great Depression) that propelled the affiliated firm. Given that one strand of our story is how money—and the moneymen—in America became entwined with political power, it's worth noting that the English branch became intertwined with political power and policy before New York's Brown Brothers. The influence of both Collet and Montagu Norman on the banking policies of England, and the presence of both William Brown and Alexander Hargreaves in Parliament, made Brown Shipley a bridge between finance and government. The English house shaped British economic and national policy, sometimes for the better and sometimes not. Of course, Montagu Norman proved unequal to the task of confronting the onset of the global depression in the late 1920s, but he nonetheless presided over a vital part of the global financial system until nearly the end of World War II. Brown Shipley established the mold that Brown Brothers then emulated.

In the waning years of the nineteenth century, however, it didn't even occur to the partners in New York to consider public office, either appointed or elected. The Gilded Age is often portrayed as a time when money ran rampant, while state governments and Washington were largely supine. That isn't quite accurate. The Sherman Antitrust Act passed in 1890 was the first attempt by the federal government to curtail the power and concentration of capital in the trusts that had grown so huge in so short a time. But it is true that the titans of finance and industry in these years did not tend to seek public office, nor did it seem to them a necessary outlet for their goals and ambitions. They preferred, for the most part, to wield influence by supporting politicians rather than going into government, and before the expansion of federal agencies with the progressive reforms under Theodore Roosevelt and then Woodrow Wilson, there were far fewer appointed offices, especially at the highest levels.

The back-and-forth of businessmen going into government and then returning to the private sector accelerated during the New Deal and became a torrent during World War II and after. That revolving door would have seemed alien and odd to James and John Crosby Brown as well as to a whole host of business leaders in the late nineteenth century. For them, government was a messy, at times sordid, and at heart dull business, to be tolerated but not joined, to be influenced but not steered. And to be honest, government during the last decades of the nineteenth century seemed a mediocre place, with a succession of weak executives, their power curtailed after the Civil War. Brilliantly, albeit a tad unfairly, Thomas Wolfe, son of Asheville, in the 1930s described the presidency in these years as a march of forgotten men, "Their gravely vacant and bewhiskered faces mixed, melted, swam together in the sea depths of a past intangible, immeasurable, and unknowable. . . . And they were lost. For who was Garfield, martyred man, and who had seen him in the streets of life? Who could believe that his footfalls ever sounded on a lonely pavement? Who had heard the casual and familiar tones of Chester Arthur? Where was Harrison? Where was Hayes? Which had the whiskers, which the burnsides? Which was which?"

These occupants of the White House were more capable than later reputation would suggest, but at the time, they epitomized the sense that the engine of the country was not on the Potomac but in New York and the West opening up with thousands of miles of railroad track linking the continent and making possible a scale and pace of economic expansion unknown anywhere in the world before. As John Crosby devoted himself to the stability of his family firm and the morphing structure of finance that made him and his so rich, New York became the locus of a potent (and for some, toxic) merger of finance and rails, of money and industry. The trusts were one stunning example, and the rise of an unlikely railroad baron who built little but managed an empire was another. His fate, and his life, were detached from Brown Brothers, but would ultimately merge with it into one. It was, as marriages often are, an odd graft, of an attention getting and seeking man who was all sharp edges and intensity with a family and firm that cultivated the opposite. And as such marriages often are, that odd graft proved surprisingly durable.

CHAPTER 7

NOTHING IS IMPOSSIBLE

The year was 1899. On a desolate stretch of track in the middle of Wyoming, only recently made a state, the Hole-in-the-Wall Gang (named after a mountain pass) held up a Union Pacific train. The gang held up a lot of trains, stealing the safes containing payrolls, but the Union Pacific had recently acquired a new owner, and he was determined to get the better of the band of latter-day Robin Hoods that was capturing not only his money but public imagination.

That much is fact. It was vividly embellished in the 1969 Hollywood blockbuster *Butch Cassidy and the Sundance Kid*. Having halted the train, Butch and Sundance try to persuade the clerk to open the door of the payroll car instead of having it blown open by dynamite. The timid clerk, Woodcock, proves not so timid. "I work for Mr. E. H. Harriman of the Union Pacific Railroad, and he entrusted me—" Butch interrupts: "Will you shut up about that E. H. Harriman stuff and open the door?" Woodcock refuses. "Mr. E. H. Harriman himself, of the Union Pacific Railroad, gave me this job, and I got to do my best, don't you see?" "Your best don't include getting yourself killed," Butch tells him, but Woodcock stays firm, holding fast as the gang blows open the door and takes the money.[1]

The movie may be fictional, but E. H. Harriman was real. He was as abrasive and aggressive and public as the Browns were reserved and diplomatic and private. Understanding the legacy of Harriman is an essential part of the story not just of the firm but of the evolution of American capitalism. Just as Alexander Brown imprinted himself on Brown Brothers, Harriman was a man who could inspire a clerk, one of thousands of his employees, to hold fast in the face of armed outlaws not known for their mercy to strangers. Harriman was never one to give in or give up. He was as tenacious as he was ambitious. Having been robbed one too many times, he not only put armed Pinkerton detectives on his trains, but he also bought horses and created a posse car so that when his trains were attacked by gangs, the horses could be let out with their armed riders to pursue the attackers. The cost of those posses was often far greater than whatever was stolen, especially with insurance covering many of the losses. That wasn't the point; for Harriman, losing, and being defeated, was intolerable. That made him a complicated man.

Harriman was known as a railroad baron, but it's more accurate to say that he was a financier who ended up owning railroads that had already been built. Many other parts of the world saw railroad construction in the last decades of the nineteenth century, but the United States surpassed them all. Given the sheer size of the country, that is not surprising, but even so, total U.S. railroad miles surpassed *all* of Europe and Russia in these years. Between 1865 and the end of the century, the United States went from about thirty-five thousand miles of track to two hundred thousand miles of iron and steel crisscrossing the continent.

That work required men and materials, but above all it required capital. Some came from the U.S. government. The construction of the first transcontinental lines and the formation of the Union Pacific were essentially a government initiative, made possible by the massive land grants given to the railroad companies and then providing them with additional subsidies so they could lay thousands of miles of track through deserted lands and lands inhabited by Native American tribes who were violently removed. The Union Pacific ultimately received as much land as New Hampshire and New Jersey combined, which it sold or leased to homesteaders in order to finance construction.[2] Completed in 1869, the first transcontinental line (which wasn't really that at all, extending only from the Pacific to the Mississippi) was a financial disaster, but it did spur further the settlement of the West and intensified military action against Native Americans. Subsequent lines in the 1870s and 1880s were funded by a combination of debt (mostly bonds) and equity, all of which required ever more elaborate forms of financing and ever more paper and prospectuses.

The railroad boom was both a mechanical marvel and a financial one, and it led to the growth of the first industrial conglomerates, the development of thousands of miles of the West, and the emergence of the United States as the most productive economy in the world. Money for the iron roads came from Americans, from their pockets and tax dollars, from the financial engineering of a rapidly growing Wall Street and satellite banks throughout the country, and from British and Western European financial houses looking to hitch a ride to American growth. It also spawned an investment mania in the United States. As we've seen, there had been bubbles and schemes before, in land and in nascent industries, but the railroads were of a different order and consumed far more resources over far more years. Government grants and guarantees shielded some investors from steep losses, but the bulk of the early companies formed to lay those tens of thousands of miles and outfit the lines with rolling stock, engines and passenger cars went bankrupt. Bondholders were lucky to recoup cents on the dollar, and many equity investors lost everything. The ones who made the fortunes were those who sold rail companies the iron and steel or who started industries that served a middle class that, because of the railroads, could now obtain goods at less cost than ever. Even greater fortunes were made by those who arranged financing for the first wave in the 1860s and 1870s and then restructured the rail companies after that wave went bust. Of those who picked up the pieces of failing lines, none excelled more than Edward Henry Harriman.

The unique ability of American capitalism in the first half of the nineteenth century to generate capital that was then used to fuel economic expansion was put to the test after the Civil War. The amount needed for the first stages of the B&O Railroad (a few million) or the Collins ship lines, or for that matter, for Commodore Vanderbilt's steamships or then for J. D. Rockefeller's wells and refineries, was paltry compared with the billions of dollars needed for the railroads. The flexibility and fluidity of the American financial system was the necessary precondition. While Brown Brothers played only a minimal role in the actual financing of late nineteenth-century rail lines, they had helped create the mold of private firms that made the rapid railroad boom possible.

Given the risks, however, and the fact that the long-term promise of the railroads was not matched by their short-term economic viability, the type of men who gravitated toward the industry tended to be entrepreneurial at best and shady charlatans at worst. Jay Gould, of the 1869 gold corner infamy, sought control of several railroads, starting with the Erie Line, before acquiring the flimsy assets of the vast but shoddily built Union Pacific. Collis Huntington and Leland Stanford both became rich and famous for their part in building lines in California and on the West Coast—the Central Pacific and the Southern. Huntington in particular was ruthless and self-serving, leaving himself immensely wealthy and his rail lines barely functional. He was described by the muckraking Matthew Josephson as "passionate and vindictive, he pursued his ends with bluntness . . . and infinite guile."[3] Even those with less of an axe to grind recognized Huntington as a force of nature driven to make himself a man above others at almost any cost. Railroads were his path to wealth and power, but he would have become an aquarium magnate if that had offered a better path.

Behind these early titans were the financiers, several of whom rose in lockstep with the new lines. They earned fees from government bond issues and corporate ones. They made commissions from raising equity and then some more from warrants and more yet from restructuring. In a world without laws governing conflicts of interest and self-dealing, little precluded these same financial intermediaries from granting themselves blocks of shares heavily discounted that they then sold at full value, or from issuing themselves warrants that would then convert into ownership at favorable prices. Hence why famed (and in their time infamous) bankers such as J. Pierpont Morgan ended up not just financing construction and restructuring but eventually owning the companies. They encouraged others to stake their capital while conserving their own, hardly a Brown Brothers tenet but one that effectively marshaled enough speculation to get the lines built.

Given that all of those financial activities were vital, many of those fees were earned, but it was not long before the larger society began to resent the few who were pocketing millions while the laborers were paid a pittance and operating companies went bankrupt and wiped out middle-class investors. Year by year, the gaps widened between rich and poor, between the few who seemed to have their hands on the levers of capital and the many who eked out a precarious wage-labor existence, who worked those rail lines or in the company mining towns in West Virginia or steel towns in central Pennsylvania, or out West, where workers were paid mostly in kind, their meager wages credited toward beds and food and clothes, leaving them in de facto indentured servitude.

Those gaps bred resentment and animosity, which erupted into violent strikes and violent reprisals. The strike at Carnegie's Homestead Steel Works in 1892 led to a pitched battle between thousands of workers and armed Pinkertons culminating in an occupation by the state militia and martial law. The great Pullman railroad worker strike of 1894, suppressed by federal troops called out by President Grover Cleveland, saw 250,000 workers refuse to man the nation's passenger cars, paralyzing national transport. The sense of economic injustice and widespread insecurity propelled the rise of the passionate progressivism trumpeted by Bryan in his 1896 speech to the Democratic Convention. It also gave rise to unionization and to a mass socialist movement in the United States and the party of Eugene Debs, which eventually captured more than 5 percent of the national vote.

Into this fray came E. H. Harriman, seemingly out of nowhere in the late 1890s, when he acquired the remnants of the Union Pacific, a vast network of crumbling lines with even worse finances. Edward—Ned professionally and Henry to his family—was born in 1848 in New York City, son of an Episcopal pastor. Harriman was a slight, slender child who grew into a slight, slender man. For two years as a teen, he attended the venerable

Trinity School in Manhattan, until he announced to his father that he preferred the school of life and dropped out to make his way in finance. "I am going to work," he informed his distraught father, and so he did, becoming, at the age of fourteen and in the midst of the Civil War, an office boy in a brokerage firm.[4] For the next twenty years he learned that trade.

In the 1880s, as the overall economy was recovering from the dark depression in the wake of the Panic of 1873, Harriman quietly acquired control of the Illinois Central Railroad. There he perfected the tools that he would use so powerfully a decade later: refinance the company to lower the cost of debt and capital; invest heavily and aggressively in new rails, new equipment and more efficient routes; and then use the improved system to carry more freight and more passengers at less cost and with more profit.

Had he stopped with the Illinois, Harriman would have been wealthy and successful, but he would not have been famous. It took being at the right place at the right time to catapult Harriman to the apex of American industry. In 1895, the proud and problematic Union Pacific was again at an impasse, needing yet another round of financing. Its backers by this juncture were financial houses, not a true railroad operator among them. It had sold off many of its miles to keep the core operation alive, shrinking to barely half of the eight thousand miles it had at its peak, but it had been born of a political mandate and had never truly functioned as an independent enterprise.

Unable to meet yet another set of obligations and payments due, the board of the Union Pacific turned to the banking house of Kuhn, Loeb & Co. and to the German-born émigré Jacob Schiff to manage a restructuring. Schiff was the leading Jewish banker of his day, and it took skill and subtlety to navigate a world where that was not an asset. A plan was in place by early 1896, one that needed the agreement of Harriman because of the overlap between his Illinois line and the Union Pacific. But Schiff was finding it difficult to get all of the needed constituents to sign off. J. P. Morgan, who held a considerable stake in the Union Pacific but was sufficiently disenchanted that he had allowed Schiff to take the lead, learned that obstacles were being created by Harriman, whom he barely knew but whose involvement he saw as a colossal nuisance. Morgan gruffly informed Schiff, "It's that little fellow Harriman . . . you want to watch him carefully."[5]

The punctilious Schiff scheduled a meeting with Harriman, who got right to the point and said that he was indeed trying to prevent Schiff's reorganization plan. Asked why, Harriman answered bluntly, "Because I intend to reorganize the Union Pacific." Schiff was not amused, given that the Kuhn, Loeb consortium, with Morgan in the background, controlled the shares. Harriman replied that he would be able to use the strong credit of the Illinois Central to get better terms for funding, which the Union Pacific board would have no choice but to accept. Schiff asked what his price was to lay off. "There is no price," replied Harriman. "I am determined to get possession of the road."[6]

Harriman was not specifically motivated by money, and he seemed acutely aware that every cent needed to be earned. "Money comes hard," he told his children Averell and Roland. "It should go wisely."[7] But he was driven to imprint his story on the country and its history. The reorganization of the Union Pacific in 1895–96 gave him an opportunity. His iron, arrogant determination combined with his pragmatic approach to both financing and reviving the line convinced a reluctant Schiff that a Union Pacific with Harriman at the helm was the most viable option. Harriman demanded to be made chairman; Schiff refused, saying that position was already filled but telling Harriman that if he joined the board and succeeded in refinancing the line and presenting a plan for how to revive the company, he would likely become chairman in due course. And that is what happened.

In later years, as Harriman rose in prominence and attracted critics, it was common for adversaries to dismiss him as purely a moneyman who found himself in the right place with enough backing to buy undervalued assets that would have gone up in value no matter what. "Harriman didn't create the Great West," said one critic who wanted to see Harriman's businesses more regulated by the federal government. That is certainly true, but Harriman did more than just buy low. He bought low and then invested in lines that prior owners had neglected. He attended to every detail, from the curve and composition of the tracks to the weight of the freight cars to hiring diligent clerks in the mold of the fictional, pathetically loyal Woodcock.

Harriman had revived the Illinois line, but the Union Pacific was larger and more decrepit. George Kennan, who was commissioned by Harriman's widow to write his biography, countered the accusation that Harriman was "only" a moneyman with the observation that while God may have created the Great West, "He didn't make it accessible. . . . Most of Mr. Harriman's great fortune was made out of the increase in the value of the properties he managed," and that increase was a direct result of the money he was willing to invest, and risk, in building and expanding the physical plant, not just reorganizing the financial one.[8]

When Harriman inserted himself into the Union Pacific management with Schiff's blessing, the business was worth $100 million. Harriman proposed spending $25 million to upgrade the track and the railroad stock. The goal was to make the line more efficient, safer, faster and able to carry more freight tonnage as well as more passengers in greater comfort. More tonnage, however, necessitated heavy cars that could handle the increased loads, which in turn required sturdier track and fewer twists and turns. That meant the routes had to be altered, which was as costly as building an entirely new line. Spending that kind of money to upgrade an existing road was unheard of. Given the valuation of the whole line, Harriman's plan was seen by many as an absurd gamble. Yet Harriman had a vision and the ability and self-assurance to articulate it. He convinced the board, and then he persuaded a consortium of bankers to lend at favorable rates. He was every bit the impresario as Edward Collins but far more adept at managing the business. In only two years, across thousands of miles, he remade the Union Pacific. The result in terms of more freight and more passengers was almost immediate: not only was the company able to service its millions in debt but it was able to start paying down the principle with startling ease. That, in turn, gave Harriman ammunition for the next phase of his plan to dominate.

If Harriman ever shared the doubts of his detractors, he gave no sign, and his friends and family recorded none. He conveyed a preternatural confidence in his ability to execute on his vision. "Nothing is impossible," he told one of the foremen on the Utah branch of the line who objected to what he thought was an impossible new route. That was the governing philosophy of his life and business. Harriman's formula, as an early railroad historian observed, was simple: "borrow huge sums of money and build up his property physically . . . to buy for his line, even at enormous cost, high efficiency."[9] For decades, the rail business had relied on initial investments backed by federal and state governments that were then refinanced at lower values and managed by businessmen and bankers who had no feel for the rails and played the losing game of cost cutting to preserve capital. Harriman came along and flipped the script. He understood that to earn you needed to spend, which seems like the most obvious thing in the world, except it wasn't.

By 1910, more than a decade after Harriman had wrested control, he had spent $160 million revitalizing the Union Pacific and adding new spurs to it. It hauled twice the tonnage and far more passengers. There is, of course, a chicken-and-egg question, whether its success was due to the economic boom experienced by the West in the first decade of the twentieth century or whether that economic boom was sparked by the railroads (of which the Union Pacific was just one, albeit a vital one). Without question, Harriman benefited from timing, but it was also timing that he had anticipated, having charted economic ebbs and flows as an investor and then operator for decades before taking the helm of the Union Pacific. In an age without national economic statistics, without forecasting based on anything more than guesstimates, part of what set Harriman apart was his acute ability to analyze the available data and extrapolate changes in the economic wind. In that, he was similar to the Browns, who had long since perfected their internal systems to absorb and process information.

Unlike them, however, he craved an empire. He took what he achieved with the Union Pacific and set in motion a plan to craft a national rail network under his control. His ambitions were so immense that he triggered one of the first federal antitrust actions, ruptured his relationship with Theodore Roosevelt and became a target for the entire progressive movement.

The subsequent assault on Harriman and the railroad trust he assembled was understood at the time as a signal moment when the populist backlash against large corporations and concentrations of wealth was finally embraced by the federal government. But the story, like all important stories, is not quite so simple. Before they became adversaries, Harriman and Roosevelt had much in common and considered themselves friends. They were both rooted in New York City. They worshipped at the altar of American exceptionalism, and they shared a passion for preserving the wilderness. Of course, without the American drive to conquer and settle the continent, that wilderness might have stayed perfectly intact. Both Harriman and Roosevelt believed that it was the destiny of the United States to bestride the continent, and those ambitions unleashed the flurry of human activity that then imperiled the wilderness. The irony was lost on them. Harriman had grown up in the city, but with his wealth, he acquired a large estate north of New York on the Hudson, at Arden. He plunged into the role of the country squire. Just as he had studied every mile of track on his railroads, he wanted to learn all he could about his land. He had relished his weeks camped out in the West along his railroads, and he delighted in the natural world. To that end, in the midst of his greatest business venture, he set off in the summer of 1899 with a large retinue to explore the Alaskan wilderness.

The simultaneous exploitation, conquest, settlement and preservation of the American West neatly encapsulates the contradiction of America and American capitalism, at once rapacious and empathetic, ruthless and nurturing. The evolving ethos of the WASP elite treated money as a precious fuel to be consumed, not just for personal gain but for the greater good as well. That ethos was then woven into the conservation movement, a movement championed by Teddy Roosevelt as president and supported ardently by Harriman. Harriman's 1899 Alaska expedition was not just an expensive foray by a financial and industrial titan; it was a deliberate exercise in exploration and scientific observation. Sparing no expense, Harriman hired two dozen scientists and naturalists, including the already famous John Muir. He outfitted a special train to take the coterie to the Northwest, and then transformed an exploration ship named the *George W. Elder* into a "floating university" to take the group up to Juneau and toward Sitka and then Homer. Others might have made the expedition a show of wealth. Harriman wanted it to add to collective knowledge.

In bringing such a large retinue of scientists, Harriman was emulating another man of grand ambitions, Napoleon Bonaparte, who in 1798 set off for Egypt before he had become the Napoleon of history, to conquer what was then a backwater of the Mediterranean. Napoleon assembled not just an army but also two hundred scientists, artists and engineers whose study of Egypt marked a new age of inquiry. Harriman intended, like Napoleon a century earlier, to make a comprehensive study of a vast land that was still largely unknown and unexplored by westerners. He approached Dr. C. Hart Merriam, the distinguished chief of the U.S. Biological Survey in the Department of Agriculture, told him that all expenses would be paid, and asked for help assembling a team that would come to include the celebrated Muir and the equally famous John Burroughs as naturalist and historian. The expedition produced one of the most comprehensive studies of Alaska ever undertaken.

Harriman's immersion in the physical aspects of building a railroad empire set him apart from many of the New York financiers who acquired railroads. J. P. Morgan did not ride the rails to study the topography, nor did Jacob Schiff explore the West. Even so, the timing of Harriman's Alaska expedition was extraordinary. At the peak of his business powers, in the midst of a crucial time for the Union Pacific, he took a three-month break at considerable expense to head to Alaska. As one of his biographers observed, "It was as if Caesar, approaching the Rubicon, stepped back and sailed instead to Egypt for a lengthy junket with a party of friends." But the motivation may have been more prosaic. Harriman even then was struggling with health, often laid up by one illness or another, and he likely needed some respite. His son Roland later explained that Harriman had been told by his doctor to take an extended rest from work. "His idea of a rest was to charter a steamship out of Seattle and take a group of distinguished scientists on a three-month jaunt along the Alaska shore." Traveling seven thousand miles into the wilderness is not usually what people think of when they want a break.[10]

The Scottish-born sixty-one-year-old John Muir was far better known than Harriman, who was a wealthy but as yet mostly unheralded New York railroad baron. While it was always nice to be invited to be part of a paid junket, Muir signed on mostly out of respect for Dr. Merriam, whose name has not survived but who was renowned in his day. Muir had already traveled far and wide. He was in part responsible for the creation of Yosemite National Park in 1890, had founded the Sierra Club and was its president, and had already made six trips to Alaska. Widely lauded as the "prophet of the wilderness," Muir was not easily impressed, and it's likely he was skeptical of Harriman's motives, wondering if the scientific advantages would be outweighed by a rich man's ego. Those concerns were allayed once he joined the group in Seattle. Muir wrote, "I soon saw that Mr. Harriman was uncommon. . . . He was taking the trip for rest, and at the same time managing his exploring guests as if we were a grateful soothing essential part of his rest-cure, though scientific explorers are not easily managed and in large mixed lots are rather inflammable and explosive." As with his businesses, Harriman's preferred method of managing was to tell the group to prioritize for itself what the agenda should be and then to form committees, draw up recommendations, and submit those to him for approval, which, given the competence of the group, he generally agreed to.

Over the next weeks, Muir provided a foil to Harriman, the austere Scot raising an eyebrow to a man who believed that even the wilderness must bend to man's will. Harriman wanted to explore, but he also wanted to hunt and bring back trophies. He coveted a bear trophy from the island of Kodiak, legendary for the size of its brown bears. When the Harriman expedition arrived at Kodiak on July 4, Ned succeeded in bagging two, and his joy at the conquest was offset only by the disdain of Muir, who thought that trophy hunting was cruel and unnecessary. He didn't try to change Harriman's view, but he did persuade Harriman's children, eight-year-old Averell and four-year-old Roland, never to do the same—or at least to promise that they would not.[11]

The expedition was not without its moments of drama and occasional danger, from the *Elder's* nearly foundering on a low shelf in the Bering Sea to floating ice surrounding landing boats, but for the most part, the weather was kind and the ship was able to manage the itinerary as planned. While Muir and Harriman did not exactly become fast friends, they did grow to respect each other, to the point where Muir was able to poke fun at Harriman's robber baron ascendency. Most evenings, there were spirited discussions not just about the natural wonders they'd encountered but about the state of the world. One night there were presentations debating a theory then much in vogue, "the blessed ministry of wealth," which grew out of Andrew Carnegie's controversial article "The Gospel of Wealth," published in 1889. Carnegie articulated a vision of a society where the rich viewed their wealth as a public trust that should be used philanthropically for the good of all. "I believe the day is coming when a man who leaves more than a million at his death, except for public uses, will be regarded as not having properly administered that for which he had only the trust," Carnegie explained. Extolling the new class of the uber-wealthy, whose success was the product of a "talent for organization and management" that only a few possessed, Carnegie did not condemn the wealthy for their wealth (which would, of course, mean condemning himself). He lauded the new rich for providing vital goods and services for the commons: railroads, oil wells, merchandise, steam power, electricity, financing. He did, however, articulate a social contract that those with exorbitant privilege were morally bound to give back, and to give back with purposeful intent during their lifetimes rather than leaving fortunes to their heirs.[12]

The Browns, whose humility and a strong Protestant ethic of service made them natural philanthropists, lived much of what Carnegie preached, except for the demand that the bulk of the money be given away in a lifetime rather than passed on to next generations. Harriman was more conspicuous in his consumption, with his sprawling and lavish estate, yachts and many of the outward trappings of wealth. Yet when he was twenty-eight, before he had considerable means, he had founded the Boys' Club of New York. In 1876, he heard about an unfortunate boy who was part of a small gang that spent days on the streets with nothing to do. The boy had thrown a rock through the window of the Wilson Mission School for Girls on Avenue A and had then been roughed up and hauled off by the police. Something about the story affected Harriman deeply. "I can't blame the boy any more than I blame the rock. The boy was there; the rock was there. But for the want of excitement and something to do, he wouldn't have thrown it."[13] And so he created the Boys' Club, which at first was little more than a gymnasium where poor boys could let off some steam. That was all Harriman could afford. Later, when he had more means, he purchased an entire building for the Boys' Club on the Lower East Side of Manhattan and contributed ever more money as the club expanded and as Harriman grew richer. At the time of the Alaska expedition, Harriman was still climbing the ladder of power and wealth, unlike Carnegie a decade earlier, who had achieved the heights and had started to reflect on what it all meant. Harriman was rich, but newly so. His focus in 1899 was on accumulating more, but he was not as unidimensional as many of his small cohort. The same mind that was always racing ahead of others was also able to take a step back and assess the meaning of what he was doing.

That evening in Alaska, as Carnegie's philosophy was debated, some stood up to give speeches celebrating the wealth that made the trip possible and to laud Harriman's generosity (though whether Carnegie would have recognized funding an expedition, no matter how many scientists there were, as philanthropy is an open question). Muir was bemused, and interrupted one of the "wealth laudations," saying, "I don't think Mr. Harriman is very rich. He has not as much money as I have. I have all I want and Mr. Harriman has not." Harriman later came up to Muir and said, "I never cared for money except as power for work. I was always lucky and my friends and neighbors, observing my luck, brought their money to me to invest, and in this way I have come to handle large sums. What I most enjoy is the power of creation, getting into partnership with Nature in doing, helping to feed man and beast, and making everybody and everything a little better and happier."[14]

By the end of the trip, Muir had come to a grudging respect for Harriman, even as he also saw him as a direct threat to the wilderness he so cherished. Harriman certainly became rich, but his attitude toward money was much as he said: it was power to be used for something more than personal enrichment. The story of the Browns in the nineteenth century was how this abstract thing called money came to be channeled into the building of America; Harriman was the perfect iteration of that. He took his experience in finance and turned it into fuel that fed the next wave of the railroad boom. He translated his skill at financial engineering into physical engineering. Harriman didn't build the first railroads, but he defined the next generation and made possible the explosion of transcontinental transport in a way that the first wave of builders after the Civil War could only have dreamed of.

Having tasted what he could do with the Union Pacific, Harriman returned from Alaska and bought up a controlling interest in the Southern Pacific, which ran down the West Coast to San Francisco. The opportunity arose with the long-awaited death of Collis Huntington; Harriman pounced when news of Huntington's passing hit the wires. Then he turned his sights to the competitors of the Union Pacific and their thousands of miles of rails that provided alternate routes to the West: the Northern Pacific and the Chicago, Burlington & Quincy Railroad. The latter had recently been acquired by Morgan in alliance with James J. Hill, the tycoon who had almost single-handedly created the Great Northern, running from Duluth to Puget Sound along the northern border of the United States with Canada. Hill was a railroad man through and through and not a creature of the financial world. He had set down roots in Minneapolis and St. Paul and was as passionate and ambitious as they came. He also recognized the contingency of life, once advising a young man to read everything, study math and engineering, get out in the world and be prepared because "some opportunity will come to every man in his lifetime," and only a few are ready to make the most of that when it does.[15]

If Hill was the consummate railroad man, J. P. Morgan was the consummate moneyman, and together they made a formidable team. Hill didn't need lessons from Morgan about keeping operating costs low,

dividends high, and the cost of credit manageable, but like all railroad magnates, he had an endless thirst for more capital. Morgan knew better than
to dictate to a maven such as Hill. Given how well the Minnesota man
managed his empire, Morgan never had to school him or scold him. They
shared a mutual adversary in Harriman. Morgan had already felt the ripples
of Harriman's ambition when Edward wrested control of the Union Pacific
and gained the support of a not easily impressed Schiff. That didn't make
Morgan a fan; there was only so much room for so many egos. When Harriman made a move to gain control of the Northern Pacific as well as the
Great Northern, Morgan was prepared to fight, which was just as well because Hill was going to fight no matter what.[16]

In May 1901, Harriman launched a raid on the shares of the Northern Pacific with the backing of Schiff. That was immediately countered
by Hill, Morgan and a large syndicate determined to keep the line out of
Harriman's hands. Some of the fight was personal; Morgan just didn't like
Harriman. But more of it was strategic. If Harriman gained control of the
Northern Pacific, he would largely control the transcontinental network in
the middle of the country. That would give him the leverage to squeeze Hill
and Morgan, whose Great Northern route was brilliantly managed but ran
through less habited territory such as Montana and Northern Idaho and
could never command the same level of freight or passengers as the routes
to the south.

What played out in May was pure Wall Street drama. Both Harriman
and Morgan rushed to buy as many shares as possible of the Northern Pacific. Within forty-eight hours, the two syndicates held more than six hundred thousand of the eight hundred thousand outstanding shares, with
neither able to command enough of a majority to take full control. Meanwhile, traders and speculators tried to get in on the action. Many sold shares
short in anticipation that the sharp climb in value caused by the aggressive
buying of Harriman and Morgan would end soon and the shares would
then plunge as the losing side divested. In that scenario, the short sellers
would make a killing. But as is often the case when Wall Street gets into a
tizzy, far too many miscalculated when and by how much those shares

would decline. Speculators were left with massive calls on capital they didn't have. The result was a market panic, which Harriman and Schiff, Hill and Morgan recognized and which they then took aggressive measures to halt before it engulfed both of them and their franchises.

Market losses were still steep, and both sides were blamed. Public sentiment had soured both on railroads and on Wall Street in the 1890s, with increasing animosity at the few who were profiting outlandishly. The defeat of William Jennings Bryan in 1896 by the business-friendly Republican William McKinley energized rather than deflated Bryan's supporters. Large swaths of the country were embracing what would soon become known as progressivism, with multiple state legislatures enacting laws to make companies and capital more accountable to labor. The Wall Street battle in May 1901 over who would control a railroad sparked a backlash. The contest was depicted as the height of robber baron arrogance, as titans battled with no regard for the collateral damage or the millions of workers who stood to be harmed if the market crashed and companies went bankrupt.

In response to the near market meltdown, *The New York Times* editorialized, "If the gentlemen composing the groups known respectively by the names of Mr. Harriman and Mr. Hill delude themselves with the belief that fighting for the control of a railroad is their own private business and none of the public's . . . it will be prudent for them to get rid of that delusion without delay. . . . If panics and disasters such as that which have just convulsed Wall Street and projected a shadow of doubt and demoralization over a financial and business condition of great prosperity . . . are to be viewed as necessary incidents of capitalist consolidation, then strong popular disfavor . . . may presently rise to a pitch of anger that will cause them to take thought, not how they may control railroads, but how they may save themselves."[17] These sentiments were echoed in publications throughout the country. They proved prescient.

The contestants for control of the Northern Pacific were far too absorbed in their battle to notice that theirs was but a foray in a larger war that they were about to lose. If they paid any heed to sentiments such as those voiced by *The New York Times*, they gave no sign. Instead, they went on the offensive against each other, with Harriman and Schiff accusing Hill of being an "autocrat" and "a bad neighbor" to the Union Pacific, and Hill firing back through interviews that his adversaries were craven speculators.[18] The battle was proving costly, however, with no end in sight. These men had access to considerable capital, but not endless capital. At the urging of cooler heads, the parties agreed to cease their public relations campaigns against each other. And then, rather suddenly, they had a breakthrough. With no love lost between them, they concluded that their mutual interests could be better served in a loose alliance rather than endless fighting. Morgan apparently wanted nothing more than to get on with his planned vacation in Europe. He didn't need the money or the aggravation, and he was still tired from the exertion of creating the U.S. Steel Trust a few months earlier. Harriman recognized that the fight would be protracted at best; Hill wanted to preserve his control of the Great Northern; and Schiff alternated between playing Iago and acting as a consoling diplomat.

After a month of financial duress and public opprobrium, on May 31, Harriman, Schiff, Hill and Morgan's representatives met at the rococo McKim, Mead & White Metropolitan Club on Fifth Avenue and Sixtieth Street, opened only a few years earlier with Morgan as its president and primary backer. The men agreed not just to a truce, but to create a new holding company called Northern Pacific Securities that would control the Great Northern, the Northern Pacific and the Chicago Burlington lines. The agreement was a handshake, soon formalized, that established a behemoth trust, a $400 million company, second in assets only to U.S. Steel. Harriman received $82 million in stock—the equivalent of $2.5 billion in today's dollars.

At the same time the agreement went into effect in September, President McKinley was at the Pan-American Exposition in Buffalo, New York. Out of the crowd, a young, angry anarchist named Leon Czolgosz pulled out a gun and shot him. McKinley took eight days to die, and when he did, Theodore Roosevelt, son of New York, onetime police commissioner of the city, governor of the state, and eager rough rider in the brief Spanish-American War, became the youngest person ever to occupy the Oval Office. Harriman's greatest triumph was thus juxtaposed not just with a national tragedy but with the ascendency of a man who had once been a friend and would soon be a scourge.[19]

Within six months of becoming president, TR broke with the center of the Republican Party, embraced the rising tide of progressivism domestically even while remaining an ardent American imperialist internationally, and in 1902 instructed his attorney general Philander Knox to take action against the newly formed Northern Securities trust and its immensely unpopular trio of Harriman, Hill and Morgan. Using the provisions of the Sherman Antitrust Act, the administration charged Northern Securities as an unlawful combination that was inhibiting competition, exercising monopolistic control and harming American workers and citizens. There is little question that had McKinley remained in office, there would have been no action taken. McKinley's main adviser, Mark Hanna, was himself a shareholder in the company and when asked by TR what he thought of the trust, he replied that the combination was an unalloyed good for the country.

Roosevelt disagreed, rather vehemently. He denounced Hill and Morgan as "representatives of privilege" who were trying "to profit from governmental impotence." Reflecting on the case a dozen years later, in an autobiography published as he was trying to wrest control of the Republican Party and position it once again at the center of social and economic reform, Roosevelt explained that in going after Northern Securities and Harriman, he was motivated by the injustice of economic concentration of power. "In no other country . . . was such power held by the men who had gained these fortunes. . . . Of the forms of tyranny the least attractive and the most vulgar is the tyranny of mere wealth, the tyranny of plutocracy." That was the language used by his administration in its presentation to the Supreme Court in late 1903. It argued that the Northern Securities trust was both anticompetitive and inimical to democracy. "To suggest competition is possible where competition is useless is an absurdity. And if this be not a restriction of trade, then no combination whereby competition is limited ever was."[20]

It took until the spring of 1904 for the Court to hand down its decision. It ordered the trust to be dissolved. The narrow 5–4 ruling, however, was somewhat undercut by the vociferous arguments of its opponents. The great jurist Oliver Wendell Holmes Jr. penned a memorable dissent that enshrined a phrase that has ever since been a touchstone for the courts: "Great cases, like hard cases, make bad law." His point was that as appealing as the decision was to a public inclined to view trusts as harmful, the antitrust laws on the books spoke only to restraint of trade and said nothing about competition per se. Holmes took pains to draw the distinction, and his argument resonated. Supporting Holmes, one critic of the Court's majority decision chimed in to argue that "competition, as a regulatory principle of the railways . . . has failed in every country of the world where it has been given a trial." Harriman and his cohort believed in natural monopolies, in the idea that a few large organizations well run and working in concert with one another would lead to a more efficient and less costly transportation network. Given the haphazard and incoherent rail lines of the 1840s and 1850s, with different track gauges, different schedules, and incompatible equipment, and then the chaos of the 1870s and 1880s with many of the same problems, they may have had a point. But the concentration of wealth and the power of those who controlled the consolidated rail lines was seen by millions of Americans not just as inherently antidemocratic but as directly damaging to society, and as an act of robbery by an indifferent mercenary elite who had enriched themselves at the expense of the rest.

Having instructed the Justice Department to move against Northern Securities, Teddy Roosevelt then found a ready adversary in Harriman, whose gruff demeanor was easily read as disdain for the common man. Even with the Court's decision, Harriman retained most of his railroad empire, but he spent his few remaining years on the defensive. He believed his work had strengthened the country and that the country was ungrateful. In 1904, as Roosevelt was preparing his presidential campaign, he asked Harriman for support, and things turned openly sour. Harriman wanted TR to support his chosen candidate for the New York Senate in return for campaign donations, which Roosevelt was unwilling to promise. In a series of letters between them, Roosevelt accused Harriman as being nothing more than "a crook," who wanted only to buy and sell members of the government, including the judiciary, for his own ends. "It shows a cynicism and deep-seated corruption. . . . It is because we have capitalists capable" of such venality, Roosevelt concluded, that the entire system needed broad reform.[21] Running against Alton Parker, who was an honorable New York judge but a weak Democratic candidate, Roosevelt won a resounding mandate in the 1904 election.

In his second term, however, TR limited most of his attacks on trusts and big capitalism to rhetoric. His one major victory, against Northern Securities, established him as a trustbuster, a reputation he used to good effect. But the only other major trust broken up thereafter was Standard Oil, and then not until 1911 under the administration of William Howard Taft. For TR, Harriman came to represent all that was flawed in the status quo, but Roosevelt was no revolutionary. He worked to pass new laws regulating big business, but he had no interest in destroying the system overall. Harriman was the sacrificial lamb.

As Roosevelt basked in public adulation, few tears were shed for Harriman. As *The New York Times* editorialized in 1906, "In the short time of Harriman's rise he has succeeded in making himself the most cordially disliked man, personally, in the whole financial community. . . . His brusqueness of manner, inversely proportional to his physical size, has gone along with an absolute intolerance of dissenting opinion." After the Northern Securities imbroglio, Harriman half-heartedly tried to find ways to gain control of lines he did not yet run, but he focused most of his energies improving the rails he already owned. Because of multiple ailments and illnesses, he also spent months recuperating at his compound up the Hudson in Arden. The day-to-day operations of the empire were increasingly handled by "Judge" Robert S. Lovett, a very able Texas lawyer who had worked tirelessly in the background as general counsel for the Union Pacific and then for Harriman's myriad dealings. In the last years of Harriman's life, Lovett also became the guardian of Harriman's image and a force in the lives of his two sons, who in turn formed a bond with Lovett's only son, also named Robert, who would ascend as high as any of them, in due time.

In part because of Harriman's illnesses in his final years, he spent considerable time with his children, who were devoted to him, as was his wife. Ed Harriman may have left a sour impression in public, but he was treasured by his family, and he treasured them, passing long and languid summer days with them in Arden and on trips to visit the boys at Groton for rowing and races, with chartered yachts at the ready, the proud father ever attentive. Training and mentoring the young boys who would become the young men who would lead the next generation had been one of Harriman's passions, from the founding of the Boys' Club to his own role as a paterfamilias. He was purposeful in what he taught his children, just as Alexander Brown had been. In much the same way that the royals of the Old World understood the necessity of training princes and princesses how to rule lest they attain power ill prepared, badly formed and prone to disastrous decisions, E. H. Harriman raised his sons with an acute sense not just of their wealth but of the imperative of doing something for the greater good.

Both Harriman's oldest son, Averell, and the younger Roland were to play key roles in the formation first of Harriman & Co. in the 1920s as an investment house that channeled the Harriman fortune into the deals of Wall Street, and then of the combined Brown Brothers Harriman, where Roland assumed a more prominent position while Averell focused increasingly on politics. They both inherited a view of money from their father that echoed Harriman's response to John Muir on the epic Alaska trip, namely that money was a tool for the betterment of society. In that, they also absorbed Carnegie's gospel of wealth, though not the specific injunction to give away their money during their lifetimes. In an interview with the editor of *Forbes* in 1920 when he was twenty-nine years old, Averell reflected on his father's legacy, "The young man who uses the dollar as a yardstick to measure the success, or non-success, of his activities, and who doesn't take very much broader—national—considerations into account is not the highest type of citizen, nor does he get the fullest satisfaction out of life. I am striving to do the thing which I believe is the best and most important thing I can do for the interest of America. I love work—I cannot see how anyone would prefer to be idle."[22]

The construction of the elite was not the product of one individual or one self-conscious group. There was no meeting of a task force, no secret society (though as we will see, they did create exclusive societies at Yale), and no deliberation about what should and should not be included in the list of attributes. Harriman was not much like the Browns in demeanor and temperament, yet his children—much like subsequent generations of Browns and an entire cohort that would move out of finance and into the halls of Washington and out in the larger world—internalized a way of thinking about themselves and the larger society that was remarkably similar: a quiet but strong faith, public affirmations of modesty, abjuring obvious greed, the gospel not just of wealth but of work, and a strong belief that with privilege and power came responsibility.

In that, E. H. Harriman was not so different from John Crosby Brown, whose letters to his children form a private primer on the values that mattered and the vices that were to be avoided, whether smoking at too young an age or not taking full responsibility for choices at any age. Though the two men never met, they were connected by their children and the business they forged, and they died within months of each other. John Crosby passed peacefully at the end of June 1909 at the age of seventy-one, surrounded by family at his summer home in West Orange, New Jersey, and comforted by a sterling reputation. Harriman, a decade younger, died from cancer in September. In death, his image softened, briefly. Eulogized by *The New York Times*, he was dubbed "a little man with an ambition bigger than the ambition of any American before him, who proposed to put himself in command of the transportation business of the entire American continent . . . and he was in a fair way to see it accomplished when his starved body said to the brain . . . I can go no further. This is the end."[23]

Until the early twentieth century, those in the world of money rarely wanted to enter the world of politics. It wouldn't have occurred to J. P. Morgan to run for office or take an appointed position. He had more power as the head of his banking house than he would have had as secretary of the treasury. That was amply demonstrated when he almost single-handedly organized the response to the Panic of 1907, making sure that there was enough liquidity and capital to prevent a complete financial meltdown. In an age after the Second Bank and before the Federal Reserve, he and Harriman and the Browns and Kuhn, Loeb and a cohort of others *were* the Federal Reserve. Politics was seen by them as a world of second-raters, and Washington was a chaotic place where too many other voices and interests competed for attention. Having created a system of money that made manifest the material expansion of the United States in the nineteenth century, this loose group then pivoted to politics in the twentieth, behind the scenes at first and then, with the Depression and the Second World War, more explicitly. And Brown Brothers Harriman was a training ground and a conduit.

One spur, of course, was the public's reaction against the wealth and privilege they had acquired. The proliferation of new laws and regulations designed to redress the power imbalances and tame unbridled capitalism was a wake-up call to that elite. In the face of a progressivism that was capturing statehouses, Congress and the White House, they realized that if they didn't step into the political fray, they could be deluged by the tide.

And, of course, just because this emerging class perceived itself as virtuous and on the side of the angels—doing right by themselves, their families and society—that did not mean that they were. Partnerships may have kept greed and risk in check, along with the resulting value system that demanded care and caution before expending capital, but they were not a check on human nature. Firms such as Brown Brothers abhorred speculators, but they did not abhor protecting their own interests even if those interests were not, in fact, in sync with the public good. As they grew richer and more powerful, they looked to the federal government for assistance.

That opened a new chapter in the early years of the twentieth century. Brown Brothers, which had stayed blissfully behind the scenes and out of the news, on purpose, which had not followed the Harriman path of making headlines as a business strategy, came to use the wealth it had built over the previous century to persuade the federal government to come to its aid in a foreign country where the laws of the United States did not apply. Brown Brothers, which had steered clear of the limelight, helped maneuver the U.S. government to invade and take control of a small Central American country for the sole purpose of making sure that Brown Brothers did not lose a few million dollars. It wasn't the first act of American imperialism, and it would certainly not be the last.

CHAPTER 8

THE REPUBLIC OF BROWN BROTHERS

In 1935, looking back over his long and complicated career as a soldier in the service of the United States, Smedley Butler, major general of the Marine Corps, many times decorated for valor in battles that spanned three decades and multiple continents, penned one of the great antiwar memoirs: *War Is a Racket*. In it, he excoriated American missions oversees, from the Philippines to Central America and beyond, as acts of greed and rapaciousness. A onetime believer turned penitent, Butler called out the chronic hypocrisy of the American elite and punctured the myth that they used force only sparingly to restore order and preserve prosperity.

In 1912, Butler, not yet disillusioned but well on his way, had been ordered by the War Department to lead several thousand Marines on an expedition to the civil-war-torn nation of Nicaragua. The mission lasted only a few months. It cost few American lives, but it put more than 2,000 Nicaraguans in an early grave. Butler's mission was to defeat a rebellion and shore up a government that viewed with favor not just American military assistance but financial intervention. Butler, who had earlier been part of a contingent of Marines dispatched to Nicaragua in 1910, carried out his mission with typical efficiency, but he was disgusted with the whole affair. In a harbinger of his later recantations, he wrote to his wife, "It is terrible that we should be losing so many men fighting these battles . . . all because Brown Bros. have some money down here."[1]

The story is more complicated, but at its core, Butler was correct. For much of the nineteenth century, finance and politics were distinct realms. There was little overlap between Washington and Wall Street. Economic interests may have dictated certain policies, ranging from the treaties with Native American tribes that were disregarded under pressure from miners and settlers to Northern acquiescence to Jim Crow laws in the American South. But only with the dawn of the twentieth century did the elites of politics and the elites of finance converge into one cohort. There was no dramatic moment when that shift happened, but there was no more dramatic illustration that it had than the invasion and occupation of Nicaragua under the aegis of President William Howard Taft and the influence of what had until then been a decidedly apolitical Brown Brothers.

As E. H. Harriman was building his empire, Brown Brothers was undergoing another generational shift, this time from John Crosby Brown to his son Thatcher Magoun Brown, who resolved his youthful dilemmas over study habits and smoking to his father's satisfaction and had been brought into the family business. He was made partner at the age of thirty. He had pressured his aging father for his own stake, writing to him in 1906, "It will be a great help and inspiration to me to have a share in the business, and I hope it will bring with it a new sense of responsibility and desire to work hard for the standing and success of our business in other ways than financial ones. You know Father how fond I am of the business and my pride in you as its head is very great." On learning that John Crosby had agreed, Thatcher expressed his gratitude, saying, "I shall always remember what you said about the business, what it has been in the past, and your hope that the same motive—higher than mere money getting—would animate those of us who will start to bear some of the responsibilities."[2]

The next generation of family partners was also anchored by Thatcher's first cousin, James Brown, grandson of the first James Brown. Ten years older than Thatcher, James maintained an even lower profile. Fluent in French, educated at Swiss boarding schools and then Columbia University,

James was a compact, elegant man, fond of tailored clothing that conveyed style without flash. Shorter by a considerable degree than the gangly Thatcher, he more than made up for what he lacked in stature with "ramrod posture and elegance" that commanded attention and respect. He was culturally cosmopolitan yet also parochial, believing that the natural order was a global hierarchy with Europe and the United States at the apex. Thatcher agreed. The two Brown cousins would be the primary family partners until the 1930s.[3]

The Brown creed of modesty, of abjuring gain for its own sake and believing that the work of money had a higher mission and purpose, was not confined to their offices at 59 Wall Street. It was the keystone of an emerging governing class. Had you been able to ask Thatcher, for instance, if these were "mere" words disguising, as General Butler would later claim, baser motives, he would have vehemently refuted the accusation. He was certain that his actions, and those of his firm and his business partners far and wide, were taken for the financial gain of the firm but even more for the good of society, for the expanding prosperity of the United States and for the onward march of that amorphous thing we call civilization.

Those values proved fully compatible with a Darwinian view of the world. The Browns of this era believed that there were those better fit to exercise power and those less so, those who could be more trusted with a contract, a loan or a mandate to govern and those who were simply not up to the task, either by temperament or background or training. Anyone could, over time, and any culture could, with the right influences, learn to govern themselves and manage their affairs, but not everyone was equally able and equally ready. As Brown Brothers ventured beyond the shores of the United States, they confronted an anarchic world unevenly developed, and they called on Washington to use diplomatic leverage and lethal force to protect their private business affairs.

The emergence of naked imperialism celebrating the strong over the weak during the height of the greatest period of social justice reform in the United States is nothing if not ironic. The Progressive Era domestically was marked by the ascendency of reformers who had been agitating since the

1880s for more guarantees for labor, more action by the federal government to ensure that corporations and controllers of capital did not capture all of the gains of the economic expansion, and more regulations at the state level to protect the mass of citizens who worked under challenging conditions. The myriad reforms ranged from minimum hours and restrictions on child labor to workplace safety and curtailing large trusts and monopolies. They included the recall of governors and senators seen as unresponsive to the needs of constituents and legislation to defend unions. Law after law was passed to protect the powerless, and that agenda was embraced by Theodore Roosevelt and by large swaths of both Republicans and Democrats.

At the same time, Roosevelt was unabashed in his enthusiasm for the muscular use of power abroad. He saw no contradiction in fighting for democracy and equality at home and seizing control of other countries abroad. Both progressive reforms and imperialism were supposed to advance civilization, and the onward march of civilization justified the use of force, whether by more government at home or by troops abroad. The Spanish-American War of 1898 was initiated by William McKinley, but its legacy was cemented by TR, who as president championed not just the acquisition of overseas territory but a vision of the United States as a country destined by its unique strengths and virtues to bestride the world. The American flag would, he stated, "bring civilization into the waste places of the earth."[4]

The nations of Europe, France and Great Britain in particular, had already colonized large swaths of the globe using similar justifications about bringing civilization to the uncivilized. Roosevelt and the United States were rather late to that party. Noble rhetoric notwithstanding, the rise of western imperialism was a contest between nations for global dominance, and the sense that much of the world had already been divvied up added urgency to Roosevelt's ambitions. With little room for American expansion in Africa or Asia, Roosevelt articulated a new variant on the Monroe Doctrine that a century earlier had warned Europe against interfering in the internal affairs of any country in the American sphere of influence.

Roosevelt's Corollary to the Monroe Doctrine set a new course for American foreign policy in the Caribbean, in Central America and in South

America. In his December 1904 message to Congress, Roosevelt declared that revolution, disorder and chaos in any country in the Western Hemisphere posed a potential threat to the stability of the entire region. Americans were not, he said, motivated by the desire for more land. The only thing the United States wanted "was that the other republics . . . shall be happy and prosperous; and they cannot be happy and prosperous unless they maintain order within their boundaries and beyond with a just regard for their obligation towards outsiders." To that end and to ensure that order was maintained and creditors were paid, the United States would henceforth reserve the right to intervene and "exercise international police power" in the case of revolution or turmoil.

What followed were decades of U.S. involvement and intervention, justified by Roosevelt's corollary. The idea that a more advanced, more powerful nation had the right and even an obligation to intervene in the internal affairs of societies less developed or simply less potent was a familiar one in Europe in the late nineteenth century. Critics of imperialism have long excoriated those views as a convenient—and flimsy—fig leaf masking rank ambition and greed. It sounds better to say you are occupying another country and taking over its affairs because of a civilizing mission than to claim, baldly, that you can and therefore are. It is easier to rationalize your actions as selfless than to assert, as Thucydides said the Athenians did in their brutal occupation of the island of Melos, that the strong do what they want and the weak suffer what they will.

Other than a coterie of ardent anti-imperialists, Americans in the early twentieth century believed in the use of military might abroad provided it could be morally justified. The nineteenth-century conquest of the American West and the subjugation of the Native Americans was unabashedly self-interested, but by the turn of the twentieth century, American elites were less comfortable with sanctioning the use of force solely to gain wealth and territory. Generations of Browns had stressed that their business was about more than the pursuit of profit. Their class, of which they were founding members, saw the extension of American power first in the Western Hemisphere and later, after World War II, globally, as having a higher purpose.

They weren't bringing Christianity, although there were a fair number of American missionaries who fanned out through Africa and Asia. They were bringing order where there was chaos; they were bringing civilization to societies that lacked it.

Nowhere was that more purely expressed than in the policies of Roosevelt's successor and onetime protégé, William Howard Taft. Born to a sterling pedigree, his father secretary of war to President Grant, Taft went to Yale, which subsequent generations of Brown Brothers Harriman partners would make their own club, and was initiated into the selective society of Skull and Bones. He went on to serve as governor-general of the U.S.-occupied Philippines. Brutal and complicated though that occupation was, it did not sour Taft on the idea of imperialism. He was then asked by Roosevelt to become secretary of war, thirty years after his father had filled the same office. Taft and Roosevelt forged a close bond. Roosevelt, with his immense standing in the Republican Party, chose Taft as his successor, and in 1908, he defeated William Jennings Bryan, for whom the third time running as the Democratic Party standard-bearer was not a charm. But the relationship between TR and Taft deteriorated once the protégé was now president, and Roosevelt came to see his handpicked successor as a weak executive who was betraying the agenda of domestic reform. That led to a split within the Republican Party and to TR's presidential campaign as the head of the Progressive Party in 1912 that denied Taft a second term but led to the election of the Democrat Woodrow Wilson. Taft would then ultimately fulfill his life's ambition when Warren Harding appointed him chief justice of the Supreme Court in 1921.

A conservative who soft-pedaled progressive reforms domestically, Taft largely continued the policies of Roosevelt internationally. He formulated a policy known as dollar diplomacy, which remained the governing philosophy of American foreign policy long after Taft left office. Dollar diplomacy encapsulated the civilizing mission of the United States. Having built a formidable economic system in the nineteenth century, the United States held that it now had an obligation to help other nations organize their affairs financially. Without sound financial management, no society could progress and prosper. And who better suited to provide the needed tutelage than American financiers and bankers, who had through painful trial and error figured out a Goldilocks formula for economic success: enough paper money but not too much to allow unchecked speculation, enough risk for gain but not enough to imperil the system. As they went out in the world, Americans carried the self-assurance that they had a model that should be widely adopted. The core idea of dollar diplomacy, articulated by Taft in his annual message to Congress in 1912, was "to substitute dollars for bullets. It is one that appeals alike to idealistic humanitarian sentiments, to the dictates of sound policy and strategy, and to legitimate commercial aims. It is an effort frankly directed to the increase of American trade upon the axiomatic principle that the Government of the United States shall extend all proper support to every legitimate and beneficial American enterprise abroad."[5]

Inflection points sometimes come with fireworks, but often they are notable only in retrospect, appearing rather banal and unremarkable at the time. Taft's dollar diplomacy speech came after more than a decade of practicing such policies. Few snapped to attention as if he had announced a radical departure from prior practice; he had not. But he did make explicit what had been implicit. American foreign policy in the Caribbean and Central America had for some years been characterized by the U.S. government as supporting, encouraging and ultimately protecting the financial interest of American businesses and bankers. The official justification was that these policies were in everyone's interest. As Taft explained in his address, "The United States has been glad to encourage and support U.S. bankers who were willing to lend a helping hand to the financial rehabilitation of . . . countries because this financial rehabilitation and the protection of their customhouses from being the prey of would-be dictators would remove at one stroke the menace of foreign creditors and the menace of revolutionary disorder."

In his development of dollar diplomacy, Taft was ably assisted by his secretary of state Philander Knox, the onetime corporate lawyer who had served as TR's attorney general in pursuing the breakup of Harriman and

Morgan's Northern Securities trust. The Progressive Era was marked by social justice movements juxtaposed to imperialism, and Knox was both a defender of democracy against the concentrated economic power of the trusts and a defender of concentrated economic power when exercised abroad. As he saw it, beyond America's shores, "true stability is best established not by the military but by economic and social forces. . . . The problem of good government is inextricably interwoven with that of economic prosperity and sound finance; financial stability contributes perhaps more than any one factor to political stability."[6]

That was certainly consistent with how men like Knox viewed financial stability at home. After the flurry of antitrust rhetoric in his first term, the Roosevelt administration had reached a modus vivendi with the large corporations that dominated American life, but in his second term, he again ratcheted up the rhetoric against these bastions of privilege. In 1907, he launched a blistering attack on "the malefactors of great wealth" who in their pure pursuit of greed were endangering the prosperity of all. William Jennings Bryan had twice failed to win the presidency, but these sentiments were very much his, just as they echoed the decades-long populist attack on the money lords. But those were attacks from outsiders against what seemed a relatively impregnable system. Coming from a popular sitting president, Roosevelt's words caused major ripples, which culminated in yet another financial panic, in October 1907.

The Panic of 1907 was confined to a small coterie of banks and financial institutions, but for several weeks, it seemed almost certain that the contagion would infect the entire economy. What prevented it from metastasizing were the herculean efforts of J. P Morgan, who in the absence of a potent central bank, took it upon himself to make sure that the financial system didn't collapse. For several weeks, Morgan was the most important man in America, calling on multiple others—including Harriman—to pool their resources and act as the lender of last resort. Under Morgan's direction, they collectively acted as the backstop in a way that would soon become the purview of the Federal Reserve System, which was created in 1913 in large measure to prevent something like what occurred in 1907 from happening again. Without the assiduous efforts of Morgan in those weeks, acting as a self-appointed guardian of a system that, yes, had enriched him but which was in dire need of governance, it is likely that the Panic of 1907 would have been as destructive as any of the prior waves that had deluged Wall Street and the whole country throughout the nineteenth century.[7]

The schizophrenic relationship between America and its financiers—lionized one moment, villainized the next—was hardly new. As we have seen, from the founding of the republic, attitudes oscillated between grudging respect for what the captains of finance could do and utter contempt for what they often did. Admiration for men of money and paper, and what they were able to unlock, gave way to disgust after 1819, 1837, 1857, 1873 and 1893. The back-and-forth of the Progressive Era generated intense whiplash. Morgan was lauded for averting collapse in 1907, and he and his were then condemned a year later with a prescient warning: "The time is coming," one publication editorialized, "when the bank will take the place of the railroad at the center of popular interest and agitation."[8] In 1911, the House of Representatives, which had flipped to Democratic control, launched an investigation into the "money trust" that was alleged to be pulling the levers of the American financial system. The dapper congressman Arsène Pujo of Louisiana was tasked with heading the committee in charge of the hearings. At the end of 1912, Pujo called on J. P. Morgan as his star villain. Ailing and angry, the seventy-five-year-old Morgan made for a reluctant witness. He knew he was being led to the slaughter, and while there was nothing much he could do, he was determined not to show weakness. He answered the hours of questions in as few words as possible, often in monosyllables. He was depicted in the court of public opinion as the malevolent prime mover of the "money trust" that was using its influence to shape government policy to protect its own privilege. Within four months, Morgan was dead, his reputation already buried.

The backdrop to the Pujo Committee was a surge in American intervention in Central America that followed logically if not inevitably from dollar diplomacy. Morgan testified in December 1912, four months after the Marines commanded by Smedley Butler had occupied and pacified Nicaragua.

Morgan himself had little to do with that, but he was undone by the backlash. Brown Brothers had everything to do with that, and yet they escaped public ire.

In their own accounts of how the firm became so intimately involved in the finances of a small Central American nation, the partners of Brown Brothers in later years claimed that their role was overstated and that they were one cog in a larger wheel. In their telling, they were approached in 1911 by the State Department and Secretary Knox and asked to make a small loan to the Nicaraguan government on fair and by no means usurious terms. Another investment house, J. & W. Seligman, was also approached. Seligman had been one of the primary bankers for the Vanderbilt family, and its partners had managed the sale of U.S. government bonds abroad. That had positioned them to raise much of the debt to build the Panama Canal. By 1911, when the loan to Nicaragua was suggested, Seligman, unlike Brown Brothers, had been deeply involved in the finances of Central America for years.

Brown Brothers took a more circuitous path. In the 1890s, a Boston lumber merchant named George Emery had won a lumber concession from the government of Nicaragua. Several years later, an English bank had lent a considerable sum to the Nicaraguan government of President José Santos Zelaya. Brown Shipley in London knew of the loan, having been approached by the syndicate that originated it. The syndicate wanted out and was looking for buyers. Partners at the Brown Brothers branch in Boston were familiar with George Emery, who was also looking for an exit strategy after Zelaya was suddenly overthrown in 1909.

Americans at the time depicted Zelaya as a petty dictator of a rinky-dink country that could not manage its own affairs competently. That characterization, however, said more about American (and by extension European) attitudes than it did about Zelaya himself. The later years of the twentieth century would indeed be chock-full of brutal mediocrities ruling a host of Latin American countries, but Zelaya was more of a modernizing autocrat than a corrupt despot. He invested in education, tried to copy the latest best practices from Europe and the United States in creating a technocratic,

competent bureaucracy, and invested in roads and rails through the cano-
pied jungles that covered the country. He took on substantial loans and
granted multiple concessions to foreign businesses, but very little seems to
have been for his personal enrichment.[9]

Nicaragua had a population of barely half a million people, most eking
out a meager agrarian living from sparse plots of land surrounded by dense
rain forest. A small percentage lived in the capital of Managua and in coastal
ports such as Bluefields and San Juan. Like most Central American countries, Nicaragua was interesting to American and European business interests because of its cash crops, primarily coffee, with plantations on the Pacific
Coast. As in neighboring Honduras and then Guatemala, bananas (on the
Atlantic Mosquito coast) were also key to the economy, hence the later pe-
jorative "banana republics."

Nicaragua, however, was not just a coffee and banana republic; it offered
a perfect route from the Atlantic to the Pacific. In the last half of the nineteenth century, it was a prime candidate for an alternate canal that would
allow ships to pass from one sea to the other without the complicated and
costly lock system required in Panama. The need for a canal linking the
Pacific to the Atlantic was obvious. In order to get from Europe or the Eastern Seaboard to California, ships had to sail thousands of miles south, make
the turn around Cape Horn at the very tip of Patagonia and then head thousands of miles back north. Reducing that by months would be a considerable boon to trade. Ultimately, the Isthmus of Panama became the first
choice, but even as that canal was being constructed in the first decade of
the twentieth century and even as the Roosevelt administration intervened
against Columbia to ensure Panamanian independence, an alternate route
was still planned for Nicaragua. The Nicaraguan canal would offer an even
shorter passage to the West Coast, and it would be easier to build and maintain, with much of the route crossing the vast and already navigable lake in
Nicaragua's west. The potential for a second canal meant that Nicaragua
received much more attention from America and assorted European nations as a future boondoggle. With canal building would come immense
spending and plenty of graft. Multiple parties jockeyed for a lucrative canal

concession, while the Nicaraguan government tried to strike the best deal, hoping that soon enough a second route parallel to Panama would be started with all of the attendant investments.

In 1909, with these machinations very much in play, Zelaya was overthrown. Washington, through its representatives in Managua, supported the planners of the coup with promises of economic aid and closer diplomatic ties. Though he was maligned as a dictator, Zelaya had never relied on military force to rule Nicaragua. His army consisted of fewer than 2,000 men, few of them well armed, scattered throughout the country. Overthrowing him was relatively easy once a bare quorum of opponents decided to act, and once American diplomats made clear that the plotters would have the financial and, if need be, military backing of the United States.

The new government, however, had only a tenuous hold on power. Much of the Caribbean coast was beyond the reach of Managua, and the American business community there held considerable sway. Zelaya had been ousted, but the situation was chaotic and unsettled. The Americans on the Caribbean side of Nicaragua at the port of Bluefields appealed to Washington for support. That led to Smedley Butler's first mission to the country, with a small force of a few hundred soldiers, who remained for several months until Zelaya had fled the country and the new government had consolidated power. In response to the turmoil, the Taft administration used Nicaragua as a test case for dollar diplomacy, building on the precedents established by Roosevelt. In 1905, the government of Santo Domingo (the present-day Dominican Republic) had defaulted on its debts to France and Germany. In response, Roosevelt warned those countries not to take military action and in the spirit of his corollary forced Santo Domingo to accept U.S. oversight of its finances. Taft's dollar diplomacy would follow a similar script in Nicaragua, extending loans to help the government consolidate power and rebuild, loans which would be secured by customs duties collected with American oversight. American money and American financial know-how would, so the theory went, help the Nicaraguan government institute sound fiscal management. Official oversight of customs collection would ensure that the American creditors would get paid back.

It remains something of a mystery who approached whom and when. Seligman later claimed that it was Brown Brothers who initiated the idea of a syndicate loan to the Nicaraguan government. Brown Brothers claimed it was the State Department. The State Department said that it was the bankers. Brown Brothers' later demurrals, however, do not hold up. In February 1911, the firm wrote directly to Secretary of State Knox, saying, "We understand that the Government of Nicaragua is considering the advisability of a new loan for the purposes of refunding her present indebtedness and of providing for other governmental needs. We also understand that, in order to secure such loan upon advantageous terms, the Government of Nicaragua is desirous of enlisting the good office of our own Government. . . . Should this information be substantially correct, we beg to say that, as bankers, we shall be glad to have the opportunity of negotiating for such a loan. . . . We beg to add that we are interested in the George D. Emery Co.'s claim against Nicaragua."[10] For its part, the State Department wanted to push out European creditors and replace them with Americans. That was the undercurrent of dollar diplomacy. If the Monroe Doctrine had drawn a line, unenforceable at the time, against European armed intervention in Latin America, Roosevelt and Taft drew a new line against European financial intervention. Nicaragua had millions in outstanding loans to English bankers, as well as multiple interests sniffing around for a canal concession. Using Brown Brothers and Seligman, the Taft administration hoped to slam the door on European involvement in Nicaragua and in the rest of Central America, Honduras especially.

The construction of the Panama Canal gave these policies added impetus. With the completion fast approaching, the U.S. government became even more determined to maintain its implied control over the region, whether by freezing out other nations economically or by intervening militarily. Dollar diplomacy was cheap and easy. It was defended as an altruistic policy designed, as Taft said, to enable the governments of the region to end years of turbulence and instability and "take their rightful places among the law-abiding and progressive countries of the world."[11] Under American tutelage, countries could jump-start stagnant systems and attain progress.

And who better to provide that tutelage than American bankers who knew how to structure loans, set up banks, issue paper money and price risk? American supporters of dollar diplomacy saw it as a win-win. The countries of Central America would advance economically and stabilize politically. American companies would find new markets, and the United States would increase its influence in world affairs.

The overthrow of Zelaya led to more political instability in Nicaragua, and lack of capital was one reason. Zelaya was replaced by a succession of weak governments, each desperately short of cash and looking to curry favor with the Americans. They could print money, but none of these fleeting governments could collect revenue, which devalued the paper they issued. They couldn't pay civil servants enough to be honest, and customs' revenue and other taxes found their way into multiple pockets before the remainder trickled into government coffers in Managua. In 1911, Adolfo Díaz, who had previously worked for a British mining company near Bluefields, became president when his alcoholic predecessor was forced to resign after only a few months in office. The government was broke and unable to pay either its soldiers or its civil servants. Aware that his tenure might be equally brief unless he found a way to replenish the treasury, Díaz turned to the United States for help. The U.S. government then turned to Brown Brothers.

In the spring of 1911, the State Department worked in concert with the banking consortium of Brown Brothers and Seligman to draw up a detailed plan to aid Díaz and recapitalize Nicaragua. Under the terms of a convention negotiated with Managua by Secretary of State Knox and his counterpart, Salvador Castrillo, the bankers would lend the Nicaraguan government $15 million. The government would use the proceeds to retire the debt still held by non-American creditors and then use the remainder of the funds to develop the country's resources, including the construction of a railroad network and the creation of a national bank. The loan would be secured by the country's customs receipts, which in order to halt the rampant graft would be overseen by a collector general chosen by the president of Nicaragua from a list of names provided by the U.S. State Department at the suggestion of Brown Brothers and Seligman.

The convention (known as the Knox-Castrillo Treaty) required both governments to ratify the terms. In Managua, opponents denounced the pact as an American plot to take over the country. "Let us try to die as free men, not as slaves with chains riveted upon us forever," one deputy in the Nicaraguan Assembly decried. But the convention was narrowly ratified, in part because many Conservatives saw no other viable fiscal path and because some felt that the printing of money had gone too far and was creating runaway inflation favoring a few speculators and impoverishing most others.[12]

But the convention faced a steeper hurdle in the U.S. Senate. Despite Taft and Knox lobbying hard, the Senate would not ratify the agreement. Even though the Senate was controlled by the Republicans, vocal Democrats warned that the convention would set the stage for the U.S. government to act as a collection agent for New York bankers. Their concerns proved prescient, and when the Democrat Woodrow Wilson, who inveighed against imperialism on the campaign trail, became president in 1913, he ended up following policies barely distinct from Taft's and Roosevelt's. But in 1911, the Democrats in Congress stood firmly against more U.S. entwinement in the internal affairs of Central American and Caribbean countries. In making their case against the convention, they drew on the age-old tradition of animosity to the privileged few of finance. Georgia's Democratic senator Augustus Octavius Bacon warned prophetically that the sole purpose of the convention was "to enable certain American capitalists to go into Nicaragua and reap a very high profit out of an enterprise which would ordinarily be considered as hazardous . . . but which would be absolutely safe when guaranteed by the Government of the United States."[13]

The Senate delayed action on the treaty, but the bankers and the State Department were undeterred. The treaty was desirable but not strictly necessary. In the fall of 1911, Brown Brothers and Seligman still hoped that a revised treaty might eventually pass Congress, but they were unwilling to forgo a prime opportunity whose risk seemed limited by the implied assurances of the U.S. government. They offered Nicaragua a bridge loan of $1.5 million. Even though the amount was one-tenth of the initial proposal, the conditions were essentially the same. Under its terms, the loan would be secured by the collection of customs duties, with a collector nominated by the bankers. In addition, the government agreed to a new Bank of Nicaragua, which would be capitalized with the proceeds of the loan and would, as the national bank, have the sole authority to issue official paper currency backed by gold. But that bank would not be owned by Nicaragua. Fifty-one percent would be owned by Seligman and Brown Brothers, and it was to be incorporated in Connecticut, subject to Connecticut law, for a period of no less than ninety years. James Brown was made president, and Thatcher Brown was named director. James Brown and Seligman also were allowed under the agreement to purchase a controlling 51 percent stake in the Pacific Railroad of Nicaragua and were appointed to the national railway's board of directors.[14]

In short order, therefore, Brown Brothers and Seligman became the financial overseers for the government of Nicaragua, the owners and governors of its national bank in charge of issuing money, and the controlling shareholders of the country's major railway. The terms of the loan itself were not particularly onerous or usurious, at interest rates of 5 to 6 percent, which compared with Nicaragua's domestic rates of 12 percent on a devalued local currency were perfectly reasonable. Less reasonable, however, was that a significant portion of the money lent by Brown and Seligman was used not for domestic Nicaraguan development but to retire the outstanding claims and concessions that Brown Brothers had acquired. The firm had bought the old Emery concession and the outstanding English loan to Zelaya for pennies on the dollar. They lent the Nicaraguan government $1.5 million, some of which was then used to pay Brown Brothers for those loans, plus interest. In short, the partners of Brown Brothers took their own capital, lent it to a foreign government in return for control of its central bank and its national railroad, and then received some of that capital back almost immediately, plus interest, to pay par value for loans that they had bought at a discount.

No one should be shocked, shocked to learn that American banks structured foreign loans to their own advantage. Bankers often arrange financing to ensure that their capital occupies a privileged position, that they are the first in, the first paid and the first out. That is one way they make money. The terms negotiated in Nicaragua were similar to the terms Brown Brothers would have asked for in dozens of other deals, particularly in riskier situations where more guarantees and assurances were needed. Nor were Brown Brothers and Seligman unique in how they did business in Latin America. J.P. Morgan and Kuhn, Loeb were involved in similar arrangements in Honduras. Using a physical asset such as a railroad as collateral was also fairly standard, then and now.

But not all aspects of the deal were so standard. Brown Brothers required the Nicaraguan government to use the loan proceeds to cash out Brown Brothers. They had earlier purchased the Emery and English loans because they made a calculated bet that those would be worth something someday, and the flow of funds from the Nicaraguan treasury directly into Brown Brothers shows that their loan to Nicaragua was primarily a way for them to cash out an investment. And yes, the Zelaya administration had signed those covenants years earlier with an English bank and a Boston businessman, not with Brown Brothers, and wisely or not, the Nicaraguan government had made a legally binding obligation to pay back the holder of the debt. Nonetheless, if you were a Nicaraguan at the time, you could be forgiven for viewing the entire $1.5 million loan originating from New York bankers as a not so subtle way to indenture the country, sign over the national banking system as well as the usually inalienable right of a sovereign to print money, and hand control and the bulk of the profits of the primary transportation link for the entire country to a small group of foreign financiers backed by the full force of the U.S. government. To make it that much more intolerable, you also had to listen as the U.S. government and its representatives preached that their primary goal was to help Nicaragua become a more stable, more prosperous country, which may have been a genuine desire but which seemed to be hollow words masking more self-interested policies.

By 1912, Brown Brothers, with James on point, was deeply involved in the day-to-day management of the finances of the Nicaraguan government.

That included a complete restructuring of the financial system, using the newly constituted National Bank of Nicaragua as the vehicle to retire and remove from circulation all of the previously issued paper money, much of which was as worthless as any of the paper issued by an American wildcat bank in the early nineteenth century. James took the lead in designing a gold-based monetary system with a new currency called the *córdoba* in honor of the Spanish conquistador who had started Spanish settlement in the country in the sixteenth century. Nicaragua's gold and silver coins were to be minted with the same metal proportions as the U.S. dollar.[15]

The bankers also assumed responsibility for the management and expansion of the national railroad. The rail system was, not surprisingly, in deep disrepair. Boxcars didn't have doors. Their flimsy roofs were sieves in the torrential rains, and tarps had to be used in a largely futile effort to keep freight and passengers dry. There were no air brakes, and security was so bad that the trains were regularly robbed. The tracks were rusted and corroded and hadn't been designed well to begin with. Several million dollars were allocated to improve the line—not Union Pacific kind of money, but not nothing for a modest network in a small country. The lines quickly began to generate more income, and pay dividends. Brown Brothers and Seligman profited nicely as a result. Rounding out their interests in key aspects of the economy, Brown Brothers also obtained a stake in the steamer that crossed the inland lake off the Pacific Coast. The firm didn't control coffee or banana plantations (they had had enough of plantations during those years in the 1840s), but the partners did earn small fees on shipments within the country and from the interior to ports on the coast.[16]

It could be argued, and was, that the investments made under the direction of Brown Brothers improved the financial and physical infrastructure of Nicaragua. There is more than a kernel of truth in that. After all, if the new bank and upgraded rails and more efficient steamship service hadn't functioned, there would have been no revenue to pay for those loans and recoup those investments. The loans made Brown Brothers money, but that money also benefited their client, which had always been their mantra.

But if Brown Brothers was just doing business as usual, it was remark-

able how closely it coordinated with the State Department and how intimately policy in Nicaragua was shaped around the needs of the bankers.
Not only were the customs collector and the chief diplomat negotiating
further loans and agreements appointed at the behest of Brown Brothers,
but the State Department was in regular communication with the bankers,
both via official correspondence and through unofficial meetings in U.S.
diplomatic offices in Managua. So closely did Brown Brothers work with
the U.S. government that the State Department allowed the firm to use
official diplomatic wires for money transfers and communications. Brown
Brothers informed the State Department of the terms of each new contract,
each revision of loan terms, and every discussion about spending on transportation, issuing currency and instituting reforms. The State Department
in turn wove those discussions into its policy matrix. By mid-1912, the
Nicaraguan government was again low on funds, and the bankers were
willing to float additional loans to cover expenses. That, too, was presented
to the State Department for approval, which was duly granted.

Even discounting American involvement, Nicaraguan politics were
hardly collegial and placid, but opponents of Díaz and his party seized on
the government's deepening entanglement with American bankers as a rallying cry. In March 1912, Secretary of State Knox took a "goodwill" trip
to Managua (as part of a larger Latin American tour), and later described
the visit as cordial and productive. That may have been true of his heavily
guarded state dinners in the capital, but in the streets, Knox had to be hus-
tled by armed guards through large anti-American protests, and a plot to
blow up his train nearly caused lethal damage. Díaz threw several newspaper editors in jail and prevented the publication of damning editorials
during the visit, so that he could tell Knox how much he and Taft were
admired, and so that Knox, largely clueless about the storm around him,
could proclaim with a straight face, "We are especially interested in the
prosperity of all the people of Nicaragua."[17]

With multiple factions jockeying and the government's tiny army only
in control of portions of the country, concern grew that the property and
safety of Americans in the country could be in jeopardy. For all the chaos

of the past few years, foreigners had been able to go about their business, but in the summer of 1912, that changed. At least three competing factions formed, each attempting to wrest control of Managua. The result was a haphazard and low-level civil war. In late July, the Liberal faction seized control of parts of the railway along with a few lake steamers and some of the customs houses and whatever coin and money were stored there. The Brown Brothers–appointed head of the National Bank in Managua wired to James Brown in New York that he was now concerned about the security not just of the bank but of Americans in the city. Brown, in close touch with the State Department, assured him that help was on the way. The bankers officially "applied for protection" and requested immediate action by the U.S. government. The teetering government of Nicaragua also appealed to Washington for military assistance. And so the Marines were dispatched.

Led again by Smedley Butler (who was not thrilled to be sent one more time to what he had once dismissed as "a third rate Central American" country), the first wave of Marines was more of an eddy, consisting of a battalion of about four hundred men who landed near Bluefields on the Caribbean coast in mid-August. President Taft then authorized a larger expeditionary force, the Tenth Infantry stationed in Panama, but it would take several more weeks for it to arrive, which Butler feared would be too late to save the Managua government and protect American interests. With the rebels controlling half of the train engines, logistics were a challenge, but the dissidents had very few men at arms and were only able to mount sporadic opposition. Butler was able to transport his Marines to Managua, not an easy two hundred miles, and then station them around the American legation.

With the leader of the opposition suffering a debilitating bout of rheumatism, Butler received his surrender. Butler then continued north to the city of León. It took longer than expected. The railroad tracks had been torn up, and his men were reduced to walking alongside the trains, clearing debris where they could. Butler was as tough as advertised; faced with an armed mob in León, with one of the leaders confronting the rather slender American general with a revolver, Butler stared him down, and in a move that would have made Indiana Jones proud, grabbed the man's revolver from his hand and pointed it back at him. The crowd burst into uproarious laughter and dispersed. By the end of August, the fighting was by no means done, but the rebellion was scattered and the remaining weeks were little more than a bloody mop-up. Years later, Nicaraguan mothers would scare disobedient children by telling them that if they didn't behave, "Major Butler will get you!"[18]

At the end of August, with reinforcements having arrived from Panama, more than 2,000 American troops occupied strategic areas of the country. Taft had considered an even larger invasion but was assured by Butler that the immediate danger had passed. All was not entirely well, however. Taft was distracted by the escalating political insurgency led by Roosevelt, who had just been nominated by the Progressive Party convention in Chicago. Nicaragua was a nuisance, but a time-consuming one given the exposure of American troops. If things went awry for the expeditionary force, it would further hamper Taft's chances at winning reelection. He lost anyway, but in late August he still had hope. He expressed concern to friends that the situation in Nicaragua was tenuous, and that further loss of life was entirely possible if not probable. The administration was also unable to control the public narrative; with typical hyperbole, one paper reported, with no evidence, that "125 American planters feared massacred." There were rumors of "untold horrors" in the country, and Taft privately told friends that the situation in Nicaragua reminded him of the Boxer Rebellion in China—the anti-imperialist uprising that had cost tens of thousands of lives and was squelched by a multinational army of Europeans.

Those fears proved unfounded. The fighting petered out by late fall, with skirmishes diminishing in intensity and the rebellious factions eventually giving up. In an excess of caution, and from a desire to retain control, Taft ordered that a contingent of troops be left in the country. They would remain there for more than a decade. Taft's open-ended use of force was challenged by Georgia senator Augustus Octavius Bacon, who had earlier opposed the Knox-Castrillo Treaty. Bacon introduced a resolution questioning whether Taft had the authority to station troops in Nicaragua without the express consent of Congress. Congress, however, was unable to muster a consensus. Taft's use of executive power as commander in chief went unchallenged, setting a dangerous precedent.

Roosevelt's ire at Taft succeeded in sinking the chances of both men in the election of 1912, which was won by Wilson with only 41 percent of the vote. Assailing Taft and Knox, Wilson campaigned aggressively against dollar diplomacy and the use of American power to protect private interests. Once in power, he made a nearly complete reversal. That was surprising, but not nearly as much as the about-face of his secretary of state. To mollify the progressive wing of the Democratic Party, Wilson had appointed the adamantly anti-imperialist William Jennings Bryan as secretary of state. Campaigning for Wilson in 1912, Bryan denounced "gold-standard imperialism," a neat swipe at the currency reforms championed by Brown Brothers in Nicaragua. A year later, in a position of power, he was suddenly less troubled. It is easier to inveigh against a system from the outside than it is to change it once inside. Though Bryan promised a thorough review of the policies of his Republican predecessors, he dropped much of his previous opposition, which left dollar diplomacy alive and well in Managua.

The Nicaraguan civil war failed to topple Díaz, but it left his government even more pressed for cash. Brown Brothers, fortified by the presence of U.S. Marines in Managua, was willing to extend additional bridge loans totaling hundreds of thousands of dollars, secured by taxes on tobacco and liquor. And the firm had the prospect of assuming the remaining 49 percent of shares of the national railroad and of the National Bank should interest payments falter. Even with that collateral, Brown Brothers had made clear in various letters and private conversations that any change in the staunch support of Washington would lead them to reconsider their commitment. Their representatives communicated the same to Díaz, who then conveyed that to the U.S. minister, who then wired the State Department in February 1913: "Although Brown Brothers may have seemed to him [Díaz] ultraconservative at times, he would like to continue dealing with them. But they will not advance another dollar or entertain a new proposition until they are certain that the incoming administration at Washington will continue the present policy." Rumors abounded that once the U.S. presidential transition occurred in March, Wilson would leave Díaz in the lurch. Knox, in his last weeks but in close contact with Bryan, dismissed the possibility. As he explained to the American minister in Managua, "There is no foundation for the rumor that the incoming administration will change the present policy of the United States toward Central America." Brown Brothers, Knox concluded, should feel comfortable proceeding with their plan to buy the remaining shares of the national railroad and to continue lending the government money, money which could then be used to repay Brown Brothers for the remainder of the outstanding English loan.[19]

After the Marine occupation in 1912, the firm was in a stronger position than ever. Dollar diplomacy had been a smashing success, for Brown Brothers. As they continued to broaden their interest in Nicaragua, James and Thatcher began to look for other opportunities in Central America. In 1915, a Mercantile Bank of America was organized as a Brown Brothers–Seligman joint venture that would use the template of Nicaragua—lend governments money in return for assuming control of the financial system and key resources and then restructure the domestic economy. The Mercantile Bank made some strides, but its progress was interrupted by the outbreak of World War I, and it eventually went bust when the Caribbean sugar market hit hard times in 1924.

In 1916, the United States and Nicaragua finally concluded the treaty that had long eluded them, this time signed by Bryan, who copied the language of the failed treaty of 1911 that he had denounced at the time. The new treaty included more loans as well as the granting of a ninety-nine-year canal concession and enshrined the right of the United States to intervene to maintain order when it deemed necessary—a clause which it triggered multiple times over the coming years and which mimicked other U.S. treaties with countries such as Cuba and Haiti. The canal concession was never used, but the treaty remained in effect until the 1970s, when it was formally terminated at the request of the staunch American anticommunist ally and dictator Anastasio Somoza. Somoza's family had ruled the country since the 1930s, when his father outmaneuvered and executed Augusto Sandino, who had led a widely popular nationalist movement founded on removing foreign financial interests from the country. Sandino failed, but his name was adopted by another insurgent nationalist movement in the 1970s, the Sandinistas, who eventually rose to power, fueled by the bitter memories of the financial protectorate of the United States and Brown Brothers. The Sandinistas' demonic vision of dollar diplomacy was as two-dimensional and distorted as the defense of it as a benign force in the economic development of Central America, but it shows how deeply the fiscal and military intervention of 1912 and beyond shaped Nicaraguan history as well as the evolution of the entire region.

By the time of Sandino in the 1930s, Brown Brothers had long left the scene. All told, the firm had recouped not just its original investments but millions more in fees and interest as well as being made whole from the early claims it assumed. It reaped additional millions in dividends from managing the National Bank and the railway. A few hundred American troops were kept in the country, first to prop up the shaky Díaz administration and then subsequent governments, until 1925, when they finally departed. A year later, Americans troops returned, and then left again, a pattern that would be repeated until Somoza came to power as a staunch American ally and an effective if brutal ruler. Franklin Roosevelt would famously refer to him as "a son of a bitch, but he's our son of a bitch."

The partners of Brown Brothers averred that their part in the story had been exaggerated. Their defense? They had engaged in a series of business transactions negotiated openly and fairly and at standard rates with the government of Nicaragua. The U.S. government had been helpful at a dicey time but no more or less than it was in multiple other countries over the years when American lives and property were in jeopardy. While there had been short-term turmoil in Nicaragua in 1912, the country had been riven by factions and weak governments before the firm became involved. And the subsequent decades showed dramatic improvement in the material conditions in the country. In one of the company's files, there is a letter from the interim president of Nicaragua some years later comparing the fiscal situation before the bankers became involved and after. Before, he said, the country was insolvent and bankrupt, with a worthless currency and no national banking system. After, by 1924, there was a gold-backed currency honored everywhere, a viable banking network, a good railroad, reduced debt and interest paid on time with international creditors willing to lend.[20] While that assessment skimmed over the continuing political instability, it was, in those basic facts, correct.

At the same time, it is extraordinary how the interests of a private firm became inextricably entwined with the policies of the U.S. government. Theodore Roosevelt had governed with an eye toward keeping business in check. While his rhetoric as a trustbuster and a protector of the working class against the rapaciousness of the rich and powerful was stronger than his actions, it is still in marked contrast to what happened after he left office. Under Taft and Wilson and continuing thereafter, there was a marriage of business and politics, which is the larger significance of the story of Brown Brothers in Nicaragua. For the bulk of the nineteenth century, it would not have occurred to Brown Brothers or to any other prominent financial firm in the United States to work closely with the U.S. government as a de facto strategic partner in foreign ventures. Such close coordination was unusual even in domestic affairs, though the federal government certainly created conditions for large industrial projects such as the expansion of the railroads. For the most part, however, the two realms—business and government—stayed separate.

If the nineteenth century saw the emergence of money and a financial system that gave the United States some unique advantages, the twentieth saw a convergence of finance and politics that propelled the United States into the economic stratosphere. The rise of a WASP elite that moved seamlessly between government and finance cemented the bonds between money and political power. That met stiff opposition from populists and progressives who saw dollar diplomacy and then the invention of the Federal Reserve as corrupt and dangerous and who believed that the financial world was inherently self-dealing, self-aggrandizing and inimical to the welfare of the bulk of American citizens. The Great Depression seemed to vindicate that view. But as the about-face of Bryan and Woodrow Wilson shows, those views were more potent as notes of opposition. Once progressives were in power, they tended to change their tune, and the interests of the financial and business community assumed pride of place. That, too, was a tension later on during the Depression years.

In trying to define the links between various power groups, academic historians have used the term *corporatism* to describe a system in the United States and elsewhere whereby the leaders of each power center work together to drive policies and steer the state. At times, that meant smoke-filled rooms at political conventions where power brokers would gather over cigars and whiskey to decide who would run for office and who would get the spoils. Usually, however, the reality was more prosaic and less organized, with society loosely governed by small groups of people with overlapping interests.

What seemed relatively unremarkable at the time—bankers and the State Department intimately coordinating and shaping the foreign policy of the United States—was in fact a new page. It wasn't just Brown Brothers and Seligman in Nicaragua; it was National City Bank of New York (the progenitor of today's Citibank) in Haiti setting the stage for the U.S. occupation in 1915. It was J.P. Morgan and Guaranty Trust Company in Cuba and Honduras. It was Chase National Bank in Cuba and Panama. And that does not include the banana companies, and the coffee companies, and the import businesses. The financiers, however, occupied a particularly central place in the firmament of American foreign policy. As dollar diplomacy evolved and expanded from Taft to Wilson, as it became simply "American diplomacy," Brown Brothers and a handful of firms became the de facto deputies of the U.S. government, and the government became the de facto agents of these financial interests.

That does not make this some dark conspiracy. It was an organic evolution of American power, which in some ways resembled all power over time and in other ways was a novel evolution of a tight group of elites whose interests were aligned without being tightly coordinated. It would be a few decades before this alignment morphed into the revolving door between Wall Street and Washington, when Brown Brothers Harriman ascended to its apex of influence. The nineteenth century witnessed the way that money was the fuel for American power; the twentieth saw the people who channeled that money and governed the financial system acquire political power. And with the emergence of a uniquely wealthy United States after World War II, these men then created a financial and political framework not just for the United States but for the entire world.

The evolution of Brown Brothers from a small family partnership into a private bank with business ties globally and deep influence in politics has been fodder for all sorts of conspiracy theories, especially as the partners of the firm assumed national roles at the highest levels of government after World War II. Nicaragua was only the beginning. To the partners of the firm at the time, it seemed like just another business deal, yet it set a new path and precedent. That was clear to opponents of the way those with money and those with political power appeared to be congealing into an overclass more than it was self-evident to the members of that class at the time. In a 1922 issue of *The Nation*, which had been partly founded by Brown Brothers money but which had moved in a rather different direction by the 1920s, the involvement of the firm in the U.S. occupation of Nicaragua was presented as a dark tale of bankers and "their grip forever fixed upon the throat of Nicaragua," with the country reduced to the same state as the chattel slave, never able "to choose another master. . . . This is American imperialism, approved by both parties. This is The Republic of Brown Brothers."[21]

Who knows what the trajectory might have been absent the outbreak of the first major cataclysm of the twentieth century, the war that began in August 1914 and eventually roped in every major power in the world, including the United States in 1917. Even before Americans mobilized for war, however, what would become known as the First World War presented a new challenge not only to the financial stability of Europe but to American businesses that had become increasingly enmeshed overseas. Like previous wars, this one disrupted businesses and trapped money behind enemy lines, but the scale in 1914 was much greater. How that was managed, behind the scenes, was a dry run for the more public and more dramatic responses three decades later. And quietly, almost invisibly, Brown Brothers was at the story's center.

CHAPTER 9

SAVING MONEY

In December 1914, James Brown sailed to England for a meeting in London. Even in calm times, an Atlantic crossing was often not smooth. The Browns had never forgotten the sinking of the *Arctic*, and it had only been two years since the *Titanic* had gone down. Now, however, there was the added peril of German U-boats, which were supposed to steer clear of neutral ships but often didn't. As Alexander's great-grandson, James was now one of the leading partners of the firm, but his trip to London was made in a different capacity. James was part of a delegation appointed by the newly created Federal Reserve Board to prevent a problem from becoming a crisis. The world was mired in the catastrophe of a war that was supposed to have been over in a few months but which had already taken millions of lives and upended decades of placid assumptions. The First Battle of the Marne alone, lasting a week in September as the French hurriedly assembled to prevent a German march on Paris, saw more than 500,000 casualties.

The Federal Reserve had barely begun to figure itself out when the war started, and one of the first challenges was how to repatriate American assets trapped in various capitals of Europe, not just in Germany and Austria and Russia, but also in France and England. There had never been transparent exchange rates, but by the summer of 1914, an equilibrium had evolved. Brown Brothers and others published their own rates, which were then widely used. Cross-border investments had been growing steadily, and after decades without a major European war, few had anticipated that the vast flow of funds across countries and secured by paper promises could suddenly be halted. August 1914 shattered many things, including the gentlemen's agreements that had formed the exoskeleton of international exchange, which had seemed just fine that July but was rendered useless only a few months later.

That December in London, James Brown, along with Benjamin Strong (president of Bankers Trust and the first governor of the New York Federal Reserve and thus the de facto head of the new system) and Albert Wiggin (president of Chase National Bank), met with the British chancellor of the exchequer, David Lloyd George, who was soon to be prime minister, and the governor of the Bank of England, Walter Cunliffe. Strong, still in his early forties, young and ambitious, was then at the outset of what would become a long and complicated career punctuated by the market collapse of 1929. Lloyd George was already starting to lose confidence in prime minister Herbert Asquith and was chafing at playing a circumspect financial role during a time of total war.

James Brown was in rarefied company, but he gave no indication that he felt out of place. And why should he have? He was one of the scions of a now-hundred-year-old family firm, entrusted with a charge to shore up the shaky foundations of a financial system whose stability was essential to whatever order remained, and uniquely suited to act as a behind-the-scenes intermediary given his family's reputation for discretion and the firm's long connection to the finances of Great Britain. He was favorably impressed by Cunliffe, soon to be made the 1st Baron Cunliffe, whom he described as "a very reserved and taciturn man but very cordial and absolutely frank in his expressions and in the confidential information he imported." Brown was struck by the degree to which Cunliffe treated him as a valued ally in the mutual task of shoring up the transatlantic financial system. He only later realized that Cunliffe extended that confidence not just because of who James Brown was but because of one of the firm's other partners, Montagu Norman of Brown Shipley.

Though Brown Shipley remained linked to Brown Brothers in a complicated partnership web, the English house had become more connected to
British finance after it moved to London in 1867. One of its nonfamily
partners, Mark Collet, had become governor of the Bank of England. Collet's grandson was Montagu Norman, an elfin, often ailing, eccentric character who sported a distinctive Van Dyke goatee. Norman worked for
Brown Brothers in New York for several years and became a Brown Shipley
partner in 1900. By 1914, however, Norman was focused on ascending into
the inner circles of London finance more than on his role as a partner. He
was a director of the Bank of England and when he wasn't attending meetings at the bank's Threadneedle Street offices, he was battling what seemed
to be a constant stream of illnesses. Norman, a contorted soul in the best of
times, was advancing his career but creating considerable tension within the
Brown partnership.

James was focused on how to ensure that capital continued to flow between the United States and the United Kingdom, as well as to and from
the continent. The United States was still officially neutral, but American
sentiment skewed strongly toward the Allied powers of Western Europe
and against the empires of Germany and Austria-Hungary. The financial
ties were also much stronger and deeper, although ties of similar magnitude
between Germany and England in the years leading up to 1914 did not, as
it turned out, preclude cataclysmic conflict. Still, you would have been
hard-pressed to find anyone on Wall Street who was rooting for the Central
Powers. Nasty rumors suggested that the house of Kuhn, Loeb and its aging
head Jacob Schiff maintained allegiance to the country of his youth, Germany, but those whisperings had more to do with the sotto voce anti-
Semitism of the time. The vast majority of the moneyed class sympathized
with France and Britain.

As part of that triad of Strong and Wiggin and because of his relationship with Norman, James was a pivotal voice in figuring out how the U.S.
banking community would assist the British and how the British banking
community would help Americans repatriate assets. But he was also in London for another equally delicate mission: to negotiate with Brown Shipley,

and with Montagu Norman in particular, a revised partnership agreement that would allow Norman to withdraw from the firm and still preserve the bonds between the two houses. A new British death tax, which raised rates to more than 20 percent on estates greater than one million pounds, threatened the financial balance of the company's Anglo-American partnership. Given the way the partnership was structured, the U.S. partners could be liable for hefty taxes on the English partners' estates. Norman, however, was an even stickier problem: he wanted out, but on terms he dictated. Norman was never an easy man and was even more difficult when it came to his own affairs. He was often clinically depressed. He would later be central in the drama of the global Great Depression as governor of the Bank of England, but in the fall of 1914, it was his personal emotional state that concerned James Brown. Eventually James was able to make Norman understand that a gradual withdrawal from the firm was in everyone's interest, and James left England with a loose agreement to preserve the partnership. It would last only a few more years.[1]

The December trip was emblematic of the essential role that bankers played in the war. Writing the financial story of World War I raises the same challenges as the financial history of the Civil War, or any war. The history of war is the story of battles won and lost; of governments victorious or overthrown; of heroism on the battlefield or home front; of territory gained and property seized or destroyed. The role of money is rarely front and center, and perhaps that is as it should be. Bankers in times of high drama provide little. Just as there are few heroic epics of quartermasters and supply lines, how wars are funded and what happens to money behind enemy lines are footnotes at best.

The outbreak of World War I ended what had been a remarkably peaceful century in European history after the final defeat of Napoleon in 1815. European powers fought numerous small wars outside of Europe thereafter, in the Balkans, the Crimea and South Africa, but the continent itself was more placid than it had been in a thousand years. A century of relative stability had led to a gradual intermingling of money and credit between the various capitals of Europe and the rest of the world, New York especially.

When lines were abruptly and sharply drawn in the fall of 1914, billions of dollars were suddenly trapped on either side of those lines, billions that had until then been expected to flow from Berlin to Paris, London to New York, back again to Vienna, St. Petersburg, Rome, and then on again to London and Paris and from there throughout the world. With no serious anticipation or preparation for a cataclysm, there were no contingency plans for what to do if that flow was interrupted, the conduits between those centers severed.

One of the most significant innovations of the twentieth century was the architecture of a global financial system linking banks and transcending nations after World War II. The Bretton Woods framework established an international set of standards and an infrastructure, governed by the United States and relevant everywhere. As with the creation of the United Nations, what informed the people who created the post-1945 system was the experience of the earlier great war—everything that went wrong and the few things that went right. One thing that went quietly but spectacularly right was the decisive action by a small set of financiers in 1914 to make sure that the outbreak of the war did not trigger financial chaos. No one won medals for that. Preventing a crisis never gets the same attention as responding to one; staving off a war doesn't garner the same accolades as winning one. Perhaps if we spent more time focusing on those who toiled to maintain the floodgates, we might be less prone to the deluge.

James Brown represented two key constituencies in 1914 that together helped keep the Allies economically stable while maintaining public confidence and barely denting the American economy. The new U.S. Federal Reserve System passed its test, with James Brown one of its emissaries in London, while the Wall Street community became for the first time a banker to the world, with Brown Brothers part of the consortium. The ingredients were there in the fall of 1914 for panic and hoarding of capital, which would have made the damage caused by the war that much worse.

The United States was arguably in a better economic position in 1914 than at any point in the previous thirty years. Not only was the overall economy stable and expanding but a series of progressive reforms had begun to address the disruptions of the late nineteenth century. Woodrow Wilson had barely won a bitterly contested election, but between his Democratic coalition and Theodore Roosevelt running as the candidate of the Progressive Party, a large majority embraced a continuation of the reform agenda, with just shy of 70 percent of the electorate voting for either Roosevelt or Wilson. Democrats took majorities in both houses of Congress and were poised to enact sweeping new laws to strengthen the antitrust powers of the federal government, enhance labor protections, provide robust farm aid and guarantee wilderness conservation. And yet for all that reform fervor, the first major piece of legislation was the Federal Reserve Act in 1913.[2]

The absence of a central bank in the United States had been keenly felt during prior financial panics. Many saw the lack of a central bank that would act as a lender of last resort and as a firehose of liquidity in times of panic as a glaring weakness of the United States, especially in an era of rapid industrialization that demanded unprecedented amounts of capital. The United Kingdom, France and Germany all had such institutions. The Bank of England was among the best and had developed a stable system of gold reserves backing up all paper promises. In a similar vein, one of Bismarck's first reforms in a unified Germany in 1871 was to institute a gold standard. His goal was to bring stability to an incoherent system of competing and overlapping banks that often spurred inflation and deepened the divisions between German states. The United States was a notable outlier. Decades of bitter debates had pitted proponents of greenbacks and paper money against advocates of a mixed silver and gold standard who in turn fought against those who championed gold. Wilson entered the White House with that argument unresolved.

It was common then, and has been typical in retrospect, to see the absence of a central banking system as a critical weakness in an otherwise vibrant United States. Without question, the economic history of the United States in the nineteenth century had been tumultuous and at times hugely destructive to millions who suffered every time banks collapsed and the financial system contracted and money became scarce or devalued. But there was a reason it was so challenging to establish a centralized financial system: second only perhaps to slavery, it was one of the most bitter debates dividing Americans, from Hamilton and Jefferson on. Would the United States be governed by a central economic authority, or would American passion for independence from government preclude that? Who would reap the preponderance of rewards as America grew richer? Would the farmers and workers receive their fair share, and would a central bank founded on "hard money" benefit only the wealthy on Wall Street and the robber barons and the industrialists? Those were core issues, and they could not be resolved on purely financial terms.

Much of the financial class, Brown Brothers included, saw the absence of a central bank as a liability and a competitive disadvantage with the nations of Western Europe. Paul Warburg, who was not only heir to a family banking firm in New York but also linked by marriage to Kuhn, Loeb and Jacob Schiff, adamantly believed that the American system of decentralized banks governed by the National Banking Acts passed during the Civil War was "stupid, bewildering and strange." If you had suggested to him that the decentralized system might have allowed for more money to flow, which in turn fueled the rapid industrialization of the country and generated more wealth, he would have dismissed you as a rube. After the Panic of 1907, Warburg was introduced to the long-serving Republican Rhode Island senator Nelson Aldrich. They both viewed the panic as proof that the United States needed a potent central bank, and Aldrich made it his mission to get a banking bill through Congress.[3]

The Panic of 1907 had been a near miss of something far worse, and few were happy with the idea that the only thing standing between a complete meltdown and stability were a handful of wealthy private citizens such as J. P. Morgan, E. H. Harriman, and the Browns. There was no official lender of last resort and no central authority like the Bank of England that could provide a backstop in the case of financial panic. Morgan had stepped up, but what about the next time? Even progressives believed that something had to be done at the federal level to redress the deficiencies that 1907 had conclusively exposed.

But though there was a broad consensus about the basic need for a central bank, there were sharp disagreements over how centralized and how powerful it should be and who would exercise control. Wilson and Bryan had campaigned in 1912 decrying the concentration of power and money in the United States and vowed to rein in Wall Street titans. But as with his abrupt change of heart toward dollar diplomacy, once in the White House Wilson was friendlier to vested interests. Some of that can be put down to the exigencies of office and the realities of wielding power rather than aspiring to it. History is replete with onetime revolutionaries who act eerily like those they replaced. Wilson was never a radical, but he was a reformer who ultimately governed more in sync than not with the domestic order he inherited.

Establishing a coherent banking system was one of Wilson's priorities. He did not support the Warburg-inspired Aldrich plan that would have vested control of the new central bank with private bankers. He preferred a bank governed by the White House. But he put aside his fiery campaign stance and endorsed a compromise hybrid system that was less centralized and more controlled by private banks than by elected officials in Washington. The Federal Reserve Act established twelve regional reserve banks, each with officers and a board elected by the local banking establishment. Knitting those together was a Federal Reserve governing body appointed by the president. The hodgepodge was not what progressives had advocated, nor did it fully satisfy the desires of bankers to be self-governing, but it has proved to be a remarkably durable system.

Conservative Republicans and progressive Democrats in 1913 agreed on very little, but they both agreed that there was something deficient about the American banking system and that capital needed to be regulated. They disagreed about how much oversight was necessary, but not that some was. That consensus made the Federal Reserve Act possible, and it has arguably been a factor in subsequent financial stability. But the chaotic fluidity of American banking in the last decades of the nineteenth century had virtues as well. The lack of regulation and centralization were part and parcel of the massive release of energy in the industrial age, and the sheer ungovernability of money and banks may have given the United States distinct advantages compared with the more rigid systems in Britain, France and Germany. The loose rules established during the Civil War were enough to keep things from spinning hopelessly out of control, but not enough to stem the tsunami of capital in myriad forms, from greenbacks to local bank notes to letters of credit to coins and IOUs and debt bought and sold so many times that its original holders had long since passed from the scene. The periodic busts when capital drained were terrible, but the booms that preceded them were magnificent. It's not clear there could have been one without the other.

That is more evident in hindsight. In 1913, American reformers on all sides of the political spectrum interpreted those prior financial crises as a sign of serious deficiencies, and not a few looked wistfully at the European banks as emblematic of a more functional system. That overlooked, however, the strength that those deficiencies masked, namely the lack of barriers that could have constrained the explosion of capital and creativity that characterized the United States in the nineteenth century. A panoply of ills was unleashed along with that energy, hence the waves of populism and then progressive reform meant to redress the harms that were done. Yet the lack of a coherent system had its own virtues. The compromise of 1913—with a central bank that wasn't quite so central, a role for the government juxtaposed to a role for private banks—was a messy American solution that attempted to tame the unfettered flow of money and to strike a balance between public good and private gain.

The creation of the new system was heralded as the dawn of a new era of peace and prosperity. One Democratic congressman from Alabama declared that with the Federal Reserve in place and Democrats in power, "this Republic can shake off temporary business disturbances like dew drops from a lion's mane. . . . Labor is employed, wages good, the earth yields abundantly, the Democratic Party is in control, God reigns, and all is well with the Republic." Soaring words but the timing was not ideal. Like those who proclaimed the dawn of endless prosperity just before the market crashed in October 1929, the sense that crises were a thing of the past, seemingly reasonable at the end of 1913, proved about as wrong as humanly possible.[4]

The new system wouldn't be fully tested until the onset of the Great

Depression, but the outbreak of war in August 1914 did create the immediate problem not just of money trapped in various capitals but of people stranded with no access to the funds. There were no ATMs, no digital banking, no easy way to wire funds in different currencies across national borders and no protocols for travelers and businesspeople on the wrong side of the line between combatants to get home with their assets intact. Brown Brothers had long been financing travelers abroad, and by 1914, that business had grown large. The last decades of the nineteenth century and early years of the twentieth saw tourism boom as trains became faster and more comfortable, steamships more reliable and ubiquitous, and as more people with more wealth ventured across the Atlantic to explore Europe. Brown Brothers and its travelers' letters in turn helped companies such as Thomas Cook in England, which specialized in organizing tours. The travel boom, however, unfolded during decades of peace in Europe and the United States, which meant that when war came, suddenly and sharply, these industries were wholly unprepared.

The outbreak of war in August immediately stranded at least five thousand travelers whom Brown Brothers alone could count; thousands of others were being serviced by other firms. Within days of war being declared, Americans in Berlin and Vienna, for instance, couldn't get money from local banks drawn on London pounds (which was the universally accepted way to get foreign exchange) even with trusted letters from Brown Brothers. Those travelers inundated the local consulates and embassies, which could do nothing except telegraph back to London and New York expressing the urgency of the needs and asking for help.

The war caught almost everyone off guard. Thatcher had his own story of surprise, not remarkable but emblematic. He later wrote in his unpublished memoir, "My brother and I were on vacation in Pasque Island, Massachusetts. . . . We were in swimming that morning in an inlet of Buzzards Bay, when a Portuguese fisherman . . . called to us that he had heard there was a panic in New York, and the Stock Exchange had closed. We had no telephone at Pasque and received mail only twice a week. We couldn't imagine why a panic." They soon found out what had happened.

It took them more than a day to get back from their rustic Pasque idyll to New York, where they went directly to the Metropolitan Club, the ornate Fifth Avenue den of New York City financiers that had been founded by Pierpont Morgan. Brown Brothers was being flooded with requests from stranded Americans in Europe who couldn't access their money. The issue was acute enough that Treasury Secretary William McAdoo went to the Metropolitan Club conclave to help coordinate the efforts of both the bankers and the American government to get people and their money out of the war-locked countries of Europe. Adding to the difficulties was the fact that the stock exchange had closed, along with the major bourses of Europe. Most New Yorkers expected a closure of days or perhaps weeks. As with expectations of a short, sharp war over by Christmas, that proved wildly optimistic. The stock market remained closed for nine months, not opening again until April 1915.[5]

With exchanges frozen, the only thing that could bail out the thousands of travelers was gold, and lots of it. Thatcher and James, along with J.P. Morgan & Co. and Kidder, Peabody, aided by Benjamin Strong and McAdoo, arranged for an emergency shipment to London of $4.5 million in gold bullion, which could then be used as hard currency to reassure counterparties in Europe to advance funds to stranded Americans. This initial response proved to be a dry run for a significantly larger "gold fund" raised in the coming months to facilitate exchanges between sterling pounds and dollars that had been disrupted by the onset of war.

World War I began the tectonic shift of the United States from being a debtor nation to a creditor. The entire history of Brown Brothers had unfolded over a century in which Americans looked to Europe for loans and investment capital. World War I reversed that. After 1915, the United States started its rise as banker to the world. When the British government soon after August suspended gold payments for pounds in order to preserve its resources for the war, the United States was thrust into a new position of being a source of funds. As *The Times* of London put it, the suspension meant the "temporary abandonment of our historic claim as an international monetary centre," and propelled New York to fill that vacuum.[6] The war was also the beginning of the end of a monetary system that pegged currencies to gold, though that end didn't happen quietly and didn't come quickly. The conservative limitations of the gold standard, capping the supply of government money to the amount of gold, wouldn't work to fund a multiyear all-out war. Typically during wars, countries nominally maintained their adherence to gold and borrowed heavily in the meantime to meet military needs. The gold system functioned during shorter wars that were limited in scope; borrowing could be repaid without too much systemic stress. The financial demands of the Great War were many magnitudes greater. The efforts of American bankers to provide gold and liquidity to Great Britain and France permanently altered the financial and political relationship between the United States and Europe.[7]

It wasn't just travelers stranded without money that posed a challenge. It was the abrupt closure of securities markets on both sides of the Atlantic halting one of the primary conduits of capital without mechanisms in place to coordinate responses. The new Federal Reserve was designed to give New York financial institutions more clout in international finance, force more transparency in the market for letters of credit, and allow New York to compete with London as a financial center. The growing economic power of the United States might have eventually altered the balance even without the Great War, but after 1914, the shift from London to New York as the apex of the global financial system accelerated. Not until 1945 would the transition be complete, but World War I upended the status quo.

The nascent Federal Reserve was, however, more nascent than federal. It wasn't yet fully staffed in the fall of 1914. Its powers were broad but vague, and it wasn't able to react quickly and coherently. Just as J. P. Morgan had been the lender of last resort in 1907 because of the absence of a central bank delegated with that responsibility, shoring up the international financial system after August 1914 was initially left to private banks in conjunction with government. In the name of strict neutrality, the Wilson administration tried to prevent American banks from lending to the European powers. But that proved untenable. There were too many links, and those could not just be dissolved. And so it was that James Brown went to London as the equal of Benjamin Strong of the New York Federal Reserve.

Bailing out travelers proved to be a small matter compared with shoring up the system of exchange, preventing American businesses from suffering catastrophic losses, facilitating the surge in exports to a Europe in immediate need of American goods and capital, and keeping people and banks from panicking. In October, McAdoo used his convening power as treasury secretary (and as Wilson's new son-in-law, having married Eleanor Wilson a few months earlier in May) to gather New York's bankers and the new Federal Reserve governors to arrange another gold fund, this one of up to $200 million, that would act as a reserve fund for all transatlantic trade. Already, U.S. exports to Europe were soaring, which was only the beginning of that change in the relative position of the Old World and the New. James Brown in August had worried that while the war would lead to a short-term boost in American exports, the turmoil of financial markets and European nations hoarding capital would be bad for the United States as a debtor nation. That would have been true, except that James did not foresee that it wasn't just crops and goods that Europe needed from the United States; it was money as well, and lots of it.

The U.S. government did not want Wall Street providing financial lifelines to any of the combatants, but it especially did not want to help Germany or Austria-Hungary. Britain was demanding that no American banks arranging loans to the Allied powers could lend money to the Central Powers, and the British government lobbied the Wilson administration to enforce that restriction. The British were suspicious of financial houses with German roots and were concerned that American firms such as Kuhn, Loeb and Goldman Sachs would lend to Berlin and Vienna. While neutrality laws meant that the Wilson administration could not take an official stance on British demands or enforce them, McAdoo nonetheless communicated to the banking community the concerns the British government had expressed to him. The fact that Brown Brothers was about as Anglophile as one could get, with the affiliation between the New York house and Brown

Shipley still intact and with Montagu Norman moving ever more into the epicenter of British financial policy, meant that the war was an unexpected boon for the firm and helps further explain why James was selected for that December trip to London.[8]

It wasn't just London that needed help; the French were in a serious financial bind by early 1915. The war had settled into lethal trench warfare along the France-Belgium border, and millions of Frenchmen were dead or wounded. Paris had never been as central as London to the global financial system. By 1915, the French government and its bankers could not meet their financial needs no matter how creative they might have been, and they were not known for their creativity. Long past were the days when the demands of the French army could be filled by a handful of private bankers such as the Rothschilds. Instead, the French turned to what had been the largely untapped American market for cash and credit, and in 1915 Brown Brothers took the lead in conjunction with the French banking house Crédit Lyonnais and with the legal assistance of the law firm Sullivan & Cromwell to cobble together the financing for a major French loan of $20 million. Much like the later World War II Lend-Lease program, the loan enabled the French government to buy food and munitions without having to sell an equivalent amount of goods to the American market in order to pay for those. It was not a huge amount, but it marked the first trickle of what would soon become a flood of American credit to finance France and England. By 1916, those loans would be in the hundreds of millions of dollars each, with all major banking houses participating.[9]

By 1916, the United States was inching closer to entering the war. American sentiment was still largely against becoming an active participant in what had become a bloody stalemate, but large segments of the population demanded that the United States be more prepared for hostilities. Wilson ran his reelection campaign on a continued promise of neutrality, with the slogan "He Kept Us Out of the War" invoked repeatedly as a reason to vote for him and the Democrats. But Wilson also supported more spending on preparedness to modernize and expand the modest American military so that it could be ready to be deployed abroad. American banks and financiers were by then deeply engaged in lending money to the Europeans, with most going to Britain and France. Now they had to meet the needs of the American government as well, which had to borrow in order to fulfill the requirements of military preparedness at home. That meant issuing more debt not backed by gold, which was not unusual in wartime but sat uneasily with conservative bankers uncomfortable with the exposure. The multiplicity of funding needs also demanded that banks work closely with one another, both within their respective countries and across national borders. Banks had always been clients of other banks, and national banks had come to one another's aid before in specific moments of duress. During the collapse of the storied Baring Brothers firm in London in 1890, for instance, the Bank of France provided some emergency funds to English banks, but those episodes were one-off events. World War I necessitated ongoing open-ended commitments, across borders, in different currencies, with no one governing body, and only the constant communications between bankers and relevant officials in each country keeping the dance going.[10] Brown Brothers was deeply involved.

In 1916, James Brown was part of another consortium formed for a substantial loan to France. Its reserves exhausted, the French government proposed using its national railway lines as collateral. James wrote to his partners wondering if that was wise, given that it was inevitable if France managed to win the war that it would need far larger loans to rebuild and would have expended vital collateral. It was a valid point, but neither James nor anyone else had a viable alternative. He also wondered whether Wall Street bankers should support the plans of the U.S. government to go to the American bond market to raise money that it would lend to Britain and France, which would in turn lend to their allies such as Belgium or Italy. There was no precedent for the U.S. government going into debt to make loans to their onetime creditors in Europe so that those in turn could make loans to support the Allied war effort. But that is how substantially the financial and political status quo had been upended.[11]

In the later years of the twentieth century, international banking institutions would be created, first the Bank for International Settlements (BIS) in the 1930s and then the multifaceted post–World War II edifice of the World Bank, the International Monetary Fund (IMF), the General Agreement on Tariffs and Trade along with the Bretton Woods system. The partners of Brown Brothers Harriman would be central in those efforts, seeing them as integral to peace and stability and to the role of the United States as the leader of the free world. By then they would accept as unquestioned the idea that the U.S. government would be the economic backstop for the world, starting with the allies of Western Europe but by no means ending there. It took the experience of World War I to alter how the United States viewed itself. While U.S. GDP was almost certainly the largest in the world in 1914, there were as yet no actual statistics showing that, and Americans still saw themselves as junior to Europe. The wartime experience of shifting from being a nation that looked abroad for capital to being a country that provided the capital was transformative for Americans such as James and Thatcher Brown. They suddenly found themselves as the prime source of funds, not just to small countries such as Nicaragua, Cuba and Honduras, but to the wealthiest and most powerful countries of Europe. In retrospect, the transition from Wall Street firms underwriting American industry to Wall Street firms in conjunction with Washington underwriting the world looked smooth and seamless, but at the time, it struck bankers and government officials as odd and unsettling that they might use the American bond market to lend money to the British treasury so that the British government might lend money to some other government or that the French state should sign over its interest in its national railroads as collateral for a loan. It was one thing culturally and historically to have the president of Nicaragua implore you for capital, but something else when it was the chancellor of the exchequer of the British Empire coming to you cap in hand.

The fact that American finance became so central to the Allied war effort did not sit well with opponents of U.S. involvement in a European war. Later conspiracy theories would see the burgeoning financial connections as part of a Wilsonian plot to maneuver the United States into the conflict so that Wall Street and industrialists could reap a windfall. The commercial bonds cemented by Wall Street supplying capital and American businesses supplying goods were a powerful factor tilting the United States to support the Allies. The fact that Germany was willing to provoke war with the United States in the spring of 1917 by unleashing unrestricted submarine warfare itself demonstrates how vital American capital and commerce were to the Allied war effort. Listening to Wilson's call for a congressional declaration of war, Senator George Norris of Nebraska, heir to the tradition of William Jennings Bryan (who himself resigned from Wilson's cabinet in protest), condemned the move, saying, "We are going into war on the command of gold."[12]

The experience of World War I was a first taste for Americans of a world where they were at the center and no longer an adjunct to Europe. Welcomed as heroes in France when they arrived at the very end of 1917, the American doughboys fought and died, but the price Americans paid was small relative to what their Allies and the Central Powers had lost. The United States itself was untouched physically, and it thrived economically as the conflict had raged. At the end of the war, in 1918, the United States was in the strongest position it had ever been, with an economy bolstered by war mobilization and its traditional allies reeling. But the United States was not willing to assume a central global role. Wilson's determination to have the United States take active leadership of a new postwar order met stiff opposition domestically. The resulting American isolation of the 1920s did not preclude continued intervention in the Caribbean, nor did it lead to any diminution in American investments abroad. But it did mean that the United States refused to take its place at the head of the table. It was not just a matter of rejecting Wilson's crowning ambition of leading the League of Nations. Overall, Americans were simply not ready. They were not ready to participate in global governance as one of the world's premier powers, and they were not yet able to abandon the mentality of being a debtor nation and embrace their new reality as the world's creditor. That adjustment came slowly to the United States in general and to Wall Street bankers in particular. World War I was a dip in the pool. The Great Depression and then World War II proved to be the dive into the deep end.

The war did not end the preeminence of the British pound in international commerce, but it did mark the ascent of the dollar. The larger story played out in microcosm when the century-old bond between the English and American houses of Brown Brothers finally dissolved. The partnership had been salvaged in 1914, with a disgruntled and prickly Montagu Norman moving out of the Brown partnership and into the leadership of the Bank of England. But what seemed like a halt to the drifting apart proved a temporary respite. In 1917, another law posed a hurdle to how the partners on either side of the Atlantic would be taxed, the Excess Profits Tax Act passed by the U.S. Congress. The goal of the bill was to prevent wartime profiteering by imposing heavy tax penalties on companies that showed unusually high profits. That perfectly legitimate goal, however, spelled the end of the shared profit structure of Brown Shipley and Brown Brothers. Under the act, the U.S. partners could be liable for the excess profits of Brown Shipley and vice versa. In many ways, this was simply the cutting of the final thread of a relationship that had been fraying for many years.

The two partnerships agreed to separate without rancor, only sadness. Brown Shipley wrote to James, Thatcher and the handful of other New York partners in December 1917, "The ties of blood and the intimacy of private friendships, expressed as they have been by common partnerships, have always been a legitimate pride with us, and although these will remain, it is a melancholy reflection that, at the moment when your country and ours have become united in the fight for civilization, circumstances over which neither of us has control should have forced a rupture which we all must deplore." The New York partners replied, "We must express to you more fully our sincere appreciation of the manner in which you finally accepted what appeared to us to be inevitable but which proved so difficult to explain to you clearly yet concisely." The partnership formally dissolved in January 1918. The two now independent firms remained each other's agents in numerous dealings, but the separation was more than technical. Partnerships dissolve all the time, sometimes with anger and recrimination, and sometimes with barely a whisper. But like divorce and death, the end of a long relationship, where lives and fortunes have been interwoven intimately and intricately, is a passing. For the American branch, the formal severing of ties with England was long in coming but still notable when it did. It was also symbolic of the larger shift between the two countries.[13]

If the morphing power dynamic between the United States and Great Britain was one outcome of the war, another was the tempering of a cohesive, clannish American elite. That was less about actual combat, which was undeniably intense for the 2 million American troops in France by the war's end, with more than 100,000 killed and 200,000 wounded. The fighting mattered, but not as much as the experience of the United States being seen as a savior for the European nations that had been the countries of origin for the vast majority of Americans. Clichéd though it is to describe that shift as the time when the child became the parent, that was what many Americans experienced, implicitly if not consciously. For a generation of young Americans who came of age during the war, it meant a radically new sense of the relationship between America and the world, and between America and the Old World especially. Having been treated as heroes in London and Paris, young Americans began to consider a world led not by Europe and perhaps by no one, a world where the United States would carve its own unique path, whether that meant neutrality and disengagement or something else. And among the young men who were formed by the war was a generation of Brown Brothers partners who would catapult the firm not only to the center of Wall Street but to the epicenter of a global system that they themselves designed.

Alexander Brown and his sons, George, John, William and James

The famous, though small, first B&O Railroad engine and car

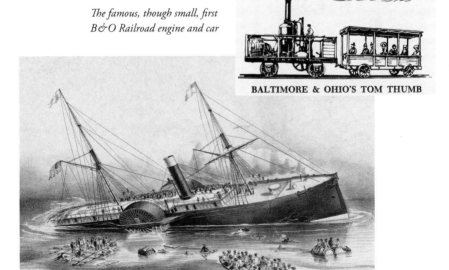

The wreck of the SS Arctic, 1854

The Brown family (James and Eliza), painting by Eastman Johnson

A portrait of William Brown as a member of Parliament, 1858

John Crosby Brown in his later years

A STUDY OF HARRIMAN,
Master of Railroads,
AND HIS METHODS OF WORK

The New York Times *studies E. H. Harriman, August 1, 1909*

Theodore Roosevelt and William Jennings Bryan cartoon "The Puzzled Chicks,"
from Puck, *June 19, 1907*

The Skull and Bones "Tomb" at Yale

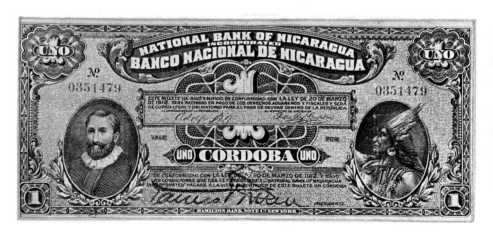

The 1912 Nicaraguan currency signed by James Brown

A spry Thatcher Brown

BIG BANKING HOUSES DECIDE ON MERGER

Brown Brothers & Co., W. A. Harriman & Co. and Harriman Brothers & Co. to Unite.

BUSINESS IS INTERNATIONAL

To Be Brown Brothers, Harriman & Co.—All but One of Old Partners Continue.

Announcement was made last night of the consolidation of Brown Brothers & Co., W. A. Harriman & Co., Inc., and Harriman Brothers & Co., effective on Jan. 1. These are all international banking houses with connections extending throughout the United States and several foreign countries. The new organization will be known as Brown Brothers, Harriman & Co.

The announcement was made last night by the banking groups involved. The combination will bring together three of the most important financial organizations in Wall Street, and under the arrangement that has been agreed upon the Harriman and Brown interests will continue to operate in their respective fields.

The announcement set out that the fusion of interests in the special type of service which private financial houses render will effect a combination of resources and facilities with growing requirements of modern business. Brown Brothers & Co. have been engaged in the private international banking field for nearly 100 years, while the Harriman firm was among the first to see the opportunities in this field following the World

Continued on Page Six.

The New York Times front-page story, December 12, 1930

Robert Lovett Time *magazine cover, March 29, 1948*

UNDER SECRETARY OF STATE LOVETT
First the world, then the cobwebs.

Prescott Bush as senator

The 1930s ad campaign

Averell Harriman (right) with Churchill and Stalin in Moscow, 1942

Averell (left) and Roland Harriman at home

Brown Brothers Harriman partners in their office, 1945

Brown Brothers Harriman front entrance, 59 Wall Street

CHAPTER 10

THE TAPPED

I t happened every May, on a midmonth Thursday. The juniors of the college had been talking about it for months, anticipating what might happen, wondering if they would be included and anointed, or left out and humiliated. The ceremony had originally been private, done in the shadow of night, with rumors of who was picked and who was not only gradually trickling out later. But in the 1870s, the juniors had had enough of waiting nervously in their rooms; instead they grumpily marched out to the Old Campus to wait together. So began the public spectacle of Tap Day that had grown by the turn of the twentieth century to involve hundreds of students and onlookers crowding the streets and cramming the windows of adjacent buildings, covered by major newspapers with the same gossipy passion of the Ivy League football games that had come to define the clubby group of Northeast colleges that trained—if not schooled—the young men who would, it was assumed, lead the United States. And of those exclusive schools, Yale in those years was the most exclusive of all.

The ceremony itself was simple enough, albeit agonizing for the juniors assembled. All college juniors gathered under a stately oak tree near the Victorian Battell Chapel, waiting till just before the clock struck five, when a small group of derby-wearing seniors, blue suited with the gold pin of membership shining in their lapels, began to weave in and out of the crowd.

Quickly, briskly, they would tap a select few and utter one simple command: "Go to your room." The ones chosen would scatter, while the others were left to face the rest of the year still part of the select but not eligible for the inner sanctums. Even in elite circles, there are rooms within rooms.

Three "secret" societies, none particularly secret, and called at Yale "senior societies," would choose on that May day fifteen juniors apiece, for membership in Skull and Bones, Scroll and Key, or Wolf's Head, or any of the other clubs. In the case of Skull and Bones, the most coveted, that meant a place in the Tomb, the society's neogothic clubhouse, fitting for a group whose alternate name was the Brotherhood of Death. The first decades of the tap ceremony had been a Yale-only affair, but with the rise of American wealth and power, fascination with the lives of the elite grew. Tap Day became a regular feature of *The New York Times* and other major papers, with reporters keeping a running ledger of who was picked and publishing their names the next day along with colorful commentary.[1]

Being tapped was the peak of a Yale student's career. It was admittance to the ultimate club, more selective than any club that these men would later join. Once in, they would be embraced by a tight group bound by honor and privacy, where they could all drop the pretense of who they were supposed to be and be as they were. They could, safely, confide their feelings, hopes, dreams, fears, knowing that whatever they said would be guarded and never revealed beyond their fraternity. That made the external hoopla all the more striking in contrast. Being a member of a senior society meant the freedom to be yourself; being selected was the ultimate public demonstration of who you were supposed to be.

Just after five p.m. on May 12, 1912, one of the last men tapped for Skull and Bones was the lanky, handsome and reserved W. Averell Harriman, Edward's oldest son and already a campus celebrity because of his father's fortune, which had now passed to him, his mother and his brother. The senior societies amped up the drama of the day, leaving some of the more famous candidates to the last, making them and the galleries wonder whether they would be spurned. But Harriman was not left out; he would never be left out. A senior Bonesman approached him, tapped him and snapped, "Averell Harriman! Go to your room." A cheer went up from the crowd, "Harriman goes to Bones!" In the phlegmatic fashion that would become his hallmark, earning him the nickname "the Crocodile," Harriman wrote to his mother informing her of the news, "It must be a marvelous institution for these men to take it as seriously and to make as much of it as they do." In later years, he confessed that it meant more to him than he let on. "It gave me a purpose. . . . To get into Bones, you had to do something for Yale." Harriman, downplaying the significance yet acknowledging the accomplishment as a product not of birth but effort, would have done his father proud. Edward Harriman never ceased emphasizing work over status, service over money. And like his father, Averell never lacked for ambition. Said his longtime partner Robert Lovett, "He was the fellow who liked to make the goal." That didn't make him the easiest man, but it helps explain his trajectory. It was also in contrast to his younger brother, Roland, who was more genial and charming but as unquestionably adept. Four years later, Roland would be tapped as well, to the surprise of no one.[2]

Averell would later look back at that day as an apex, and that from a man who would soar quite high. He had gained entrée into the preeminent club for his class based on who he was. He had not, or at least he did not think he had, bought his way in. He was not admitted because his father had pulled strings. Yet he was also blissfully unaware of the currents then swirling around him. At the very moment of his initiation, the senior societies and their rituals were coming under fire. The public spectacle of who was in and who was out grated on much of the student body at Yale and had led to charges that the societies created hierarchies that undermined the values and mission of the college to educate all young men of the college equally. The case against the societies was encapsulated in a novel, *Stover at Yale,* published in 1912, whose protagonist goes through agonies as he prepares for the fateful day, not knowing if he will be among the select or the left out: "When a boy comes here to Yale . . . and gets the flummery in his system, believes in it—surrenders to it—so that he trembles in the shadow of a tomblike building, doesn't dare look at a pin that stares him in the face . . . when he's got to the point that he's scared to think, and no amount of college life is going to revive him. That's the worst thing about it all, this mental subjugation which the average man undergoes when he comes up against all this rigmarole of Tap Day." The book was written with a purpose in mind, and it exceeded its expectations. It sold briskly and hit a nerve. One Yale graduate claimed that the book was to elite college education what *Uncle Tom's Cabin* was to slavery.

Notwithstanding the irony of a group of mostly privileged students objecting that some among them were more privileged than others, the commotion over the Yale societies was echoed at other elite institutions. At Princeton, Woodrow Wilson (who had been the school's president before going on to become New Jersey governor and then president of the United States) had tried but failed to reform the dining clubs, and similar moves were afoot at Harvard (which had a more scholarly reputation). The Yale societies ultimately were not abolished, and indeed were barely changed, but the tension they generated was a harbinger of a much greater revolt against the elites that would happen decades later, in the heat of the 1960s, against a world that had been crafted by the generation tapped in the years just before World War I.

These controversies barely dented Harriman's consciousness, any more than a French aristocrat of the ancien régime might have noticed the privation on the other side of the carriage curtains. John Crosby Brown had lived through years of labor revolts and rising class tensions as if those were distant echoes of faraway struggles, and though Averell's father had worked his way up from a clerk to a titan, Averell, like John Crosby, was to the manor born. The reformist impulses of the Progressive Era along with egalitarian demands of the populists had led to myriad new laws at both the state and federal level, and yet had impinged on the growth of a robust and self-confident upper class hardly at all. In fact, that class had only deepened its sense of rightful place at the top of a social and economic hierarchy, a place cemented not by the titles and lands of Old World nobility but by an ingrained belief in the responsibility of those with money and hence power to serve and to lead. In that sense, at least, they were distinct from the aristocrats of Europe. The new American aristocracy of money had no discomfort with inequality, but they understood that only in a country where everyone could prosper would they prosper.

It may have been because the Harriman brothers had been taught from a young age not to make a show of their wealth; it may have been that their father constantly drummed into them the mantras that "great wealth is an obligation and responsibility" and that "money must work for the country"; and it may have been that neither the brothers nor their peers in the inner sanctums of the inner sanctums gave any public indication that they were aware of the vast gulf between their lives and the lives of so many others.[3] But in their bubble they had imbibed a worldview of money, power and service that by the early twentieth century had evolved into a governing creed. Alexander Brown would have at once recognized the sensibility and yet been surprised by how deeply it had seeped into the bones of not just the Bonesmen but of an entire class that now numbered in the many thousands.

Nowhere was the new elite more explicitly identified and its values explicated than at the Groton School for boys on the outskirts of Boston. Founded in 1884 by Endicott Peabody, it was not the first school in the United States modeled on English public schools (that field was already crowded with the likes of Lawrenceville Academy, St. George's in Rhode Island, Milton and Philips Academy Andover outside of Boston, to name only a few), but it may have been the most important in the late nineteenth and early twentieth centuries. Peabody was barely out of his twenties when he created Groton, but he was well connected, his father having been a partner of Junius Morgan's in London and Endicott himself having experienced English education firsthand. Groton, along with those other private boarding schools of the Northeast, became the incubator of a new overclass, seeped in a stew of Protestantism, duty, honor, work and responsibility. The school motto said it all, *Cui servire est regnare*, "To serve is to rule."

Sports were a key component, just as they were at equivalent English schools at the time. Athletics reinforced a social order maintained not just by the headmaster and teachers but by the older boys training and hazing the younger. Peabody once said that given a choice between sports and academics, he would chose sports. "I'm not sure I like boys who think too much. A lot of people think a lot of things we could do without." It seemed unlikely that the generation of young Americans at the end of the nineteenth and into the early twentieth century was going to be hardened by war; the United States barely maintained a military after the end of the Indian Wars in the 1880s, though it did begin to build a naval fleet. But if they weren't going to be made men by war, then a combination of sports and the cruelty of upperclassmen might season them. The Groton schedule was rigid and regimented. Peabody admired the ancient Spartans, and the school was short on creature comforts. Whatever Peabody was selling, the upper class was buying. In a few decades after it opened its doors, Groton trained not just the Harrimans, but most of the Roosevelt clan, including Franklin Delano and two of Theodore's sons.[4]

The education was grounded in the classics, with an emphasis on the rote learning of Greek and Latin, along with history, philosophy and Christian theology funneled through an Episcopal lens. Imbibing the wisdom of the ancients was more important than questioning its precepts. Students could probe and analyze, but challenging the basic fundamentals was no more welcome than questioning the divinity of Christ would have been in chapel. Everyone attended chapel daily, along with Sunday services and a mandatory "sacred studies" course in the first year. Groton's moral framework of honor, duty, work was a distillation of the Western tradition, though not the only one available. Peabody could have emphasized love, compassion and humility in the face of the unknown splendor of God's creation, but that was not his bent. In that, he was certainly more severe than the Browns, James and John Crosby especially, whose private faith was altogether gentler and more compassionate.

We will never solve the chicken-and-egg question of whether the curriculum and mores of these preparatory schools and colleges such as Yale shaped this class, or whether this class shaped them. Alexander Brown hadn't attended these schools, yet his messages to his sons were indistinguishable from much of what Groton inculcated. The same could be said of E. H. Harriman's autodidactic philosophy. A dash of Brown, a pinch of

Harriman plus a liberal heaping of Plato and Cicero and Seneca and Aquinas were the core ingredients. It's often been said that these schools molded the ethos of the new American elite, but it's equally true that the ethos of their parents and grandparents molded these schools.

Groton was the prelude to the Big Three—Harvard, Yale and Princeton. Each had been around for more than two hundred years, and Harvard was approaching its third century. Their early roots, like those of all colleges, grew out of the church. But they changed dramatically in the late nineteenth century, increasing not just the size of their student bodies but also the scope of their influence and the nature of their curricula. By the end of the century, 65 percent of New York's upper class sent their sons to one of three, and nearly three-quarters of Boston's upper crust did the same. While only a very few Americans attended college at the turn of the twentieth century (only fifteen thousand bachelor's degrees were awarded in 1890), one component of the reform movements sweeping the country was an emphasis on education. That ranged from more formal and rigorous curricula to the move toward universal public education for grade school and then high school. The Big Three were swept up in these shifts. More students clamored for admission, though those numbers pale in comparison with the early twenty-first century. In a world where more people were entering colleges and universities, one way the Big Three maintained their preeminence was by emphasizing who went there—and who was not admitted—more than on what was taught in the classroom.

Yale especially cultivated an aura of selectivity, and Tap Day was the pinnacle. As the education became more secular, the school focused ever more on its mystique. As Harvard professor George Santayana put it in his disquisition on higher education at the time, "Nothing could be more American—not to say *Amurrcan*—than Yale College. The place is sacred to the national ideal. Here is sound, healthy principle, but no overscrupulousness, love of life, trust in success, a ready jocoseness, a democratic amiability, and a radiant conviction that there is nothing better than one's self. It is a boyish type of character, earnest and quick in things practical, hasty and frivolous in things intellectual. But the boyish ideal is a healthy one, and in a young man, as in a young nation, it is perfection to have only the faults of youth."[5]

There was a curriculum, of course, and the Yale faculty and administrators took it seriously. At the turn of the century, a recently tenured economics professor named Irving Fisher issued a report warning about a severe decline in academic standards. Fisher, who would later become famous for his work on inflation and economic theory and infamous for stating that the stock market had reached a permanently high plateau on the eve of the crash in October 1929, was acutely aware that the rise of sports and other extracurricular activities was not only competing for student mind share but winning. Yes, incoming students still had to pass a language proficiency exam in ancient Greek and Latin and continue those studies. That, however, mostly had the effect of weeding out the applicant pool and keeping it confined to the small circle of private schools such as Groton that insisted on the rote learning of those long-dead languages.

Yet those languages were the conveyor belt for the wisdom of the ancients, which self-taught men like E. H. Harriman had read themselves in translation but which their children along with generations of upper-class and aspiring schoolboys in England and America had then studied in the original. In addition, at those private schools, the boys were required to study mathematics, philosophy, American and European history, and some economics. The goal was not to produce scholars (to the dismay at times of a faculty that might have preferred that). The goal was to train the rising generation of leaders.

That was not something whispered. It was explicit and unabashed. The United States may have been a democracy, but at the turn of the century and into its first decades it was a democracy with an increasingly confident and self-conscious elite that saw itself as bound to lead and that defended its privilege and treasured a set of values that Groton and Yale, Lawrenceville and Princeton, Collegiate and Columbia, Boston Latin and Harvard nurtured and reified. Charles William Eliot, the president of Harvard in the 1890s who served as head for forty years, wrote in 1897 that his "community does not owe superior education to all children but only to the elite—to those having the capacity, proven by hard work that they also have the necessary perseverance and endurance." That elite wasn't necessarily one of birth or class; its membership was fluid, and theoretically open to those who showed by their intellect, acumen and ambition that they were worthy. But it happened that most who constituted Eliot's elite were not only rich but white, male and Christian. That did not especially trouble him or his peers. Training the rich (and not women, almost never men of other colors, and only a limited quota of Jews) was seen as a noble and needed calling, because, in Eliot's words, "the country suffers when the rich are ignorant and unrefined."[6]

The self-confidence of America's newly wealthy was evident in the next generation, those children of the captains of industry who were taught modesty but who still imbibed a sense that the first rank was their birthright. Far from shying from that, they embraced it. Theodore Roosevelt embodied the more aggressive forms of that confidence when he talked of the duty of the rich and powerful toward those who had less. Domestically, that meant helping those less able and using both charity and the levers of government to allow for more opportunity to more people. That helps explain why very wealthy people embraced aspects of the progressive movement. Internationally, Roosevelt's noblesse oblige meant a paternalism that easily morphed into the imperialism of dollar diplomacy, "a duty," as Roosevelt put it, "toward the people living in barbarism to see that they are freed from their chains, and we can destroy those chains only by destroying barbarism itself."[7] And how better than to instill that duty in the young than by sending them to colleges that saw that as their mission.

Once at these schools, the leveling factor was social and athletic, not academic. Said one Yale graduate and later faculty member, "Money counted, social standing outside counted, yet the son of a shopkeeper could get as far on athletic prowess as the gilded child of privilege on his family momentum. Good looks counted also. . . . Wit, and the gift of being amusing . . . were very helpful; and so was political sagacity."[8] The reliance on sports to help sort character and leadership wasn't a product of Yale. That had been evolving over the course of the nineteenth century, first in

England and then the United States, but it reached an apex at Yale in the years leading up to World War I. The use of athletics to determine manliness was not just a proxy for armies and war; it was also a way to socialize young men into a rules-based hierarchical system that at once demanded conformity to the group and rewarded individual achievement.

The tension between academics, social activities and sports was never resolved, and the triad was rarely in balance. In the immediate pre–World War I years, that balance had skewed too far toward the social and athletic poles, hence the warnings from faculty that Yale's academic standards were slipping and the widespread student pushback against Tap Day. In response, a few changes were made to modernize the curriculum and focus the undergraduates more on academics: the ceremony of Tap Day was made less stressful and embarrassing by de-emphasizing the public nature of it (hence why by the mid-twentieth century, the societies had become more secretive, and Tap Day was no longer a public ceremony, with the tapping instead done privately in each junior's room). But then the war interceded, and by the time some normalcy returned in 1920, some of the more pressing concerns had receded.

Roland Harriman, younger than Averell by four years, nicknamed "Bunny" either for his childhood habit of keeping pet rabbits or for a life-long habit of twitching his nose, described his Yale experience as a lesson in life. "Yale did more than give me a modicum of a good education. It gave me an interest in outside affairs and taught me how to conduct myself in a grown-up world as well as how to pick and choose men as friends and associates." And the friendships he formed at Yale would prove instrumental to the future of Brown Brothers and to the emergence of the United States as the steward of the global economic system: Prescott Bush, Knight Woolley, Ellery James and above all Robert Lovett, Yale students all in the same few years, all tapped, and all connected for life.[9] In the 1920s, twelve of the seventeen partners of Brown Brothers' and Harriman's firms had gone to Yale, and eight of those had been tapped for Skull and Bones. One group coalesced around the Harriman brothers, the younger Roland especially; another group was older but of the same ilk, Moreau Delano and Thatcher

Brown especially, all members of one of the senior societies, all later bound together in Brown Brothers Harriman. And of course there were others at Yale at the time whose lives would intersect in later years, and none more important to the rise of the United States as a global power than Dean Acheson, who would help define American foreign policy in the first years of the Cold War.

For the Browns, the imprint of Alexander Brown remained indelible, and his sensibility was reinforced by these schools. For the Harriman clan, the risk taking of Edward was leavened by the molding of Groton and Yale, smoothing the rough edges but not to the point of dullness. Above all, these young men were socialized into a class that by virtue of common experiences and similar educations blended into a coherent group with a narrow range of mores. Yes, there were differences in backgrounds and wealth, and yes, these schools were not cookie cutters, but once funneled through a few dozen boarding schools and even fewer colleges, these thousands of young men became a more defined set than America had seen in a century. Just as the tobacco planters of Virginia and the merchants of Boston had been close-knit groups sharing similar understandings of how the world was and should be, this group of privileged white Protestants emerged from these schools with a cohesive worldview that they then exported to the rest of the globe after World War II, when they assumed positions of political leadership.

The eventual merger of Brown Brothers and the Harrimans may never have happened without the relationships forged at Groton and Yale, though one of those relationships began earlier: the lifelong friendship between Robert Lovett and Roland Harriman. They met because of their parents, when Robert's father, Judge Lovett, became Edward's closest adviser. Edward took his children with him as he scouted the world, and one of those excursions was a 1903 trip to Texas inspecting various rail lines. As always, he traveled on his own private car, named the *Arden* after his New York estate. On one of the many inspection stops, Judge Lovett, "a very distinguished gentleman in a square derby," met the train and brought along his young son, who started exploring the car, with the seven-year-old Roland eyeing him.

E. H. Harriman was an early fitness buff. In an age before gyms on every corner, he made do with calisthenics, push-ups, sit-ups and chin-ups. He had a pull-up bar installed on the *Arden* next to his bedroom, and young Bob Lovett (barely a year older than Roland) took one look at it and jumped up. According to Roland, he did twenty-five pull-ups, and then did some flips, which impressed Roland. Unfortunately, it also impressed Harriman, who turned to his son, pointed to Lovett and said, "Roland, why can't you do that?" That didn't go over well. Roland later wrote, wryly, "It was a wonder I ever talked to the boy again." Instead, it was the beginning of a lifelong friendship and partnership that lasted nearly seventy years.

Like all selective memories, that one said volumes about each person in the story: Judge Lovett, quiet, dignified, taciturn or at least not speaking such that anyone recalled his words; E. H. Harriman, a coiled bundle of energy, physically and emotionally hard, demanding of himself and of his sons. Roland did not recall his father's words as a gentle nudge but as a challenge and an admonition: do better for yourself and do better than the other person. The other person could have been anybody, but in this case, it was Robert Abercrombie Lovett, intense, competitive, energetic and focused even as a child. And Roland, the younger son, gentler, watchful and cosseted, wanting his father's love and approval but secure in his place in his life, then and always.

Born in Huntsville, Texas, the younger Lovett lived most of his life in New York City, where his father moved in 1904 to become Harriman's chief aide and the president of the Union Pacific after Harriman's death. Lovett had a rather different memory of his first meeting with Roland. In later interviews, he described the younger Harriman as "a charming fellow . . . he was a delightful soul . . . very friendly, well-disposed toward everyone." But perhaps that was in the light of looking back after many years. Tales of Lovett's competitiveness were legion, as were his gifts as an unlicensed physician; he was forever trying to diagnose his friends' ailments, or those of anyone in his proximity.[10] He was also an amateur thespian, fond of Shakespeare in particular and always eager to act. More animated onstage than off, Lovett struck some of his college peers as aloof and arrogant and some as charming and engaged. To most, however, what made him tick was a mystery.

Lovett's life would be comingled not just with the Harrimans but with the Browns as well, long before the merger. As the senior Lovett assumed control of the Harriman empire, he moved into the center of New York society, and as such, bought a sprawling home in Locust Valley on the north shore of Long Island, later made famous, along with Manhasset and Oyster Bay, by F. Scott Fitzgerald as West Egg, the scene of Gatsby's mansion with its lavish parties and glamorous guests. These ocean enclaves were to the adults of the early 1900s what the senior societies were to the students of Yale: places where like could congregate with like, gated not by walls but by codes of privacy and shared economic status, connected by a web of clubs and dinner parties and days on the beach.

In one of those languid summers just before Bob went off to Yale, he met a girl. She was one of the three daughters of James Brown, who had his own summer place in Oyster Bay. James liked to throw tennis parties, and the spry Lovett, who played each point as if it were the match, was a regular invitee, as were Roland and the older Averell. The youngest of the Brown's daughters, Adele, took a liking to Lovett, and he to her, though he wasn't particularly adept at making his feelings known. As she later recalled, "When he kept coming over, I thought he wanted to see one of my sisters, but when he *kept* coming over, I found out that he wanted to see me all the time."

Lovett and Adele began dating. She was a frequent guest at Yale parties, including the over-the-top festivities of Junior Promenade Week, seven decadent days of prom, dancing, drinking, picnicking, and then more dancing and drinking. The week saw a bevy of young women descend on the campus, along with chaperones. The logistics were months in the planning as each family weighed the pros and cons before giving assent. The February 1917 prom included a host committee with Bob Lovett as one of its key organizing members as floor manager. The event concluded with seven hundred couples, outfitted by bespoke tailors and dressmakers, at an all-night dance.[11]

Bob and Adele eventually married in 1919. Judge Lovett gave his son a multivolume set of the writings of German philosopher Immanuel Kant as a wedding gift. His father valued the dense epistemology of an eighteenth-century thinker, and wanted his son to have not just a fit body but a sharp mind capable of nuance and critical thinking.[12] Yale was the natural choice for college, but Lovett wasn't tapped in New Haven. After that glorious prom week, in 1917, he enlisted in the navy to train as an aviator, one of two dozen Yale students who had formed the Yale Aero Club. The club was created by an upperclassman named Trubee Davison (son of Henry Davison, a J.P. Morgan partner), who had served a stint as a volunteer ambulance driver in the summer of 1915 in France and witnessed the birth of aerial war. He came back with a passion for flying and a suspicion that the United States would soon find itself at war. Lovett jumped at the opportunity to fly, and at the prospect of being part of something great. The Yale Aero Club was an extraordinary initiative by a group of young men barely out of their teens, animated by fun and by a desire to serve the country. Trubee Davison later became assistant secretary of war under Coolidge and Hoover, the same position Lovett would eventually hold under FDR. Davison then left government to become president of the American Museum of Natural History, whose board Roland would later chair.

When Wilson asked Congress for a declaration of war in April 1917, the Yale club was converted into the First Yale Unit, and its members were commissioned as junior officers and sent to West Palm Beach to begin training. The secretary of the navy praised the young men for their willingness to sacrifice. Flying, however, was not an option for just anyone. Separate from aptitude and courage, it was hideously expensive. The Yalies were dubbed "the Millionaire's Unit." But they were widely admired and envied by their classmates. In honor of their service, an upperclassman traveled down to Florida one day in early May 1917 and tapped Lovett for the Bonesmen. Sent to the front in France in 1918, they retained many of the benefits of their special status. Knowing of his fondness for nice clothes, Lovett's mother gave him a tailored suit of long underwear made of Angora wool to withstand the frigid air in flight, and he then had thirty uniforms made in New York along with a special trunk (to keep them pressed and dry), which followed the unit into battle.[13]

The young flyboys were attracted by the adventure and the adrenaline, but it was only thirteen years since the Wright Brothers and their first successful flight at Kitty Hawk. Flying was exciting in theory, but it was frequently fatal. With aviation strategy being invented and refined as the war in Europe dragged on, the reality of air war was far grimmer than the giddy dreams of the Yale men. Almost all the aircraft were biplanes—with two stacks of wood and canvas wings; these couldn't withstand many bullets and were easily damaged. The average pilot in Europe at the time lasted three weeks before being shot down. The sole reason the Yale unit was spared more fatalities was that they only saw combat at the end of the war in the summer of 1918. Even then, two of them were shot down, one captured and one dead. Lovett was forever shaped by the experience.

Graduating from Yale in absentia, Lovett returned to the United States at the end of 1918 to marry Adele. He enrolled at Harvard Law School but decided that he had neither the patience nor the calling to be a lawyer. Instead, his father-in-law, James Brown, arranged for him to get a job at a bank, as a prelude to a job at Brown Brothers, which followed soon after. With no sons, James looked to his son-in-law to carry on his line at the firm. Lovett not only obliged but took to the role with the same focus he had displayed for much of his young life. By the time he was in his midtwenties, he had already exemplified that blend of wealth and duty, discipline and commitment that Groton and Yale and the Bonesmen so valued. He had taken his gifts and advantages, used them for the greater good of his classmen and country, married well and worked hard.

Meanwhile, at the end of 1918, Woodrow Wilson had entered Paris as a conquering hero, and he accepted the accolades as his due. He had a grand vision of a postwar world cemented by a League of Nations, governed by the most powerful nations but open to all, a forum to resolve conflicts between countries before they became lethal, a process for emerging nations to join the international community, and a system of collective security that would end the vicious cycle of wars that had plagued mankind. Most of that was embraced and codified at the Paris Peace Conference, but Wilson had not fully reckoned with the strength of the resistance in the United States. He was asking Americans to break with the long tradition of standing apart and steering clear of entangling alliances. Wilson's treaty for the League faced opposition in the U.S. Senate, and rather than agreeing to amend it, Wilson demanded all or nothing. Nothing is what he got. The United States did not join the League that he had crafted, and Wilson was personally devastated. His political defeat did not, however, mean an American economic retreat. The war opened a new era for American investment abroad, beyond the Caribbean and the Western Hemisphere. The wartime experience of Brown Brothers and numerous other financial firms whetted their appetites for more, and the 1920s saw Americans extend their financial range beyond Europe and into Soviet Russia and East Asia and the Middle East.

As that Groton and Yale generation entered their young adulthood, they were uniquely poised to build on the foundation that money had built in the nineteenth century. A United States brimming with affluence, overflowing with capital and graced with a nimble financial system capped by the new Federal Reserve, had a phalanx of young men with a deep sense of duty and an equally deep sense that they were bound to lead. They had been schooled with the values of humility, but their innate elitism also instilled an arrogance, a belief that they could and should shape the world, for its betterment. They were born into a secure cocoon of privilege with a clear value system and an innate conviction that they knew what other peoples and other societies did not. For them, there was Europe and America on one side of the civilizational ledger; on the other were the Nicaraguas of the world. And unlike the elites of Europe, they believed it was their duty to improve life for everyone and not in their interest to rule anyone, at least not directly.

After a brief and painful postwar economic downturn in 1919, Brown Brothers thrived, and so did the new banking business created by Averell Harriman with his younger brother, Roland, along with a coterie of their Yale classmates. Harriman used his inheritance to launch an investment firm. He was initially seen for what he was: an inexperienced young man with a fortune surrounded by equally inexperienced friends and family. Compared with Brown Brothers, Harriman & Co. was an upstart, but one that had to be taken seriously if only for the wealth at its disposal. In contrast, the partners' room at Brown Brothers headquarters at 59 Wall Street, with its roll-up desks and tea service, was notable for its Anglophilic quaintness and its attachment to tradition. As 1920 dawned, it was led by the steady, dapper James Brown, now fifty-seven years old, and by his cousin Thatcher Brown, now no longer so junior at forty-four, who had become in middle age a study in mannered gentility, as much the steward of reputation and rectitude as his father, John Crosby, his grandfather James and his great-grandfather Alexander.

The first bout of American internationalism ended with a totem of Brown Brothers accompanying Woodrow Wilson to the Paris Peace Conference: a traveler's letter of credit. To cover his expenses, Wilson carried with him in January 1919 a $10,000 Brown Brothers letter, which he knew, as anyone in those years knew, would be honored abroad as surely as any paper money or gold. By then American Express and its traveler's check were gaining market share, but Brown Brothers letters of credit carried more cachet, had higher limits and were accepted everywhere. You couldn't just go to Brown Brothers in New York, or to Brown Shipley in London, and get one; the partners had to approve of you. Much like membership in one of New York's elite clubs, possessing a Brown Brothers letter was its own form of social validation in addition to being a valued form of money.[14]

Wilson was not much interested in material things. His greed was for remaking the world, not buying fancy clothes or expensive baubles. At the end of his time in Paris, he had used barely half of the $10,000, and he returned to the United States loaded with promises to end war but light on luggage. His proposed League of Nations, grounded on the Fourteen Points he had enunciated in January 1918 that enshrined the sovereignty of states, delegitimized war and established the idea that nations would act collectively to guarantee peace and security, held its first meeting in 1920 with the United States conspicuously not a member. Wilson—incapacitated by a stroke, president in name but hardly able to speak—could only watch silently as his dream was simultaneously realized and crushed.

But for Wall Street and American business, there was no retreat from the world. The United States had made a permanent shift from being a debtor to a creditor, a lender rather than a borrower. As American finance extended its tendrils to more parts of the globe, the Harrimans and their new firm were particularly aggressive, but so were most of the houses of Wall Street, old and new, Brown Brothers included. The Groton and Yale set had been prepped for service and unsentimental competition. They were tempered by the war but not scarred by it. The conflict had given them a taste for internationalism, even as it had dampened it for the country at large. As the roaring twenties began, America found itself apart and powerful, while the new elite looked to a wealth of opportunity that their parents and grandparents could only have imagined.

CHAPTER 11

THE BUSINESS
OF AMERICA

Woodrow Wilson may have been an ambitious idealist who wanted to remake the world, but he also was an American nationalist who saw his country as on the rise. During his brief moment as the belle of the Paris peace ball, he attempted to craft a treaty and a League that would simultaneously serve America and serve the globe. In one of his many, ultimately doomed, attempts to convince the American people that their future was linked to the world beyond, he argued that America's "industrial fortunes are tied up with the industrial fortunes of the rest of the world." Given that, "America minding her own business and having no other" made no sense, not just to the financiers and the elite, but to any manufacturer or importer or merchant, indeed any American engaged in business. "I am looking after the industrial interests of the United States," Wilson promised, urging his countrymen to support his plan.[1] They did not.

But while the Senate did not ratify the League of Nations, Wilson's internationalism was not safely tucked away. A crop of America's youth had tasted what it was like to be immersed in the wider world, and there was no going back. The 1920s are often portrayed as a fantasy moment of wild prosperity as the United States turned inward even as the world began to descend into financial chaos and political darkness. It's an appealing narrative—a United States consumed with its own affairs as the rest of the world spins off its axis. It is not, however, a particularly accurate one.

All was not immediately smooth sailing. The United States did experience a brief, sharp and expected postwar recession. Rarely do nations end wars without an economic bubble popping after years of hypercharged production often accompanied by price controls, explicit or implicit. The end of the war saw both economic contraction and rising prices in the United States. The country, and much of the world, also had to contend with the deadly "Spanish" flu pandemic that erupted in the spring of 1918 and then intensified again in the fall. By the time the flu had burned itself out in 1919, nearly three quarters of a million Americans had died out of a population of just over 100 million people. Tens of millions more perished globally, on top of the tens of millions who had been killed during the Great War.

Unlike the war, the flu pandemic struck the United States at home, and, given its ferocity, it is startling how quickly America rebounded. After 1921, the American economy grew and grew, though in an age before the creation of the GDP and the measurement of it, it is challenging to say with certainty by precisely how much. Most later estimates put the rate at close to 5 percent a year, which is even more impressive considering that inflation was tame. For the first time, more Americans lived in cities than on farms or in the country, and that in turn sparked a revolution in consumer goods. "A change has come over our democracy," wrote one observer. "It is called consumption-ism."[2] From there, it was only a small step toward consumerism. Fewer and fewer Americans made their own things. Most now bought what they needed. Real wages for workers and even for beleaguered farmers also increased, as did economic inequality. Stocks surged, and more people began trading, though stock ownership remained confined to a fraction of the population.

The idea of fortress America was more fiction than fact. If anything, the efflorescence of the United States economically in the 1920s went hand in hand with more economic engagement with the world at large. With its new status as a creditor, the United States in the twenties was a prime source of capital for the rest of the world after the war, and that placed Wall Street and American banks in a plum position. Capital accumulation became a national sport. Having helped steward a domestic empire of money, Brown Brothers and their cohort went global. Their attitudes toward money and finance also went national. The lure of capital and the idea of saving money and building up assets became more widespread throughout the middle class. The push for mom-and-pop ownership of wartime government bonds certainly played a role, as did the booming stock market after 1921, which most didn't participate in but which still spurred a greater public awareness of saving money in its more abstract forms—paper money, bonds, stocks—rather than storing away value in homes and gold and things. Thomas Nixon Carver, a Harvard professor of economics in the 1920s whose work enjoyed a broad readership, argued that the next leg up for society would come when workers started using their wages to buy shares so that they could benefit directly from the profitability of the companies they worked for. That argument was not without controversy in those years, but it pre-saged a new turn in the way Americans overall viewed capital and labor.[3]

"Everybody I knew was in the bond business, so I supposed it could support one more single man." So announced the fictional Nick Carraway in the novel of its day, F. Scott Fitzgerald's *The Great Gatsby*. The business wasn't really for him; he found himself bored to sleep by the stock ticker and could hardly even feign interest, preferring instead the seductive company of Gatsby. But the idea of Wall Street as a clubby place that was none-theless open to an ever-expanding coterie of young men making their way in the world, seeking fortune and the good life, was woven into the 1920s gestalt along with the speakeasies that flourished in the shadow of Prohibi-tion, the flappers who were the icons of the free-wheeling age, the sudden emergence of women as a political force armed with the vote, and the un-smiling countenance of President Calvin Coolidge hovering above it all.

Though it was the affable, go-along-to-get-along Warren Harding who succeeded Woodrow Wilson, it was Coolidge who stamped the 1920s with his peculiar blend of Yankee primness, free-market mantras and moralisms. Although he was a popular figure, Harding had detested being president and felt overwhelmed. "I knew this job would be too much for me," he told one friend, and in 1923, he became the third president to die in office from natural causes. Coolidge appeared unfazed by the sudden turn of events. Never one to waste words, he was known as Silent Cal, and so sour did he often seem that he was famously derided as having been "weaned on a pickle" (a quip attributed to Theodore Roosevelt's famously quippy daughter Alice). Coolidge saw his reputation fall and then rise in later years, especially because of his innate affinity for the way that government and business could intersect for the greater good of society. Coolidge set the tone for an America in the corporatist mold, where business was good for America and America was good for business and the role of government was to ensure that the economic engine kept humming and to adjudicate when interests conflicted.

While Coolidge never quite said that "the business of America is business," he did say in a 1925 speech that "the chief business of the American people is business." That has usually been taken as the sum total of his philosophy, but it was a good bit more considered than that. He elaborated in that speech that Americans "are profoundly concerned with producing, buying, selling, investing and prospering in the world. I am strongly of the opinion that the great majority of people will always find these the moving impulses of our life." That was not, however, the end of the story. Channeling Alexander Brown, he continued, "Of course, the accumulation of wealth cannot be justified as the chief end of existence. . . . As long as wealth is made the means and not the end, we need not greatly fear it. . . . But it calls for additional effort to avoid even the appearance of the evil of selfishness."

And in his conviction that America was a nation devoted to making the world better, Coolidge was not so far from Wilson. The goal, he believed, was to balance personal desire for gain with the needs of society at large, which could entail self-sacrifice and which always demanded some compromise of individual ambition and desire. "It is only those who do not understand our people who believe our national life is entirely absorbed by material motives. We make no concealment of the fact that we want wealth, but there are many other things we want much more. We want peace and honor, and that charity which is so strong an element of all civilization. The chief ideal of the American people is idealism. I cannot repeat too often that America is a nation of idealists."[4]

That mélange of idealism and avarice, of financial internationalism and political isolationism, of duty to country and enrichment of self, hard work and the greater good alongside languid summer days on yachts defined the financial class that was at once lionized and scorned not just by the fictional Nick Carraway but by the culture at large. As the war and the fervor of the final years of the Wilson administration faded, the early twenties gave way to the normalcy of Harding and then Coolidge. That normalcy didn't preclude corruption and scandal under Harding and his ill-enriched cronies, didn't sidestep the harshness of Prohibition or Attorney General Mitchell Palmer's Red Raids that presaged the Cold War McCarthyism after World War II, and didn't do anything in the face of a Jim Crow South and a reborn Ku Klux Klan that enforced a system so oppressive for African Americans that they fled north in droves in the Great Migration that forever changed the demographics of the cities of the Northeast and the Midwest. The Red Raids of November 1919 and January 1920 were extensive, with thousands rounded up on suspicion of communist and revolutionary intent using evidence that today would be considered flimsy at best; many of those arrested were brutally beaten in custody, and aliens caught in the dragnet were summarily deported. The red fever broke quickly, but its outbreak tells us that it was an age where violence, state sanctioned, could still flare with breathtaking intensity. Still, the postwar years ushered in a "normalcy" of economic calm and increasing affluence, as the modern megacorporation came into being and the locus of economic dynamism moved into cities and their peripheries while farmers mounted a doomed rearguard action to preserve their way of life.

It was also an America of America First. The phrase had actually been used by Wilson's 1916 presidential campaign, when he ran on a slogan of having kept the United States out of the war and thus placed "America First." Harding's campaign promised to exalt "Americanism" with the bedrock principles of America First and pride in a "selfish nationalism." That was not just an expression of pride in America but also a dog whistle for a white American nationalism that was isolationist, segregationist and anti-immigrant and would culminate in one of the most exclusionary laws in American history, the Immigration Act of 1924, which vastly curtailed legal immigration to the United States for decades. While Harding genuflected in the direction of American economic engagement with the world, his campaign and his short presidency marked a retreat from the hyperinternationalism of Wilson's second term.[5]

Yet Harding's skepticism about internationalism was only one note in a more cacophonous chorus. Brown Brothers and the Harrimans saw opportunity abroad, and they ventured even more into the world. While their economic ambitions abroad were in direct contrast to the political isolationism of the era, American businesses met no resistance from the federal government. Yes, the Harding and then the Coolidge years saw higher tariffs, which penalized foreign imports and purportedly protected American farmers, but these leaders also presided over domestic tax cuts and welcomed foreign investment in the United States, which was in the interest of both Wall Street and burgeoning industrial companies.

Thatcher Brown had ended the war much as James Brown had begun it, with a trip to Europe in late 1918, not as part of any peace conference but to settle unsettled accounts, especially business interests in Scandinavia and France, where Brown Brothers had assembled substantial loans. Writing in November, Thatcher explained the reason for the trip: "It had been apparent for some weeks that the war was drawing to a close and it became necessary to send a partner to Europe promptly to trade and negotiate out and settle many war casualties involving the shipment of commodities to Europe." But while open business needed to be wrapped up, Thatcher wasn't in Europe to unwind the firm's foreign commitments; he was there to expand them. The French government was in immediate need of funds. The reparations soon to be levied on Germany would eventually help France reconstruct its devastated northeast, but in the interim, it was strapped. Brown Brothers was one of several American banks that could arrange and package multimillion-dollar loans, which it did not just in France but throughout Northern and Western Europe.

For the next decade, Brown Brothers would find itself constantly solicited for funds by governments of countries such as neutral Sweden, allied Canada, and former enemy Germany, all of which turned to American bankers for the liquidity and loans. Countries throughout Latin America also became even more active clients, no longer concentrated in Central America and the Caribbean but now extending all the way to the Straits of Magellan and including the governments of Chile and Argentina. There had, of course, been American businesses throughout the Southern Hemisphere in the late nineteenth century, but the pace picked up substantially after the war as British investment became scarcer. As Europe contracted, the United States and its bankers and companies expanded.

Averell Harriman, meanwhile, began to flex his own muscles. E. H. Harriman had left a fortune of nearly $100 million (the equivalent of well over $2 billion today). With the war over, Averell persuaded his mother, who still had considerable control of the family purse, to back his push into acquiring ships that were coming onto the market as war booty. He was convinced, rightly, that the end of the war would be a boon for American exports. Within a year, he had cobbled together a company that controlled dozens of vessels. The keystone was the Hamburg-American Line, which had been among the world's most significant shippers prior to the war but whose entire fleet had been confiscated at the war's end. Harriman saw the revival of the line as an opportunity, particularly because he was able to buy low with an option to sell high. The managers of the Hamburg line were in desperate need of capital from the Allied side in order to resurrect the business, and Harriman was able to provide that at a heavily discounted valuation.[6]

That entrepreneurial coup earned Harriman considerable press, though the subsequent performance of the line would disappoint. On the heels of the deal, he sat for that *Forbes* interview where he preached the gospel of giving back and the virtues of hard work, especially for those with means. "It is . . . indefensible for a man who has capital not to apply himself diligently to using it in a way that will be of most benefit to his country. . . . Idle capital or capital misapplied is as destructive economically as the conduct of the loafing workman or the bomb thrower. It is the duty of everyone, rich and poor, to work."[7] And that work, he said repeatedly, should benefit not just the self but the nation. He was singing in the same amen choir as Wilson, Coolidge and leading industrialists such as Henry Ford and Andrew Mellon (who then became Coolidge's secretary of the treasury), all of whom spoke from the same hymnal about honor, wealth, duty, each to his place, government and business working hand in hand with labor to build a better world.

After that worldwide recession in 1920–21, American businesses and finance adjusted to the new status of the United States as both a lending nation and a repository for the world's gold. The troubled economies of Western and Central Europe sought out the relative stability of America with its liquid financial markets and thriving economy. As the recession faded, the world's stock market began to rebound, and in the United States, a new era of speculation and stock ownership began, slowly at first, and then picking up pace year after wonderful year.[8] Wall Street was both a physical place and a symbol of money and power. That explains the bombing of September 16, 1920. Set off from a horse-drawn cart just as workers were streaming out of J.P. Morgan's headquarters at 23 Wall Street, just doors away from Brown Brothers at number 59 (with its new thirty-six-story extension a symbol of the firm's success), the bombs killed more than thirty people and wounded several hundred more. The target was the House of Morgan, a symbol of international finance and already a font of conspiracy theories about how a cabal of financiers was running the world, fomenting wars and then profiting from chaos. But while lethal to the people walking on Wall Street on their lunch breaks, mostly clerks and secretaries, the bombs dented business not at all. Those responsible were never found, though the violence came on the heels of the vicious Red Raids and a bout of mass hysteria that the United States was on the brink of a communist insurrection. The public reaction to the bombing, after years of war, influenza and domestic turmoil, was surprisingly muted, as it was the following year when hundreds of African Americans were killed by white mobs in Tulsa, Oklahoma. Normalcy then was not what most would consider normalcy now.

Harriman built on his shipping empire and extended his interests into the Soviet Union. As a young man in a hurry, he was drawn to high-risk enterprises, but he rarely skimped on due diligence, emulating both his father's appetites and his passion for detail. At a time when the business and political classes of the West were staying far away from the Soviet Union and its Bolshevik rulers, Harriman saw an opportunity, as did the Soviets. They were in dire need of assistance to exploit the mineral resources of the country, and Harriman offered to invest to build up various extractive industries, especially manganese mines in the Georgian Caucasus. With Moscow having consolidated power after the last of the post-1917 civil wars, the transportation infrastructure of the country was rudimentary at best. Much as Edward Harriman had set off into the West and then Alaska, Averell embraced the adventure of exploring the Soviet Union and the rest of the world, and his money followed wherever he went. His investments ranged from German cable and wire companies to Silesian mines between Poland and Germany to a wild bet on fellow Bonesman Juan Trippe and his dream of launching a commercial passenger airline. After a few rocky years, Trippe's venture blossomed into Pan American World Airways, one of the great success stories that redefined international air travel after World War II. Averell, along with Roland, also backed a visionary young newsman named Henry Luce, another graduate of Yale, and another Bonesman, slightly younger than the brothers, thirsty for a small amount of capital so that he could create *Time* magazine.

Ultimately, neither Harriman's Hamburg shipping company nor his Soviet mining gambles paid off financially. The ship line underperformed, and the manganese mines fell victim to internal Soviet politics in Moscow, losing Harriman more than $3 million.[9] By contrast, the domestic investment in *Time* paid off handsomely over the years, both in dividends and in positive press. The Harriman brothers had such a good experience with that news investment that they then put money into another fledging start-up called *Newsweek*. Remarkably, it would be Averell's foreign economic adventures that marked him the most. While they didn't pan out as hoped, they ensconced him in the international postwar world and would later be one of the cornerstones of his life as a roving diplomat and Cold War architect. Few people have ever been as connected as Harriman, and he used those connections—along with his inherited wealth—to great effect in his later career.

As he traversed Europe, Russia and the Americas in the 1920s, Averell was welcomed into every circle. In Paris, he met with the leaders of the International Chamber of Commerce, which had been created at the end of the war and which had asked Harriman to be on its board of directors. Its goals for business were similar to the political goals of the League of Nations, to create a neutral space for businesses from multiple countries to coordinate rules and also resolve issues through an agreed-upon system of arbitration. It was, in many ways, a precursor to the more robust series of institutions that would emerge at Bretton Woods toward the end of World War II, and which form the exoskeleton of multinational business today.

Harriman later recalled that the Paris dinner exposed to him what role the United States could play economically as the world's leader if it chose to:

> One evening I remember that I met with the leading bankers and industrialists of the principal countries. I remember the British and German, the French. . . . It was quite a small dinner. . . . I asked them why they thought that the United States was moving ahead as we were in the mid-twenties, you remember, whereas Europe was stagnant with built-in unemployment. They said it was because we had a continent of free trade. And I said, "Well, if that's the case, why don't you with all your influence in different countries make the changes that are necessary to get freer trade in Europe?" The answer was that unless there was a military understanding, freedom of trade

could not exist. Because there wasn't a military understanding of some kind, every country, for its own security, demanded to be as autarkic as possible. And I think one man said, "From castings to forged big guns, to buttons on the uniform."[10]

From that, and a host of other encounters, Harriman drew the lesson that military security and economic security would, in Europe at least, need to be linked. It may be, of course, that he picked that memory in later life to support what would become the American security and economic imperium post–World War II, but he was hardly the only one to draw from the 1920s a clear set of conclusions about what would be best for global economic and political security that was then used as the cornerstone of the post-1945 world order.

The observation about free trade was both true and untrue. From a European perspective, the United States was a country-as-continent, and goods flowed freely between the states. But the United States of the 1920s was hardly a bastion of free trade as that idea was understood. The theory of free trade emerged in mid-nineteenth-century Britain in the centers of industry and commerce—Manchester, Birmingham and Liverpool especially. Its most articulate proponents, John Bright and Richard Cobden (and also William Brown), advocated a world without tariff barriers and without government subsidies to industry. They were not just utopians. They had economic motives as well: the textile industries of those areas of England were the most advanced in the world, and free trade everywhere would only benefit them. But they were also driven by an idealistic drive for peace and progress, and a belief that a world with fewer barriers separating men and nations would be a world of fewer wars and greater prosperity.

Free trade was not the bedrock of American policy in the 1920s, which instead maintained high trade barriers and even more stringent immigration barriers to the outside world. And the challenges facing Europe were less about trade per se than the fact that the continent had been riven into multiple new separate countries such as Hungary, Czechoslovakia and Poland, which had been carved out of the Austria-Hungarian and German empires at the end of the war. Each new nation wanted to build its own independent domestic economy. They were trying to construct viable nations in a time of political upheaval with little domestic consensus and hobbled by weak economies that had been shattered by the war. The hurdles were immense.

Harriman's business interests in the twenties intersected with most of the major firms on Wall Street. They also required the support of a bustling industry of lawyers and law firms that finalized those deals. Some of those firms had been around for decades, while others either formed or remade themselves to handle the increasingly global, complex and lucrative expansion of American business. The firm that eventually became Cravath, Swaine & Moore counted nineteenth-century titans such as William Seward among its partners, but it took Paul Cravath in the early twentieth century to turn it into a Wall Street powerhouse. Other firms, Sullivan & Cromwell above all, emerged in these years as their own incubators of power, privilege and wealth as they wove together the volumes of paper and promises that were the foundations of so many of the deals brokered by Harriman, Morgan, Brown Brothers and the rest.[11]

Averell was a dealmaker, but in order to complement the direct securities and investment business of his firm, W. A. Harriman & Co., in 1927 he created a banking partnership with his younger brother, Roland, along with Roland's Yale classmate Knight Woolley. The new firm was called Harriman Brothers and Company. Though the titular head of both firms, Averell was not a competent manager or collaborative partner. He had less passion for paper than he did for tangible assets: ships, railroads, planes, mines. That left the behind-the-scenes work of finance to Roland and the other partners, which helps explain why Harriman's financial business, though well capitalized with the family fortune, was not as successful as Brown Brothers and a passel of older, more established Wall Street houses. In his tendency to keep his own counsel and plunge into far-flung investments, Averell emulated his father, but E.H. had brought highly skilled operators such as Judge Lovett into his inner circle. Averell was less adept at that, which Roland noted. Roland felt that the Harriman ventures, many of which were successful, ended up less than the sum of the collective parts because Averell was not adept at partnership.

Roland communicated his concerns directly to Averell, saying, "To put it in a nutshell, you are continually interested in getting new business and . . . handicapped by not having the proper means in the way of organization to carry out any unusual or new focus of business outside the regular routine."[12] Rather than putting together an organization that could take the connections Averell was so good at making and building on them, Averell instead remained a lone wolf, pursuing his contacts and passions and handing them off to Roland and the others who worked for the firms when it suited him. But that was not the same as a partnership, and it was markedly different from the culture that Brown Brothers had nurtured and cultivated over the course of a century. Harriman could afford to do business that way because of the fortune left to him and his brother. Both Averell and Roland were capable and smart, but Averell's inability to create a tight organization—which seemed neither here nor there during the boom times of the 1920s—proved a dramatic liability when the crash and the crunch came after 1929.

Brown Brothers, on the other hand, remained a smooth partnership, with Thatcher and James doggedly managing the franchise and fielding an ever larger number of requests for deals, loans and investment capital. James kept a detailed diary for the entire decade, and while he never editorialized in those entries, they form a microcosm of the swirl of activity that the twenties offered to American businesses and financiers. In the summer of 1919, while the world's diplomats milled about in Paris, James recounted a dizzying variety of meetings in New York. These included more discussions about a Swedish loan of $2 million involving Jacob Wallenberg, meetings on a Canadian loan of nearly $100 million being bundled by a consortium of Morgan, Brown Brothers and Otto Kahn (the new driving force of the German-Jewish-American banking house of Kuhn, Loeb since the passing of Jacob Schiff), and lunches and discussions with his partners about the continued ups and mostly downs of the Mercantile Bank that had been formed on the heels of the Nicaragua intervention.

There were also repeated discussions and multiple meetings to arrange a loan to the Kirby Coal Company in West Virginia, to consider an underwriting request from the American Coke and Chemical Company of Illinois, another to arrange financing for Duquesne Light & Power, and another to assess the creditworthiness of the Burroughs Adding Machine Company of St. Louis. Burroughs began life as the American Arithmometer Company and then evolved into a mainframe computer maker that later became the multibillion-dollar Unisys Corporation. It had been founded by William Burroughs, the grandfather of William Burroughs of beat poet and drug-induced writing fame, thereby linking Brown Brothers not just to twentieth-century technology giants but to the pop culture of the sixties generation that rejected everything those companies stood for.

There was a $2 million loan to the Republic of Columbia, still recovering from civil war and led by a government avidly pursuing industrialization and soliciting more investment from the United States; a possible loan to pay for twenty thousand tons of flour bound for Greece; another loan for the city of Copenhagen; and another for a Norwegian bank on behalf of the government of Norway. James also had meetings to discuss the firm's potential interest in a project being proposed by the British Eastern Telegraph Company, which was among the largest cable operators in the world, to lay cable connecting Latin America to East Africa and then to the Suez Canal down to Aden and from there to India. James also mulled a modest investment in a Boston-based wool-scouring plant in Boston, met with the Chilean ambassador to the United States at the behest of former treasury secretary, Woodrow Wilson's son-in-law and now lawyer and private businessman William Gibbs McAdoo (who would narrowly miss out being the Democratic presidential candidate in 1924), and held a series of meetings to consider a loan to an engineering concern in Australia. And that was only the activity of two months in the summer of 1919. James's diaries continue in that vein for the next decade.[13]

The ratio of meetings and discussions about ventures that did not come to pass to those that did was high. In January 1920, for instance, James was approached by representatives of a very young Prince Albrecht Radziwill, heir to the Polish-Lithuanian family, who wanted to sell one million acres of land they had acquired near Monterrey, Mexico, stretching along the border of the United States in Texas. James took the meeting but expressed no interest in the transaction.

James also advised Benjamin Strong on how the Federal Reserve should set the discount rate, especially in light of what European banks were doing. Recognizing that the United States was not in a monetary vacuum, James and Strong debated how much to factor in the rate policies of the Europeans in determining those of the United States. Given the lack of formal coordination between central banks and a rudimentary staff at the Federal Reserve, policy was the result of numerous conversations, informal and unofficial, between central bankers such as Strong and influential private players such as the Browns. James reiterated to Strong how much he had disagreed with the low discount rate during the war, even though he recognized that it allowed the U.S. government to borrow more cheaply. Given that he had disagreed even then, when there were compelling wartime reasons to lower borrowing costs, he did not support a low rate after the war's end. He believed that lower rates, by making the cost of capital cheaper, only encouraged speculation. And we know how the House of Brown felt about speculation.[14]

As the twenties progressed, the relationships between finance, industry and governments foreign and domestic continued to tighten. Most of that was entirely informal, as scholars of corporatism have pointed out. Connections were nurtured without any international institutions to maintain them. But in many ways, they presaged what would be created and codified after 1945. In that sense, the formal international economic and political system these men later crafted did not spring out of whole cloth from the devastation of World War II but instead had been incubated informally in the twenties. That period of relative peace and prosperity—albeit unevenly distributed between the United States, Europe and the wider world—saw an ever more intricate web of connections that involved business and finance leaders such as the Browns and Harriman sitting down with counterparts in Europe and with officials such as Benjamin Strong or Andrew Mellon or Herbert Hoover (who was busy turning the Commerce

Department into the main hub of economic policy making in Washington) and debating what policies, tariffs, interest rates or regulations would best serve the greater good of American business and prosperity and by extension the stability and prosperity of the globe.

For later critics, skeptics and conspiracy theorists, these cozy relationships between elites were proof that a small interconnected ruling class pulled the levers of American policy. And not just pulled but did so for venal reasons that enriched them at the expense of others. Those graduates of the Ivies who then fanned out to law firms such as Sullivan & Cromwell (John Foster Dulles, the Princeton graduate who later became Eisenhower's secretary of state; and his younger brother, Allen, who became director of the CIA, being Exhibit A), to banking firms such as Brown Brothers and Morgan and Chase, and then to high positions in government seemed to prove that point.

Even more troubling to later critics were the business connections between Harriman, Brown Brothers and their law firms with German industrial companies such as Thyssen and Krupp in the twenties. Those linkages became the foundation of a deep belief in some circles that American businesses were complicit with the rise of the Nazi Party. It's certainly true that well into the late 1930s, American financial relationships with German companies continued, even as those companies were key to the rearmament of Germany under the Nazis. Some later social critics and historians saw the rise of fascism as the dark side of corporatism and argued that business titans in Germany preferred the strong rule of the Nazis to the chaos of the democratic Weimar Republic. From there, it was only a dotted line to connect them to American enablers. While it's true that some of the industrialists who supported the Nazi war effort had ties with Wall Street in the twenties and thirties, that is a far cry from the more insidious claims that Wall Street purposely aided the rise of the Nazis.

The belief that a small clique of elites pull the strings has never gone away. It flared in the nineteenth century when economic depression hit the heartland, and it has usually centered on the coastal elites that the Browns and Harrimans epitomized. It waxed and waned throughout the twentieth century, but the tight bonds between this small group of people and their companies were seen as proof of a hidden network, a cabal of families and businesses that controlled the country behind the scenes. In 1927, for instance, Harriman helped bring a Texas company, Dresser Industries, public on the New York Stock Exchange, and his firm took a stake in Dresser. It was a successful public offering, and Dresser thrived with the growth of the Texas oil industry. Dresser then eventually merged with Halliburton, which was led in the 1990s by Dick Cheney, secretary of defense under President George H. W. Bush and vice president to George W. Bush. And who had been a junior partner in Harriman's firm when Dresser went public? Prescott Bush, the family patriarch. For those prone to see pernicious patterns, these dots connected themselves.

While it's undeniably the case that the number of Yale, Harvard and Princeton graduates was tiny relative to the population, and that there were only a small number of people with ocean estates on Long Island, and that many of these people knew one another and had intermarried, and while they were indeed rich and often exerted political power, the centrality of this cohort can be overstated. This stratum was one hub of a series of spokes. Henry Ford and his auto empire in Detroit, the rise of scientific management he championed that followed the theories of Frederick Taylor, the boom in Florida real estate, California's Pacific Gas & Electric, J. B. Duke's American Tobacco Company, and hundreds of others all represented powerful nodes that intersected only occasionally with the Northeast elites personified by the Browns and Harrimans. They often had different agendas, whether supporting higher tariffs or Jim Crow laws or anti-immigration policies that the Browns and Harriman did not. But because the Browns and their class went on to be a driving force behind the post–World War II order that cemented the American century, their centrality in American life even before is easily exaggerated. They mattered greatly, but they weren't the only ones who mattered greatly.

Having survived a tumultuous nineteenth century where many other partnerships—formed with the best of intentions by families determined to leave their mark or provide for future generations—had failed or simply faded or been acquired, Brown Brothers in New York decided to hold a rather grand (and for them anomalous) party in honor of the hundredth anniversary of the opening of the New York office by the first James Brown. Yes, the firm had been around for more than twenty years by the time the New York branch was opened, but for the partners and descendants then managing Brown Brothers, the New York office held a special place.

The celebration was held on December 19, 1925, at the University Club, another palace designed by the Gilded Age architects McKim, Mead & White. The club still stands at Fifth Avenue and Fifty-fourth Street as a paean to its era, its burnished wood and downward lamps giving off a glow barely sufficient to read the afternoon papers but more than enough light and shadow to project an image of affluence. The Brown's anniversary dinner was hosted by James Brown, fitting given that the party was partly in honor of his grandfather. The event was almost a cliché of what you would imagine such an event to be. If it had been filmed for a movie, critics would surely have panned the scene as unimaginative and derivative. But it was true to its time and place. The menu consisted of Clear Green Turtle Soup au Xérès, (a demi-glace then at the height of French culinary fashion), Queen and Ripe Olives, Filet of Sole, Supreme of Pheasant with Currant Jelly, Salad Florida with French Dressing and Cream Cheese, and Biscuit Tortoni with Marrons and Macaroons. The theme of the meal was "a century of service."

Speaking on behalf of the firm's staff, Mr. W. E. Blewitt declared, "Through the whole period of 100 years, the outstanding family characteristic of the Firm has been that of reserve, and a dislike for the limelight. . . . The history of the firm is especially remarkable when you consider it had to do with the building and development of a new nation, at a time when so many of the early business enterprises were really experiments of a speculative nature." He went on to explain that the creed of the Browns is that commerce is grounded in "good faith and fair dealing." If Alexander had been listening, he would have smiled.

After their feast, in the dining room with those soaring ceilings that would have been dark by the evening's end, with the faintest ghosts of light flickering from the table's candelabra, James Brown rose to give the final speech. "I believe that a business, like an individual, has a soul. Strong as the forces are which can lead one to work for gain, for the comfort and happiness of one's family and dependents, there needs yet to be a stronger motive—a motive for unselfish service, and a desire to give a better return than the other fellow for what is offered. Brown Brothers & Co was started and perpetuated by God-fearing men, who had the interest not only of their business but of their community and country at heart. If this is so in the future, I believe that the firm will go and prosper." And so it did. The next week it was back to work.[15]

The Browns were men of their class, with its attendant virtues and flaws. In March 1925, Thatcher confronted a problem. John Crosby Brown had built his "country" house in West Orange, New Jersey, and that had passed to his wife, Mary, and then, when she passed in 1918, to Thatcher and his brother James Crosby, who was then a partner in the Philadelphia office. Thatcher still cared about the old West Orange neighborhood, but he and his brother were not interested in keeping the house. That March, a man approached James Crosby about the sale of one of the parcels of land that had belonged to Mary. James explained what happened next in a letter to Thatcher. "A man named Dicks, from Hamilton Company, Orange, came in today to see about buying the remaining land that we have at Orange. In answer to my question, he said his principal was Leopold Meyer, who is a Jew, and who wants to buy the whole piece, including May's five acres, and would pay $50,000 cash. I told him that we would not sell to a Hebrew under any conditions." Thatcher concurred, "I quite agree with you that we do not want to sell the Brighthurst lot to a Jew for residence or any other purpose." Doing so might create tension in the community and alienate the neighbors.[16]

There was nothing particularly unusual about these sentiments. Wall Street itself had long been partitioned between the Jewish firms—Goldman Sachs, Lehman Brothers, Seligman and Kuhn, Loeb—and the Protestant Morgans, Browns, and Harrimans. The fact that they would not and could not be members of the same social clubs did not preclude them from doing business together, which they did constantly. Nor did what was then garden-variety prejudice preclude social interaction. But residential areas were a different matter. For the most part, if you were a member in good standing of the WASP elite, you could certainly package a loan with the Lehmans or Otto Kahn; you would not likely yacht with them; you would not live next to them; and by no means would you let your children marry theirs.

Or so it seemed. In truth, not everything was quite so set. Social segregation was as often breached as honored. In 1927, Averell decided to underwrite a new golf club at Sands Point, Long Island. He and a few others put in the initial capital of a few million dollars, and then helped assemble a marquee list of founding members. These included a who's who of some of the leading financial and business elites of the day: Cornelius Vanderbilt IV, Bernard Baruch, Irving Berlin, Walter Chrysler, Harry Guggenheim, E. F. Hutton, Marshall Field, James Forrestal, William Paley, John Schiff, Robert Lehman.

The list is striking not just for the aggregate wealth of its members, but for the fact that so many were Jewish: Baruch, who had served in Wilson's wartime administration; Irving Berlin, the most famous American composer of his day; Bill Paley, who was then making money from his family's cigar business and only starting to carve out the media empire that became CBS; Harry Guggenheim, heir to his father's mining and oil fortune and a Yalie; John Schiff, Jacob's son; and Robert Lehman, who would soon lead his family firm. The others were not: Edward Francis Hutton, who founded the eponymous brokerage firm and married heiress Marjorie Merriweather Post and then built an estate for her in Florida called Mar-a-Lago; Marshall Field, heir to the Chicago department store family fortune; Vanderbilt, the soon-to-be-dispossessed scion of his family's widespread businesses; Chrysler, founder of the Detroit motor company that bears his name still; and Forrestal, then an executive at an investment firm that became Dillon, Read and later the first secretary of defense.[17]

The prosperity of the decade, of course, did not cure all ills, but it took the edge off social and political tensions. American politics remained fractious, with harsh racial suppression in the South and farmers and rural America as bitter as ever about the coastal and urban elites who appeared to be thriving at their expense. Even so, the presidential election of 1928, between Republican Herbert Hoover and the Democratic governor of New York, Al Smith, was not much of a contest. The strong economy would have been a headwind for any Democratic nominee, and Smith's Catholicism and opposition to Prohibition did him no favors in a country where anti-Catholic sentiment was virulent. Faced with Hoover, who could call on his years of experience and could take personal credit for the good times as a guardian of economic policy as the head of the Commerce Department, Smith fared as well as could be expected and as poorly as one would have predicted.

If there was any question about the breadth of Hoover's victory, the changing tune of formerly vociferous opponents showed how much the country had come to accept the gospel of prosperity. For decades, Lincoln Steffens had been a fierce critic of big business, a champion of government reform and regulations, one of the original muckraking journalists who had raised public awareness of the imbalances of unfettered capitalism and helped pave the way for the rise of the federal government as a protector of labor and the average citizen against the rapacity of industrialists and Wall Street. Yet in 1928, the sixty-two-year old Steffens surveyed the United States and announced, "Big Business in America is producing what the Socialists held up as their goals: food, shelter and clothing for all. You will see it during the Hoover administration."[18]

Even the Browns, despite their years of prudence, were not immune from this bout of irrational exuberance. Flush with the confidence of a strong economy and a competent Republican administrator entering the White House, Thatcher Brown, along with executives from the mining conglomerate W. R. Grace, set off on a multimonth tour of Latin America at the beginning of 1929 to see what opportunities the Southern Hemisphere might offer. Thatcher later recalled in his laconic manner, "We thought it wise to have partners visit these countries and decide whether this business was worth going after and to look perhaps into commercial banking with these countries."[19] This visit culminated with a line of credit of $50 million to the government of Argentina. The timing was not good. Within a year, the Argentine government would be overthrown in a military coup, the United States would be facing its worst economic crisis ever and that credit would be nearly worthless.

Hoover's first six months in office were his only time of respite. The stock market crash that began with a fall of 11 percent on October 24, 1929, forever known thereafter as Black Thursday, would turn out to be more than a market calamity. It was the beginning of one of the worst economic downturns ever, both for the United States and for Europe and significant parts of the world. There has never been consensus about what caused what and why the various variables combined to produce what was eventually called the Great Depression. The plunge in stock prices over that week in October was extreme, but it had followed an extraordinary bull market that had seen stocks rise tenfold in the mid- to late 1920s—Union Pacific's stock, the source of most of the Harriman fortune, had been at 129 in 1920; it peaked just shy of 300 before the crash and paid a dividend of 8 percent. In the week after October 24, stocks posted double-digit percentage losses on both Black Monday (October 28) and Black Tuesday (October 29). By the end of that week, equities had plunged more than 30 percent. Then Wall Street mobilized. Major institutions and individuals started buying to establish a floor. By November, the market had calmed down. But the match had been lit.

James Brown's diaries from these weeks chart the unease and mild panic, but discussions about new deals continued much as before. At an October 29 meeting with executives from the Central Union Trust, James noted that there was, "considerable discussion around the table with regard to panic conditions in the Street." But he also noted that there was "no special trouble reported: loans on margins came in freely and the company had not been to the Federal Reserve." The next day, on October 30, as the market remained precarious after dropping almost a third in less than a week, he wrote after a meeting with his partners that, "conditions continued from bad to worse, but it seemed to us that the decline in prices had gone too far.

We were, therefore, willing with reservations to recommend purchases of many standard stocks for a long pull and so cabled to London and Paris." November was volatile but not quite as dramatic as those October days. Stock prices stabilized; some of the excess margin loans that had fueled the bubble were flushed out; and after Christmas, the index began to rise again. In early 1930, the firm's recommendations to its clients that they buy into a weak market seemed vindicated.

CHAPTER 12

FROM THE ASHES

The year 1930 began with hopes that the worst had passed. It ended with faint hope that it couldn't get any worse. The brief respite and stabilization of the New York Stock Exchange masked the sudden deterioration of the financial system. By Christmas of 1929, everyone from President Hoover to the financial press was saying the country "was back to normal." If only that had been true.

There was as yet no central clearinghouse for information, and in spite of constant communication between the central banks of England, France, Germany and the United States, gauging financial stress was almost impossible aside from comparing anecdotes and balance sheets. Everyone knew that some of the growth of the 1920s had been boosted by loose credit and speculation, but no one knew how much. The flow of gold out of England and Europe and into the United States had already raised alarms in financial policy circles, and not a few on Wall Street were concerned at the signs of too much froth in equities. But that was a far cry from a sense that the financial and economic systems of the Western world were about to implode.

The economies of the West had done well in the twenties, even if the bloated gains of equities were discounted. Wages had gone up; cities had thrived; industries had churned out new products that were snatched up by new urban middle classes; automobiles had transformed transportation, with ten million cars in 1920 and nearly thirty million by 1929; roads and bridges were built across the country to pave the way, literally, for the motor age; manufacturing productivity had soared; domestic taxes had been aggressively lowered even as tariffs on foreign goods remained; construction boomed; a new era of radio advertising hypercharged commerce. Some things were bought on credit, yes, but many were purchased with the hard-won cash of hard-earned wages. Those things were not mirages.

By the end of 1930, however, it was clear that what had transpired in the markets a year earlier was a harbinger, not a correction, not an anomaly, not a healthy purging of a speculative binge, and not a welcome reversal of the flow of gold and money from Europe into the United States. In 1928, to combat the perceived surfeit of speculation, the Federal Reserve had begun to raise short-term interest rates. That has been taken by generations of subsequent forensic economists as one of the prime factors leading first to the market crash in 1929 and then to the real-world economic contraction that began in 1930 and accelerated rapidly in the United States before spreading to Europe. Tight credit choked off market speculation, and at the time, that was seen by firms such as Brown Brothers and by the long-serving and ever rigid treasury secretary Andrew Mellon as a good thing. Thatcher had wanted more rigorous standards and tighter credit for a decade and had watched disapprovingly as the excesses of the twenties mounted.

You could not, however, tighten credit just for the financial markets. Tightening had real-world effects. In 1930, demand for consumer goods started to drop. Prices fell, and then they started falling for agricultural goods. Farmers had already been struggling to balance increased demand with falling prices as everything in the twenties became more plentiful and cheaper. Many farmers had taken on high levels of debt, backed by land and equipment, in order to stay viable. But the plunge in farm prices in 1930–31 combined with escalating bank failures was too much. A wave of farm foreclosures went hand in hand with businesses cutting back jobs and production. Banks closing, higher interest rates, and then even higher tariffs with the passage of the Smoot-Hawley Bill in the summer of 1930 combined to make a bad situation considerably worse. And then France, England and, worst of all, Germany started to contract sharply, with their own central banks struggling to maintain their gold reserves and working at cross-purposes with each other. The death of longtime New York Fed leader Benjamin Strong in 1928 had not helped matters. The Federal Reserve was not rudderless, but Strong's successor, George Harrison, another Yale graduate and Bonesman, did not have the gravitas and respect that Strong had acquired. It was a recipe for indecision, though it's entirely possible that had Strong been alive, his decisions would have been no better.[1]

The false calm of early 1930 did not last. By summer, it was quite clear that the stock market crash had set something in motion, and that something was not at all good. Watching as conditions deteriorated, the partners of Brown Brothers, at the offices at 59 Wall Street, were relatively sanguine about their position. So too were the Harriman brothers and their firm. Over the course of a century, the Browns had prepared for and endured multiple panics and crises. They had outlasted embargoes and the War of 1812. They had weathered the Panic of 1819, and while they had almost gone under in 1837, they believed they had learned a lesson in how much exposure they could afford at any given moment. They had emerged stronger after 1857, survived the Civil War, navigated through the severe shock of 1873 and its aftermath. They had seen the once-great Baring Brothers collapse, and then had done just fine as the country reeled from labor unrest and the Panic of 1893. They had supported Morgan when he came to the rescue of the financial system in 1907, and they had managed their way through the Great War and the end of the transatlantic partnership with Brown Shipley. Things looked grim in 1930, but they had been grim before and the firm had survived and thrived.

Averell and his two linked firms were even more secure, or so they thought. They were capitalized well beyond most of their more established peers and competitors. While Union Pacific's stock price had taken a dive at the end of 1929, that was after years when it had doubled and doubled again. Neither Brown Brothers nor the Harrimans had participated in the speculative excesses of the late 1920s. Brown Brothers had repeatedly declined invitations to join "pool" purchases of securities, an innovation then in vogue that allowed for a few large institutions to buy a substantial portion of a company's stock and then resell the shares to the individual investors clamoring for them. Knight Woolley, the Harriman partner with the most substantial market experience, forbade the use of company investment funds for the purchase of securities, even though that would have considerably augmented the firm's capital. With the Harriman fortune, the risk wasn't worth it, and the crash of 1929 seemed to vindicate the wisdom of that stance. Numerous brokerage houses that had used their own capital to speculate and then used leverage were squeezed by margin calls after the crash and collapsed.[2]

Even with their strong foundations, both Harriman and Brown Brothers were being buffeted by larger forces. So too was Washington. The popular image of Herbert Hoover is that he did nothing as the markets and the economy collapsed. His defeat by Franklin Roosevelt in 1932 forever cemented the picture of Hoover as a rigid free-market ideologue who, bolstered by the even more rigid Andrew Mellon, believed that market spasms and economic downturns were inevitable glitches in capitalism that were best dealt with by allowing them to run their course. Those attitudes were hardly marginal. Said Oklahoma's senator Thomas Gore (grandfather of Gore Vidal), recessions and downturns were "an economic disease. You might just as well try to prevent the human race from having a disease as to prevent economic grief of this sort." Hoover might have said the same, but the picture of him as aloof, stubborn and above the fray is radically incomplete; his efforts to confront both the market crash at the end of 1929 and then the escalating economic crisis that intensified in 1930 were substantial, especially compared with past precedent. They were not, however, sufficient.

Hoover was akin to the Harrimans and the Browns in his attitudes about government, its role and the role of private industry and citizens. They shared more with Hoover than they did with Roosevelt. That is hardly what one might have expected, given that FDR was a product of Groton and Harvard and had more in common culturally with the financial elites than did the technocrat Hoover, who was raised as a Quaker in

Iowa, had gone to college (Stanford) on the West Coast and then lived outside the United States for years. Hoover was an acolyte of modern measurement and management. His passion for data and organization was rather distinct from the chummy world of personal connections and relationships cultivated by the East Coast financial and business elite. But like the Browns and the Harrimans, Hoover believed in the "ideal of service" and understood society to be a delicate balance between the individualism that made America so potent and the need to attend to the greater public good that all stable, powerful societies required. His reluctance to use the coercive power of government to attempt to halt what was initially seen as a normal albeit painful economic correction stemmed from the conviction that it was up to interested groups and individuals to act in times of duress, with the federal government and the executive branch using its convening power to bring those together.[3] In 1921, when he was commerce secretary, Hoover organized a conference on unemployment that led to the first measurements of a national unemployment rate so that both government and industry could gauge what was happening more accurately and respond more effectively. That template—convene, gather data, and nudge private groups to act with government as a backstop—informed his responses at the end of 1929 and into 1930.

Unlike Mellon, who infamously advised that the best course of action was to "liquidate labor, liquidate stocks, liquidate the farmers, liquidate real estate," Hoover believed that the federal government had a responsibility to halt panic. And so he brought business leaders and bankers to Washington, urged them to bolster capital spending and lending in order to offset the fear caused by the market panic, and attempted to mimic the events of 1907, when Morgan had galvanized the business community and provided just enough liquidity to halt the panic. As financial markets stabilized into the spring of 1930, in fact, Hoover received nearly universal plaudits for his efforts. With markets calm and public fear receding in early 1930, *The New York Times* concluded that "a helpful reassurance has gone out from the White House to permeate the whole land."[4]

It proved to be a false dawn. By the middle of 1930, bank failures were accelerating. Even though the Federal Reserve had loosened conditions once again, only a third of banks were part of the Federal Reserve System in 1930. Most were stand-alone, given that branch banking was in many places not allowed. Bank failures had been relatively common throughout the 1920s, but the pace quickened measurably in 1930, and by the fall, the crisis had spread to Europe. The deterioration in Europe forever colored how Hoover himself understood the causes of the Great Depression. In his mind, as he wrote in his memoirs, "the great center of the storm began in Europe." The Great Depression that in his view commenced at the end of 1930 was a European import, albeit aggravated by speculation and a weak banking system in the United States. Because he misdiagnosed the problem, his response was inadequate. But it is not true that he stood idly by, and by 1932, he had begun to consider many of the policies that would be foundational to the New Deal launched by FDR in 1933.

It was, though, an epic case of too little, too late. Hoover's belief that the United States would have weathered its own storm had events in Europe not spun out of control ignored the domestic depression that was deepening by the summer of 1930. The business and financial community recognized that whatever the specific origins of the downturn, by the middle of 1930, the United States was deteriorating quickly. The situation in Germany was also dire, which helped explain the sudden rise in popularity of the once-marginal National Socialist Party led by Adolf Hitler, which catapulted from the fringe to the second-largest party in the Reichstag in the elections of September 1930. Americans were also hurting, and they punished Republicans in Congress in the November midterms. Hoover lost his majority in the House, and Republicans barely retained the Senate that November.

What really changed the equation for the United States was the beginning of a bank panic in the fall of 1930. Unemployment had already been spiking by millions, though without reliable statistics in 1930, hard numbers were impossible to come by. What was measurable was the number of bank runs, which sharply accelerated in the fall. Six hundred banks folded in 1929; in 1930, the number more than doubled, and larger banks began failing. These waves of bank runs and failures nearly destroyed the American economy.[5]

And so it was that the idea of merging Harriman's firms and Brown Brothers went from casual banter on a train heading from New York to New Haven for a glorious Yale reunion weekend to a matter of urgency by that December. The reunion and the train ride make for a good story, but the train ride was not the first time that the subject had been broached. Roland, who was often opaque and elliptical, was unequivocal about that in his memoirs. He recalled that "the merger discussions all started long before the country began to move into the Depression." There is no reason to doubt his assertion; in his waning years, Lovett, too, confirmed that discussions about a possible merger had been ongoing for years.

The young men on the train to New Haven that day had befriended one another as college students, and other partners, Lovett and Roland in particular, had known each other since childhood. It would have been utterly natural for one of them to say, over drinks perhaps, late into the evening after one too many coupes of champagne or an excessive number of gin and tonics, "We really should work together. It would be grand fun." Ellery James, who started at Brown Brothers in 1919 after serving in France as an artillery captain, had been friends with Roland almost as long as Lovett, and his apartment on Park Avenue, inherited from his wealthy lawyer father, served as a crash pad for friends such as Prescott Bush and Knight Woolley.[6] Woolley, expert not just in bankers' acceptances but in the whole arcana of paper derivatives that helped propel Harriman and Brothers, and also something of a dandy, fond of pipes, pin-striped suits and a good party, would have wanted nothing more than to merge the firms. How many times over the years prior to 1930 had he urged his friends to think about working together?

Then there was the basic fact that the senior members of Brown Brothers—Thatcher and James—were growing older. They had helmed the family firm with aplomb and managed its finances wisely, assisted by James's son-in-law, Lovett, but the onset of the crisis was troubling. James was nearing seventy, and he did not relish the coming storm. Thatcher was more than a decade younger, but he understood that this time, unlike the crises faced by his father and grandfather and great-grandfather, might be the one that proved too much.

What was most troubling was that neither firm had taken on excessive risk. They had, by their lights, done everything as they should have, and yet they were now in trouble. Brown Brothers had an uncomfortable exposure to Argentine bonds, which did indeed go bad. Those bonds were the subprime loans of their day, lucrative in fair weather and worthless in foul. But while the losses were painful, they were not lethal. Brown Brothers had managed their exposure. Indeed, both firms had carefully conserved partner capital, and even the Harrimans were mindful that a huge fortune could easily become a small fortune if not stewarded well. Yet with the rapid descent of the banking system in the second half of 1930, none of that much mattered. Brown Brothers, recalled Thatcher, was stuck with what he politely called "undigested securities," namely stocks and bonds that had been issued at reasonable prices but were now trading at unreasonable lows, which meant that the firm had less capital than it had anticipated. It also was facing the retirement of senior partners such as James, as well as needing to buy out the estate of James Crosby Brown, Thatcher's brother, who had died that April and had managed the Philadelphia branch. "It became clear to us," Thatcher later wrote, "that we were doing too large a business for our capital." And so, he concluded laconically, "we turned our minds to securing additional capital."[7]

The Harriman firms were better capitalized, to be sure, but beneath that placid surface there were unsettling ripples. The many loans the firm had extended and the ventures that Averell had formed in Germany, Austria and Hungary were now vulnerable in ways that could not have been foreseen. Business that appeared sound at the time the deals were concluded and the financing arranged were now in question. The Harrimans were new to Wall Street, with their father's name and money but with little track record of their own. As the Browns had long ago understood, in times of duress, trust and reputation become their own form of currency, and the Harriman firms had only a small account of each. The Browns had a surfeit. Hence it made eminent sense that, as *The Wall Street Journal* observed, "To the large resources of the century-old Brown firm [should be] added the tens of millions available to the Harriman interests."

The final negotiations took only a few weeks. Given the multiple connections and close friendships, the terms of the merger were relatively simple. Most of the discussions took place at the Park Avenue apartment of Brown partner Charles Dickey. As Thatcher recalled, "Assets of the respective firms were valued at market—if there was a market—and the assets difficult to value, where questions of judgements were involved . . . were left by the respective firms to a senior partner, in each firm, to trade out and agree on." These issues of valuation are often the most contentious in merger discussions, but with high levels of mutual trust, they proved no stumbling block. It was, Lovett recalled, a relatively simple arrangement: "Harriman had this little business and too much capital; Brown Brothers had too much business and little capital. So the merger was perfectly obvious. We wanted capital; they wanted business. We had business; they had capital. Perfectly normal things. We were all friends. We had known each other well. It was the simple thing to do."

The only real challenge was what to name the new partnership. Suddenly, ego reared its head in place of the usual sublimation and protestations of modesty. Thatcher and James were adamant that the firm their family had run for a century bear their name. But the Harriman brothers were equally proud of their father and their family. To settle matters, the parties agree to ask three outsiders for their input. One voted to call it Brown Brothers; the other said it should be called Harriman. The third made the reverse Solomonic decision, and it was agreed the new entity would be called Brown Brothers Harriman.[8]

From there, the next step was to inform clients and the public and to make the physical move. It was agreed that Harriman and all its employees would decamp to the spacious headquarters of Brown Brothers at 59 Wall Street, which had recently been substantially enlarged and which had the virtue of seeming to be a rock-solid institution. Reporters were invited to Thatcher Brown's apartment on December 11, 1930, at 775 Park Avenue, where they stood in the library to await what turned out to be the surprise announcement of the firms' merger, with all the partners in attendance.

Not all the questions asked were friendly. The reporters wanted to know, naturally enough, what had precipitated the move and whether the firms were hiding pending insolvency behind the scrim of the merger. But the following day, the press was mostly positive, with *The New York Times* simply noting in its front-page story that the merger would likely facilitate the ability of both firms to meet the expanding business of a more global world. It was a marriage of "financial aristocrats" said another publication, between a new arrival and "a veritable banking power whose history is closely linked with American history." Next to the happy story of the merger in *The New York Times* blared another headline: BANK OF U.S. CLOSES DOORS. The banking system was about to experience a new meltdown, and the creation of Brown Brothers Harriman was a rare bright spot.[9]

All that remained was to move offices, with those clerks trundling the paper assets of the Harriman firm into the Brown Brothers offices. The combined staff of the new firm numbered more than five hundred, most of them employees of Brown Brothers.[10] Not all of them were kept on. There was some culling of the ranks, made a tad less painful by the pension plan that both firms had introduced in the 1920s. The new partners of the combined firm, less than a dozen of them in toto, assembled in the storied Partners Room, with its rolltop desks close to one another and the portrait of Alexander watching over the four Brown Brothers. There were no palatial offices for the partners, just a beautiful room of functional desks. "We were not simply custodians," Roland remarked in his memoir. "We were not managing stockholders money. We were managing our own money, and that is quite a difference."

It remained to be seen whether the cultures of the firms could merge as easily. It was said that "if the Brown Brothers went camping because they wanted to know if a railroad should be built, E. H. Harriman built a railroad because he went camping." The entrepreneurial individualism of E.H. and Averell contrasted strongly with the reserve of Thatcher and James, although that was bridged by Lovett and Roland and Prescott Bush who were used to supporting roles, albeit crucial ones. In 1931, it was an open question whether those disparate qualities would blend seamlessly or at least without too much friction. Some tension would have been normal, and expected. What is perhaps most remarkable about the conjoining was how little friction there was. In the end, the underlying similarities of culture, education and mores proved more powerful than the personality differences between Averell and Thatcher, or between any of the younger partners. In this case, their differences were surface; their similarities were deep.

As a result, there was no postmerger clash of culture; no partners senior or junior departed in a huff; staff did not decamp en masse, even as some were let go. Of course, the United States was plunging into an economic chasm, and opportunities for other employment were shrinking fast. But even as the economy recovered after 1933, the merged firms retained talent, partners and staff, and cohered into one close-knit partnership rather than distinct organizations. It was, as Roland concluded, "a happy marriage arrangement," made happier by each group appreciating what the other brought, Harriman providing needed liquidity, and Brown Brothers offering a deep reputation and a plethora of relationships. That sentiment was later echoed by Prescott Bush, one of the more junior partners at the time, who recalled that it was "a very happy merger because we had so many friends." It was an organization with "no officers, and its functioning smoothly was dependent upon the ability of the managing partners to get along easily with each other, without jealousies or anything like that."[11]

The merger did change one thing forever: the centrality of the Brown bloodline faded. While Thatcher Brown continued to be a partner until his death in 1954, and while his son Moreau Delano was a partner, as was his grandson, after 1930 the firm became less of a family affair. Yet even as the bloodline ceased to dominate the partnership, the culture meticulously created by Alexander Brown, his sons and their sons and theirs, remained intact. The new firm embodied the Brown ethos even with the new Harriman partners joining the ranks. Brown Brothers had more than a century of culture and a way of doing things; the Harriman firms were barely a decade old. While Averell was always and ever his own man, the spirit of Edward and his aggressive drive to build an empire was not as evident in his sons. Averell was intensely ambitious and realized many of those ambitions, but the partnership culture of the combined firm strayed only marginally from what Alexander had established: service, focus, trust, reputation. Of the elite and for the elite, but guided by the belief, flawed or not, that doing well would ultimately do well for society, for country and for the onward march of Western civilization. And of course, they would make money in the process.

All was not yet quite well in their world. In early spring of 1931, Knight Woolley and Ellery James were dispatched to Europe to wrap up outstanding loans and businesses, even at a loss. They were celebrating their near escape from a swath of deals that could have sunk the new firm and were on their way back to the United States when they learned that the Austrian Creditanstalt, one of the major European banks founded by the Rothschilds, had collapsed. That set off a chain reaction of new bank failures throughout Europe and the United States. Germany saw an immediate run on its gold reserves as companies and central banks attempted the financial equivalent of pulling up the drawbridges and isolating themselves.[12] The collapse of Creditanstalt was the moment when the Great Depression truly went global.

Brown Brothers Harriman struggled. Its capital dipped into the red, and several partners had negative balances, on paper at least. It reached a point where in 1932, Averell and Roland quietly turned to their mother, Mary, who still controlled substantial portions of the Harriman estate, for an emergency infusion of $1 million (approximately $18 million in today's dollars). They refused to make a show of it, or to ask for any alteration of the partnership terms. They also kept the problems secret outside of that small circle of partners; any whiff of how thin the ice was could have severely harmed the nascent firm in the eyes of its clients and crushed morale internally. Most of the staff remained unaware. James, though mostly retired from the day-to-day affairs, was grateful. He wrote to Averell, "It is difficult for me to find words to express my appreciation and my admiration for the courage you are showing under such uncertain conditions. The contributions you have made . . . at such great sacrifice to your personal fortunes is something no partner of the firm can ever forget. . . . Such actions deserve high reward."[13] For several years, a number of the partners owed money to the firm, which Harriman had personally recapitalized. They were known internally as the "red partners" and were not able to make their partnership accounts whole until later in the 1930s. It's not clear how close the combined enterprises came to collapse. Subsequent memoirs are opaque, and while the partners later hinted at trouble and went personally into the red, it would seem that the threat was significant but not as dire or potentially lethal as the near-death experience of Brown Brothers in 1837, when only the timely intervention of the Bank of England saved Alexander's sons from shuttering their business.

The viability of Brown Brothers Harriman was in stark contrast to the economic devastation swirling around them. The Great Depression was the ruination of thousands of local banks. It saw perhaps 25 percent of all workers unemployed, and others only eking out a living. It saw unpaid veterans of World War I massing in the Washington Mall looking for aid, only to be routed and scattered brutally on the orders of President Hoover by soldiers led with excessive zeal by a general named Douglas MacArthur. It witnessed shantytowns in major cities housing families, destitute workers and children shabbily clothed, huddled around fires burning in metal drums. These makeshift camps were derisively named Hoovervilles in mockery of the impotence of the president to ameliorate the situation. The crisis saw farmers, facing the double-barrel of foreclosures and drought, head in droves to California in search of a new promised land, which some found and many did not, and whose plight was searingly immortalized by John Steinbeck in *The Grapes of Wrath*. And it saw a cratering of U.S. industrial output along with a concomitant breakdown in Europe that led to the rise of fascism in Germany, the victory of the Labor Party in Great Britain and a collapse of the Versailles war reparations system that had held sway since 1919.

Even so, most major financial institutions as well as the large corporations that had emerged in the 1920s were not felled. Dented, certainly, but the brunt of the Depression fell on those least able to bear it: the farmers and wage laborers and factory workers and city workers catering to the growing but still small service economy of food and leisure. Stores shuttered; plants were idled; the upper middle class slid back and cut back; the middle class slid further and had less room to cut. "Brother, Can You Spare a Dime?," the song written in 1932, became the ballad of the Depression, along with the haunting images of the Dust Bowl later captured by *Fortune* magazine photojournalist Margaret Bourke-White, who had started with the first issue of Henry Luce's *Time* spin-off. *Fortune* was launched in February 1930 to celebrate the glories of American capitalism and industry but soon shifted gears and then dispatched White to document the ravages of the collapse. The magazine would eventually return to Luce's intended triumphalism after World War II.[14]

The onset of the Depression was yet another moment when the volatility of money overwhelmed the rudimentary guardrails meant to contain and channel its antinomian energies. The rigidity of the gold standard; the lack of coordination between governments globally; the lack of clear lines of control and authority within the U.S. financial system, even with the new but largely untested Federal Reserve System; the easing, then tightening, then easing gyrations of central banks around the world as they grappled with a situation that was spiraling out of control; the opaque flows of money across national borders; the beggar-thy-neighbors policies of multiple countries, including the United States, with higher tariffs and suspended payments; and the naive belief that the fever would break on its own—all combined to fuel an economic cataclysm.

One key aspect of the crisis was the relationship between money—paper promises made by private financial firms such as Brown Brothers and by governments—and gold. As the crisis deepened after 1930, governments tried, often futilely, to preserve their gold reserves, at least until Britain abandoned its gold standard in 1931. The shiny metal was widely perceived as having lasting value, but actual economic activity was backed either by trusted governments or reliable firms. Gold limited how much paper and money could be put into circulation, but there had always been a shadow money system running parallel to the gold system. The exclusive private firms in the business of paper and promises—underwriting, issuing, creating—were in these years often the most conservative in their approach to money. As speculation ran amok in the late 1920s in the stock market, firms like Brown Brothers were not part of the scrum, because they saw more clearly than most, being as they were at the epicenter, just how mercurial money could be. Best to ride it with a tight tether and not let it ride you.

The lack of panic even at the height of the crisis at the partners' desks of Brown Brothers or the offices of the Harrimans or, for that matter, in the halls of Kuhn, Loeb or the corridors of Morgan and the nooks of Lehman Brothers reflected the degree to which the bastions of Wall Street were not as personally exposed as many of their clients. Yes, there were countless investors who lost nearly everything in the crash that began in 1929 and intensified after the summer of 1930, but the myth of brokers leaping to their death as the market plunged obscures the fact that the ones who suffered the most during the Depression were mostly not the ones manipulating the levers on Wall Street. Partnerships were less inclined to take outsized gambles for the simple, basic and obvious reason that it was their money, their firm and their reputation on the line. They were quite capable of advancing bad loans or making bad judgments, but they were almost never overexposed on any one deal. Only in a situation when everything was going bad simultaneously were their balance sheets stressed, and even then usually not to their limit. And that is what you would want from your financial stewards: that they be more conservative than their clients, more cautious, more willing to forgo upside in order to avoid crushing, debilitating, destructive downside. With something as potent as money, a combustible fuel for good and for ill, there was something to be said for staid bankers. Theirs was a sustainable model of capitalism even as the fate of capitalism hung in the balance.

It's important to see the formation of Brown Brothers Harriman and its first years in the context of the worsening Depression and the rise of Franklin Delano Roosevelt and the New Deal. Not only did those shape the trajectory of the firm, but the Roosevelt years became their entrée into Washington and made possible the emergence of the firm and its partners as central actors. As the economy deteriorated, even Republican support for Hoover diminished. With the nomination of Roosevelt by the Democrats in 1932, many business and financial leaders were concerned at the populist turn that his election might portend, but FDR was also a man of their class and background. His views were protean, and he was adept at playing to multiple sides, denouncing greed and the captains of money at one moment and then calling those selfsame people the next day soliciting advice. He won an overwhelming electoral victory in November 1932, winning nearly 60 percent of the popular vote and forty-two states. That was as much a rejection of Hoover as an endorsement of FDR, given the widespread sense that Hoover had utterly failed to meet the situation. But up until Inauguration Day in March 1933, no one, even in his inner circle and perhaps not always FDR himself, knew what to expect in terms of policies. It was a fluid crisis, unprecedented in depth and scope, and there was no playbook, until FDR made one up.[15]

And at first, he enjoyed wary support among the financial class. They knew reform and regulation were inevitable. In the Senate, a series of hearings in the banking committee excoriated Wall Street firms for their role in the collapse. Those findings would form the core of the Pecora Committee report that was instrumental in shaping future legislation. FDR's rhetoric was a challenge for Wall Street. In a campaign speech in the fall of 1932, he assailed the concentration of wealth: "We find two thirds of American industry concentrated in a few hundred corporations and actually managed by not more than five human individuals. We find more than half of the savings of the country invested in corporate stocks and bonds, and made the sport of the American stock market. We find fewer than three dozen private banking houses, and stock selling adjuncts of commercial banks, directing the flow of American capital. In other words, we find concentrated economic power in a few hands. . . ." In 1933, a group of alarmed bankers plotted to overthrow FDR and approached Smedley Butler, now a fierce anti-imperialist after years of suppressing rebellions in Nicaragua and throughout Central America, to lead a coup. It was never clear how serious they were, but Butler would have none of it. Aside from the right-wing fringe that feared FDR was going to create a socialist dictatorship, the prevailing sentiment in the financial community was that dramatic change was imperative to save the country. "Wall Street wanted to be led out of the wilderness," quipped one writer, "and was in no mood to be particular about the character of its savior."[16]

Still, the New Deal saw an intensification of the same fissures that had rent American society in the nineteenth century in the battles over central banks and hard money and easy credit that pitted the heartland against the coastal elites, the urban against the rural, the working class against the moneyed class. Over the years, Roosevelt and the New Deal have become a Rorschach test where everyone sees something different. Some on the left see FDR as a savior of the working class. Others decry the limitations of his reforms and criticize him as a patsy for the financial and business class that did nothing to change the have and have-not reality of American capitalism and left unchallenged the Jim Crow racial caste system in order to keep the Southern Democrats in his tent. On the right, he was excoriated for being "a traitor to his class" who opened the floodgates to the politics of economic resentment and redistributive government policies. Those debates raged in the 1930s, and they have never quieted since.

Throughout 1932 and into 1933, Brown Brothers Harriman stayed in close contact with the officials tasked with easing the strains on the financial system. Just as James had counseled Benjamin Strong, the firm's partners gave input to the Federal Reserve, and their advice was part of the mix. Recognizing that the winds in Washington might be shifting against them, they also began to take more concerted political actions. The substantial increase in the federal budget in 1931–32 alarmed those who believed that the economic crisis would end only when spending was brought in line with what the government generated in tax revenue. The genial Roland was a Republican, and he was the most conservative of his partners (though no one at Brown Brothers went to extremes). His conservatism was primarily fiscal, and he feared that the federal government would soon succumb to the pressure of reckless spending. He had enough of his father in him to do something. Rather than moan over dinner about "that man" Roosevelt, he assembled an informal group of like-minded Republicans. They held meetings at the Harvard Club, and to add more oomph, Roland named the group the National Economy League. Its members included Archibald Roosevelt, Theodore's grandson and FDR's cousin. Roland then urged FDR through several of his advisers to reform the veterans' pension system and thereby slash the federal budget. The veterans' pension plan was then consuming a substantial portion of the budget without distinguishing benefits for veterans who had been wounded from benefits for those who had not. Roland and his ilk wanted Washington to spend more on the former (who were few) and less on the latter (who were many) and thereby bring balance to the federal budget and alleviate the Depression without destroying the creditworthiness of the United States and the dollar. The veterans' program mattered to them purely as a means to an end. If you could eliminate government profligacy, you could free up funds and then channel those toward temporary programs to get the country through its rough patch.

Roland's efforts seemed to bear fruit when Roosevelt and Congress passed the Economy Act in March 1933. One of the first steps taken by FDR, the act reduced pensions and cut the salaries of government workers. That followed a tax increase that had been passed under Hoover. The Economy Act belies the image of the New Deal as an unabashed embrace of spend, spend, spend. Ultimately, FDR did champion rafts of emergency spending, but the Economy Act shows that it was never quite so simple and that *reducing* government spending other than for stopgap measures and short-term boosting of the economy was still part of the mantra that guided many of those making policy, at least initially.

Soon enough, of course, the New Deal plunged into more spending and more government. Before the 1930s, the federal government was relatively small and comparatively lean. The budget in 1932 was about $4 billion; by 1936 it was more than $9 billion. Federal expenditures in 1932 were around 5 to 6 percent of overall GDP (already more than in 1930 due to Hoover's emergency programs in 1931–32). By comparison, by the early twenty-first century, federal government expenditures had ballooned to more than 20 percent of GDP. The unleashing of government spending was facilitated by another New Deal move that would prove a harbinger. In April 1933, Roosevelt issued an executive order instructing all individuals and institutions to turn over their gold to the Federal Reserve. Then he took the United States off the gold standard, which meant that the dollar became, for the time being, purely government paper with no rights to redeem in gold. The rationale was simple: in order to jolt the economy, the government would need money, and the gold standard was restricting its supply. In the same spirit that the Union during the Civil War had issued greenbacks not tied to gold, FDR paved the way for new government programs by relying on government paper.[17]

Armed with money, the White House and Congress proceeded to tame its guardians. The common view in 1933 was that speculation had caused the onset of the Depression, and that speculation had been recklessly fostered by banks and brokers. The first act passed under Roosevelt was a "bank holiday" to halt the panic. The brief holiday was mostly symbolic— a few days pause was not structural change. But it was seen as a great success, providing relief to a stressed system and to thousands of small local banks that had not yet faltered but were vulnerable. And it was small banks that FDR wanted to help, not Wall Street. In FDR's inaugural address in March, he held Wall Street responsible for the calamity and pledged to neuter the financial class. The speech is best remembered for the statement that "the only thing we have to fear is fear itself," but it then continued in a more condemnatory vein:

> The unscrupulous money changers stand indicted in the court
> of public opinion, rejected by the hearts and minds of men. . . .
> They know only the rules of a generation of self-seekers. They
> have no vision, and when there is no vision the people perish.
> The money changers have fled from their high seats in the tem-
> ple of our civilization. We may now restore that temple to the
> ancient truths. The measure of the restoration lies in the extent

to which we apply social values more noble than mere monetary profit. Happiness lies not in the mere possession of money; it lies in the joy of achievement, in the thrill of creative effort. The joy and moral stimulation of work no longer must be forgotten in the mad chase of evanescent profits. These dark days will be worth all they cost us if they teach us that our true destiny is not to be ministered unto but to minister to ourselves and to our fellow men.

The first item on FDR's legislative agenda was to stop the financial rot that he and his advisers believed lay at the heart of the problem. Hoover to the end believed that the worst of the Depression was exported to the United States by contagion from abroad, but even he had sympathy for the idea that speculation had run amok. There had already been bills percolating in Congress to address that problem and attempts to curtail it in the future. Their champion was Senator Carter Glass of Virginia, and the bill he crafted altered the trajectory of Brown Brothers Harriman almost as much as the Depression and the merger.

Self-taught, physically slight, vertically challenged, passionately progressive, deeply ambitious, and all too comfortable with segregation, Glass served in government for more than forty years. It is hard to find a more significant American public servant who has received less attention. His career is a reminder that the Groton-Yale Northeast WASP elite were by no means the only center of power in the early twentieth century. Glass was first a newspaperman in Lynchburg, Virginia, before being appointed to the House of Representatives in 1902, where he served for eight terms and was instrumental in the legislation creating the Federal Reserve System. Wilson asked him to be treasury secretary in 1918, and then Glass was again appointed to an open congressional seat, this time as a senator, where he remained for twenty-six years and was almost his party's nominee for president in 1924.[18]

Starting in 1931, Glass began to cobble together legislation to address the financial causes of the Depression. By the time of FDR's ascension, he had a working framework for how to reform the banking sector, and in the House, the long-serving Democrat Henry Steagall of Alabama proved to be an able partner. Winthrop Aldrich, son of Republican senator Nelson Aldrich, who had been so pivotal in crafting the Federal Reserve Act (and was uncle to both David and Nelson Rockefeller), was also intimately involved in the legislation, which is an indication of how much some key figures of the Establishment were in favor of reform and regulation. The chaos of the banking collapse had nearly engulfed the entire industry, and even the more conservative among them saw some virtue in setting better rules and having more oversight. The resulting banking bill, the Glass-Steagall Act, was signed into law in June 1933. It upended the landscape of banking and investing, and it forced the happy Brown Brothers Harriman marriage to undergo a divorce.

The stated purpose of the act was "to provide for the safer and more effective use of the assets of banks, to regulate interbank control, to prevent the undue diversion of funds into speculative operations." There were two major provisions: the creation of bank deposit insurance in the form of the Federal Deposit Insurance Corporation (FDIC), which was designed to assure depositors and prevent bank runs, and the mandated separation of commercial banking—deposits, loans, money management, mortgages—from investment banking. That meant that a deposit bank couldn't issue and underwrite securities or act as an institutional broker, and the managers of one couldn't sit on the board of another or use other backdoor means for control. Every institution that had both functions was given a year to decide which would be its focus. The act also created the Federal Open Market Committee, which would come to assume responsibility for setting targets for short-term interest rates.[19]

The Glass-Steagall Act was the most important financial reform bill of the New Deal, and perhaps of the twentieth century. The separation of commercial and investment banking remained in place for decades, and has widely been credited with helping prevent future financial crises until 2008, by which time most of the act had been repealed or gutted. It was not the only New Deal piece of financial legislation. Along with it, Roosevelt signed the Securities Act of 1933, the "truth in securities" law, which required companies to disclose more public information about their business when issuing shares and made those companies liable for information that was deceptive or fraudulent. A year later saw the creation of the Securities and Exchange Commission (SEC) to oversee and enforce this new wave of regulations. As its first head, FDR appointed Joseph P. Kennedy, who had made a fortune trading stocks in the 1920s and had once remarked, "It's easy to make money in this market. . . . We'd better get in before they pass a law against it." His appointment was greeted with howls. It was, said one outraged liberal critic, "setting a wolf to guard a flock of sheep." The SEC became Wall Street's cop, and its creation helped propel the Kennedy dynasty into politics.

These laws were passed because of the widespread belief that the clubby nature of Wall Street and the close bonds between the various firms had allowed for the easy exchange of inside information and the issuance of fraudulent or overvalued securities backed by the hard-earned deposits of real companies and actual people. It is undeniably true that the 1920s had seen more banks get into the securities business, aggressively buying and selling stocks and bonds. That was seen as having fueled the bubble that triggered the crash and the damaging bank collapses, and, voilà, the Great Depression. Later work suggests that while speculation was indeed out of hand in the late 1920s, the involvement of commercial banks was not a fundamental reason for the Depression. But in 1933, the perception was nearly universal. Hence the regulations and agencies designed to curb those people and tame their insider culture to ensure that never again would they be allowed to endanger the public good for their own private gain. No one invoked a cross of gold, but William Jennings Bryan, fervent believer in fate and providence, surely was smiling down from the heaven he prayed he would be in, surrounded by a chorus of populist angels singing amen.[20]

As it turned out, it was deposit insurance and the FDIC rather than Glass-Steagall that had the most immediate palliative effect. Knowing that your savings at your local bank were now backed by a federal guarantee removed the primary reason for bank runs and failures. By 1934, the number of bank collapses had shrunk to insignificance. Perhaps that was because the weakest banks had already failed, but in the years following, the FDIC guarantee acted as a powerful security blanket. Since 1932, there has never been an equivalent rash of bank failures triggered by widespread panicked withdrawals.

For Wall Street, and for Brown Brothers, Glass-Steagall was dramatic. It forced firms to decide what business they wanted to be in and which to divest. For the newly christened Brown Brothers Harriman, it meant a separation and a radical change. "That affected us quite severely," Prescott Bush recalled. "I mean, we were cut right through the middle."[21] Prescott and Roland, Republicans both, supported the law as sound policy, even as it negatively affected them. So too did Bob Lovett, who wrote to Harriman in 1933 that in his judgment, "the Glass-Steagall Bill is not all bad by darnsight. It seems me to take a decided step forward. . . . The real opportunity the legislation offers is for some unified banking system. And I am all for that. . . . Our forty-eight different types of banking legislation simply make for confusion and unnecessary risk. While I am prepared to admit that you cannot legislate good banking practice into a man's head, I likewise believe that you can legislate a bad banking machine out of a man's hands."[22]

The firm, unlike so many on Wall Street that raged at the New Deal, was open to reform and to thoughtful regulation. The partners recognized that public confidence was at a nadir, and that there was a social license to operate that no financial institution could do without. In the wake of the crash and the Depression, financial firms were once again in the crosshairs of public ire. The pain of the shotgun divorce mandated by Glass-Steagall would be mitigated by restored trust. The suite of new laws also established some clarity, and Lovett for one was glad that henceforth, the firm would not have to contend with an endless thicket of regulations from forty-eight different states. The increase of federal power and oversight were short-term inconveniences that would, in the long term, cost Brown Brothers and the industry less.

But breaking up was hard to do. The partners took their time to assess their options. It was not a decision to be made lightly, and the partners were divided over which business to choose for the primary entity. Had it been up to Averell, Brown Brothers likely would have elected to be an investment bank; that was his area of focus in the 1920s. It was not, however, where the bulk of the merged firm's business lay. According to Thatcher's unpublished memoir, "As we analyzed our business over the past years, we found that about 65 percent of it had been regular banking business and only 35 percent underwriting and selling securities." That made the decision clear, even if it went against the desires of the one person who was able to provide emergency working capital. The partnership chose commercial banking and would spin off the investment bank.

On June 6, 1934, the firm announced that pursuant to the new law, it would split into two: Brown Brothers Harriman as the commercial bank and Brown Brothers Harriman & Co., Inc. to be the investment bank focusing on underwriting and dealing in bond issuance and other securities. The $5 million in initial capital for the spin-off was provided for by, no surprise, the Harriman fortune. If it seemed messy that the names were so similar, it was. Recalled Prescott, "It was a great mistake, because there was immediate confusion . . . it was constantly annoying and troublesome." The investment bank took some employees from the legacy firm, but while the capital came from Harriman, many of the personnel came from National City Bank of New York (later Citibank). Like Brown Brothers, National City spun off its securities division, and its president, Joseph Ripley, was one of Averell's college friends. The Brown Brothers Harriman and National City investment banks merged into one with Ripley as its head. After a few years of testy requests by Brown Brothers, it renamed itself Harriman Ripley, which they had resisted because while Ripley was a fine name and all, it didn't have the cachet of Brown Brothers.[23]

What seemed optically dramatic, of course, ended up being somewhat less so in practice. The separate firms could no longer underwrite securities and then take deposits and use those to underwrite more; they could no longer use their own accounts to fund large purchases and issues. But the same individuals could still work with each other as long as their firms were distinct legal entities. A partner of Brown Brothers Harriman could not act as an investment banker, but he could certainly do business with investment bankers. The legal separation mattered, but not as much as it appeared. Brown Brothers was unusual, however, in choosing for its primary business commercial banking, which was usually less lucrative albeit more stable. That played a significant role in determining the future evolution of the firm, and one reason, in addition to its sustainable culture of enough, that it did not become a behemoth in assets or personnel. In Baltimore, Alex. Brown & Sons, its now-distant cousin, became an investment bank, as did prominent houses such as Lehman Brothers and Goldman Sachs.

Though the partners of the independent firms continued to work closely with one another in ways that would later be seen as violating the spirit if not the letter of the laws, they did not act in bad faith. In their dealings, they used information and connections and access to financing that the vast majority of the public did not. There were no laws then to prevent that, and there were not yet many layers of mandated disclosure, even with the Securities Act demanding some. The small number of people involved in high finance meant that relationships and personal connections mattered hugely, before the New Deal reforms and after. J.P. Morgan spun off its investment bank division into Morgan Stanley, which included the partners of Drexel & Co., founded in Philadelphia by portrait-painter-turned-banker Francis Martin Drexel, whose son Anthony Joseph had set up the initial Morgan firm with Junius Morgan, Pierpont's father. Morgan Stanley opened its offices in 1935 at 2 Wall Street, a few doors down from the main J.P. Morgan offices at 23 Wall Street, and continued to use office space in the old firm.[24]

It is true that the passage of these acts led to less frenzy on Wall Street, fewer new issues and a general tendency to conserve capital. The number of shares traded on the New York Stock Exchange stayed far below 1920s levels. Although the worst for the financial system had passed by 1934, the Depression still gripped the country overall, and animal spirits remained in hibernation. Investment banking was a fine business in the thirties, but not an extraordinarily lucrative one. Commercial banking, however, thrived.

Brown Brothers Harriman began to innovate and create new lines of business to replace both its waning franchise in travelers' credits (made redundant by the emergence of American Express and travelers' checks) and its lost underwriting fees. The New Deal attack on the power of money, which echoed earlier assaults, reshaped corporate structures but did less to disperse the concentrated power on Wall Street. New Deal laws dampened stock speculation and the more egregious forms of corrupt dealing, and deposit insurance began an era free of widespread bank panics. Even so, the populist surge did not dent the profitability of Brown Brothers and their brethren. The priests of the temple had faced an existential threat of insolvency and had, in the end, muddled through.

The New Deal faltered at the end of FDR's first term, and the economic recovery stalled. The rhetoric against concentrations of money and power then intensified once again. Even though banks were now more regulated than at any point in American history, the relative prosperity of capital versus labor, of the owners of companies rather than the workers, and the continued struggles of rural America propelled Roosevelt to take a harsher stance in his reelection campaign against Alfred Landon, the Republican nominee and popular governor of Kansas. In a fiery speech in New York's Madison Square Garden, FDR unleashed a torrent of vitriol against those who had attempted to thwart the New Deal and had successfully undermined the signature reform of the time, the National Recovery Administration, which had been tasked with coordinating the reforms and granted extensive powers to do so. Roosevelt vowed to continue "to struggle with the old enemies of peace—business and financial monopoly, speculation, reckless banking, class antagonism, sectionalism," and he denounced as "tyrants" those who warned of economic collapse should he be reelected.

Roosevelt, of course, was swept to another victory in the fall of 1936. But his verbal sallies against the temples of money and the captains of industry did not translate into crippling actions any more than his cousin Theodore's presidency had seen trustbusting become ubiquitous. After the flurry of reforms in the first years of the New Deal, the financial infrastructure of the United States had been more or less set, with some subsequent tweaking but no major additions, not during the remainder of Roosevelt's presidency and not for many decades thereafter.

And so Brown Brothers Harriman was left to tend to its own business, keeping a low profile as was the firm's wont. That served it well in a time when a higher profile could have invited a punitive backlash. As the battles raged over the shape and course of the New Deal and as the economic downturn stayed intractable, Brown Brothers Harriman and its partners put their heads down and created new businesses that would shape the financial world for the rest of the twentieth century. And they began as well to move into politics, where they would shape the political and economic order that would define the globe.

CHAPTER 13

"WE WERE VERY HARD WORKERS"

The United States in the mid-1930s entered a twilight period. The worst of the Depression had passed, and FDR had succeeded in lifting the public mood out of stark fear and panic into mild optimism. The present remained challenging, but Roosevelt assured the public that the future would be better. By his second term, however, it was clear that the New Deal had not succeeded in restoring the economy, at least not fully. In spite of some promising signs, economic growth in 1937 stalled even as the sense of immediate collapse subsided. There were fierce debates about whether American democracy had run its course, and whether it was time for a reconsideration of a capitalist system that could create such crises and hardship. Meanwhile, most firms simply got back to business. Brown Brothers Harriman was no exception.

The new old company, now solely a commercial bank, needed to find fresh clients and new lines of business if it was to remain viable. Harriman money provided some breathing room, but it was not an endless well. The point was to make money, not to lose it, and not to rely on being bailed out by a partner's family. While Roland assumed a key role in the firm's leadership, Averell increasingly turned his attention to Washington and to his chairmanship of the struggling Union Pacific. The sprawling line was facing dire circumstances because of the sharp decline in freight and passenger traffic as well as the rise of the automobile as an existential competitive threat to the railroads. Dozens of rail companies were going bankrupt, and others survived only because of government subsidies that kept them from insolvency. Baltimore's B&O, whose stock price peaked during the pre-1929 bubble at $145 a share, plummeted to $3 by 1932 and received an emergency government loan of $31 million.

Averell's answer to what ailed the Union Pacific was to spend more. Contrary to what many do when faced with a business losing customers and bleeding money, Averell didn't try to cut his way to profitability. Instead, like his father, he invested. He did trim costs by closing stations, but he did not skimp on maintenance and new equipment. As he took more active control of the business after Judge Lovett died in 1932, Averell also invested more in passenger services, especially dining cars. While buses and automobiles had many advantages over rails, especially in the freedom they afforded, railroads could offer a more relaxing, pampered experience. But there had been little innovation since the heyday of the Pullman cars, and by the early 1930s, the Union Pacific was dusty and dingy. So Averell decided to allocate $50 million to upgrading passenger service. "We set ourselves the job of regaining public confidence. . . . We had been afraid of innovations, afraid to disturb the picture. . . ."[1]

The result was a stunning transformation. The Union Pacific introduced streamlined passenger cars using lighter materials. An engineering overhaul allowed these sleek new cars to travel faster, and the radical upgrade in speed and comfort succeeded in attracting attention and traffic after 1932. Hundreds of thousands of people turned out in Washington, Baltimore, Chicago and other stops to see a prototype of the new train. Averell got even more publicity by breaking the record for the fastest transcontinental journey of seventy-one hours that had been last set by his father in 1906. On October 22, 1934, his train left Los Angeles and arrived in New York City fifty-six hours later. The next day, almost sixty thousand people came to walk through the cars at Penn Station.[2] A new superfast train, powered by a diesel engine—which was touted as the next big thing in transportation—touched all the right chords in a society still mired in a deep economic slump but eager to see the potential of new technologies and human invention.

Harriman was eager to maintain the momentum. What he did next was unexpected, but it turned out spectacularly. While modern new trains with amenities and creature comforts could attract passengers, people would only travel great distances if they had somewhere to go. To that end, Averell mulled the idea of a destination that only the Union Pacific could offer. The line already generated some revenue as the prime conveyance for tourists who wanted to visit Yellowstone Park, but what if there was another place tourists could visit, a resort owned and developed by the railroad itself? And so, in the late fall of 1935, Averell began to scout locations throughout the West for a ski resort proximate to the Union Pacific's routes.

He had recently met a young Austrian skier on a family hunting trip, and on a lark offered him a stipend to find the perfect spot. Skiing was then becoming more popular, boosted by the success and publicity of the Lake Placid Winter Olympics in 1932, and Harriman saw economic possibilities where Roland, Robert Lovett Jr. and the senior management of Union Pacific did not. Yes, there were modest ski resorts in upstate New York and New England, and some out west at Lake Tahoe, Mount Rainier in Washington, and Mount Hood, Oregon. But these were few and far between, and none had the glitz and luxury of the alpine resorts of Europe. At best, Averell's colleagues thought it would be a quixotic venture that would waste some money; at worst, they thought it would be an expensive failure that would tarnish the company's image.

The young Austrian was named Felix Schaffgotsch, who may or may not have been a minor aristocrat with vestiges of family money but who insisted on being called a count. Felix took to the task: he spent months looking for locations across thousands of miles of mountain area near to the Union Pacific lines. He was about to inform Harriman that he'd found nothing suitable when he was told of a perfectly set bowl nestled in the mountains around Ketchum, Idaho. He trekked there and recognized its possibilities within hours. He wired Harriman that he had, at last, found it.

Harriman immediately set off in February 1936 with his wife and young daughter, along with his close friend Bill Paley of CBS. He took one look at the place and fell in love.

In less than a year, Averell had persuaded the board of Union Pacific to plow millions into building a grand hotel and funding an aggressive and what proved to be uniquely successful marketing campaign. The area was renamed Sun Valley. The luxury lodge was built, and to ensure that the grand opening scheduled for December 1936 was an event that every paper and newsreel would cover, Harriman encouraged his advertising gurus to market to the glitterati of Hollywood. If Sun Valley became associated in the popular mind with the glamour and mystique of Hollywood stars, it could become the premier winter spot of the United States. And so it did.[3]

Sun Valley, however, faced unexpected competition from the New Deal. One of the many projects of the Works Progress Administration (the New Deal agency charged with investing in the nation's infrastructure) was to build up a resort and trail complex at Mount Hood in nearby Oregon. That made it even more important for Sun Valley to stand out. There was no snow when the guests assembled in late December, which meant a few weeks of food and booze to entertain the likes of Claudette Colbert, Errol Flynn and the powerful producer David Selznick. The guests at least got to ride the newest innovation, the first chairlift in the United States. And then it snowed.

From then on, Sun Valley became a paparazzi paradise. It was where the rich and the famous gathered to be seen in winter, and maybe to ski. In 1939, Harriman invited one of the most famous novelists of the day, Ernest Hemingway, to come to stay. There he finished *For Whom the Bell Tolls*. Hemingway brought luster to Harriman and Sun Valley; Sun Valley and Harriman gave Hemingway a place to write and drink. In the five years between the grand opening and America's entry into World War II, the resort generated hundreds of thousands of dollars annually for the Union Pacific in passenger fees alone; its train was the only viable way to get there. But the passenger rail fad of the 1930s proved to be more a blip than a trend, with automobiles surging as the dominant mode of transport after

World War II and then air travel taking off. Sun Valley remained a lucrative resort but on a small scale next to the bottom line of Union Pacific as a whole.

The images of dust-destroyed farms in the Great Plains and hard-bitten families looking blankly into the camera lens of Margaret Bourke-White and Walker Evans, the lines of the hungry waiting for food, the face of Henry Fonda's Tom Joad in the stark John Ford 1940 film adaptation of *The Grapes of Wrath*—those rightly mark our sense of the Depression years. But not all was bleak all of the time, and Hollywood thrived in part because people needed hope and escape. The flourishing advertising industry catered to those needs and hopes, and papers full of gossip about what the privileged were up to, smiling gaily with martinis in hand, acted as a balm, if not a soporific, to soothe people in a troubled time. It may have been largely a fiction, but then again, there were many millions in a middle class that did not suffer deep privation, who could afford a trip west, maybe just to gawk, in Sun Valley and elsewhere. The Harrimans, the Hollywood stars, the Wall Street elite, became celebrities and would become only more so in the years to come.

The Union Pacific was unexpectedly graced with another source of revenue, unplanned, unexpected, and ultimately worth billions of dollars. The company had acquired a large tract of land near Long Beach in California. Adjacent to the port and not particularly appealing as a residential area, it was designated an industrial zone. A portion was sold to the Ford Motor Company for a factory. The Los Angeles basin was already home to several active oil fields, and in 1932, the Union Pacific licensed prospectors to drill exploratory wells. They found oil, and not just some oil. The Wilmington Field beneath the railroad's land turned out to be the largest oil basin in California and the third largest in the United States.

The discovery happened at the perfect moment. As industrial production slowly recovered nationally, demand for oil picked up, and in fact accelerated faster than overall growth because of the boom in energy-intensive industries ranging from autos to construction. To maximize output, Harriman authorized further expenditures on the field, as did Edsel Ford for the adjoining tracts owned by Ford Motor. Dozens of wells were drilled, dotting the landscape with pumpjacks known as nodding donkeys, metronomically going up and down, with an eerie quiet. The Wilmington Field ultimately produced more than two billion barrels, not all of which were controlled by Union Pacific but which netted the company tens of billions in revenue. As passenger traffic collapsed after the 1930s and the cost of maintaining the freight system skyrocketed, these oil holdings were spun off, and spun off again, ultimately ending up in the hands of Chevron.

When not focused on building his ski resort and managing the affairs of the Union Pacific, Harriman turned toward a life in government. He had been sometimes smart and usually lucky in his business ventures, but his ambitions were not sated by augmenting the fortune he had inherited. He was one of the few men of his class and industry to support FDR, though he was hardly a radical. Harriman agreed with the basic contours of the New Deal, its regulatory framework, and the expansion of a Washington bureaucracy designed to manage the crisis, put people to work and oversee the raft of new agencies. But more than anything, Harriman wanted in, and his acquaintance with FDR, fraught though it was because of the vestiges of the old animosity between Teddy Roosevelt and E. H. Harriman, gave him his entrée. He took a small role in the signature agency created by the New Deal, the National Recovery Administration, and his primary attention turned away from the firm.

That was not without some negative ripples. Most of the firm's partners were Republican and had little love for FDR, nor did most of their clients. Those clients were not particularly fond of Averell cozying up to the New Deal Democrats, and that posed a business challenge for the firm. But whatever their private misgivings, the partners defended Averell from barbs. Prescott Bush fielded an inordinate number of calls from angry clients saying, "What the hell is your partner doing down there with this Red bunch of Communists or Socialists? We'd laugh it off and say, 'Well, Averell feels he wants to devote some time to the national interest. He's done a lot in industry and he's become interested in trying to do something for his country, and if the President wants to use him, why, fine, he's going to do it.'"[4]

While Averell shifted his energies toward Washington, Brown Brothers Harriman began to change the way it did business. It was steered less and less by Thatcher, who after the retirement of James in 1934 was now the only Brown family partner of his generation. Instead, the locus of the firm shifted to the younger partners, Bob Lovett, Roland Harriman and especially the most recent member of the group, Prescott Bush. They did not change the culture of the firm; if anything, that culture changed them. None was descended from Alexander Brown, but they embraced his mold as surely as any of the sons and grandsons.

His later prominence notwithstanding, Bush was probably the least privileged of his cohort, though in relative terms he was privileged indeed. He was born in Columbus, Ohio, his father a railroad executive who then became president of one of the many Rockefeller companies, a business called Buckeye Steel Castings that made parts for the railroads. Unlike many of his later peers, Prescott attended public schools, which exposed him to a diverse world of students from different classes and backgrounds. He told his oral history interviewer, "We had representatives of most every ethnic group in the public school, and I always felt that that gave me a sense of balance about these ethnic problems that was useful to me in later life, and particularly in political life."

For high school, Bush, by now a six-foot-four young man whose physical stature and patrician mien his sons would inherit, went to St. George's in Rhode Island, the storied old boarding school that predated Groton. There he was cast into an altogether more rarified orbit that he seems to have adjusted to with about as much friction as a well-worn pair of slippers. He became a member of the civics club, which he cited later in life as the germination of a passion for political life.[5] From St. George's, he slid into Yale in the fall of 1913 and floated into its inner circles: the Whiffenpoofs choral group, the Glee Club, baseball teams and assorted sports. To no one's surprise, he was tapped in his junior year as a Bonesman, where he befriended Roland and Knight Woolley and the others. He planned to go into politics and was intending to go to law school when the war intervened. He went into the army, became a field artillery captain and was in France in June

1918 at the tail end of the Meuse-Argonne offensive. "It was," he reminisced, "quite exciting and of course a wonderful experience."

The war over, Prescott attended his first Yale reunion in the fall of 1918 and was offered a job at a hardware company in St. Louis by one of his classmates. Not every Yalie went directly into a dream job. But Prescott had the right connections and soon met Dorothy Walker, the daughter of George Herbert Walker, a wildly successful local businessman and investor with second homes in New York City and on the North Shore of Long Island, where he'd socialized with the Harrimans. Walker also served as president of the United States Golf Association—whatever he may have felt at first about Dotty's beau, at least the young man played golf. Prescott and Dorothy fell in love and got married in St. Louis. Then, in a move that would inadvertently shape the course of American politics over the next century, George Herbert Walker went to work with Averell Harriman as president of Harriman's new investment firm.[6]

Walker was not an obvious choice for Averell. The match was born of friendship and mutual interests such as breeding and racing horses more than business affinity. Walker proved able, though his impact on the Harriman firm was muted by Averell's tendency to go it alone and to rely on his brother Roland for the day-to-day. With a prominent title and not much impact, Walker made money. He bought and built more homes and expanded the family estate in Kennebunkport, Maine. The house on Walker's Point became the summer refuge for generations of Bushes.

Prescott had a winding career. He moved back to Columbus after the sudden death of his mother to be of help to his father. He took a job with a rubber flooring company, stayed in Columbus for two years, and made sure his father would be all right. Then he accepted an offer as a junior executive at another rubber company in Massachusetts and then in New York City at the United States Rubber Company, one of the first companies to be included in the new Dow Jones Industrial Index in the 1890s, which later changed its brand name to Uniroyal, which was ultimately bought by Michelin. But Prescott was not destined for a life in rubber. As a young executive living in Greenwich, Connecticut, with two young children, including

George Herbert Walker Bush, he was offered a position at his father-in-law's firm along with his Yale classmates already there. While it was not yet common to call these associations the old boys' network, that was precisely what it was.

While Prescott was as deeply entrenched in his class as anyone, his background in business and the Midwest did set him apart from many in the financial world in these years. Not only had he grown up in a different world, though of a similar class, he had also been a middle manager and was attuned to the demands of an operating business that needed to make and sell products. In subsequent years, that made him particularly adept at tailoring the offerings of Brown Brothers Harriman to the needs of its nonfinancial clients, and particularly good at speaking about business in a way that seemed savvy and often was. It also served him well when he turned to electoral politics, which called on his skills as a salesman as well as a statesman.

As cornerstones of the service industry, banks and financial firms were not primarily in the business of products. Hence the distinction between, say, a manufacturing or retail business and the service industry. True, travelers' checks and letters of credit were in their way "products" that were made, packaged and sold at a profit. The financial industry, however, made money mostly on activities that were derivatives of an operating business. Trading securities, handling deposits, extending loans and mortgages— these derived from and supported the activities of individuals and companies. That was true of large financial institutions, and even more so for local banks, whose primary franchise was to take in deposits and then provide credit to local companies, developers and homeowners. Local bankers, ensconced in the community, were connected socially and personally to the men who ran those companies. Credit decisions were often made based on those connections. The best Wall Street firms operated much like local banks, in the sense that relationships were a key element in assessing risk and making decisions. Most bankers, however, rarely had the experience of actually working in the companies they underwrote. Prescott did, and that may explain why he proved so adept at reframing the business of Brown Brothers Harriman after the investment banking split in 1934.

Parts of the financial world in the 1930s hadn't changed much from a century earlier. The buying and selling of stocks, arranging loans, the issuance of bonds, letters of credit, and banker's acceptances to facilitate trade looked then much as they had in the nineteenth century. Brown Brothers Harriman had met those needs for generations and knew how to. In the 1930s, however, there was nothing resembling what we now call wealth management or investment management. In the decades prior, people with assets usually kept gold or cash in a bank, bought real estate and jewelry, had a few bonds and invested directly in businesses. Some bought stocks and had been burned if they didn't get out before the middle of 1929. And some of those who invested directly in stocks and bonds relied on the advice of a trusted adviser or broker, who was compensated with commissions on the trades and only very rarely with fees. Wage earners were not part of the picture. Large companies such as General Electric and U.S. Steel had started providing pension plans for their employees, and the passage of the Social Security Act in 1935 gave working Americans their first guaranteed income in retirement. But almost none of them managed their retirement funds directly.

For the affluent, the demands were different, and in the 1930s were not adequately addressed. Prescott's insight was to recognize an unmet need. Under his leadership, Brown Brothers Harriman became one of the first established firms to emphasize investment management services for its clients, and to charge fees for doing so. It hardly seemed a radical move at the time, more an organic outgrowth of informal business already being done, which could then be routinized and commoditized to the pecuniary benefit of the firm and its clients. But it would prove in its way as transformative of the financial industry, and by extension American society, as the early use of letters of credit for trade and travel and the paper architecture that had enabled the economic and industrial expansion of the United States.

The new avenue seems to have been opened accidentally and was primarily a product of Bush's skill as a salesman. Averell had recently befriended the thirtysomething Bill Paley, head of the small but fast-growing Columbia Broadcasting System, or perhaps it was Paley—younger, Jewish, less connected—who sought out Averell as the entrée to the Establishment that he wanted to be part of. Paley's father was a Ukrainian cigar maker; Averell's had built one of the largest railroad empires in the United States. Paley wanted to change the world; Averell already owned much of it. One of the first pure radio companies, CBS was founded in 1927. The twenties were the era of the radio. The first commercial broadcast was only in 1920, after the wartime ban on civilian radio was lifted, but there were few listeners because there were so few sets. As mass production picked up and prices for the sets dropped, home ownership of radios started accelerating. By 1930, nearly two-thirds of American households had a radio. That was why FDR could become the first radio candidate and why he was able to use radio to communicate directly with people. It was also why so many millions felt they had an unusually direct and intimate connection with him: his voice, in those fireside chats, broadcast into their living rooms. CBS rode that wave.

Soon after the founding of CBS, Paley turned to the Hollywood studio Paramount Pictures for additional capital. Averell brokered the deal, and Paramount bought a minority stake. As part of the agreement, Paramount retained the right to purchase the rest of CBS on favorable terms, but then the Depression hit and Paramount filed for bankruptcy. Instead of buying the rest of CBS, Paramount now had to sell its stake. CBS was not quite the radio powerhouse it would soon become, but it was valuable and growing steadily. Paley had an option to buy back the 49 percent of CBS that Paramount owned, and he turned once again to Brown Brothers Harriman. This time, with Averell no longer handling most of the business, Paley worked with Prescott on the buyout that would make CBS a wholly independent company.[7]

It was not a huge transaction. CBS had only a few dozen stations and lagged behind RCA's National Broadcasting Company (NBC). But Paley was ambitious and connected. He had a vision for CBS not just as a broadcaster but as a creator of content. Paramount needed to unload its shares quickly rather than at a premium, and Paley seized the opportunity to gain full control. Paley almost certainly would have spoken with Averell first, privately, not in a formal meeting at 59 Wall Street, and Averell almost certainly told him that his firm would love to help and that he should arrange the specifics of the deal with Bush. Paley had about $2.5 million lined up to buy out Paramount, but he needed to come up with a total of at least $5 million, which he didn't have. Brown Brothers and Prescott were able to assemble a consortium in short order. Averell put in some more money personally, as did Lehman Brothers, which at times was a rival and at other times joined with Brown Brothers for joint deals. Paramount took the money, and Paley gained full control of CBS. Harriman, Bush and their firm acquired a client. Over time, that investment would reap the firm many, many times its initial investment.

As a result of the deal, Prescott joined the board of CBS, where he remained until he became a senator in 1952. Being on the board tightened his connections with men such as Richard Dupree, the new CEO of Procter & Gamble, who was focused on building his brand through advertising. Where better to advertise than radio? Dupree asked Prescott to join his board too. And so it went. Later, as many started to question the motives and behavior of the Establishment, Bush had no doubts that he had behaved honorably and conducted himself with the utmost integrity. By his lights, the web of relationships cemented by money were inherently constructive. Rotating sets of people, in overlapping concentric circles, provided funds, sat on boards, went to dinner, served in companies. Glass-Steagall may have removed one conflict of interest, but it didn't disrupt the personal webs that were vital to future business. Brown Brothers in the nineteenth century had existed in a tight community bound by economic bonds and often linked by social connections. Joseph Shipley could not have walked into the offices of the Bank of England in 1837 had it been otherwise. The firm cultivated a deserved reputation for discretion. The client came first, and because the partners put up their own capital when financing a venture, they would gain only if the deal did well for their clients and suffer if it did not. That is how the partners saw their world. Prescott Bush was new to the firm, but in that respect Brown Brothers Harriman had changed little over the years.[8]

Brown Brothers was never about size. In 1934, as part of the new raft of

New Deal regulations, the partnership was required to disclose its deposits for the first time. It reported barely more than $20 million, well behind the behemoths such as Chase National and National City, though still enough to place Brown in the top one hundred of the largest banks in the country out of nearly fifteen thousand. Size alone was not the sole or even the most significant criterion for influence; relationships were, and because of those relationships, the firm stumbled into wealth management.[9]

As a result of the CBS deal, Paley and CBS kept accounts at Brown Brothers. As CBS grew, so did the size of its accounts at the bank. The question then was how to put those to more productive use. "We were very hard workers," Bush recalled, and with the spin-off of the investment bank, the partnership was focused on finding additional revenue and new business. The firm had a seat on the New York Stock Exchange and so could buy and sell securities directly. In Bush's telling, people began approaching the partners and asking, "Look, I have half a million dollars. I don't know what to do about this market. What should I do?" In response, the partners would say, "Well, why don't you let us do this for you? We're doing it for the Harrimans, our own partners, so and so's wife, and the children and my own wife. . . . We can do for you just what we're doing for ourselves, if you think that's good enough."[10]

The crisis of 1929 undoubtedly created a need. Bewildered by the seemingly endless descent of the stock market and the collapse of commercial activity across the board, clients sought advice. As always happens, for guidance they turned to experts they trusted. As the crisis eased, the partners realized that advice was itself a service they could offer and charge for. That was the prosaic beginning of a multibillion-dollar industry that grew over the twentieth century to guide and oversee trillions of dollars of investments, from massive pension plans to the retirement accounts of schoolteachers.

In response to the demand, Brown Brothers created an Investment Advisory Department. While wealth management would in time grow to encompass not just the high-net-worth world but large swaths of the middle class, the partnership was uninterested in small accounts. They may have inadvertently planted the seeds of the larger, more democratized wealth management industry to come, but that was not what the partners were interested in. They were exclusively focused on high-net-worth individuals. They wanted minimum amounts of $200,000, which could generate at least $1,000 in fees per year, half a percent on each dollar under management; that was the equivalent of about $3.6 million in today's money generating $18,000 in fees. In order to boost the fledgling business, the firm sought celebrity clients, on the same theory that Sun Valley looked to Hollywood stars as its first guests: celebrities were free advertising and helped burnish the brand as exclusive, desirable, trusted by the rich and famous.

The idea of charging fees to advise clients about how to invest was novel. Brokers made their money from commissions on transactions rather than from fees based on assets under management. Since then, what was novel has become standard. Charging a fee based not on buying and selling but on how much money was under management followed a simple principle: doing so would provide an incentive to the adviser to see that pool of money grow. Brokers could earn commissions on the purchase or sale of stock whether or not that transaction was in the best interests of the client; a broker gets paid whether the stock goes up or down, whether the client does well or poorly. Charging an asset-based fee was thought to align the client with the manager. Brown Brothers could honestly say to its clients that they did well only if the client did well. The firm's wealth management business grew rapidly after the first small experiments in 1931. By the mid-1930s, the investment management division was not only substantial but also highly profitable. What began as an experiment morphed into a more formal business line. Given that it needed to scale to be truly lucrative, the firm began doing something that it had largely avoided over the years: it advertised.

The 1930s saw a boom in the advertising industry. In spite of the Depression, or perhaps because of it, companies avidly sought new ways to reach customers. In response, Madison Avenue advertising firms began to refine their methods of reaching consumers and tailoring and targeting messages. The famed ad man Edward Bernays, who later applied those skills to public relations and American foreign policy, helped large corporations such as Procter & Gamble market their products more effectively. Brown Brothers, which had thrived in the reputation and word-of-mouth world of nineteenth-century banking, decided in 1934 to launch an ad campaign in *The New York Times* announcing its new wealth management offerings. The first ad was titled "What the Private Banker Does." The next ones went on to enumerate the answers to that question, and the final one touted the firm's exclusivity, "A Limited Number of Clients."

The financial press took notice. In the words of *The Wall Street Journal*, "Superficially, but superficially only, [Brown Brothers] thus makes a radical departure from the ways it has been accustomed since 1818. In other respects, its practice of private banking still anchors on the bottom principles which, by all reasonable inference, explain its survival: A body of business precept and procedure which has outlasted the financial chaos of early America, the long struggles out of wildcat banking . . . the inauguration of a national banking system . . . and finally the wrenching dislocations of a World War and its aftermath."[11] Charging for acumen and advice based on a century of experience came naturally to the firm, as did its approach to investment management and private banking. The mutual fund industry was barely in its infancy, so helping clients preserve and augment their assets meant deciding the right blend of stocks and bonds and then selecting the specific securities for a client's portfolio. To do the research on a wider array of companies outside of the business relationships the firm already had, Brown Brothers hired analysts and became the first of what would later be called on Wall Street buy-side firms because they were in the business of buying securities, whether for clients or their own accounts, as opposed to the investment banks that sold them.

To augment the marketing material beyond a few ads, Prescott penned a lengthy pamphlet titled "Scattered Wealth." It was astute, and manipulative. It had a picture of Alexander Brown on the cover, to remind any who might otherwise be unaware of the legacy. The booklet played on the legitimate fears people, even those of means, had of market volatility and the prospect of losing one's hard-earned, or inherited, wealth. It began by puncturing the myth that putting money in a safe deposit box is safe; over time, it warned, as have generations of wealth managers and private bankers in the decades since, that inert cash in a box, used to purchase gold, or left under a mattress, will steadily lose its value. At the time, there were no reliable or consistent statistics on inflation; the statistical agencies were in their infancy, and no one thought in terms of things like GDP, inflation, or purchasing power. But if they lacked those terms and the statistics to undergird them, most people with some money and a desire to save it and pass it on to heirs grasped the basic concept.

Even those who felt they understood stocks and bonds, Bush warned gently, might be resting on a false sense of security. Too much had changed and was changing too quickly for one to be complacent about one's sagacity about money and investments. Unless you had a staff to keep the pulse of the markets and analyze meticulously the movements of companies, their stocks, their bonds and the overall contours of the financial system and the regulatory framework, you were likely to come up short. The arguments he made then are in essence indistinguishable from what investment advisers still tell their clients. The world, Bush, concluded, was being convulsed by "sweeping federal legislation, designed to control and regulate business as never before." What's more, "scientific and technological advances in recent years are recognized as revolutionary. New inventions and new industries usually cause dislocations of labor and other social and industrial readjustments; international and political relations are on a new interwoven dimension. All of which will increase the difficulty of managing investments."[12]

In touting the firm's offerings, Bush touched on what would soon become familiar tropes: the idea that managing money requires skill that few laymen possess; the world is rapidly changing in ways that make old assumptions outdated; only those who devote themselves to making sense of what can be bewildering changes can identify the right stocks and bonds and the appropriate mix tailored to the individual needs of clients and their appetite for risk. Many of these statements contain considerable truth, but the way they were presented spoke to not-so-latent anxieties about having money and losing it. The underlying message was that professional money managers and private bankers are the best bulwark against bad decisions.

Having helped make the money of the nineteenth century, having acted as trusted stewards for the quicksilver of paper promises only sometimes backed by solid assets, hard specie or firm government commitments, Brown Brothers Harriman made a natural move to use its skills and reputation to help clients navigate a world of money that had become more complex and remained intensely volatile. In a brochure from 1938 titled "The Album of a Bank," the firm emphasized the qualities it believed would appeal most to its clientele: the fact that Brown Brothers had a handful of partners and—that phrase from its earlier ads—"a limited number of clients"; that every client is unique and that offerings must be tailored to those specific needs; that the firm was, among all other choices, heir to a long heritage that would stand the test of time. And so even as it was launching a new business line, it tethered that to the old. Its new investment advisory business would more than replace the investment banking that Glass-Steagall stripped from it.

One never knows how much a company believes its own marketing, but Brown Brothers had a somewhat looser culture in private than its public mien of gray eminence. After publishing the investment primer, Prescott circulated a parody memo to the partners titled "Shattered Health." In it, he wrote that "there is nothing about a book on investment that looks particularly hard to write. . . . Of course this is a joke. Maybe you have never tried to edit such a book, let alone write it; but I have." That was a send-up of the opening line of "Scattered Wealth," which said: "There is nothing about bonds and stocks that looks particularly hard to manage. . . . Only this is an illusion." He went on to lament that in writing a book as one in a partnership, everybody had an opinion and an edit but no one wanted to take responsibility and put their name on it. "Three of the partners in New York think the whole idea is lousy and should be abandoned in favor of a Christmas card." He ended the memo saying that "I don't give a damn what anybody thinks and so this book is going to be printed and in your hand no later than January and if you don't like it you can write a letter to Alexander Brown who died in 1834."[13]

"Shattered Health" is a reminder of how much of the color of these men was hidden. Behind the muffled doors of those clubs and inner offices, in the drawing rooms on Park Avenue and on the shores of Long Island, there was another world, an extension of those weeklong dances at Yale, an outgrowth of an all-male-school world that was cruder and ruder and more jocular. In public, their rough edges were occluded, their feelings tucked tightly away. Their culture was one of a certain way of presenting oneself to the world, with the private self at times a very different animal, though that, of course, depended on the individual. For a man such as Alexander Brown, the person who comes through in letters and business dealings was likely much who he was in the privacy of his home; the same was true of John Crosby Brown. But for others, for Averell Harriman and Prescott Bush and Bob Lovett, there were more irreverent, coarser, funnier, lustier versions of themselves that rarely peeked through the public façade of reserve. Averell could be stiff and aloof professionally, but he was also known as a bon vivant with a hyperactive social life. He wooed, dated and married a succession of high-society women, culminating with Pamela Digby. Lovett was a college dandy who had courted his wife, Adele, dancing and drinking, and as a couple, they were frequent clubgoers in Prohibition New York and afterward. Prescott's memo hinted that they did not always take themselves seriously, that they could be self-deprecating and petty about their clients, that they were complex and kept secrets. They were also very, very good at making sure that what went on in private stayed private, forever. Brown Brothers Harriman is unique not just in its longevity, influence and continuity of its culture, but in the complete absence of errant partners who made scandalous waves.

As the firm took on more business, it acquired a marquee set of high-profile clients whose wealth the firm managed. The work included not only structuring investment portfolios but tending to mundane needs such as tax returns and estate planning. There are several folders dedicated to "famous people" in the archives of the firm, replete with mundane and occasionally entertaining correspondence. One was Archibald MacLeish, Pulitzer Prize–winning poet, writer and playwright, an editor at *Fortune* before being appointed as the Librarian of Congress under FDR. MacLeish later helped recruit scholars for the wartime intelligence agencies that were a precursor to the CIA, joined the Office of War Information, and then, briefly, filled the post of assistant secretary of state for public affairs. He was also long connected socially to Lovett, who had been close to Archibald's older brother, Kenneth MacLeish, a member of the Yale air unit who had been killed in action in 1918. Archibald was a walking set of contradictions, at once at home in the world of money, secrecy and class, but also prone to essays and plays that took bankers to task for the collapse of the Depression. Lovett wasn't just an old friend; he was an investor in one of MacLeish's plays, an investment that went to zero but which Lovett dismissed as well worth it nonetheless. Brown Brothers handled Archibald's taxes and investments, and it was the former that caused the most problems. Even though the income tax was barely two decades old, Americans quickly adapted to the new regime with the familiar mix of evasion and resentment as well as the headache of keeping good records, which, in a time when everything was simply reams of paper receipts, could be trickier to keep track of unless you were well organized, which Archibald MacLeish decidedly was not.

In that vein, he wrote to the firm confessing that he could not meet the perfectly reasonable requests for documentation. "As regards the allowance for expense," he wrote, "I keep no books of expenditures in connection with lectures, trips etc. and the figure I have given you is a figure based upon my recollection of railroad fares and living expenses in connection with trips to Chicago, Iowa City and to many other nearer places. . . . All I can say of the item is that it represents my best memory and is certainly considerably less than actual expenses incurred." Imagine how the junior tax person assigned to him at the firm must have felt, picturing the discussion with the IRS and having to assure the auditor that the numbers must be correct because their client said that was what he remembered paying. MacLeish frequently appealed directly to the partners, including complaining to his old friend Lovett, who once phoned the firm's tax department and told them to waive the $25 fee for annual tax service "in view of the fact that Mr. MacLeish was at the moment irritated about something else that had happened . . . and this would just serve to increase his irritation."

Also amusing was the correspondence between the firm and the husband-wife duo of Dorothy Parker and Alan Campbell. Parker had become famous in the 1920s as the impresario of the boozy New York literary Algonquin Round Table, writing first for *Vanity Fair* and then for *The New Yorker* under its founding editor, Harold Ross. Parker was known for her acerbic wit. She once quipped, "If you want to know what God thinks of money, just look at the people he gave it to." She wrote poetry in a time when writing poetry could make you famous; she married, divorced, had flings—all of which were fodder for gossip columns hungry for details about the group that coalesced around her. She also befriended a fair number of the city's financial elite, and Averell, Lovett and Adele enjoyed the occasional evening out with the Round Table group in the 1920s. One might cynically say it made the bankers feel cool and the artists feel rich, but there was clearly an affinity.

Parker's social set dissipated with the onset of the Depression. The public mood was muter, and Parker and her friends were getting older. It was around then that Dorothy met Campbell, a less lauded writer and would-be actor, and together they decamped to Hollywood in the early 1930s for greener paychecks as screenwriters. Having sold out, they did rather well and were both nominated for an Academy Award for their script for the first version of *A Star Is Born*, in 1937. But while Hollywood rewarded them lucratively, they remained connected to New York. The literary knights of the Round Table may have gone their separate ways, but they still could make mischief now and then. In 1938, Parker and Campbell hosted an after-party at the Algonquin for Philip Barry and his acclaimed Broadway production of *Here Come the Clowns*. Barry also happened to be a Brown Brothers client, but the party created something of a kerfuffle. The Algonquin sued Parker and Campbell for unpaid bills and associated costs. According to an account in *The New York Times*, "The Campbells remembered to leave $50 for the help but forgot about the $488.22 for the 732 drinks that were consumed at the party." Matters were eventually settled.

Like many screenwriters, Parker and Campbell lived a feast-or-famine existence. They were nominated for an Academy Award in March 1938, but the ensuing years were lean. In March 1940, Campbell wrote to the tax department at Brown Brothers, "I am returning post-haste the two income tax papers, and we are delighted at what low taxes we have for the year 1939. In our delight, we forgot that the reason for it is that we didn't work. Anyway, it was pleasant."[14] Parker remained famous, but fame in those days did not always carry a paycheck. In the 1950s, she was caught in the Hollywood blacklist against supposed sympathizers with communism. She and Campbell divorced and remarried and were estranged again when Campbell died of an overdose in 1963. Parker never lost her sharp wit, which if anything became sharper with the struggles of time. And always she maintained an observer's detachment, even from her own life. "You make money writing on the coast," she once concluded. "But that money is like so much compressed snow. It goes so fast it melts in your hand."[15]

Celebrity clients were diverting, but, like aperitifs, best in small quantities. The main business was elsewhere. As the firm redefined itself and took on a much wider range of deposits, the partners continued to build their public image. Robert Lovett stepped out from behind the curtain and penned a widely read article in the popular *Saturday Evening Post* in 1937. The piece was called "Gilt-Edge Insecurity," which was keyed off the phrase then in vogue of "gilt-edged security," which referred to a high-quality bond, usually issued by a national authority such as the Bank of England. Like Bush in "Scattered Wealth," Lovett examined the promises and perils of investing, and he did so by looking back at the misguided conventional wisdom of investors over various periods beginning in 1901 and ending in 1936. His conclusion, not surprisingly, was that "securities are not secure," and that what people believe to be a smashingly good idea at the time frequently proves to be terrible.

The average investor in 1936 (who statistically would have been in the upper echelons of income) would have, according to Lovett, held a portfolio of blue-chip names such as American Radiator, Anaconda Copper (closely associated with Brown Brothers), General Motors, Sperry Corporation, Standard Oil of New Jersey (now Exxon), Consolidated Edison of New York, and others. Given conventional wisdom in 1936, that portfolio looked solid. That is the problem with most investing. What looks solid in the present often proves to be foolish in the future, and you know that only in hindsight. Take a similar snapshot of a portfolio in 1901. At that time, fewer people owned stocks and corporate bonds and fewer companies sold shares to the public, but using the records kept at Brown Brothers, Lovett demonstrated that a portfolio of diversified, dividend-paying stocks equivalent in quality would have performed disastrously. "After having his capital at risk for thirty-five years of enormous industrial progress and national growth, our investor would show an aggregate loss of about 25 percent." It looked marginally better for the investor in 1919, who bought during a post–World War I lull, but woe to the investor who bought in 1926 as the market was climbing its bubble mountain and credit was being issued willy-nilly by companies that had no business raising debt and in time defaulted. In short, Lovett argued, even meticulous investors whose choices appeared wise and conservative at the time more often than not lost money. Of course, Lovett concluded that some investors did quite well, though no one was unscathed in 1929–32. Those who did well did so because they avoided emotional investing and because they understood that nothing should be considered safe and permanent simply because it appears shiny at the time. Only constant and assiduous focus on what is sound and what is ephemeral, what is noise and what is signal, could lead investors to make money over longer periods. And implied, though not explicitly stated, was that a firm such as Brown Brothers Harriman could be, and always had been, the guide and the steward that everyone needed.

What pertained in financial markets, as it turned out, pertained to politics as well. Ingrained in these men was the belief that their experience in the financial world could translate seamlessly into the public sector. The New Deal offered opportunities for government employment, but most of

Wall Street maintained a wary distance, shaping legislation where they felt they could and should. The flurry of financial regulations calmed down after 1934 and left the industry altered but not fundamentally changed. Another set of laws, in 1940, established a framework for investment advisers and for the newfangled products such as mutual funds. But by then, the focus of the country was turning elsewhere, to the wars in Europe and Asia.

With the rise of Adolf Hitler in Germany and the Empire of Japan in East Asia, the call to service exerted a powerful pull on our cohort. They had engaged the world, in the Caribbean and then Europe during the First World War, and after that in finance in the 1920s. By 1941, they were ready to answer the call, and no one answered more readily than Robert Lovett, son of a Texas judge, a product of the Ivy League, content in his role as a captain of finance until the war presented him with an unparalleled opportunity. He seized it.

CHAPTER 14

A CALL TO SERVICE

Work," Bob Lovett once observed, "good work, I mean, is something you do because you enjoy it. It's interesting, fun. All this talk about working yourself to death—you can bore yourself to death too. Why not work and remain interested?"[1]

No one could accuse Robert Abercrombie Lovett of not working. From the competitive boy who showed up young Roland Harriman in front of both of their fathers, to the Yale student who learned to fly planes and then volunteered to go to the front, to the junior clerk muscling his way to senior partner, Lovett had worked hard all his life. He was born into great wealth, the only son of an ambitious father who rarely scrimped when it came to his progeny. But Lovett, who was described in a *New Yorker* profile as "tall, slender, and well-tailored, with a face like a humorous monk," worked anyway, and he never did find that work dull. And why should he have? Between Wall Street in the 1920s and 1930s and Washington in the 1940s and 1950s, Lovett lived a life at the epicenter.

For a man who became so famous in his time, Lovett has left a light footprint. He begat no biographies. Histories of World War II and the beginnings of the Cold War mention him frequently and prominently, but he is never the pivotal player. In that sense, he resembles Averell Harriman, who had an even more storied résumé, mentored a generation of policy advisers and senior officials, and yet was not seen as the central character in anyone's play save his own. The qualities that made Lovett, Harriman and many of their cohort so prized as the U.S. government exploded in size, scope and influence, first with the New Deal and then with the war and its aftermath, also made them opaque. Yes, they were at the epicenter, later dubbed "the wise men" when they were called on by Lyndon Baines Johnson to offer their advice about the Vietnam War and then dubbed, with more ambivalence, "the Establishment" by 1960s voices questioning the role of elites. But in their heyday, they lived with an untroubled, unruffled dichotomy that the public and the private were separate realms divided by high walls between what was shown and said to the world and what was said when the doors of the partners' room or the Situation Room were shut.

Harriman, Lovett, Henry Stimson, George Marshall, John McCloy, Dean Acheson and others lived by a code that was at once about service but also about discretion. Their omertà—epitomized by Skull and Bones—was so ingrained that nothing could shake it, to the end. Even their memoirs and oral histories possess a veneer as polished and muffled as the library of a New York club. It was not simply about the public face versus the private. While they could cut loose at parties and after one too many drinks, and while they had those hidden selves, in key respects, the private mirrored the public. For the most part, these were not people of deep introspection; they lived lives of doing, and other than a few tortured souls such as James Forrestal, who became the first secretary of defense before ending his own life, or Dean Acheson, who had an unusual philosophical bent, they tended to be as they appeared, much like Alexander Brown in his day. They lived by a simple creed of work, duty, action. They believed in the capitalism they had helped create, and when faced by war and its aftermath, they came to defend that capitalism, along with what they assumed were attendant virtues of democracy and freedom. Not until all of those were tested and challenged did they begin to crystallize a coherent system. What had been implied before 1939, a certain way of doing business, a certain way of organizing government, a certain way that individuals fit within the collective, became explicit. The American way, their American way, became the model for the world.

It's not that they weren't sometimes colorful or a bundle of contradictions. Lovett was at once "the near-perfect example of the perfect executive," and someone who could fluidly migrate from class to crass, "fluent in both the State Department and infantry versions of English." The college bon vivant morphed into an adult bon vivant who enjoyed the late-night company of poets and writers. The tough young aviator became a hypochondriac who was constantly pleading ill health. He almost never refused a challenge, but to friends and confidants, he always had a worrying, hand-wringing plaint that he would need to check first with his doctors. He was smooth and confident in public, self-deprecating about his premature balding, and exuded self-assurance. He was taciturn, yet not too taciturn, reserved but not too reserved, witty, sometimes sharp and annoyed but rarely over the top, demanding but not abusive. He had, it was said, "good horse sense." He was "so tough that he hates himself," yet he was also known for his easy sense of humor, frequent laughter and for never raising his voice even when stern with subordinates or frustrated with superiors. He relished what was hard and seemed uninterested in what was easy. One friend observed to a journalist, "Bob is happiest when he has to fix up somebody or something. He just laps up disaster."[2] With the outbreak of war in Europe, he was presented with a disaster of epic proportions.

I t wasn't just a sputtering recovery that challenged Roosevelt in his second term. His plan to reconfigure and expand a Supreme Court that had stymied key aspects of the New Deal met stiff opposition in the Senate and dented his image. The isolationism of Congress and large swaths of the American public disrupted his plans to support England and France as German aggression intensified after 1938. While the financial and banking system had stabilized, there was no love lost between FDR and the captains of those industries, who for the most part saw him as an adversary. By the late 1930s, they had by and large tuned out Washington to focus on their businesses, but the escalating crises in Europe and Asia could not so easily be tuned out. For firms such as Brown Brothers Harriman, which had extensive dealings not just in Western Europe but in Germany as well, the aggression of Adolf Hitler and the Nazi government signaled problems ahead, as war was becoming more likely with each passing month. Of the partners, Bob Lovett was the most involved with European affairs and traveled regularly. He was a powerful voice in the firm to reduce its exposure to German business in the late 1930s. One ingredient of Brown Brothers' recipe for sustainability had been anticipating crises and taking a defensive position ahead of them, knowing that the time to be prepared is before, not during. That had served the firm well in the past, and it would again when the most destructive war in modern history began in 1939.

The German invasion of Poland in September confirmed that Adolf Hitler and the Nazis would not be sated by the annexation of Austria and Czechoslovakia. Writing to Roland soon after the invasion, Lovett questioned whether the firm should continue to extend credit even to neutral countries in Europe given the possibility that they would either be invaded by Germany or that the Germans might use banks in neutral countries in order to obtain funds illicitly from the United States. The firm was in a strong position financially, and Lovett saw no reason to run such risks for a bit more business. He also concluded, correctly it turned out, that "a short war seems unlikely and there is increasing evidence that if it lasts long enough some internationally minded politicians will see the answer to their prayers and our involvement will result almost automatically." He was not keen on American involvement, but he was under few illusions about which way events were trending.[3]

As fate would have it, Lovett was in France in May 1940 when the Germans finally ended months of uneasy inaction on the Western front after the invasion of Poland. The speed of the French collapse was breathtaking. In just six weeks, the mechanized fury of the German attack, combining superiority in armored vehicles and tanks with coordinated air strikes, overwhelmed the French army. It was not for lack of focus on the part of France.

The French had been planning for another war with Germany since the last one ended. They had invested heavily in their army and navy, and with their British allies had more tanks than any country in the world. They had also spent years fortifying their border, building the Maginot Line, where they assumed the Germans would strike. But France miscalculated where the main attack would be. The French high command did not realize that the war to come would be fought, strategically and tactically, in fundamentally new ways.

It was oddly fortunate, therefore, that Lovett was there to witness what transpired. He departed France just before the fall of Paris with a keen sense of urgency about how unprepared the United States was to fight the type of war that was likely coming sooner or later. It wasn't just that he was the right man in the right place at the right time. He was uniquely qualified to assess the scope of American deficiencies, specifically when it came to airpower. He had been one of the first American war aviators, and he had maintained his intense passion for flying, which included the involvement of Brown Brothers Harriman in the birth of Pan Am and American commercial aviation. His entire career as a banker had been built on his grasp of systems and processes, long a strength of the firm he had married into. And above all, Bob Lovett was a fixer.

Those traits are what led to his first major appointment in government. In the summer of 1940, he had a long conversation with Robert Patterson, the newly appointed undersecretary of war, a graduate of Harvard Law School, a longtime New York attorney and then judge, and in Lovett's social and professional nexus. After Paris, Lovett had taken it upon himself to do a private survey of the aviation industry in the United States, ostensibly as part of his banking duties but driven more by his alarm about American readiness to defend itself in a new era of warfare. Lovett asked a simple question, "How are we going to make our air force the best in the world?" He wrote an extensive report mapping out the challenges, underscoring that there had been a revolution in airpower since the last great war and that no nation could hope either to defend itself or to conduct credible offensive military operations without a modern and large air force. There was talk in

Washington about upgrading American airpower, but Lovett was skeptical. "It is my impression," he wrote, "that the government will not get the plane production being talked about from present or planned plants."

He wasn't angling for a job, unlike his partner Averell, who had floated in and out of advisory roles during the early years of the New Deal and was now back in Washington working with the White House on improving domestic transportation of raw materials. That placed Harriman at the center of a not entirely covert but certainly hushed effort in the White House to organize America for war. Averell left a trail of ambivalence in his wake, impressing many with his supreme self-confidence and evident competence while leaving a distinct impression that you were valuable to him primarily if you were of use to him.

In the summer of 1940, Averell urged Lovett to find a way to put his expertise to use in the government. Lovett expressed reservations. He was not conflicted about public service per se. He was, as ever, worried about his health and stamina, a worry he communicated at great length. "I would not want to undertake a job unless I was prepared to work an indefinite number of hours for an indefinite number of days efficiently and contently," he confided to Averell in a July letter. On substance, he was mindful of the economic pressures that the war might create for the financial world, mirroring issues of wars past with stranded assets on each side of the hostilities but magnified this time by the collapse of France and the chance that outstanding loans made by Brown Brothers and countless others would be written down to zero for lack of any means of collecting. But as concerning as that was (and thankfully for the firm at least, it had pared its European commitments as the situation had deteriorated in the late 1930s), it was secondary to the woeful state of American air preparedness.

"I sincerely believe that the only way we can get ready," he wrote to Averell, "is to subordinate everything to our rearmament—particularly in aircraft—and that we should keep our mouth shut and tread softly until we have gained the strength to back up our statements or our demands." He was uncomfortable with some of the rhetoric from public officials urging rapid mobilization against Germany, for the simple reason that the public was not there yet. Lovett was keenly aware of the gulf between what is said by government officials in public versus what is mulled or desired behind closed doors. But he was also aware that time was not on their side, that England was in danger of falling, and that the United States would not be able to stay neutral indefinitely. For that reason, he was unequivocal: "I want to help in any way I can, as soon as I can, and if possible in connection with aviation where I have a lively recollection of the sad errors of the war."[4]

Lovett wrote up his observations and circulated those to a handful of people. One of them was Robert Patterson, another was James Forrestal, then undersecretary of the navy, who had a house near Locust Valley. They then passed the memo on to the new secretary of war, Henry Stimson. The elder Stimson, widely known as the Colonel, had been in many ways the grandfather to them all, a Yale man in the 1890s, one of the first members of Skull and Bones. Stimson was over seventy and had served in Republican administrations as secretary of war under one president (Taft) and secretary of state under another (Hoover). He had comfortably retired from government to return to his lucrative law practice and was living in New York City when Roosevelt approached him to enter government once again. FDR needed the support of the Republican Party if he was to nudge the United States toward rearmament and then toward a more confrontational approach to Germany and Japan. He knew that Stimson stood for the internationalist wing of the Republican Party and that they shared more in common when it came to global affairs than inward-looking Republican isolationists such as Arthur Vandenberg of Michigan and Robert Taft of Ohio. The war would obliterate many of those categories: Vandenberg later became an architect of the postwar world. Even in 1940, American public sentiment was already beginning to shift, not conclusively but incrementally away from isolationism toward more active support for Great Britain. Reflecting that, the Republicans nominated former Democrat and outspoken internationalist Wendell Willkie to face Roosevelt in the 1940 presidential election, which meant that FDR was not put on the defensive about his tilt toward intervention the way he might have been had he run against Taft or someone of that ilk.

In December 1940, with Roosevelt resoundingly reelected and after months of indecision, Lovett resigned his Brown Brothers partnership and moved to Washington to become a special adviser to Stimson. His mandate was to focus on airpower. At the time, Lovett could not have known what lay ahead, and resigning the partnership was a dramatic move, reflecting the urgency of the moment. In making that choice, he shifted decisively from private industry to the public sphere, but for him and so many others, the move was natural and smooth. He had served his partners, his clients and his firm, just as his father had served the Union Pacific and the Harriman family, and now he would serve his country. When asked years later how it was that three of the firm's handful of partners ended up in the highest levels of government, he replied simply that "it was the background of Yale and a sense of public duty . . . and the quality of people we had." That said it all.[5]

The skills he had honed as a banker, especially the analytical and organizational talent that he possessed, would now be used for the good of the country, and the worldview that he embodied would follow him to Washington. His partners praised his move, though Averell, who was also becoming more ensconced in Washington, did not resign his partnership. He had not been deeply involved in running the firm, but his capital was still vital and not until he was appointed secretary of commerce after the war would he too tender his resignation. Lovett, meanwhile, wasted no time getting to work. There was no gradual period of acclimatization. As he dove into the statistics and convened meetings, he was startled by what he found. The procurement system was, he said, "a hell of mess," and neither private industry nor the War Department itself was ready to produce what was needed. As he later wrote, "When I went down to Washington in December 1940 . . . I was at first shocked at the small size of the Air Force and the Army Air Corps and, secondly, amazed at the inefficient organization and cumbersome set up and with no central overall command structure adequate for war conditions." He intended to fix that. He made an immediate and positive impression on his new boss, which was no easy feat. Stimson was notoriously crusty and demanding, and he had no paucity of self-regard. He had always commanded respect but by now, his résumé alone would have intimidated most. Lovett was deferential but not obsequious, and he spoke his mind. "The more I see of him," Stimson noted in his diary, "the more I like him."[6]

Matched with Lovett was another man whose career had been equally meteoric, John McCloy, a prominent Wall Street lawyer and dealmaker at Cravath, who, like Lovett, had experience doing business in Europe and who was Stimson's neighbor in an exclusive Adirondack summer community.[7] Dubbed the "heavenly twins," McCloy and Lovett became two of Stimson's key aides, and soon each was appointed assistant secretary of war, with Lovett given oversight for the entire air capabilities of the United States. Lovett's challenge was acute and quantifiable: Germany had an air force, the Luftwaffe, of a million men and nearly four thousand aircraft in the middle of 1940; the United States had fewer than half that number of planes, many of them obsolete, and, more crucially, fewer pilots and servicemen to maintain and fly them. The main problem was one of structure and mind-set. As he told Patterson, "This is a quantitative war, but the airplane industry has so far been qualitative." Of course, Germany was engaged in all-out war while the United States was trying to avoid one, but the disparity was still stark, and Lovett was charged with rectifying it.

By the summer of 1941, Congress had shed some of its inhibitions and authorized a buildup. Lovett was key in working with factories to retool for aircraft production. It wasn't just the deficiency in equipment. The American armed forces had an antediluvian approach to airpower as an instrument of war. Lovett was an early and passionate proponent for an expansive view of airpower that eventually became settled strategy but was at the time almost revolutionary. The Germans had demonstrated how devastating airpower could be, and how a nimble use of both tactical bombing (attacking enemy troops and equipment) and strategic bombing (damaging supply chains and factories and threatening civilian centers) could turn the tide. It was up to Lovett to shake the American military from its torpor to meet the German threat.

But first he had to fight against what he called Dupe's Disease, a two-decade caesura "during which a national revulsion from the last war causes us to convince ourselves and teach our children that we would never fight another war. We were told that we were safe and to hell with the rest of the world. Unfortunately, love of peace is no substitute for the strength to insure it." As he told a small group gathered at the University Club in New York City, "Our first problem grows out of a national apathy which amounted almost to a phobia against preparedness. Anyone who favored building up the machines of war was labeled a merchant of death. . . . And the second phase of Dupe's Disease can be called fiscal flatulence. This malady manifests itself by a rapid contraction of the sphincter muscles of the national purse."[8] Throughout 1941, Lovett not only worked inside the War Department but also played public evangelist to shift attitudes about the gravity of the conflict that he believed lay ahead. Americans still had visions of the last war. They were unprepared for what Lovett called the "gangster methods" of the mechanized total war being waged by the Germans and the Japanese, with few distinctions between enemy combatants and civilian populations.

"The defense against such measures is obvious," Lovett declared in a radio speech in the summer of 1941. "It is partly spiritual and partly material. On the spiritual side all of us have got to keep in mind the clear value of the liberties we have come to accept as a matter of course. . . . On the material side, we must set our hand to the task of building up our defenses to such a pitch that no nation and no combination of nations dare to assail us. We have the money and the men—we need the mentality and the machines to save for ourselves and the world the type of life that we think is worth living." In the end, he urged, the savior would be American industry and American capital, the foundation for the vast efforts required to preserve the country's way of life.[9]

The Japanese attack on Pearl Harbor on December 7, 1941, came before those defenses could be completed, but the preparations of 1940–41 meant that the United States was closer to being mobilized than it had been in 1917. It was also more in sync with its allies. Thanks to the work of men like Averell Harriman (who had been dispatched to London), the U.S. government even before Pearl Harbor had started to integrate American aid with British needs, primarily via the Lend-Lease program that allowed the United States to arm the United Kingdom, the Free French, the Chinese Nationalists led by Chiang Kai-shek and even the Soviets. Harriman not only served as the key liaison for joint Anglo-American policy but also began to act as the primary intermediary with the other great adversary of Germany, the Soviet Union under Joseph Stalin. Harriman's prior business dealing with Russia in the 1930s gave him standing in both Washington and Moscow. In September 1941, after the Germans launched Operation Barbarossa, their massive invasion of the Soviet Union that June, Harriman in almost impromptu fashion accompanied Britain's Lord Beaverbrook to Moscow to coordinate aid to Stalin, laying the groundwork for Harriman's eventual appointment as U.S. ambassador to Moscow in 1943.[10]

Whatever divisions and debates had existed prior to Pearl Harbor evaporated after the attack. The United States embarked on total war mobilization, drafting millions of men into the armed forces and redirecting the industrial capacity of the nation toward production. While the resulting four years of war were not nearly as disruptive domestically as the Civil War had been eighty years earlier, the coordinated fusion of the home front and the war front had never been more complete.

Lovett more than almost anyone understood the dynamics of industry and the needs of production, and he had a vision for the deployment of airpower. He was a details man who valued the quantitative and relished the nitty-gritty that is particularly essential to the complex web of parts, supplies, men, fuel and logistics that airpower requires. He brought the same attention to the systems and processes of war that he and generations of Browns had applied to trade and banking. Lovett also appreciated that airpower was still a tabula rasa when it came to how it should be used. His experience in World War I gave him confidence in his judgments; he also recognized that in 1918, airpower was rudimentary at best. Two decades later, his careful assessment of American weaknesses and German and Japanese strengths convinced him that the United States could do things differently and better than either. He was on solid ground insofar as no one really knew what the potential of airpower was, for the simple reason that it was all so new. "They tell you you can't lick Germany with airpower, that it can't be done," he snapped at a reporter in 1942. "How the hell do they know? It's never been tried. The hell with the past. Our big stuff is the only thing that can deliver itself to any place in the world and go right into combat. That's the one reason I believe in the bomber—high-level, glide, dive and every other goddam kind."[11]

Lovett had to confront multiple obstacles, ranging from domestic production and supply chains to unrealistic demands from Roosevelt, who wanted the United States to ramp up to 125,000 planes in production by 1943. Lovett knew that was absurd, and not in a "setting high expectations" kind of way. "It is a little bit like asking a hen to lay an ostrich egg," Lovett told Army Air Forces chief Hap Arnold. "It is unlikely that you will get the egg and the hen will never look the same." By 1945 however, airplane output had reached 90,000 planes a year.

Lovett did more than accelerate production. He carved out a new autonomous role for airpower, which elevated it as coequal to land and sea and paved the way for the creation of a separate air force after the war. He oversaw the creation of pilot-training programs that met the sudden need for thousands of aviators. He was a champion of the construction of American air bases abroad and an advocate for their permanency after the war. Perhaps even more consequentially, he seized on long-range bombing as a new element in modern warfare, pushing for both research and development of the flying fortresses that terrorized enemy troops and wreaked havoc not just on factories and munitions depots but on civilians in cities across Germany and Japan in a controversial embrace of the same total war that Americans had decried when it was conducted by their adversaries.[12] The United States combined both tactical and strategic bombing with devastating effect against both Japan and Germany, and unleashed a torrent of death on civilian populations in both countries. The Axis powers may have obliterated the barrier between combatants and civilians, but the Americans showed no strong desire to reerect those barriers as long as hostilities continued. It was a brutal war. Lovett and others believed that winning required brutality. That was not desirable, nor, in their view, was it avoidable.

The triumph of American airpower was more directly connected to the industrial and economic might of the country than to any other aspect of the war. Building an air force composed of multiple new kinds of aircraft, each of which needed dedicated supply chains and innovation, was a task that no other country in the world could have met in so short a time. Without Lovett orchestrating, the United States might not have. In the words of Stimson's successor as secretary of war, Robert Patterson, "The fact that our air forces achieved their huge expansion in time was due more to Bob Lovett than any other man."[13] In fusing industry with innovation, by bringing together the quantitative with the qualitative, Lovett represented the apotheosis of American money married to American power. But he had no interest in remaining in government once the war ended. In September 1945, he retired from the War Department and resumed his partnership at Brown Brothers, where he was welcomed back without hesitation.

Averell Harriman, however, had no interest in returning to the life of a businessman-banker. He established a quick rapport with FDR's unexpected successor, Harry S. Truman, whom he had not met until he flew back to Washington in the spring of 1945. While Harriman had none of Truman's folksy charm and lacked the Missourian's easy way with people, Truman came to value Harriman as an intermediary, dispatching him as ambassador to London as the war ended and then appointing him secretary of commerce when Henry Wallace, FDR's spurned vice president and hero to the progressive movement opposed to the hardening of American policy against the Soviet Union, was dismissed in September 1946.

By then the world had changed again. Postwar 1945–46 did not, as some had expected, look like the postwar of 1919–20. This time, instead of rejecting robust engagement with the world, the United States embraced it, and instead of proposing a new world order only to leave it dangling, American officials drafted a postwar order and then enforced it. World War II thrust the United States into a global role, with troops and supplies stretched from the South Pacific to the Himalayas and Burma to the Caucasus, across North Africa and throughout Western and Central Europe. Rather than retreating to North America after the summer of 1945, the United States remained engaged, governing Japan and parts of Germany, trying to broker peace in the civil war in China between the Nationalists and the Communists, and acting as administrator to a new political and economic system that had been drafted in San Francisco in the spring of 1945 and at a remote resort in New Hampshire called Bretton Woods in the summer of 1944. From those emerged the United Nations as the political anchor and the International Monetary Fund and the International Bank for Reconstruction and Development (popularly known as the World Bank) as the economic ones.

The architecture of the postwar system may have occupied a lower tier in 1944 and early 1945, but with the successful Allied landing in France on D-Day in June 1944, it was evident that sooner or later, the Axis powers were going to lose and the Allies would be faced with what to do afterward. The experience of the Paris Peace Conference and the perception that it had laid the seeds for the present conflagration loomed large. Over the course of multiple summits between Roosevelt, Churchill and Stalin, many of which Harriman attended, discussions alternated between coordinating war efforts and debating the shape of the postwar world. In the spring of 1945, with battles in the Pacific still raging, representatives from nearly four dozen governments not allied with the Axis powers met in San Francisco to design the United Nations and draft the thousands of pages of text that delineated the structure and scope of the postwar institutions that would govern the international system. More explicitly than the League of Nations, the institutions that grew out of World War II married both the idea of a congress of nations and of a hierarchy among them. All nations would have a vote in the United Nations, but only five would have preeminence as permanent members of the Security Council. All countries would have a voice in the economic institutions, but the United States would have the dominant say, due to the sheer size of its economy and to the establishment of the dollar as the new global reserve currency, replacing the British pound.

That in turn paved the way for an international monetary system based on the value of American paper, and based as well on fiat money instead of gold or a system of various national currencies linked to gold and to one another at fixed rates.[14]

The other main gathering of countries to design the postwar architecture occurred even earlier, at the foot of Mount Washington at the Bretton Woods resort in New Hampshire. The goal of the conference, announced Roosevelt to the delegates in July 1944, was nothing short of creating a new world economic order. The goal was simple and profound: to prevent any repeat of the conflagration of world war as well as the cataclysm of the Great Depression that was widely seen as having precipitated it. "The program you are to discuss," he told the delegates, "constitutes only one phase of the arrangements that must be made between nations to ensure an orderly, harmonious world. But it is a vital phase, affecting ordinary men and women everywhere. For it concerns the basis on which they will be able to exchange with one another the natural riches of the earth. . . . Commerce is the lifeblood of a free society. We must see to it that the arteries which carry the blood stream are not clogged again. . . . Only through a dynamic and a soundly expanding world economy can the living standards of individual nations be advanced to levels which will permit a full realization of our hopes for the future."

While the United Nations is the more familiar result of the war's end, the Bretton Woods system proved at least as consequential and unquestionably more functional. In part, that was because it subsumed the governance of the global economy largely to one dominant player with a trusted currency. For better and at times for worse, Bretton Woods soon evolved into a system that allowed the United States and the American dollar to oversee the world economy and global trade almost everywhere the Soviet Union was not in control. That was not a foregone conclusion even at the war's end, especially with Great Britain not ready to cede its century-plus of economic hegemony to the Americans. But economic reality dictated the terms of the peace; the British won the war against Germany, and then lost their empire.

In shaping the institutions and policies at Bretton Woods, the delegates drew on the experiences of both the Depression and the only international financial institution that existed at that time, the Bank for International Settlements. That bank had been set up in Basel, Switzerland, in 1930 in order to help central banks coordinate their actions; its record had been decidedly mixed, with a thin staff attempting to help smooth the flow of money across borders in the midst of a severe crisis during which governments were attempting to wall themselves off from trade and capital flows in a futile attempt at inoculation. The bank was further undermined by the suspicion that it had turned a blind eye toward Nazi use of slave labor in industries that the bank assisted. But at the very least, the BIS did provide an example of how the financial system could be better integrated.[15]

The goal at Bretton Woods was not just to create an architecture for the coordination of the financial system; it was also to establish a conduit of loans and credit to help nations that needed capital. The paucity of capital was seen as a primary cause of economic collapse in the 1930s, and there was a palpable concern that without an ample and immediate supply of money at the end of the war to help nations rebuild and retool, the aftermath could see widespread economic collapse that would quickly descend into political chaos. That would turn the sweetness of victory into a nightmare of global deprivation that would inevitably lead to more war and likely the spread of communism. The challenge was to craft a system that simultaneously provided easy money for rebuilding and development and controlled the supply and movement of currencies. Money was a powerful tool; too much of it, and you had a deluge that destroyed value and ruined economies; too little, and economic activity would grind to a halt. The trick was to create a system that was elastic enough to channel money where it was needed when it was needed and to restrict its supply at the same time. It was not an easy balance.

The Americans, however, had an acute sense that it was up to them, and that the British Empire was waning and along with it the regime of the pound sterling that had been the fulcrum of global trade and international finance since the defeat of Napoleon early in the nineteenth century. The

British economists at Bretton Woods, and especially John Maynard Keynes, recognized the precariousness of Britain's war finances, but this view was not shared by Winston Churchill and his immediate lieutenants. The British government fully anticipated that multiple countries in Western and Central Europe would need emergency infusions of capital once the war ended. As it turned out, Great Britain would as well. Having established the primacy of the dollar as a global means of exchange, Bretton Woods was seen by those in the know as a passing of the torch, and many in Britain were none too pleased. But when the British government nearly went bankrupt within months of the war's end, it was the surfeit of dollars and the Americans' willingness to lend them that proved to be the savior. In the spring of 1946, Lord Keynes, weeks from his death, helped negotiate the terms of the loan that kept Britain afloat.

No bell rang announcing a new hegemon. There was nothing preordained about the United States becoming the leader of the free world and assuming the mantle of imperial power. It was, after all, a country that disdained European imperialism and preached its dedication to free and open markets, provided that those markets were structured in accord with rules that it had established. But almost no one in the American Establishment fundamentally questioned that the world would be better off with the United States in a key role. The lesson that had been learned from the post-1919 experience was that an international system absent active American participation was doomed, and the situation in the immediate aftermath of the war seemed to validate that. Swaths of Europe and East Asia were in ruins or had seen their industrial infrastructure decimated. In Europe, the winter of 1945–46 raised the threat of mass starvation, never mind the rebuilding of cities, rail lines and factories.

And then there was the Soviet Union. At the Yalta Conference in February 1945, the Big Three of FDR, Churchill and Stalin had been allies coordinating the war's endgame. By the time of the Potsdam Conference in the summer of 1945, suspicion had set in as it became clear that the Soviets planned to control Eastern Europe. The Americans shifted from treating Stalin as an ally to seeing the Soviet system as a threat to free society and open markets. Truman, concerned that as an accidental president he would not be taken seriously, confronted the Soviet foreign minister, Vyacheslav Molotov, that spring in language not usually reserved for diplomats. "I gave it to him," Truman recalled, "a straight one-two to the jaw." If he thought he had landed a knockout punch, he was deeply mistaken.[16]

Having laid the foundation for a postwar order led and financed by Americans and by the dollar, the United States was confronted by a Soviet Union that had acceded to neither and not only was prepared to defend its sphere but also rejected the presumptions of Washington that the postwar world would be governed by a web of institutions dominated and bankrolled by the United States. The Cold War did not begin the moment the war ended. But it began soon enough.

The relatively peaceful end to the Cold War in 1989, which many had feared would lead to nuclear annihilation, combined with the triumph of the West and capitalism, dampened the argument over who caused the conflict in the first place. But until 1989 and beginning almost as soon as World War II ended, that argument was one of the primary fissures in American society. The main fault line was between those asserting that the United States was prepared to accommodate the Soviet Union but was forced into a more confrontational stance by Stalin, and those who believed that the United States, driven by the demands of capitalism and the self-interest of business, was bent on expanding the reach of the United States and forcing the collapse of communism in general and the Soviets in particular. Over time, those who saw the Cold War as a reluctant American reaction to the Soviets aligned on the right while those who viewed the United States as the culprit tended to fall on the left. And for the left, the role of money and Wall Street was clear: the United States was driven to enlarge the sphere of capitalism, just as it had earlier into Central America and then South America. The "Republic of Brown Brothers" in Nicaragua was a model for what was to come after 1945. That became a popular perception in the 1960s, when the deteriorating war in Vietnam led to a wholescale reappraisal of the role of money and capital in the expansion of America's presence around the world.

In 1945, however, with that future still to be written, many who had answered the call to service believed that their work was now done. The war had been won, the enemy vanquished. It was time to put down arms and return to the domestic front. That did not mean isolationism, quite the opposite. But it did mean shifting back to the business of America being business. The demobilized GIs swarmed home and poured into universities as their ticket to the middle class. The domestic economy did not, as feared, contract. The United States instead became the economic engine of the global postwar recovery, amounting to more than half of all manufacturing worldwide in the years after the war, which created more prosperity than the New Deal ever had. And as the GIs returned home, so did men like Lovett, planning to put down their arms and pick up their pens.

CHAPTER 15

THE WISE MEN

Lovett in 1946 believed that his time in government was done. The challenges ahead were not only in the tempestuous global arena but also at home, ensuring that American society remained firmly committed to private and free enterprise as its foundation. While capitalism was not in immediate peril in the United States itself, abroad it appeared to be an open contest. Lovett wrote a lengthy memo to his partners summarizing what he had learned in his years in Washington, in which he expressed his gratitude for being able to work with such worthy men as Stimson, McCloy and General George Marshall. Reflecting on his years, he emphasized "the amazement at the productive capacity of this country" and his "respect for the average American businessman." He was also struck by a disparity that he had been unaware of: "The views of the rest of the country are far better represented to Executive Agencies and in the legislative councils than those of New York State. It always astonished me that one of the great industrial centers of the world, and certainly the world's greatest financial center, was virtually voiceless, and certainly ineffective, as compared with smaller communities in the South and Southwest." He may have understated how much the economic power of New York translated into political sway at the national level, but in Washington he had seen up close how many different factions jockeyed for influence over federal policy. His perspective also suggests that the conspiratorial view popular particularly in the 1970s that a close-knit clique of financial elites dictated American economic policy was not a perspective shared by those elites themselves. If anything, Lovett was acutely aware that within the government, there were multiple competing interests and that his particular bastion was often not the one that dictated policy, especially in Congress.

He returned to private life more convinced than ever about the foundational creed of capitalism and the proper role of the state. "If industry is to be capable of continuous progress, it must be healthy. To be healthy, it must be profitable. To be profitable, it must live in a climate of reasonable regulations and reasonable costs. And if we are to have a reasonable climate, the voice of reasonable people must be heard in volume at least equal to the minority of radicals who doubt the value of private enterprise. . . . If we are to look to industry to defend us in the future, I am firmly convinced that we must be prepared to defend it today."[1]

As Lovett was explicating his views to his partners, Averell's deputy in the Moscow embassy was doing much the same to the makers of policy in Washington. In February 1946, as Western Europe and Central Europe grappled with a winter of deprivation, George Kennan consolidated into one document his assessment of the Soviet Union. Rarely has policy been so clearly defined and articulated, and rarely has one document so shaped the future trajectory of a country and by extension the world. We will never know what U.S. policy toward the Soviet Union would have been had Kennan not penned his "long telegram." We do know that after it was sent and circulated in official Washington, there would be no live-and-let-live between the Soviet Union and the United States. The arc of the Cold War as a contest for global dominance was largely set.

Kennan depicted the Soviet Union as a unique, and malevolent, force. Unlike great power rivalries of the past, the standoff between the Soviets and the states of the West was not amenable to traditional statecraft or settled spheres of influence. In Kennan's ominous words, "We have here a political force committed fanatically to the belief that with US there can be no permanent *modus vivendi,* that it is desirable and necessary that the internal harmony of our society be disrupted, our traditional way of life be destroyed, the international authority of our state be broken, if Soviet power is to be secure." While Kennan acknowledged that the Soviets were far weaker militarily and economically than the United States, that was bound to change. That made it urgent for the United States to take advantage of its position of strength, to educate the American public about the nature of the menace, and to design a strategy to confront it. A vital component would be to maintain and increase the vitality of the domestic American economy and that of its allies in Europe and Asia and beyond. "Much depends on health and vigor of our own society," Kennan concluded. "World communism is like malignant parasite which feeds only on diseased tissue."[2]

Kennan's telegram was a match in a dry forest. While its contents were classified, it was widely read within the government, in part because of the assiduous efforts of Harriman and Forrestal to make sure it had the intended effect. Only weeks later, Winston Churchill, on a speaking tour of the United States after his ouster as British prime minister, stood on a podium in a high school gymnasium in Fulton, Missouri, flanked by President Truman, and announced darkly that "from Stettin in the Baltic to Trieste in the Adriatic an iron curtain has descended across the continent. Behind that line lie all the capitals of central and eastern Europe. Warsaw, Berlin, Prague, Vienna, Budapest, Belgrade, Bucharest, and Sofia, all these famous cities and the populations around them lie in what I must call the Soviet sphere, and all are subject, in one form or another, not only to Soviet influence but to a very high and in some cases increasing measure of control from Moscow." Truman had already digested Kennan's telegram. Churchill gave the ideas added eloquence, and public airing. Churchill may have intended his words to force a recognition that the world was now divided into separate economic and ideological spheres; they were taken as a call to arms to roll back Soviet power before it was too late.

Looking back, it is hard not to be struck by how quickly and almost without debate the United States shifted from viewing the Soviets as a complicated ally to an unequivocal adversary that posed an existential threat to the American way of life. Yes, there were voices of dissent, most notably from Henry Wallace, who objected to the onward rush toward confrontation and was promptly ejected from the Truman administration. On the whole, an entire phalanx of American political and business elites—Lovett and Harriman key among them—accepted that Soviet communism was a new challenge that required as much effort in its way as the war that had just been fought. This time, however, the contest would be as much economic and ideological as military.

How to explain this rush into a new conflict? The sense that Western Europe and parts of Asia were teetering on the verge of economic collapse was part of it. It was not unreasonable to look back at what had happened in the 1930s and draw the conclusion that economic chaos was a breeding ground for extreme ideologies. Everywhere in Europe in 1946, communist parties were surging. While the United States had a brief red scare at the end of World War I, communism had never become a serious domestic force, which meant that it was seen as an alien ideology. All of these factors generated a sense of urgency bordering on paranoia.

It's said that we become more aware of who we are and what we value when thrust into contact with competing views. The United States emerged in the nineteenth century when the old, familiar nations of Europe were the primary rivals. It had flirted with empire in Latin America, which was composed of states that were part of the same religious and philosophical heritage. But in confronting the challenge of communism, Americans in positions of power were forced to clarify and define their own system and values in the face of something new. There is nothing like the other to make you aware of who you are.

Lovett and Harriman, along with Prescott, Roland, the rest of their partners and most of their class, had lived their core values more than they had articulated them. Even in the depths of the Great Depression, they had not seen their worldview truly challenged. Communism was an alternate value system and more to the point an economic system that rejected the core tenets of capitalism—private property, personal profit, a system of laws protecting contracts, competition, and money for wages and for investment. What had been taken as unquestioned was therefore threatened, and the captains of capitalism reacted accordingly. Faced with a system that would upend the world they had helped craft, they responded by fighting as if their lives depended on it.

Brown Brothers and their brethren did not panic. They took stock of the situation and once again understood that they needed to serve, to protect themselves, their system and their country. Faced with an adversary, they crystallized what had been assumed, concretized what had been inchoate, and created—often on the fly, improvised more than planned—a template for how countries should be run, how the international economy should be managed, and how money should flow. The system they created soon governed the world and remains entrenched, fraying at the edge but in place, to this day.

The Soviet Union did not share that vision. The question, in retrospect, is whether the Soviets presented the level of threat commensurate with the reaction to them. Just because a country, even a large one with considerable resources, adopts a hostile stance does not mean that it can deliver on its bluster. By most subsequent estimations, the Soviets under Stalin did not have the economic or military capacity to challenge the United States. But the power of its ideas is harder to gauge. Lovett and Harriman thought that those ideas were dangerous. And they were hardly alone. There was palpable fear in the United States that Soviet and communist ideology would take hold throughout the world, and if adopted by sufficient numbers could be a lethal blow to the free and open markets that the American Establishment believed were essential to global peace and prosperity.

By 1947, any hopes that there could be a postwar modus vivendi with the Soviets were fading fast. The British Empire was disintegrating more rapidly than either the Americans or the British had anticipated. The assumption had been that the British might need temporary propping up but would remain a vibrant force globally. But much as World War I had seen the sad unwinding of the equal relationship between the two houses of Brown, the end of World War II saw the U.S.-British relationship shift dramatically as the once-mighty British Empire deteriorated. The winter of

1946–47 in Europe was freakishly frigid, which worsened an already dire situation as millions eked out a threadbare existence in hollowed-out cities and towns. The Truman administration was confronted with a naval stand-off in the Black Sea between Turkey and the Soviets, and most acutely, with the raging civil war in Greece between the Athens government and insurgents identifying themselves as communists. In response, Truman announced that it would be the policy of the U.S. government to aid those fighting against communism. "I believe it must be the policy of the United States to support free peoples who are resisting attempted subjugation by armed minorities or by outside pressures," he declared. He said that American aid should be both military, in the form of supplies, and financial, in the belief that "financial aid . . . is essential to economic stability and orderly political processes." Congress approved the policy that became known as the Truman Doctrine. The initial allocation was $400 million to be used for Greece and Turkey. As the year drew to a close, the Truman administration reacted to signs that the Italian Communist Party was surging and might win the next elections. As a result, the newly constituted Central Intelligence Agency was authorized to covertly support the Christian Democratic Party in Italy against its communist rivals. The combination of overt aid and covert action would become a blueprint for the rest of the Cold War.

In the midst of these tectonic shifts, Robert Lovett returned to government. Even through the momentous changes of 1946, he had expressed little interest in leaving his perch at Brown Brothers. But his life would be overtaken by events. Lovett had developed a close relationship with General Marshall during the war, and like Lovett, Marshall—who was almost universally admired for his role in the American victory—had resigned as chief of staff of the U.S. Army soon after the war ended and had planned a long and quiet retirement with his wife in rural Virginia. The humble, taciturn general had looked forward to "a little of home life for Mrs. Marshall and me . . . my limited activities, whatever they may be, of a strictly nongovernmental or political nature." But it was not to be. Implored by Truman to undertake a diplomatic mission to China to see what peace could be brokered between Chiang Kai-shek and Mao Zedong (none, as it turned out), Marshall was then asked to become secretary of state in January 1947. One of the first things he did was to recommend to Truman that Lovett be undersecretary. Lovett said yes. How could he not? "There are three people to whom I can never say no—my wife, Henry Stimson, and George Marshall," he quipped.[3]

But it wasn't Marshall who made the pitch. It was Truman himself. As Lovett recalled, he and Adele "were living then, in the old superintendent's cottage on my father's place out at Locust Valley waiting to sell his place. . . . And I always got up at 6:45 and went downstairs to get breakfast in my bathrobe and then dressed after breakfast. And the telephone was in Mrs. Lovett's room, not in my room upstairs, with an extension downstairs. And the phone rang while I was having breakfast, and I heard it stop ringing because she picked it up and she said, 'Bob, Washington is calling.' It went downhill from there."

And I said, "Yes."

He said, "This is the President."

And I said, "Now listen, this isn't at all funny. It's 6:45 in the morning. I'm right in the middle of breakfast, I'm trying to get the early commuter train to New York and for God's sake this is no time for jokes!"

He said, "No, this is really the President."

So I said, "Well, I beg your pardon, sir, I didn't realize that."

And then he said in effect, "I've got to get a new Secretary of State and I've signed up General Marshall on the condition which he made that you'd come down and be his Under Secretary." So, he said, "I want you to do that tonight."

And I said, "All right, sir. I've got to go and check with my partners; I've got to get permission to get out of the firm and the New York State Bank Department has to approve. But I don't anticipate too much trouble; I'll call you back as soon as I've gotten hold of my partners."

Unsurprisingly, his partners assented, though his resignation entailed another arduous divestiture process. Lovett had to sell everything he owned that related to military contracts. He later claimed that while the partners understood his motivations, they still said he was a fool to take the position. Other accounts suggested that Lovett wasn't quite so sure he should accept the job, and it was Averell who called him a "damn fool" for even hesitating. Either way, his partners may have teased him in a schoolboy manner, but they respected him for returning to Washington. As a result of his decision, he amended his earlier mantra. "The three people in the world I can't say no to—and now we've got to add to that list the President that I think has done an absolutely superb job, and I think we're in one hell of a mess. So if he thinks I can do anything—I don't think I can—if he thinks I can do any, why there isn't anything to do but go down there."[4]

Lovett was unanimously confirmed by the Senate. He was stepping into a significant role, and replacing a significant person: Dean Acheson, who was going the other way through the revolving door and returning to private life for what turned out to be a brief interregnum. The position of undersecretary in those years was much like a chief of staff. The job was to manage the burgeoning and complicated bureaucracy of the State Department. Lovett, more than the dramatic Acheson, was perfectly suited to the role, which was more heavily skewed to policy implementation than to policy making. Acheson's later memoir was titled *Present at the Creation* as recognition that those in the foreign policy positions in the government in these years created a new domestic and international system and that it unfolded every bit as quickly and radically as the launching of the New Deal. Lovett, focused on enacting and managing, was not just "present at the creation." He was, as Acheson fully acknowledged, one of the creators.[5]

Within weeks of Lovett's confirmation and appointment, on June 5, General Marshall went up to Harvard University to receive an honorary degree and deliver a commencement address. Flanked by J. Robert Oppenheimer, who was being honored for unleashing the powers of nuclear destruction at Los Alamos and who would later be stripped of his security clearances, Marshall used his address to speak of reconstruction. This was no ordinary encomium replete with genial homilies. Instead of urging the young hopefuls assembled in the yard that morning to go forth and deploy their talents, he announced a sweeping plan to rescue the economies of Europe devastated by the war. "In considering the requirements for the rehabilitation of Europe," he intoned, "the physical loss of life, the visible destruction of cities, factories, mines and railroads was correctly estimated, but it has become obvious during recent months that this visible destruction was probably less serious than the dislocation of the entire fabric of European economy." The only solution, he continued, was to restore "the confidence of the European people in the economic future of their own countries and of Europe as a whole. The manufacturer and the farmer throughout wide areas must be able and willing to exchange their products for currencies the continuing value of which is not open to question." And the only way that could be done was for the United States to distribute billions of dollars of loans and grants directly to those countries in need.

If anything encapsulated the new American worldview, this speech and the resulting Marshall Plan was it. In the postwar world, economics, and specifically the contest between dueling economic systems, would be the fulcrum. The exchange of products in a market system cemented by currencies—by money—was the foundation of capitalism, which Soviet communism rejected. Whether or not the world could accommodate two opposed systems in a live-and-let-live détente, the American foreign policy establishment by the late 1940s was convinced that states of Western Europe would not remain within the capitalist fold unless immediate action was taken to shore up their economies.

As it turned out, Lovett would be one of the main implementers of Marshall's vision, along with the deputy secretary of state, Will Clayton, and a core of others. Marshall himself struggled with an arduous travel schedule and myriad health ailments that would lead to a removal of one of his kidneys and his early retirement as secretary at the end of 1948. He delegated much of the implementation of the Marshall Plan to Lovett, whom he trusted completely. Lovett navigated months of negotiations with the French, the Benelux countries, Italy and others. It did not always go smoothly, largely because the Europeans clung to the belief that they were only in temporary duress. They also balked at the imperious attitude of the Americans. The United States insisted that because it possessed the money that Europe needed, it would set the terms of market reform, which money would be grants and which loans, and how and under what terms those billions would be repaid.[6]

There were also domestic obstacles to the Marshall Plan in Congress. Lovett built on his years of working with Congress for appropriations during the war to help the administration win over its many skeptics. In the Senate, Arthur Vandenberg was wary of an open-ended aid program of the size being contemplated, and other Republican isolationists in the House needed persuading as well. Lovett brought the same statistical rigor to making the case that he did to all of his endeavors, though he also applied a more personal touch to Vandenberg, often stopping by the powerful senator's apartment in the evenings to brief him on the latest thinking as the administration crafted its plans. In formal presentations, Lovett made an airtight case that every dollar spent or lent by the Americans would have a tangible effect in reconstructing Europe. As he later recalled in an oral history interview, "We used all IBM machines in the Census Bureau and ended up by borrowing those of the Prudential Life Insurance Company in Newark in order to make our calculations. The sheer mechanical figuring of the so-called country needs and pricing these items was beyond anything we had anticipated and far exceeded any similar effort made in government."

Lovett was joined in these efforts by Averell Harriman. After a brief tenure as ambassador to Great Britain, Harriman became secretary of commerce in late 1946. By mid-1947, he was put in charge of corralling American business leaders in order to secure their cooperation with the Marshall

Plan. While Lovett worked behind the scenes with European governments and Congress, Harriman confronted domestic opposition to spending in the neighborhood of $13 billion (more than $150 billion in today's dollars) for economic aid abroad. It was one thing to rally public opinion to buy bonds to support a war, but asking Americans to endorse a massive spending program using taxpayer dollars in peacetime to help other countries was a stretch. He had to make the argument that the Marshall Plan was necessary to construct a world that would benefit the United States. That was part public relations and part private, convening groups of business leaders, state politicians and members of Congress to make those arguments and listen to objections. Averell was a master convener.

The United States had already spent nearly $10 billion on European rebuilding, particularly in the occupied zones of Germany, and now the ask was even greater. To make matters more complicated still, there was an open question of whether aid should be extended to the Eastern bloc. While the early iterations of the Marshall Plan did not preclude aid to the Soviet Union and Eastern Europe, that was quickly shelved due to a combination of Stalin's hostility and the perceived impossibility of convincing Congress and the public that their tax dollars should assist communist countries. The more attention Averell devoted to the plan, the more it became his central focus and crowded out other responsibilities as head of commerce. In 1948, Harriman changed roles again and moved to Paris to become the official U.S. coordinator of the Marshall Plan after Congress finally approved the aid, in no small measure due to Lovett's relationship with Vandenberg in the Senate and with leading Republicans in the House. It was a sign of how crucial the Marshall Plan was to American foreign policy in that period that Harriman would step down from a cabinet position in order to administer the program. In 1948, the Marshall Plan was the signature U.S. foreign policy endeavor, one that dwarfed anything that the Commerce Department was then undertaking.

The Marshall Plan was not an act of charity, though it was charitable. Channeling American aid was designed to bolster the international economic system, as well as the political framework, for the benefit of the

United States. A stable and eventually robust Western Europe structured around free markets, anchored by the Bretton Woods currency system and aligned with the United States would be a market for American manufactured goods. American manufacturing, having amped up for the war, had significant excess capacity that more robust export markets could absorb. The plan also required the United States to import more and so provide a market for European goods. Even though parts had been devastated by the war, Western Europe was still America's prime economic partner, if it could rebuild and not succumb to the wave of communist parties and to the covert onslaught by Moscow.

Stalin's reaction to the Marshall Plan validated American paranoia. He denounced the program as "an American imperialist plot to subjugate Western Europe," which was several bridges too far but in keeping with Soviet rhetoric and propaganda that interpreted everything through the lens of a to-the-death ideological struggle. Stalin's extremism fed the same in the Americans, who took the Soviet leader at his word even though that word was at best situational and temperamental. Harriman later defended the Marshall Plan as "exactly the reverse of what Stalin claimed." The United States wanted an independent and free Europe able to thrive on its own, and financial assistance was the formula to achieve that.[7]

For Harriman and the Americans administering the aid, the self-help emphasis was paramount. It wasn't just about giving Europe money; it was about channeling the funds in a manner most likely to accelerate European domestic recovery until it could be self-sustaining. It was the economic equivalent of a jump start. The goal was to juice the economic engine of the countries needing assistance so that they would be less likely to embrace communism and then be cut off from the free-market sphere that was the cornerstone of American affluence. As Lovett remarked, "Europe was in a vacuum. Well, not only nature had caused the vacuum, but the Soviets loved one. So the best defense it became clear . . . was to move in and get those people going on the basis of self-help."[8] Rejecting the post–World War I experience of aid in the form of loans that were then never paid back, the Marshall Plan represented a major commitment by the United States to Europe, and it helped weave together a Western bloc aligned around capitalism and democracy.

There were divisions, of course, particularly between those who embraced more social programs in Europe and those who argued for less government, but it wasn't simply the Marshall Plan that cemented the Western phalanx. There was also a new military alliance called the North Atlantic Treaty Organization, formed in 1949 after arduous negotiations throughout 1948. NATO bound the states of Western Europe even more closely to the United States, and was interpreted by the Soviet Union as a move even more hostile than the ones that had come before. Lovett's role was crucial. Overcoming once again the concerns of Vandenberg and the wing of the Republican Party that abhorred "entangling alliances," Lovett worked assiduously with his European counterparts to formulate the treaty that would cement the Western alliance for the next forty years and beyond.[9]

The slew of international security arrangements went hand in hand with the birth of a new and permanent national security bureaucracy in the United States. The National Security Act of 1947 created the National Security Council at the White House, the Department of Defense and a separate air force branch to complement the navy and the army. It set up a joint chiefs of staff structure, and it established the Central Intelligence Agency to manage analysis and implement covert action. Bob Lovett's fingerprints were everywhere. He had chaired a commission at the State Department in late 1945 outlining the need for a central intelligence agency, and his work during the war made possible the autonomous air force that became the third and final pillar of the military triad that continues today.

Even with the 1947 act, however, the thrust of American policy in these immediate postwar years was not yet primarily military. It was economic and political and to an extent ideological, albeit with the understanding that the United States would need a potent military capability at the ready. It would take the Korean War, and Bob Lovett as secretary of defense, to shift the balance firmly toward an ever-expanding military establishment, with massive budgets, a nuclear arsenal and a standing army larger than any American had ever known.

In addition to the Marshall Plan, 1947 saw one other creation that received comparatively less attention at the time and yet ultimately shaped the rest of the century. As the architects of the postwar order looked to the recent past for lessons about what not to do going forward, the high-tariff regime of the 1920s and 1930s was cast into question. The efforts of multiple countries to protect themselves from the shock waves by raising tariff barriers had the opposite effect. High-tariff barriers enacted by every major country simultaneously in the early 1930s succeeded in making paupers of everyone. Taking heed of that lesson, the Truman administration convened a multilateral conference to set a new paradigm for trade going forward, one that would reduce barriers, lead to more commerce and thereby strengthen the edifice that U.S. national security strategy was erecting.

Quietly, with little fanfare, nearly two dozen nations began designing an international trade regime. One of the recommendations of the Bretton Woods agreement was to create a trade body equivalent to the World Bank, but trade raised thornier issues of sovereignty and domestic economic health. In April 1947, a meeting was quietly convened in Geneva to hash out a basic framework without attracting attention. The delegates knew that they would inevitably face domestic opposition to removing tariff barriers, and they wanted to reach a consensus before confronting the politics. Over the next eight months, representatives from eighteen countries argued and debated. Acheson and Will Clayton at the State Department were briefed regularly and guided policy, and Lovett shepherded the final stages of the negotiations. The result was the 1948 General Agreement on Tariffs and Trade (GATT), which began the process of lowering tariffs and revising trade laws over the next four decades until GATT morphed into the World Trade Organization (WTO) in 1995.

The initial agreement was not nearly as complete or comprehensive as some had hoped. There were too many stumbling blocks involving individual products ranging from American wool to French fishing reels. Rather than trying to solve everything and accomplishing nothing, the countries endorsing the general parameters of GATT agreed to meet regularly in subsequent rounds over the coming years to hash out the thousands of specific products and duties. The final stumbling block to GATT was the British system of imperial preferences and how hard the United States would push to end that. For more than a century, the British had traded with their colonies in a system that was essentially closed to other countries, with tariffs so high on, say, Indian exports to non-British countries that trade was all but banned. The British government was not prepared to concede the end of the empire (even as it crumbled), and the Americans, perhaps sensing that it was coming anyway, decided not to force the issue. GATT was ratified and came into force at the beginning of 1948. Lovett drafted President Truman's speech. The negotiations had resulted, Truman announced, in "a landmark in the history of international economic relations. Never before have so many nations combined in such a sustained effort to lower barriers to trade. Never before have nations agreed upon action, on tariffs and preferences, so extensive in its coverage and so far reaching in its effects." The conclave also endorsed the creation of the International Trade Organization, which in the end did not happen because of resistance in the United States to yet another powerful multinational body. But the idea was the seed of what eventually became the WTO.[10]

The agreement did not force the immediate removal of all trade barriers, nor envision them in the short term. That would have been politically impossible in the United States and in every other country. Even the rather limited GATT framework aroused intense skepticism in Congress, in the British and Canadian Parliaments and in every legislature of every country involved. Bowing to those political realities, the agreement eschewed a grand new plan and instead set schedules, tabled hot-button issues and products for later discussion, and established the category of "most favored nations" that would reward those countries that restructured their trade regimes. The initial agreement fell so short of loftier ambitions, however, that some officials involved in the negotiations advocated walking away, including the main point person, Will Clayton. Lovett proved to be the crucial voice convincing Truman to endorse the agreement, even with its shortcomings. Lovett had his eye on the bigger picture, which depended on a nexus of trade, economic aid and military alliances that would glue the states of Europe to the United States. He argued to Truman that a "thin" trade agreement was vital and "better than none." That argument carried the day. Lovett's pragmatism demanded a deal, not the best deal, especially because embedded in the process was a commitment to continue revising the rules over time. If contesting the Soviet Union and halting (and ultimately rolling back) the spread of communism depended on a mix of security and prosperity, then anything that moved the needle toward more commerce and closer economic integration was for the best.[11]

Given the backdrop of the high-tariff regime of the 1920s and 1930s, combined with the war years that saw a complete disruption of trade, the GATT framework was astonishing. It could never have surmounted years of anti-free-trade policy were it not for the fact that after 1945, the United States faced almost no competition for its domestic manufacturing and exports while the European nations who signed onto GATT needed the United States for reconstruction. It wasn't, therefore, that everyone simultaneously embraced free trade as an ideology as much as most understood that more trade with fewer barriers was a pragmatic solution to myriad problems. Nonetheless, the move from a world characterized by mercantilism (high-trade barriers that kept British trade with the colonies walled off from the rest of the world, for example) and draconian tariffs (such as the Smoot-Hawley Tariff Act, passed just as the Depression was intensifying) to a world dedicated to reducing those barriers was a radical break from the past. There remained considerable opposition and discomfort with the idea. While the GATT nations agreed on general principles, each one had domestic constituencies and industries that felt threatened and fought against the lowering of barriers, which is why it would take decades and multiple rounds of negotiation to form the World Trade Organization. Many of the concerns proved well founded, and domestic industries that weren't protected were disrupted. But as Lovett had argued, GATT achieved its primary purposes, which was to invigorate trade, bolster the capitalist economies of the world against the Soviet Union, and increase American prosperity.

Lovett's rotation in and out of government service continued when Marshall once again retired after Truman's gritty and surprising electoral victory against the heavily favored governor of New York, Thomas Dewey. Rallying the heartland with his folksy populism aimed at stirring up the old passions of rural America against urban elites, Truman defied the pollsters and the pundits and was reelected. He did not, however, depart from the economic security policies his administration had set in motion. To replace the ailing Marshall, he turned once more to Dean Acheson. Lovett tendered his resignation, not out of any dislike of his fellow Yalie but out of a desire to return to his life as a banker and partner. He was readmitted to the partnership of Brown Brothers Harriman in 1949. It was a short-lived reprieve. Barely a year later, he resigned the partnership once more, this time to take up the position of deputy secretary of defense when George Marshall, again playing Cincinnatus, returned to Washington to rejoin Truman's cabinet as secretary of defense in September 1950. In the interim, Marshall had served as president of the American Red Cross. When he resigned to lead the Defense Department, his replacement as head of the Red Cross was none other than Roland Harriman.

Averell, meanwhile, continued his peripatetic career, moving from point person for the Marshall Plan to the head of the newly established Mutual Security Agency in 1951, which was created to administer post–Marshall Plan aid as well as military assistance under the new NATO framework. Harriman's unique position in the government—as a minister on call—led *The New Yorker* in an extensive profile to call him the government's "plenipotentiary." Averell roamed from appointment to appointment but with a singular focus: "Harriman is constantly preoccupied with money these days, since he is in effect the paymaster for all funds appropriated by the United States to bolster the non-Communist world, but because he is not obliged to worry about his own money, he sometimes seems unaware that he has any." Averell embodied a certain WASP disinclination to spend, which Alexander Brown would have recognized and approved of. He sometimes took that too far, with an occasional disinclination to eat. His secretaries had to remind him to have a sandwich at the end of the day.

Called on by Truman and then by later administrations for his advice and counsel, Harriman epitomized the clubby, informal and consultative nature of the national security establishment in those years. Given that much was being invented on the fly and chaos and motion were the norm, multiple voices in and out of government contributed to policy debates, and the cabinet acted as the president's council and not just an assortment of grandees heading their own mammoth departments. The White House staff was comparatively lean, and Truman used his cabinet as a group of senior advisers. Nowhere was that more evident than in the framing of the signature national security document of its day, one that set the United States irrevocably on a course of military competition and confrontation with the Soviet Union.

Toward the end of 1949, two things happened that pushed the Cold War into an even more adversarial groove: the Soviets detonated their first nuclear weapon, catching U.S. intelligence by surprise, and the Communists emerged victorious in the Chinese civil war and pronounced a new era in Beijing. The reaction in Washington was to galvanize the full resources of the American government to contest the Soviet Union. Dean Acheson instructed the head of the State Department's Policy Planning Staff, Paul Nitze, another Ivy-educated Wall Street lawyer who had migrated into government, to weave the various threads from the past five years into a new and comprehensive approach.

The result was NSC-68, a nearly-sixty-page document that drew from George Kennan's earlier assessment, magnified the Soviet threat and called for the militarization of American foreign policy. Never straying far from the basic contention that the Soviet Union posed a lethal threat, "animated by a new fanatic faith, antithetical to our own, and seeks to impose its absolute authority over the rest of the world," the document stressed the need for a more muscular and aggressive American policy aiming not just at containing Russian influence but rolling it back. The bottom line was that the United States had to work assiduously so that "the free world [could] develop a successfully functioning political and economic system." That meant continued enlargement of alliances; more economic development not just in

Europe but in Asia, the Middle East and Latin America; and a substantial increase in military spending.

At the Defense Department, Lovett was one of the small circle that not only helped craft NSC-68 but was also responsible for making it the official policy of the government. Lovett was especially attuned to the public-facing function of the document, which would remain highly classified but would still inform how the administration would make its case to Congress and the American public about the need to ramp up military spending to meet the Russian challenge. He had been arguing for months that the Cold War needed more active support from a skeptical public. Powerful figures in the Republican Party, such as Robert Taft, were still not sold on the need to augment the scope and scale of government spending not just on the tradi- tional military but on intelligence and aid and on selling the American vi- sion around the world. The goal of NSC-68 was to express the threat in such stark language that the American public (which would never be able to read the exact text but which would be informed by officials using it as a template) would be scared into action.

Understanding the propaganda aspects of the document, Lovett urged that it be written "simply, clearly, and in Hemingway sentences. . . . If we can sell every useless article known to man in large quantities, we should be able to sell our very fine story in larger quantities."[12] As it turned out, Lovett himself would be in prime position to "sell it." First, the onset of the Korean War in June validated, in the eyes of these policy makers, the thesis that communism was on the rise. Even though the Russians had only indirect influence at best over the decisions of the North Koreans, for Americans at the time, it was all part of an interconnected and undifferentiated red wave. Acheson wrote later that "it seemed close to certain that the attack had been mounted, supplied and instigated by the Soviet Union," which was justifi- cation enough for the United States to enter the war to shore up South Korea. Lovett, who was as convinced as any that the Russians placed "low value on human life . . . with a ruthless barbaric attitude towards the indi- vidual" and had an unbridled "desire to expand," plunged once again into coordinating a major war from his perch near the top of the Defense Department.[13]

Even at the time, the language of NSC-68 raised eyebrows for its nihilistic assessment of the Soviets and for its uncompromising demand for mobilization to contest the spread of communism. In later years, critics of American foreign policy pointed to the document as an example of how the Establishment in the postwar years hysterically and cynically magnified the threat in order to steer U.S. policy in a more militaristic direction. In many ways, those critiques were based on how American policy evolved afterward, especially in the 1960s with the overreach of the Vietnam War and assorted covert operations around the world. In the retrospective light of Vietnam, NSC-68 became Exhibit A for the contention that American policy had been designed in secret to benefit the elite with harmful consequences for the country.[14]

But in 1950 those critiques lay decades away. In September 1951, Lovett, who had been teased in his circle for being ever the bridesmaid, was elevated to the cabinet as secretary of defense. Marshall, after fifty years in government, announced his final retirement, and Lovett was the unquestioned successor. "There is no one else in the United States who has his understanding and confidence," Marshall observed, and Truman fully agreed. Lovett spent the remaining fifteen months of Truman's term at the helm of the Pentagon. The arc of the Cold War, the shape of the national security state and the panoply of international alliances had largely been determined. The United States was deeply immersed in the stalemate of the bloody war on the Korean Peninsula, and that occupied much of Lovett's attention. On the rare days when he wasn't working with the military command on Korean strategy, Lovett as secretary attended to the reintegration of West Germany into the European system and the rapid buildup of the Air Force's Strategic Air Command, which was to be one of the pillars of U.S. nuclear policy. The tight relationship between Acheson at State and Lovett at Defense meant that there would be remarkably little tension or policy dissent during the administration's final months. In a similar vein, the long personal and professional bonds between Lovett and Harriman meant that Harriman as administrator of aid in Europe would continue to have more influence over policy than his titular role would suggest.

Lovett, even at the pinnacle of his governmental career, remained primarily an implementer of policy, which had always been his forte. The fact that he was more doer than grand strategist meant that he received comparatively less attention than Acheson or even Kennan. Exiting the war in Korea proved elusive, but the path he advocated of accepting a divided peninsula paved the way for President Dwight Eisenhower to end the war early in 1953. The doctrine of massive retaliation as the operating nuclear and military strategy toward the Soviet Union, as well as the overall approach set by NSC-68, needed thoughtful implementation, and Lovett was uniquely equipped for the task. He watched the election of Eisenhower with some trepidation, not because he doubted the general's ability but because he was wary of the man who was slated to lead foreign policy should Eisenhower win, John Foster Dulles. Dulles had been poised to become secretary of state in 1948 when Dewey unexpectedly lost, and he was almost certain to become Eisenhower's. Dulles did not entirely reject the consensus that Acheson, Lovett, Harriman and others had forged, but he appeared to them more dogmatic and zealous. He advocated an even harder line toward the Soviets and appeared to flirt with the idea of preemptive nuclear war. He seemed altogether too comfortable with the nativist anti-communism being espoused by Wisconsin senator Joseph McCarthy. Dulles was from a similar background and moved in the same New York circles, but they did not much like him, and he returned the favor.

The waves of McCarthyism that buffeted Washington in these years, abetted by increasingly influential figures such as Richard Nixon of California, first in the House of Representatives and then the Senate, echoed the nastier aspects of nineteenth-century populism. When McCarthy accused the State Department of housing hundreds of communist agents, he was speaking part fact and many more parts fiction. His language dripped with contempt for educated urban elites who attended the finest schools, controlled the levers of finance and betrayed the country. He saw in the influence of those WASP elites the same pernicious specter that Bryan had and that those who railed against the makers of money had in the nine-teenth century: a small cabal profiting immorally, undermining hardwork-ing Americans for their own selfish gain. And this time, it was in cahoots with an evil empire.

McCarthy soon went too far and was reined in, but by then, many of those he had attacked had returned to private life. As Truman left office at the beginning of 1953, Lovett stepped down and once again was welcomed back into the partnership. Acheson retired for good. Harriman left the gov-ernment after Eisenhower's inauguration and ran for elected office, win-ning the governorship of New York. Unlike Lovett's, Harriman's public career would continue for many more years, and he would become a senior policy official in the Kennedy administration, a role that Lovett declined. But then Harriman had always needed the validation of high office; Lovett, from all appearances, would have been content if he had served during the wars and then thrived as a banker once those were over.

In the span of a decade, a relatively small number of men had entered the highest circles of American national security policy making and de-signed a new world order. Many of the core people came from the same class as Lovett and Harriman and the same community as Brown Brothers. They shared a sensibility born of private boarding schools, Ivy education, a similar strain of Protestantism, then nurtured in the financial world. They wove that sensibility into the founding fabric of postwar American foreign policy. In 1941, as the United States was ramping up its preparedness cam-paign in anticipation of war, Henry Luce—who had become one of the most influential media titans in the country in no small measure due to the backing of Harriman—published an editorial in *Life* magazine titled "The American Century." Even before it was clear how the war would un-fold, Luce proclaimed that American power was such that the twentieth century was destined to be the American century, and foremost in impor-tance was the economic order. "It is for America and America alone to determine whether a system of free economic enterprise—and economic order compatible with freedom and progress—shall or shall not prevail in this century. We know perfectly that there is not the slightest chance of anything faintly resembling a free economic system prevailing in this country if it prevails nowhere else." Luce spoke for them all and encapsulated what the postwar order created by Americans attempted to accomplish: an international system that would allow free economic enterprise to thrive so that it could continue to thrive in the United States itself.

Before the war, before the rise of the Soviet Union, there had been less need to clarify basic ideas or articulate them. Yes, the Great Depression forced some self-examination, but the war and the ideological challenge of communism turned a loose set of principles into a specific set of institutions. The Bretton Woods accords with its World Bank and IMF, the General Agreement on Tariffs and Trade, NATO, the Marshall Plan, the United Nations, the creation of a permanent national security bureaucracy in the U.S. government, the buildup of the military as the bulwark and last line of defense—all of these were based explicitly or implicitly on the idea that the United States had found a formula for economic success and national power that might have been tested by the Depression but had still made it richer and stronger than any nation in the world. And that formula, at its heart, involved a dynamic unleashing of industry fueled by a steady stream of money.

In 1945, men such as Lovett and Harriman, who had made the money that made America, distilled the formula that they believed had made America rich and powerful. Much was improvised; much was in reaction to events rather than a prior plan. But as that formula coalesced, Americans in positions of power exported it globally, seeing it as a prerequisite to peace, stability and prosperity. In a few short years, they succeeded beyond all measure in erecting a system of laws and institutions and the primacy of the dollar that came to govern almost every country on the planet by the end of the twentieth century. As American power has waned in the twenty-first century, the framework has been dented and it has been contested, but it remains today the operating system in every corner of the globe.

CHAPTER 16

IN THE VALLEY

The Wall Street that Bob Lovett returned to was a more sedate one. Of the many changes wrought by World War II and the onset of the Cold War, the fading of Wall Street was hardly the most notable. But after the Depression and the reforms of the New Deal, the financial industry entered a long period of relative quiet. Not until 1954 did the Dow Jones Index, then the leading stock market indicator composed of the top thirty industrial companies, match the high it achieved in 1929. Traders made money, for sure, as did assorted brokerage firms and banks. But they did not make crazy money. In fact, in 1955, there were, according to *Fortune,* only thirty thousand executives in the entire country who made more than $50,000 a year (equivalent to about half a million dollars a year in today's coin).[1] Wall Street pay scales were akin to what top executives made at companies such as Ford Motors and General Electric. It was a very good living, but it was not notably out of sync with the rest of the country. And pay in general even for the richest was a comprehensible multiple of the average, and not as it was before the Depression and again in the twenty-first century, hundreds of times the average.

The postwar decades were times of immense change—the birth of television, the proliferation of air travel (a nod here to Brown Brothers), the explosive growth of American suburbs, years of substantial economic expansion and population baby boom, the adoption of mainframe computers in multiple industries. But for Wall Street, it was a sleepy time. In the country as a whole, the economic engine hummed, making possible not only generous domestic spending but defense budgets greater than at any period in American history outside of full mobilization, as well as hefty foreign aid and development budgets. As the middle class grew in affluence and numbers, American corporations thrived, and manufacturing was in the enviable position of acting as the factory for a world that was rapidly rebuilding but still lagged behind the United States by a considerable margin. Wall Street, meanwhile, was but one industry among many, profitable, lucrative even, but by no means a standout.

That normalization of finance was well under way by the late 1940s. The culture of Brown Brothers had always been one of reticence, and even as Brown Brothers Harriman made more active efforts to market its wealth management services, it managed to convey a message of humility and deliberateness in order to appeal to a clientele that valued discretion and would have been repelled by the idea that their bankers were motivated by greed and ego. The partners and employees may have had private lives more complicated than their public personas, but there was not much of a gap between the external image of Brown Brothers Harriman and the internal culture that the partners cultivated. During the war, the firm had started publishing a company newsletter titled "The Fifty Niner," after the address of their Wall Street headquarters. In it were articles about the firm's bowling league and a wry lament that the best bowlers were serving their country in the armed forces. The issue in the summer of 1945 began with a letter to those in the military, "All of us here are pulling together to keep the old ship B.B.H. & Co. cruising along in good style," and offered a prayer for those employees who were then engaged in the "task of freeing the world from the forces of evil." A simpler time, yes, but genuine. And it wasn't just Brown Brothers. In these years, theirs was a culture that numerous other Wall Street firms embodied or at least emulated.

With the war over and the bank once again fully staffed, its communications largely reinforced the messages of the 1930s, reaffirming the views of Lovett and Prescott Bush—who in turn channeled Alexander Brown—that stocks and bonds were ever risky and that care must always be taken to manage those risks. And as befitted a firm that had survived the ups and downs over generations, the culture also insisted that basic principles be married to flexibility to meet a changing world. In the 1953 employee handbook, new hires were told, "As you read this, remember that it describes merely today's policies that meet today's needs. The policies of Brown Brothers Harriman & Co. are not rigid. They are being changed constantly to meet new conditions and to meet the needs of people who make up our organization." The mantra as always was that the bank was only as good as its reputation. "Since a bank is primarily a service organization," that handbook concluded, "it is a fact that the character and reputation of Brown Brothers depend to a large extent on its employees."[2]

By the end of 1952, assets had grown considerably since the nadir of the 1930s: it was still among the hundred largest banks out of nearly fifteen thousand in the United States, and it was still not nearly as big as the biggest. Size, however, was never the point or the goal for the partners. Having the right business was always more important than having the most. With two of the partners (out of fewer than two dozen) shaping American policy at the highest levels, and one more—Prescott Bush—poised to enter the U.S. Senate in 1952 after failing to win in 1950, the bank could rightly view itself as more successful and influential than many of its larger peers. Per dollar, it was certainly as profitable.

Its reputation, however, was fading somewhat. A *New York Times* profile of the firm in 1958 quoted one senior executive saying, "Our friends tell us about the fine job we are doing, and then they admit they're not quite sure just what our business is." Perhaps for that reason, the firm issued a new and longer brochure the following year titled "The Personality of a Bank." Like past iterations, it described the partnership's storied history, harkening back to Alexander and then invigorated by the merger with Harriman. It also touted the advantages of a "private bank," which included "the freedom to act promptly and effectively in all situations" rather than being constrained by an inflexible public charter. The result, the firm announced, was that "today we are a bank—and yet we are more than a bank." Not only were the scope of activities broad, ranging from wealth management to loans to arranging credit lines for deals to tax services, but clients could benefit from the fact that "public service, a characteristic of the firm, adds another broad dimension to the partners' grasp of national and world conditions."[3]

Prescott Bush continued that tradition. He had been active in Connecticut Republican politics throughout the 1940s, primarily as a fundraiser. But he made known his interest in doing more and was recruited in 1950 to contest one of the state's two Senate seats, held by an interim Democrat named William Benton. Bush lost by barely 1 percent of the vote and was thus well placed to run again in 1952, this time against Representative Abraham Ribicoff. Bush was ambivalent about campaigning and had been bruised by the nastiness of politics, but he jumped in and won the election. His opponent did not slink away. One of the rare Jewish elected officials at the national level in those years, Ribicoff later served two terms as Connecticut's governor, a brief stint in John F. Kennedy's cabinet, and then finally won election as a Democratic senator in 1962, filling the seat vacated by Prescott and remaining in the Senate for nearly eighteen years.

The election was not without collateral damage for Prescott and the firm. Averell, playing his role as a Democratic Party grandee, endorsed Ribicoff, which deeply disappointed Bush. As Prescott later recalled, "We had been partners for many years. There was no blowup. We just stopped speaking." That said, the endorsement may have backfired. "Averell did me one favor. The support he gave Ribicoff kept Abe from making the obvious attack on the rich Wall Street banker." Bush then returned "the favor" and slammed Harriman as "unqualified for public service because of his surrender to the left wing of the Democratic party." Not usually thought of as quirky, Bush campaigned in an unorthodox manner, sometimes bringing along his old Yale Whiffenpoofs colleagues and breaking into a cappella songs during campaign rallies.[4]

Bush was a Republican, but that meant something rather different in those years in the Northeast. He presented himself on the campaign trail as a "moderate progressive." He was supportive of Margaret Sanger's Planned

Parenthood, which was then primarily focused on spreading access to birth control in the years before the Pill became widely available. He had no issue with higher taxes if those would serve the common good and national defense. Later he would take a vocal stand against the ardent segregationists of the Democratic Party, such as Mississippi's James Eastland, which was both good morals and good politics. In general, Bush was closer to the center of the Democratic Party even though he served as a Republican. He was fiercely anticommunist but deeply uncomfortable with the tactics of McCarthy, whom he helped curb in the Senate in 1954. But he was also rigid in his sense of public decorum and supported censuring speech he thought crass and inappropriate. In that spirit, he denounced Edward Albee's play *The Zoo Story* on the floor of the Senate for being "filthy" and entered a motion to prevent the play from being produced in foreign countries if any government money was involved. On the flip side, the cosmopolitan Bush opposed the isolationist wing of his party still led by Ohio's Robert Taft, who had failed to attain the presidency but remained a party power broker. Bush also strongly supported federal spending on domestic programs such as the interstate highway system, one of the signal domestic achievements of the Eisenhower administration that defined the landscape of the United States. With a spider web of roads crisscrossing the country and supplanting the railroads, the United States became a haven and a heaven for the cars that made possible the 1950s settlement of the crabgrass frontier of the suburbs.

Bush was self-aware enough to recognize that no matter what his policies were, he was perceived as a scion of privilege. He was a frequent golf partner of Eisenhower's, whom he regularly bested. For some, that was a sign that Prescott was one of the select, and they admired him for it; to others, his golf outings were a symbol of rank inequality, of the proximity to power unfairly enjoyed only by a few. Bush himself believed at his core that there wasn't much he could do about what people thought, except to do his best as a public servant. In 1959, at the legendary Alfalfa Club annual dinner in Washington, a club initially formed to celebrate the birthday of General Robert E. Lee but which evolved into a mainstay of the Washington social scene with its black-tie all-male dinners, Bush received the "nomination" for president. In his "acceptance" speech, he played with perfect pitch the part of the self-deprecating silver-spoon child. "It is my belief, my whole belief, that public office is a sacred trust. This reminds me to say right now that contributions for my campaign can be mailed to my trust, at the Guaranty Trust Company." He then sung the rest of his speech to the tune of *The Music Man* and concluded with a rousing rendition of "The Whiffenpoof Song."[5]

After nine years in the Senate, Bush unexpectedly decided not to run again in 1962, either because of his stated reason that he was genuinely exhausted and preferred to return to his partnership or because he sensed that this time he would lose to a resurgent Abe Ribicoff. His Senate career was not notable for its accomplishments. He passed his terms doing the people's businesses, with no scandal, no whiff of impropriety, and no meaningful legislation that bears his name. After 1962, Bush's political career was at an end, which was in its way fitting, because the age of the particular Establishment of which he was a part was also coming under siege. It would not be torn down, at least not completely, nor would it survive the sixties unscathed. He was as much a Rockefeller Republican as Nelson Rockefeller.

By the end of his Senate tenure, his class was already in the crosshairs of a culture that was beginning to question the received wisdom of the generation that had fought *the* war and the Cold War. In spite of the rosy images of a contented, thriving middle class, there were in the fifties already rumblings that perhaps all was not quite as it seemed, that the achievement of a level of economic security and employment that had proved elusive during the New Deal and that became something of a norm only after the sacrifices of World War II had not, as it turned out, produced widespread contentment. One of the bestselling books of the fifties was 1955's novel by Sloan Wilson, *The Man in the Gray Flannel Suit*. Its protagonist was one of those modestly successful denizens of the middle class, Tom Rath, who earned more than a decent salary of $7,000 a year in Manhattan, commuting each workday from the suburbs, where he lived with his wife, Betsy, and their children. The Raths were the middle-class version of the Bushes, living in similar suburbs, making a similar commute, working in similar businesses but for less money. They lacked the means of the wealthy, and while the salary was enough to live decently, it wasn't enough to live up to aspirations. A culture that trumpeted more and more and better and better left the Raths and their neighbors and friends feeling hollow, never quite satisfied and always one paycheck away from whatever else they needed or wanted. The novel ended seemingly well, with Tom in a new, better-paying job. The book begat an equally prominent film, with Gregory Peck playing the everyman, but what touched the nerve wasn't the benign arc of the Raths' lives but the barely suppressed dread that there was something incomplete about the American dream of peace and endless material prosperity. Enough was never quite enough in Tom Rath's America.[6]

A year after *The Man in the Gray Flannel Suit*, an academic sociologist named C. Wright Mills published a book called *The Power Elite*. Mills described an American society that was largely controlled by, yes, a power elite consisting of a few interlocking circles in business, finance, politics and the arts that collectively formed an oligarchy of privilege and power. Mills did not go so far as to argue—as many later did—that this elite was sitting around behind closed doors as a cohesive coterie coordinating strategy for national and global dominion. But he did assert that the flowering of this elite, including "the corporate rich" that would have included Brown Brothers Harriman and a "political directorate" of men such as Lovett, Harriman and Bush, was undermining an already tenuous democracy in the United States. Mills also charged that what this elite craved—more power and more money—were not in the country's best interests. Their claim that what was good for them was good for all was self-serving pablum. What was good for them, he vehemently argued, was good for them, and not so good for everyone else. Brown Brothers may have spoken the language of service and the public good, but at heart, Mills alleged, they were out for themselves.

While the existence of a cohesive power elite is debatable, the influence of *The Power Elite* is not. It is difficult to overstate how much the ideas articulated by Mills entered the lifeblood of American society and pop culture, first in the fifties as a counternarrative to American triumphalism and then as a more widely accepted theory of society in the 1960s. It is impossible to understand how the reputation and image of firms such as Brown Brothers Harriman, and the reputation of men such as Lovett, Harriman, Bush, along with Acheson, Kennan, and that cohort, deteriorated from respect and admiration to an entirely more ambivalent picture. And not just ambivalent. Starting in the sixties and then intensifying into the seventies, public attitudes shifted to outright animosity that recalled the angry words of the early New Deal and the denunciations of the populists, but this time a new strain was added that saw the militarism of the Cold War as proof that the elites were manipulating the system in their favor.

Soon after Mills, another sociologist, E. Digby Baltzell, called out the proliferation of wealthy men in politics. It wasn't just Harriman, then governor of New York, but also men such as Nelson Rockefeller, who was also running for governor, along with a slew of others. Baltzell noted, correctly, that the role of the rich in politics had waxed and waned over the decades since America's founding. John Hancock, the bold signer of the Declaration of Independence, along with Charles Carroll, that Baltimore grandee who was another signer and who later inaugurated the B&O Railroad, were two of the richest men in the colonies at the time. The Congress of the 1880s was notably full of wealthy men, and of course, FDR may have led the great leveling of the New Deal, but he nonetheless came from a patrician fortune. As government grew in power and scope in the 1940s and 1950s, it seemed logical that men drawn to power, wealth and prestige would find government service more attractive. As government power became more interwoven with corporate power in the 1950s, as business leaders such as General Motors CEO Charles Wilson served as secretary of defense and Cleveland steel executive George Humphrey as secretary of the treasury, the revolving door between business and government seemed to revolve with less and less friction. Baltzell was not unequivocal in his critique. "American civilization, led by businessmen of daring enterprise, has produced the highest standard of living the world has ever known. . . . The prize of power is stimulating to the old rich, and the cult of the self-made man may very well be on the wane in our world of abundant consumption. . . . This may or may not be a healthy thing for our country but after all there are few authentic log cabins for future Presidents to be born in."[7] But while Baltzell himself offered some nuance, these unflattering perspectives on the nexus of money and power indelibly affected how storied firms of Wall Street and Main Street were perceived. Much as J. P. Morgan had gone from the hero of the Panic of 1907 to the demon of the Pujo hearings in 1912, the image of the executives and financiers who entered government and then wrote the blueprint for the twentieth-century world went from lionized to demonized by the end of the sixties.

The easy flow from Wall Street and big business into government continued in the early years of the Kennedy administration. Harriman, again in search of a position after losing his reelection bid as governor of New York to fellow mogul Rockefeller, cozied up to the much younger John F. Kennedy. He was welcomed, if not warmly; his years of experience were valued. He was offered a less prominent post of assistant secretary of state for Far Eastern Affairs under Dean Rusk, who had been president of the Rockefeller Foundation and was in résumé Harriman's junior. Still, with multiple crises brewing in Laos and Vietnam, Harriman took the job believing, correctly, that he would be closer to the center of policy making than his title suggested. Over the next four years, Harriman would be part of the circle that edged the United States toward the fateful and ultimately disastrous commitment to dispatch hundreds of thousands of American troops to shore up the government of South Vietnam.

Several weeks after the election, Kennedy dispatched Clark Clifford, who had been a young aide to Truman and a legal adviser to the Kennedy family, to sound out Lovett about serving as secretary of the treasury. Lovett was still a registered Republican, but after a bruising and narrow election victory over Nixon, Kennedy hoped to assemble a cabinet that could command some Republican support. Clifford deeply respected Lovett and urged him to meet with the president-elect in Washington. Lovett demurred, saying that he didn't want the position. He later explained, "I felt for physical reasons alone it would not be possible for me to accept." Age was beginning to catch up with Lovett's hypochondria, although he would live for another two decades and die a few months before his ninety-first birthday. Lovett joked with Clifford that he thought it "would be very difficult to keep up with a group of forty-year-old touch football players," which had the virtue of being both a good metaphor and literally true, given the legendarily competitive Kennedy football games on the beach on Cape Cod at Hyannis Port. Lovett then detailed his health woes and the warnings of his doctors about possible surgery. Clifford played the encounter perfectly, with soothing, understanding words. Kennedy was also sympathetic, perhaps because of his own secret health woes.

Kennedy, however, insisted on meeting Lovett in person. In early December 1960, Lovett took a plane to Washington and a taxi to Kennedy's Georgetown town house. Kennedy apparently greeted him with a football and a Harvard sweatshirt. "That's a hell of a way to treat a Yale man," Lovett barked. The two settled into an easy rapport. Kennedy asked him for advice about whom he would recommend not just for Treasury but for State and Defense. Lovett put forth a variety of names, including the one who would ultimately fill the Treasury spot, Douglas Dillon, a prominent Republican whose eponymous Wall Street investment bank, Dillon, Read, founded by his father, was where the tragic James Forrestal had begun his career. Lovett also put forth the name of his old friend John McCloy for one of the three positions, and he urged JFK to select someone for the Defense Department who had a keen understanding of the need for meticulous statistical assessments of strategy and tactics. In the end, on Lovett's recommendation, Kennedy chose Robert McNamara, who had excelled at quantitative analysis running Ford Motors. That skill with numbers would prove problematic in Vietnam.[8]

Lovett did agree to serve as a consultant, and to be on several committees, though he joked with Kennedy that "a committee is a group of men who, as individuals, can do nothing but who, as a committee, can meet formally and decide that nothing could be done." During Kennedy's time in the White House, Lovett consistently urged him to be mindful of the close link between price stability and economic growth, whether in the United States or Western Europe or anywhere else in the world. That was Lovett's way of recommending the continuation of conservative economic policies implemented by the Treasury and also by the Federal Reserve. And it meant, for Lovett, not succumbing to the liberal economic views of economists such as Harvard's John Kenneth Galbraith, who was finding favor in Kennedy's circle. When the stock market sold off in May 1962, JFK was being urged by some of his advisers to take action and intervene. He phoned Lovett, who said bluntly that the president and the government should under no circumstances interfere and should "let the market find its own level."[9] That advice was heeded. And given Lovett's deep experience in national security policy, Kennedy turned to him not just for economic counsel but also for military and nuclear strategy, particularly during the failed CIA-organized Bay of Pigs invasion meant to topple the government of Fidel Castro in 1961 and during the tense days of the Cuban Missile Crisis a year later.

In the changing climate of the sixties, the cozy relationship between high officials and men such as Lovett, a private citizen and a partner in a storied banking house, was taken as proof positive that the power elite ruled. It began to strike many as undemocratic that vital national interests could be shaped by unelected men who had back channels to power. Adding weight to that belief was that revolving door. For the most part, in the first half of the twentieth century, men of affairs—Andrew Mellon, Bernard Baruch, Elihu Root, Stimson, Acheson, Lovett, Harriman—first made their fortunes and then went on to Washington. In the 1960s, however, high government officials started to leave Washington to make their fortunes. When men of wealth turned from business to government, that had at times led to outcries about corruption and excessive privilege. But when high public officials started to exit government for generous salaries on Wall Street, that added fuel to the simmering resentment expressed by Mills and increasingly felt by a fractious baby boom generation disinclined to celebrate the system they were inheriting.

In 1965, after considerable effort, Brown Brothers Harriman wooed Robert Roosa, the undersecretary of the treasury in the Kennedy and early Johnson administrations, to join the firm as a partner. Roosa was a Rhodes Scholar and an academic economist trained at the University of Michigan.

He had spent his entire career in government, rising through the ranks of the research division of the New York Federal Reserve before being appointed by Kennedy to head up monetary affairs in the Treasury Department. As the scale and scope of government borrowing increased dramatically after World War II, the once sleepy function of coordinating bond issues and government borrowing assumed a prominent place and had been elevated to a new position at the top of the department in the mid-1950s. As undersecretary, Roosa was also responsible for the day-to-day management of the Treasury Department in addition to overseeing all matters monetary. He worked with the Federal Reserve on the money supply, streamlined the printing of dollars and added quantitative rigor to the issuing and pricing of Treasury bonds. He coordinated with foreign governments, which, given the relative economic might of the United States in the early 1960s, often meant dictating policy to them. He was one of the few hands-on guardians of the strength of the dollar and the maintenance of U.S. gold reserves. By all accounts, he was highly competent, wonky and apolitical. For his efforts, he was paid $17,000 a year, a salary that would have placed him squarely in the ranks of a senior vice president at a large corporation.

Then Wall Street beckoned. After aiding the transition from Kennedy to Johnson following the president's assassination in November 1963, Roosa quietly spread the word that he was planning to retire from government and was looking to join the private sector. The prospect was catnip to every major bank and investment firm. Roosa had an unblemished reputation and connections with senior government officials and banks around the world. He understood the intricacies of monetary policy and the myriad ways that currencies traded and value fluctuated during a messy period when Bretton Woods still governed and the dollar remained the linchpin but the system was beginning to fray. In fact, it was fraying largely because international central banks could exchange dollars for gold. Throughout the 1960s, that link between the dollar and gold weighed heavily on U.S. officials. Trying to maintain a system where global currencies were pegged to the dollar but dollars could be exchanged on demand for gold caused considerable heartache, and many in Washington feared they were playing a losing game. With fixed exchange rates, trade restrictions easing because of GATT and the United States still committed to economic aid for its allies and acting as an export engine, there was a chronic outflow of dollars and gold to other countries. By the time Roosa ascended to his Treasury role, the dollar, a fiat paper currency guaranteed by faith in the U.S. economy and the wisdom of its government, was more vital than gold to the global economic system. But gold habits died hard.

Among Roosa's Wall Street suitors was Brown Brothers Harriman. Prescott Bush, newly readmitted as a partner after departing the Senate and familiar with Roosa from his days in Congress, took the lead in wooing him. As Bush recalled, "We decided that it would be better for him and better for us if he fitted into our picture, where he could be of use to all those other banks, and at the same time his compensation would be as good or better than it would be with them, and it would improve our prestige at home and abroad." It proved to be a happy arrangement for all of them. After many lunches and likely not a few drinks, Roosa chose Brown Brothers as his new private sector home so that he could, as he quipped to one reporter, "get some sleep and make a little money." Roosa was able to translate his experience into wealth, his power into affluence. He promptly helped expand Brown Brothers Harriman abroad and develop expertise in managing bond portfolios in a more dynamic—and presumably more profitable—manner for clients.

As Bush observed at the time, "I mean he's just as happy as he can be. Now from our point of view, our judgment in getting him was just marvelous, because it's been a wonderful thing for us. It's added to our business. We've got new business as a result. People want to talk to this man." If you were prone to see the world in terms of a small establishment and a power elite, Roosa to Brown Brothers seemed to prove the point. He augmented the firm's already extensive web of connections with other private banks and global central banks and acted as a trusted go-between. He cemented the reputation of Brown Brothers as a private bank that may have been dwarfed in assets by other behemoths but was second to none in influence.

Roosa allowed the firm to continue doing what it always had: select its business rather than chase it, work closely with clients and stay at the center of it all.[10]

The term "the Establishment" entered popular culture sometime in the 1960s. An English journalist named Henry Fairlie, who wrote for London papers in the 1950s and then *The New Yorker*, took credit for coining the phrase as a way of describing "the matrix of official and social relations within which power is exercised." Fairlie also credited Ralph Waldo Emerson with offering an even earlier iteration. By the late sixties, the term had permeated pop culture as a catchall for a close-knit community of influence that spanned K Street in Washington, Wall Street in New York and the name-brand corporations of Main Street. However defined, the Establishment was not composed of everyone. It was *them*, not us; it was the privileged few, not the working class; it was the Ivy League, and not the young men sent to Vietnam.

It was not just the cultural left that interpreted events through this new and unfavorable lens. In 1965, Arthur Schlesinger, who had served in the Kennedy White House as an aide, wrote in *A Thousand Days*, his paean to JFK, that "the New York financial and legal community was the heart of the American Establishment. Its household deities were Henry Stimson and Elihu Root; its present leaders, Robert A. Lovett and John J. McCloy; its front organizations, the Rockefeller, Ford and Carnegie Foundations and the Council on Foreign Relations." Soon after Schlesinger penned that observation, Lyndon Johnson, whose genius at Washington politics was unfortunately matched by his maladroitness at foreign policy, convened a working group at the White House of just these men, who had been present at the creation and who designed and then maintained the structures of the early Cold War. Johnson's national security adviser, McGeorge Bundy, another product of Groton and Yale, dubbed them "the Wise Old Men." Their advice on Vietnam, however, only deepened the quagmire. Lovett urged Johnson to double down. Johnson, hearing the same from McNamara and his generals and deeply worried that he would go down in history as the president who lost a war, was all too ready to take that advice.[11]

The Wise Men crystallized the reaction against them. As we've seen, throughout the nineteenth century, attitudes toward wealth and power in the United States oscillated wildly between adulation and condemnation. The turn against Wall Street and against the makers of money in the sixties, however, added a new line to the script. Before, in the 1840s and 1930s, it was greed, speculation and then economic collapse that triggered the backlash. In the 1960s, it was the disastrous consequences of the influence these groups were seen as wielding both vis-à-vis domestic inequities and international wars. The same men who had graced the covers of *Time* in the 1940s and 1950s and who were hailed as servants of the public good and defenders of national security against the communist threat were, by the late 1960s, increasingly seen as defenders of systems that enriched them to the detriment of the country. They were held responsible for the intractable war in Vietnam by the commutative property that said that if they exercised power for self-interest, then the war in Vietnam must be serving their interests. They were also indicted in popular imagination for their culture of secrecy, on the assumption that secrecy, especially in government, masked goals that could not be defended in public and behavior that would be seen as immoral in the light of day.

The change in the cultural weather did not go unnoticed at Brown Brothers or among others in their circle. In 1966, Thomas Stilwell Lamont, whose father had been head of J.P. Morgan during the 1930s, wrote to his old friend Lovett about a speech given by John Kenneth Galbraith, Kennedy's economic adviser, ambassador to India and a Harvard professor. By the mid-1960s, Galbraith had established himself as one of the most vocal critics of the drift in American foreign policy toward more confrontation with the Soviet Union and greater involvement in Vietnam, and he became a leading spokesman for Americans for Democratic Action, which had been formed in the late 1940s as a political action group that would lobby the Democratic Party to adopt more socially liberal and less militarily aggressive policies. In his speech, Galbraith laced into "the permanent diplomatic and military establishment and the New York foreign policy syndicate—the Dulles, McCloy, Lovett communion with which . . . Secretary of State

Dean Rusk would be associated and of which Dean Acheson is the latter-day associate. . . . It has credited itself with a uniquely perceptive and aroused view of . . . the international communist conspiracy. With the permanent establishment it has now guided our foreign policy for so long that many Americans unquestionably imagine it to have tenure." Liberals, Galbraith intoned, should not cede the field to that establishment and should challenge the foreign policy consensus that had led to the deepening morass in Vietnam and to conflict around the globe. Americans could be anticommunist and still find a more realistic and effective foreign policy than the one that those men had crafted. Not surprisingly, Lamont wrote to Lovett highly critical of Galbraith, though not without a wry humor. "Congratulations," he wrote, "on your membership in the Syndicate . . . I love to picture you . . . planning in some dark corner of the Club . . . your nefarious next moves in directing the nation's foreign policy."[12]

It would get much worse as the seventies began. The shift against the Establishment by liberals such as Galbraith was nothing compared with the shift in the streets by students and protesters who rejected not just elite privilege but the entire framework of capitalism. For them, Galbraith was part of the Establishment he excoriated, insofar as he was a Harvard professor and served in the highest levels of government. For the surging populist left, that made him complicit in a corrupt system and an unreliable interlocutor. Those protesters and their many more sedentary supporters reviled the foreign policies of the United States that they deemed no different from the brutal imperialism of empires past. Brown Brothers had briefly come under fire decades earlier for its adventures in Nicaragua as an adjunct enabler of government and expansion. By the late 1960s, the firm was lumped in with an unjust system ruled by an immoral country for venal purposes that far from saving the world was leaving it in ruins in the name of American power and the almighty dollar. Then came 1968, which felt like a turning point, even at the time. Martin Luther King Jr. was gunned down. Robert Kennedy was assassinated. Cities burned in anarchic riots. Johnson announced that he would not seek reelection. The Democratic Convention in Chicago was the scene of televised protests brutally suppressed. And with the Tet Offensive at the start of that tumultuous year, it was evident that the war in Vietnam, blessed by the Wise Men, had become intractable and unwinnable.

The cultural darkening may help explain why Brown Brothers then did something that was, historically speaking, out of character. That September, they threw themselves a party, a 150th birthday extravaganza, and not just one discreet event like the centennial dinner at the University Club but a wildly expensive multiday junket bringing together the world's leading bankers and businesspeople, capped off weeks later with a party for more than a thousand people in New York City. It was, *Time* observed with wry understatement, "a novel celebration." It wasn't that the parties were egregiously grand, but they were out of step with the cultural tenor of the time. Had you been part of the celebrations, you could have, at least briefly, forgotten the troubles of the world outside.

Given that Alexander Brown had arrived in Baltimore and started trading well before 1818, the idea that Brown Brothers Harriman was "only" 150 years old was a fiction. But the strict lineage of "Brown Brothers" was the opening of the Philadelphia branch by John Brown, rather than the earlier founding of Alex. Brown & Sons, which in any event was now the name of the distant Baltimore house. The first part of the planned sesquicentennial festivities was to bring more than a hundred CEOs and central bankers from the United States and around the world to Seattle and then whisk them by a special Union Pacific train to Sun Valley, where the celebration would conclude with outdoor activities, dinners and speeches by Brown Brothers' partner Robert Roosa and by the chair of the Federal Reserve, William McChesney Martin.

The firm, which by then had grown to twenty-one partners, decided not just to host an event and a party; it also invited the financial media to cover them. That, even more than the events themselves, was a break from a past when the firm only rarely trumpeted its public image outside of marketing materials. It had run ads for its wealth management services, but that was of a lesser order than using a celebration to tell the world, "Look, we're still here and we're as strong as ever." Lovett and Roland Harriman invited the financial reporter for *The New Yorker*, John Brooks, then perhaps America's most famous writer on all things financial, to come along to Seattle and Sun Valley to report what he saw. Brooks ultimately composed a long, wry profile, acknowledging that the idea of Brown Brothers Harriman combined with the Union Pacific was the very definition of old school and that the anniversary plans were "quite uncharacteristic. . . . Brown Brothers is hardly known for being low-down or modern. On the contrary it is known for paneled walls, portraits of ancestors, roll-top desks and conservative methods."[13]

The kickoff for the assembled grandees was to dine at the top of Seattle's Space Needle, the city's 1962 World's Fair vision of an interstellar future towering six hundred feet above the bay and a galaxy away from the marble floors and wood paneling of Wall Street. The next day the guests were to be shuttled down to Everett, Washington, to tour Boeing's massive hangars, where the world's largest passenger jet, the 747, was getting its finishing touches and where Boeing was developing a space division. Following the daylong tour, the guests would board two twenty-car Union Pacific trains, with each compartment marked with metal-engraved name plates and each serviced by a porter. The train would then make the nearly eight-hundred-mile trip to Sun Valley, where the guests would spend a few days at Averell's resort, though it was no longer actually his; he had sold it to a developer in 1964. Brooks was curious why Brown Brothers Harriman would take its guests on a tour of an airplane and space company when its legacy rested on the rails of the Union Pacific. Lovett, one of the main planners of the affair, explained that Boeing and Brown Brothers had a long and close relationship, and that Boeing's CEO, Bill Allen, was a friend and client. "I think they deserve a lot of credit for winning the Second World War," Lovett went on. "I remember how, as Assistant Secretary of War for Air, I bought the B-29 bomber from just a blueprint in a lousy little greasy-spoon diner in Dayton."

Speaking with Brooks, Roland Harriman, also active in the planning, joked that it wasn't really Boeing that won the war: "Boeing didn't win the war. Bob Lovett's ulcer did." Perhaps so, but the massive four-engine B-29, dubbed "the Superfortress," certainly helped. Reflecting on the seeming contradiction in touting an airplane when he was still chairman of the Union Pacific Railroad, Harriman stated what was by then obvious. "A friend said to me, 'The airlines are going to take away ninety-five percent of your passenger business.' I said, 'I wish they'd take away a hundred percent of it.' As you know, it isn't profitable." Within a few years, Union Pacific would become a freight operation only, which it remains to this day. "We all love trains," Lovett remarked, "but we don't fight the future." Of course, Lovett himself had had a lifelong love affair with airplanes, and even before he was a partner, the firm had been involved in that financing of Juan Trippe (who attended the Seattle junket) and what became Pan Am. But the choice to tour Boeing was nonetheless a striking statement that Brown Brothers understood that the bank might have been rooted in tradition but would survive only if it embraced the future. That seemed particularly urgent in the United States in the late sixties, which was losing respect for the past that Brown Brothers represented and appeared on the verge of passionately rejecting it altogether.

Fourteen CEOs of the one hundred largest companies in the United States, including U.S. Steel, General Motors, Litton Industries and Allied Chemical, accepted the invitation to attend. Even more impressive was the number of bankers. As it turned out, the junket was one of the largest gatherings of central bankers ever, along with the CEOs of international banks such as Hongkong and Shanghai (HSBC) and Barclays and Julius Baer and the chief executives of the leading private banks of Sweden and the Netherlands and Japan. After their overnight train to Sun Valley, the guests were slated for four days of work and fun, with two morning sessions devoted to serious discussions of the global economic system and U.S. monetary policy, and the remaining time spent playing tennis or golf, shooting, hiking, fly-fishing, drinking and dining and drinking. William McChesney Martin, who had been appointed head of the Federal Reserve under Truman and had already been at the helm for nearly seventeen years, gave an evening keynote shoehorned between two days of doubles matches where he was partnered with Marcus Wallenberg, the head of Sweden's largest bank and a Brown Brothers client since the 1930s.

It was, according to a lightly snarky Brooks, "four hours of formal deliberations during four days' program—bankers' hours, I suppose." Brooks scored an easy point, but he didn't quite get that the socializing and the schmoozing and the activities were part of the point, weaving the connective tissue among people who might not otherwise have assembled but who shared a common interest in the maintenance of the global economic and commercial system. The fact that Brown Brothers was able to convene such a gathering was something of a surprise even to the assembled guests, many of whom confessed bemusement and bewilderment that they themselves had accepted the invitation. Many of the foreign guests also told Brooks that they were struck by how American it was to throw a party in honor of a corporate anniversary. The head of the largest Mexican bank praised his hosts during one dinner toast, though he admitted that "any party is a success if you invite people for a free four days."

There was substance sprinkled into the festivities. Roosa, who had been a key draw for many of the central bankers along with Martin, gave—at least for a banker—an impassioned speech that with the turmoil in the developing world, it was time for a new Marshall Plan. But, said Roosa, this time the billions of dollars needed to support "the urgent capital needs of developing nations" should come from a collective of Western nations and not from the United States alone. The mechanism Roosa suggested was complicated, involving multiple countries contributing to a fund that would then be administered through the World Bank and other development agencies. His central point was that even as the world was unlocking and creating more capital than ever, a decreasing percentage was flowing to the developing world where it was sorely needed. That meant that huge swaths of Asia and Africa and South America were capital starved, which rendered them susceptible to the false promises of communism. In order to counter that threat, Roosa argued, developed nations should band together to offer capital to those countries. Only then could developing nations meet their needs for roads, bridges, communication lines, hospitals, power generation and the whole gamut of requirements to move up the ladder. Roosa warned, however, that rather than providing that capital, developed nations were increasing activity with each other to the detriment of the developing world. That, he claimed, was increasing the risks to the global system. The growing gap between the global haves and have-nots combined with domestic tumult in the United States and in Western Europe (which was seeing its own student protests and uprisings in 1968) marked a dangerous moment in the history of the postwar economic and political order.[14]

Delivered in the measured monotone of the bureaucrat and banker, Roosa's speech did not make much of an impact beyond his audience. But both his diagnosis and prognosis of the global system nailed the realities of the moment. The year 1968 would mark the beginning of a particularly tumultuous period as the developing world confronted stalled economies and unmet expectations, flirted with the Soviets and uneasily sought aid from the United States. The United States itself was about to enter a decade of economic challenges as well, made more intractable by an unsettled global political and economic environment. Even had it made more of a splash, Roosa's formula was likely too little and too late to have altered that trajectory, but at least he acutely identified the next wave of global unrest.

The other percolating crisis was the role of the dollar in global trade and its fraught relationship with gold. By 1968, the dollar was perceived as one of the only stable stores of value. Countries and businesses around the world hoarded dollars, but they also liked the option of being able to exchange their dollars for gold when they wanted to, which put continual pressure on America's gold reserves. At the same time, as the United States started spending more on Vietnam and as Germany, Japan and Western Europe began to boom, the relative position of the United States deteriorated, not enough to topple the U.S. from its pillar of economic and military supremacy but enough to generate waves of uncertainty. Those assembled in Sun Valley knew that the United States was wrestling with gold redemptions; little did they know that within three years, the gold standard would end.

Regardless of those tremors, in 1968, the dollar remained by far the most important global currency. That fact was emphasized by McChesney Martin in his dinner speech in Sun Valley. Cribbing from social critic Marshall McLuhan, Martin declared that "money talks because money is a metaphor, a transfer or a bridge . . . money is a language for translating the work of the barber, doctor, engineer or plumber. As a vast social metaphor, bridge or translator, money—like writing—speeds up exchange and tightens the bonds of interdependence in any community."[15] The dollar, buffeted by global trends though it was, represented for Martin a measure of global health—or weakness. While he didn't go so far as to say that a strong dollar equaled a strong global economy, that was implied. And he did make explicit the idea that democracy in America and throughout the world depended on a robust marketplace where individual freedoms were secured by the right to own property and engage in commerce. A stable dollar was the vital element. The takeaway, as one newspaper put it, was that the "U.S. Dollar Is Still as Good as Gold."[16]

As subsequent events would demonstrate, the U.S. dollar was better than gold. It, and not gold, was the global medium of exchange. It, and not gold, was liquid and carried the promise of unlocking economic activity, unlike gold, which bottled up potential in an inert metal that may have commanded value over millennia but could not build a road through the Sahara, a dam in Pakistan or housing in Phoenix. The world was about to enter economic rapids, and you could feel it in the shifting and troubling currents of 1968. The answer would not be more gold. It would be more dollars. Paper money, not a lustrous metal, had unlocked the potential of the United States in the nineteenth century. It would do the same for the rest of the world in the second half of the twentieth, but just as the nineteenth century had been replete with dizzying and unsettling and often nauseating booms and busts, panics and euphoria, the same would be true of a global system pegged to the dollar. The dollar was the answer to many ills, but it also created its own, especially as the gold standard came to an end.

The Sun Valley celebration concluded with the partners feeling that it had been a smashing success. There were two more things left. One was to hold a larger party in New York for Brown Brothers staff and families along with the entire Wall Street community. A few weeks after Sun Valley, the firm turned Pier 13 on the East River in Manhattan, in its waning days before it became a decrepit tennis dome and then was torn down, into what *The New York Times* dubbed "a picturesque waterfront scene . . . with a feeling of grandeur." The partners spent $75,000 on the gala, and they allocated thousands more to give every member of the staff a cash bonus. Said one secretary, "We loved the party, but loved the money gifts better." Of course, the free and bountiful food wasn't bad either, though it may not have been, strictly speaking, good: it included fifty gallons of a beef stew that was supposed to have followed "Great-Great-Great-Grandma Brown's recipe." There was plenty of drink to wash it down, including 120 bottles of Scotch, 36 bottles of bourbon, 60 of rye, and another 120 bottles of gin and vodka. Lovett and Knight Wooley dubbed the whole affair "ingenious" and "delightful," and Lovett wondered why it was the first time in 150 years that the partners had thought to throw such a splendid affair.[17]

Like many such parties, however, it proved to be the celebration of an apex. Following the public feting of what had been a very private firm, the four remaining elder partners—Lovett, Knight Woolley, Prescott Bush and Roland Harriman—decided that it was time to move aside for a younger generation. Averell had long since ascended to a passive role, and while all twenty-one of the firm's partners were equal, there were some more equal than others. To symbolize the transition, the four senior members let *The New York Times* run a story about how they would "vacate their roll-top desks in the partners' room and move up to new quarters" upstairs. *The Times*, concluding with laconic understatement, remarked that "a new outlook has developed at 59 Wall Street. The traditions of 1818 will not be discarded but neither will they suffice for the troubled world of 1968."[18]

As Brown Brothers was hosting a thousand guests on the pier that October evening, the Apollo 7 space mission was about to be launched into space, paving the way for the moon landing the following year. The Olympics were about to begin in Mexico City, remembered now for the fierce expression of black power by two American athletes who raised their fists on the victory podium and were then stripped of their medals. The Soviets were obliterating the last vestiges of a democracy in Prague; the U.S. presidential election was entering its final days and would shortly see Richard Nixon eke out a victory against Hubert Humphrey; and the student protests that were sweeping the nation took on an added edge as NYU was shut down and buildings occupied.

Those were the headlines, full of attendant drama. The currents identified by Roosa and Martin in Sun Valley were less evident in the daily maelstrom but more consequential for the future. The roiling of the developing world, its hunger for capital and the resulting political chaos, would become the story of the seventies and beyond, as would the rise of the dollar and the end of gold along with the inflation and stagnation that those shifts helped produce. And as all of that was swirling, the financial system was about to change radically. Brown Brothers, already an anomaly for lasting as long as it had and staying so much the same, was about to become a firm enclosed in amber.

CHAPTER 17

WHEN IS ENOUGH ENOUGH?

B rown Brothers Harriman made it to its sesquicentennial. Brown Shipley remained a bastion in London, and Alex. Brown & Sons continued in Baltimore as a highly successful private bank. But the path of the investment bank that branched off as a result of Glass-Steagall in 1934 was starkly different. Harriman Ripley started propitiously enough, even with the initial confusion over its name. It was well capitalized, had the Harriman moniker and was run by a respected group of experienced bankers. But Harriman Ripley found itself meandering and slowly losing luster. By the mid-1960s, it was still going, but barely. And then it did what so many firms do when struggling: it looked to another firm as a savior, or in this case it found another firm also in need of one. The result was a merger of flailing equals, both hoping the other would revive their fortunes.

Their partner was another storied bank that had faded: the Philadelphia-based Drexel and Company. Founded before the Civil War by Francis Drexel, it was then run by his son Anthony, who went into business with J. Pierpont Morgan in 1871 to create Drexel Morgan, the precursor to J.P. Morgan & Co. Like Harriman Ripley, the 1960s Drexel was a child of Glass-Steagall. Faced with their own Solomonic decision, J.P. Morgan, like Brown Brothers, decided that their primary business would be commercial banking. Morgan Stanley and Drexel were spun off as their investment banks. Thirty years later, Drexel

was alive but not all that well. Harriman Ripley's partners and Drexel's partners decided that they had complementary needs and complementary skills,
and with the successful marriage of Harriman and Brown Brothers in their
collective memory, they decided to combine. It did not go so well.

By the early 1970s, Drexel Harriman Ripley had descended to the lower
tier of investment houses. It was making some money, but it was hardly anyone's first or second choice for major deals, which was where the big dollars
were in those years of megamergers and conglomerates like Gulf & Western.
The conglomerate craze would burn out eventually, but at the time it was the
best game in town, and Drexel Harriman wasn't playing. Said one partner,
"We were afraid to open the paper every day for fear we'd see yet another deal
for one of our clients filed by somebody else." Hardly the stuff of grand tragedy, but a dwindling nonetheless. At the end of 1970, Drexel accepted a cash
infusion of $6 million from the Firestone Company, which was itself a bit odd.
Firestone was a major manufacturer of rubber and tires but had no investment
background. The firm had been a client of Drexel's for decades, but the financial press at the time was confused by the acquisition, and with good reason.[1]

Within less than three years, Drexel Firestone was foundering too. It was
a challenging time in general for Wall Street. In 1971, the U.S. government
finally conceded that it could no longer maintain the Bretton Woods balance
between a dollar world and a gold world. Growth in the United States was
slowing and inflation was rising. The brief stock market giddiness of the late
1960s had crashed to earth, and the public mood in the United States and
throughout the world was grim and getting grimmer. There was a widespread
feeling that chaos was looming globally. In America, cities were hollowing
out; crime was rising; and respect for the institutions that had held things
together was plummeting. On August 15, 1971, Richard Nixon made a nationally televised address and announced that foreign governments would no
longer be able to exchange their dollars for gold. "Prosperity . . . requires action on three fronts," he intoned. "We must create more and better jobs; we
must stop the rise in the cost of living; we must protect the dollar from the
attacks of international money speculators." He proposed a new jobs bill plus
a ninety-day freeze on prices and wage increases to fight inflation. He then

announced that after decades of helping the world become economically viable, the United States must now attend to its own issues and stop subsidizing the growth of other countries. That meant an end to other nations' using the dollar and American gold reserves as their piggybank.

The speech and the resulting plan to suspend the gold standard were dubbed "the Nixon shock," and it was shocking. Many Americans applauded what they perceived as the staunch defense of the American economy in a world seemingly spinning out of control, but other nations were roiled by the implications. Nixon initially thought that the gold suspension might be temporary, but by 1973, it was clear that there was no going back. The result was an agreement among the world's largest economies (then the G10) to create a new system based on multiple currencies, as well as a new relationship between the major countries of Europe that would form the basis of the euro. And all currencies would be floated against the U.S. dollar.[2]

In many ways, the official termination of the gold standard only ratified the dollar world that already existed. But the abrupt end of the gold standard was still disruptive. The seventies turned into a decade racked by double-digit inflation in the United States and in many parts of the world. For those who believed that a system of fiat paper money would be dangerously susceptible to inflation, the remainder of the seventies seemed to be a QED. The terra incognita of high inflation combined with low growth (dubbed "stagflation") stymied central banks, and multiple oil shocks caused by embargoes intensified the sense of unraveling. Many concluded that a world without gold anchoring and constraining the supply of money would be chronically volatile, and that even if inflation were tamed in the short term, it could at any moment in the future rear up and wreak havoc.

The turmoil made it a challenging time for investment firms. Stocks gyrated wildly; interest rates soared and moved with almost unprecedented volatility; and Wall Street was hit by waves of mergers and closures. Drexel Firestone tried and failed to do deals in a highly competitive and difficult environment. Within a few years, it was clear to Firestone that the acquisition had been a bust, and they sought an exit. In 1973, Drexel merged again, this time with a relatively new and relatively small brokerage firm that had been created in 1935 by Philadelphian I. W. "Tubby" Burnham. Burnham was seen as a minor player and an upstart, but he brought hustle and ambition and thought he could make good use of the Drexel name. Soon after, the new Drexel Burnham swallowed up the American arm of a Belgian banking house called Lambert, and the new firm was christened Drexel Burnham Lambert. Sitting at a desk in New York City watching these dizzying moves was a young bond trader trying to find a market that he could own and define. His name was Michael Milken.[3]

Even though Drexel Burnham Lambert had capital, energy and a good name, it was not a propitious time to muscle in on the higher-tier investment banks. There were massive deals to be made in the seventies, especially given the merger mania of the conglomerates and the early inklings of the leveraged-buyout boom of the 1980s. But it was already becoming a winner-take-all culture, with the firms at the top—Morgan Stanley, Goldman Sachs, Lehman Brothers, Salomon Brothers, Merrill Lynch—taking a disproportionate share of the deal spoils. That left Drexel scrambling, and Milken scrambled.

Like many young men on the Street, Milken was ambitious and hungry, and he found himself at a firm that felt marginal. But being at Drexel gave him more space to carve out his own path than he would have had at Brown Brothers, steeped in tradition and dedicated to a particular way of conducting business. Even more, had he been at a more established firm with a culture that focused on the downside more than on the upside, he would never have been given the same amount of rope. He might have made money, but it is unlikely he would have made so much so quickly, or fallen so fast.

His great insight was to identify an area of the market that was being underserved: firms and ventures with low credit ratings, high levels of debt or no clear track record. Such companies needed credit to expand or survive, and in the seventies, with rates rising sharply and many banks feeling pinched, it was hard to find anyone who would lend to them even at a high premium. Milken saw an opportunity. He began packaging loans that carried higher risks of default but also higher fees and higher interest rates, which meant more income for Drexel. These bonds, known as high yield, soon earned the moniker that made Milken famous: junk bonds.[4]

One of Milken's early financing coups was the casino industry in Las Vegas and Atlantic City. Casinos had an unsavory reputation, some of it deserved, as corrupt enterprises with connections to organized crime peddling a product that preyed on human weakness. That made it well-nigh impossible for casinos to obtain loans and credit lines from reputable banks. Milken connected with an ambitious young mogul named Steve Wynn, and in the late 1970s helped him finance a new casino in Las Vegas by raising nearly $200 million in high-yield junk bonds. No other Wall Street firm would touch the casino business during these years. Brown Brothers Harriman partners likely would have dismissed the idea without hesitation. Milken, backed by Burnham, plunged ahead, and structured the deal so that he personally stood to gain not just hefty commissions but also the upside if the new casinos succeeded. By the late 1980s, Wynn's ventures were worth billions. And so was Michael Milken.

Drexel began to thrive during some of the worst days the financial industry had seen since the 1930s. Stagflation, combined with a general malaise in the United States, crimped business activity and dampened the animal spirits that Keynes once identified as a needed ingredient for a robust economy. As others were retrenching, Milken and several young upstarts (men like T. Boone Pickens and Carl Icahn, who were dubbed "corporate raiders") were plunging into speculative ventures with an attitude of "what have we got to lose?" Older, white-shoe firms like Brown Brothers Harriman navigated the storms as they always had, but Milken and others made a fortune.

The election of Ronald Reagan in 1980, the shock therapy of sharply higher interest rates applied by chairman of the Federal Reserve Paul Volcker, and the general turn in the global business cycle led to a dramatically improved mood and a notable uptick in economic confidence and activity. The stock market started to build momentum after 1982, beginning what would be a nearly eighteen-year run. Inflation ebbed and then interest rates began to decline, beginning what would be a thirty-year bond bull market of lower and lower rates and muted inflation. As the economy strengthened and confidence rose, what had been a Milken anomaly started to become the norm.

It wasn't just corporate raiders and a wave of buyouts financed by loans at a scale that would have been unthinkable even a generation earlier. And it wasn't just more creative ways of using stocks and financial instruments to fund growth and mergers. There was a new wave of profitability on Wall Street. After World War II and through the 1970s, Wall Street was a lucrative place but not stratospherically more lucrative than any number of other industries, in New York and throughout the country. That was part of the general trend. In the United States overall in the 1950s and 1960s, there was less extreme wealth at the upper end compared to the large and growing middle class, and the income and wealth gaps stayed relatively static. But in the eighties, Wall Street and the financial industry entered a new phase of rapid and extraordinary growth, and compensation for the dealmakers and traders began to detach from other industries. Top executives in other industries also did very well, as more of their compensation was tied to their company's stock price at a time when stocks were booming. That created incentives for CEOs to maximize shareholder value above all else. And Wall Street was there to provide the capital, to issue more shares, buy back shares, issue bonds and earn colossal fees from deals. You could get rich in multiple ways in America in the eighties, but on Wall Street you could get filthy rich.

The rising fortunes of Wall Street led to a new and not always positive public image. The old American love-hate relationship with making money, lots of it and quickly, was in full bloom in the eighties, with films such as *Wall Street* and its two-dimensional yet seductive villain Gordon Gekko a composite stand-in for those like Milken who preached not a gospel of wealth but an incantation that "greed is good." The reality was more nuanced, and the benefactors and malefactors of great wealth countered, not without merit, that they were making American capitalism more efficient and more robust, and that outsized compensation was simply a side effect of a larger and positive economic transformation.

As profits soared and the markets rocketed, the financial firms of Wall Street did something that in the past they had primarily facilitated: they went public. For generations, these firms had been private partnerships— Brown Brothers, Lehman Brothers, Goldman Sachs, Bear Stearns. Merrill Lynch and some specialty brokerage houses went public in the seventies, but many of the larger commercial banks remained private. As stock markets took off in the eighties, these companies realized they could capitalize on their profits to a far greater degree and become much larger if they sold shares to the public and did not limit themselves just to financing other companies. That set off a wave of initial public offerings as financial firms went public in the 1980s at heady valuations. What had been private partnerships or regulated banks were suddenly inundated with shareholder capital and not just the carefully accrued profits of partners. One informed observer announced when Morgan Stanley went public in 1986, "It is a watershed event in the history of Wall Street. It confirms that the traditional private partnership structure of investment banking that had been the dominant form of organization is now obsolete."[5]

The shift from tightly controlled private firms to ever larger public ones had profound effects. A partnership such as Brown Brothers was always constrained by the amount of capital its partners could or would contribute. Even as that could grow very large in flush times and after deal upon good deal, the money that they deployed to finance their clients was partly their own. If a deal went bad, if they did not perform adequate due diligence, if they lent to a sketchy venture or to clients with questionable business plans and dicey character, they stood to lose personally. The fact that it was their own money also set inherent limits on how much they were willing to use for leverage. If I have a million dollars and am able to finance a deal with ten times the leverage, it doesn't take much to lose everything.

But when the source of funds becomes hundreds of millions and then billions of dollars of shareholder capital, and when a firm could start using its market valuation to generate more loans, and when the partners of a public bank could use leverage from another public bank to finance those deals, then the size and scope of those deals could expand substantially. And that is precisely what began to happen in the 1980s, which made not just men like Milken hundreds of millions of dollars individually but which added billions to the market size of numerous firms.

Drexel Burnham Lambert, however, had a different story. It did not go public. It went down. The errant child of Brown Brothers, Drexel was undone by the frenzy uncorked in the eighties, and Milken was brought low by one of his business partners, Ivan Boesky, who cut a deal with an ambitious young prosecutor in New York named Rudy Giuliani. Giuliani used questionable interpretations of insider trading and racketeering laws to extract pleas from Boesky and Milken. Milken went to jail (and was later pardoned by Donald Trump), Drexel went bankrupt, and half a dozen of Giuliani's other convictions were overturned on appeal for having misused the statutes. Giuliani had public opinion on his side but not the law.

But the collapse of Drexel was only a blip on the way to more spectacular profits and more creative unlocking of capital. By going public, the traditional Wall Street houses did what Americans had been doing since the early 1800s: make more money and unlock more capital in ways that were at once destructive and productive. In the 1820s, Brown Brothers used a public offering to build the B&O Railroad, and then too much capital led to the Panic of 1837. The wealth that was unleashed to build the railroads also triggered the Panics of 1873 and 1893. The calming effect of the Federal Reserve was one element in the boom of the 1920s, but that boom was one reason for the onset of the Great Depression.

The eighties saw an explosion of capital that carried into the nineties and then, even with the bursting of the internet and telecom bubble in 2000, continued well into the aughts. The financial services industry became one of the largest components of the stock market itself. In 1957, when the S&P 500 index of the biggest publicly traded companies was created, there were exactly zero financial services companies included. By the early 1990s, they accounted for 15 percent of the market; by the mid-2000s, nearly 25 percent. A sector whose primary historical function was to provide capital and advice to companies in the actual business of making and selling and transporting and creating stuff grew larger than almost any other sector in the economy because of the fees and profits it booked buying, selling, and trading securities that it invented, managing money that other people made, and sealing deals that other industries needed. All of that was supported by the public markets and by the stocks of those companies being bid ever higher as their profits soared and as executive compensation at the top of those firms soared even more. By 2008, the average total compensation of the top tier of the financial services industry was hundreds of times that of the average worker in the United States. The only other industry that could compare was Silicon Valley.

It is easy to decry these developments as greed run amok and yet another moment in American history when capital made the bulk of the gains while labor stagnated. That much is sadly true. It is also true that the end of the partnership model in the 1980s begat the excesses that finally became unsustainable in the 2000s. But another part of the story is that once again, vast amounts of money were made, not just by people but for society. The capital unlocked by the financial world made possible the telecom infrastructure of the 1990s that facilitated the information technology revolution of the 2000s in much the same way that excessive amounts of capital in the 1870s made the railroad boom possible, and both paved the way for a painful, destructive bust, in 1873 and again in 2008-9. Wall Street abetted both the creation and the destruction.

Finding the right balance between releasing the power of money and taming it, between making money and channeling it to productive ventures instead of into the pockets of the very few, has been a constant challenge in the United States and in most other societies. Even when that balance has been well struck, the relative wealth of those making money in banking and finance has attracted envy and animosity, especially when those rewards appeared unfair. But something changed in the 1980s, when Wall Street itself went from being a service industry—lucrative and powerful but still client centered and partner oriented—to being an industry in its own right. Then, no longer tethered by the risk to their own money, these newly flush public companies, and many private ones that benefited from the efflorescence of money in the frothy public markets, started to think of themselves as product makers and profit centers in their own right. They started to expect excessive returns and outsized compensation, and they took on levels of risk that in time came to imperil the whole system because they were without fear of substantial personal loss.

You would be hard-pressed to find Brown Brothers much in the news after their 1968 festivities. Its business was confined to relatively few clients, and the firm was not involved in issuing securities. As Wall Street entered its feverish era of growth, the partners of Brown Brothers were as wary as always during times of profit taking and speculation. So they toddled on. The older partners retired and passed away—Prescott Bush in 1972, then Roland in 1978. Averell and Lovett died within two months of each other in the spring of 1986, Averell at the age of ninety-four, and Lovett, who had been so sure so many times in the past that he was fatally ill, at the age of ninety. Long before they died, all of them had slowly withdrawn their capital to ensure that the firm wasn't burdened with the demand to pay out their estates.

Meanwhile, Brown Brothers made solid profits, as a correspondent bank, doing some lending for the worldwide commodities business, opening a fixed income desk under Robert Roosa's careful guidance, continuing as a high-end wealth manager for wealthy clients. And as the dance was getting more frenetic in the eighties, Brown Brothers Harriman stayed true to itself and its history. It stayed a partnership, which briefly expanded to more than forty partners but which by comparison with Goldman or the ill-fated Lehman Brothers was still tiny. In 2003, it sold its headquarters at 59 Wall Street and moved around the corner to Broadway. Its old building remains, now carved into apartments with retail space where the entrance used to be. Its former lobby was home for several years to Thomas Pink, a London shirtmaker with popular and global ambitions that itself overreached. The firm's new home, several floors of a 1970s office building at 140 Broadway, has a transplanted Partners Room just off the main reception area, where rolltop desks nestle against plateglass windows and the portrait of Alexander and his four sons still hangs.

Brown Brothers Harriman continues to this day as a partnership, floating beneath the public radar. It makes hundreds of millions of dollars a year, but it does few high-profile deals, does not put the financial system on the line for its own gain and wouldn't even if it could. It was and is a culture that emphasizes risk management not as a box to be checked but as a first principle. The firm has attracted remarkably little notice since the 1970s, but it has not stayed static. There is no way it could have lasted through the past decades had it not adapted to the changing world of money and technology and globalization and found areas where it could hold its own against larger, better capitalized competitors.

Their contemporary niches are the unsexy corners of the financial world: global custody, institutional wealth management, foreign exchange, fund accounting, cash management. Over the last forty years, fewer of its clients are people and most are other banks or investment firms. The firm was always, in some respects, focused on other businesses. It did take on celebrity clients in the 1930s and built a private wealth management franchise aimed at the high net worth, but since the 1970s, it has been primarily a business-to-business company. That is one reason why it attracts less attention: it is not a consumer retail bank that advertises like JPMorgan Chase, and it is not a retail wealth management firm like Fidelity that needs to build its name to attract clients. But Brown Brothers also flies under the radar because of the nature of what it does, which is essential to the smooth flow of money through the complicated webs of the financial system but is also opaque and often arcane. In the tech world, Apple gets constant attention both for its size and because its business is consumer facing; many of its suppliers are multibillion-dollar companies in their own right, but they are largely anonymous. Without them, however, there would be no iPhone.

The services Brown Brothers came to provide must be provided. As foreign investment in U.S. stocks and bonds accelerated in the 1980s, for instance, someone had to translate foreign assets into dollar-denominated securities. Someone had to act as a custodian. Someone had to price those transactions and settle trades, especially cross-border trades of stocks and bonds. And whoever did those things had to be reliable and trustworthy and meticulous and systematic, all of which were cultural hallmarks of Brown Brothers Harriman, starting with Alexander Brown. Those services were vital, and they earned small fees that over time added up to billions and billions of dollars. Many of its clients were banks, pension plans and other financial institutions that in turn were managing money and facilitating transactions for millions upon millions of ordinary people. Brown Brothers opened offices around the world, from Tokyo to London, Hong

Kong to Luxembourg, to work with clients and set up systems. The firm invested heavily in technology and in people, and it grew in numbers and in revenue, year by year by year, through today.

Brown Brothers figured out in the 1970s that it should not compete with firms such as Drexel. It recognized in the 1980s that it would not compete with a firm such as Goldman. It accepted in the 1990s that it could not deploy capital on the scale of the investment banks and venture firms that were underwriting the tech boom. And above all, its partners decided, without ever seriously considering the alternatives, they didn't *want* to do any of those things. There was never any serious discussion of going public. In part, that was because Brown Brothers was not as attractive a business for the public markets. It wasn't a dealmaker with gaudy profits and high margins. It was a steady business with a solid set of franchises in a less glamorous corner of the financial world. Even so, its direct competitors, larger—but not flashier—institutions such as State Street and the Bank of New York, went public and reaped billions. Brown Brothers was uninterested.

They were also uninterested in getting bigger for the sake of getting bigger. In the 1980s, as the buying and selling of U.S. securities accelerated, Brown Brothers found itself servicing some of the largest banks in the world: Lloyd's of London, Citibank, HSBC, to name a few. The banks kept increasing the volume of business that they were sending Brown's way. For a while, the firm invested more in people and technology to accommodate the demand, but soon it was too much. Brown Brothers began politely informing these banks that it could no longer manage the demand and asked them to find someone else. In short, faced with an avalanche of business from immense institutional customers who could pay tens of millions of dollars in annual fees, Brown Brothers did not scramble endlessly to catch up. Instead, the partners took a deep breath, and fired their clients.

Reflecting on the decision, one Brown Brothers partner remarked, "You know, we didn't do what a firm like Goldman might have. We didn't ask ourselves what size we should be to meet the business. We asked what business we should take to match our size."[6] Rather than expanding so that they could gain more business and more money, the firm opted to stay smaller because its partners believed that was their most sustainable path. In a Wall Street characterized by a relentless push for more business, more profit and more money, that decision is almost unfathomable. It is also why Brown Brothers thrived over the next decades. By the 2010s, it was generating more than $2 billion in revenue and at least $500 million in profit in a good year. If it had been publicly traded, its market capitalization could easily have been close to $10 billion, which is modest in a world of financial behemoths, but for a firm with fewer than thirty partners and several thousand employees, where all the employees shared in the profits, that is more than considerable. The firm made money for itself, for its employees and for its clients. It did so without fanfare, performing essential tasks for reasonable fees. What more can one ask? And why, exactly, should one ask for more?

At the end of 2021, the partners made yet another momentous decision: they sold more than two-thirds of their business to State Street, a large Boston-based bank that specializes in custody of assets, for the sum of $3.5 billion. With the sale, Brown Brothers Harriman divested itself of not just its custody business but also its investor services arm, which had provided securities processing, accounting, and technology services for banks and institutional investors around the world. The slimmed-down firm has fewer than fifteen active partners and fewer than one thousand employees, bolstered by a large amount of capital, building for the next century as they have for the last two.

Much as it had done in the 1980s, the firm in 2021 arrived at a clear calculus: the only way it could compete in an increasingly commoditized business would have been to hire more, invest more, get bigger, even as the services being offered commanded lower fees. Rather than playing that game, the partners did as they had always done, as Alexander and his sons had done in moving out of the physical trade of goods and as the firm had in divesting its investment bank after Glass-Steagall in the 1930s: they chose to stay private, small and flush.

In a world where the financial system brought multiple economies to unprecedented heights and then brought them down to epochal lows, it's worth going back to one of Alexander Brown's favorite homilies,

"Shoemaker, stick to thy last." The role of the banker, he believed, was to serve clients and to preserve the capital of the partners, in that case his own family. Over the generations, that mantra expanded to embrace the ideals of service, to clients and to society. It was an ethos that propelled the partners of Brown Brothers to the highest echelons of the government, and it was also an ethos that prevented them from using other people's money for their own self-enrichment. They became rich, for sure. They were complicit in slavery and the cotton trade, culpable in taking advantage of Latin America, and too certain that their way was *the* way. At times, they confused the formula that had made them wealthy for the operating system of all stable, successful societies, and thus treated the challenge of communism as an existential threat. But they never departed from the core belief that making money carried with it responsibilities and that they would only be of service if they remembered that they were in the business of facilitating the work of others.

There needs to be some risk-taking for innovation to thrive, and sometimes that means losing money. A financial world comprised only of Brown Brothers might be too risk averse. But the contemporary sense that Brown Brothers Harriman is a wistful tale of a once-great firm is itself a troubling sign of how capitalism came to be seen as an engine only for more. The relentless pursuit of profit came to crowd out other imperatives and meant that unless you got bigger and more profitable, you were failing. But in what universe does surviving and thriving over the course of more than two hundred years constitute failure? In what healthy system does never becoming too big to fail get judged negatively? Why is sustaining a culture that shuns the spotlight and remains both viable and modest not valued, while becoming a behemoth is both celebrated and reviled? Why is Michael Milken a parable, while Brown Brothers a faint echo? Those judgments say more about how capitalism came to be defined than they do about how a family partnership such as Brown Brothers Harriman should be understood. Over the centuries, they made considerable money, and much of that money made America. For two hundred years, the firm stuck to its last. It might have been better if more of us had. And it might be best, as we head into our tumultuous future, if more of us do.

ACKNOWLEDGMENTS

The story of Brown Brothers Harriman is in many ways a microcosm of the story of the rise of the United States from a colonial periphery to the most powerful nation in the world in the mid-twentieth century. The history of the United States and of the evolution of money has been told countless times, and likely will be told many times more, but to be able to juxtapose the story of one firm over two centuries with the evolution of the nation as a whole, well, that is special.

I've always gravitated toward topics that allow for a specific narrative to make a larger point—to shed light on how we in our present came to be in the world we're in—and when I mentioned to my editor and onetime agent, Scott Moyers, that I wanted to find a way to narrate the big story of the United States, money and the rise to global power, he immediately suggested I take a look at Brown Brothers. It proved to be the perfect idea, and this book is the result. We all owe debts to our editors, but in this case, Scott has been not just taskmaster and prodder-in-chief but muse as well. Thank you isn't sufficient, but it will have to do for now.

I learned a lot about the worlds of finance from my years at Fred Alger Management and Envestnet, and to colleagues there I am deeply thankful. This book brings together my years as an academic, as a historian and as a would-be scholar with my years in the world of finance, and I will forever be grateful for the teachings of my mentors at Harvard, Ernest May, Joseph Nye, Bernard Bailyn, Samuel Huntington and Akira Iriye; at Oxford, Roger

Owen and Albert Hourani; and at Columbia, Richard Bulliet, Rashid Khalidi, Eric Foner and Jim Shenton.

Several people graced me with their input on early chapters of the manuscript. As always, they get credit for whatever is better in the final book; for whatever is not I bear sole responsibility. Once again, my dear friend Timothy Naftali and my father, David Karabell, were invaluable sounding boards. My onetime coauthor and forever sparring partner Jonathan Rosenberg gave me needed help in making sure I was up-to-date on historiography. *Foreign Affairs* editor Gideon Rose (I knew him when) and Fareed Zakaria (him too) made sure I did at least partial justice to Yale. And my wife, Nicole Alger, in a heroic act of either marital dedication or sacrifice or both, read every chapter, caught numerous errors of grammar and style and pushed me to make sure that the narrative read smoothly for those not totally marinated in the world of finance. Finally, Taylor Bodman of Brown Brothers not only read the manuscript and called out places where the history or characterization were lacking but also was a vital resource and source of insight over the several years this book evolved.

My agent, Andrew Wylie, not only once again made the trains run on time to a degree that E. H. Harriman would have admired but provided his usual professionalism and steadiness in a tumultuous time for all of us.

Early on, Nick Serpe (now at *Dissent* magazine) and Andrew Battle did yeomen's work gathering supplementary documents and articles, and later on, Toby Greenberg ranged far and wide to help me gather photo images and the attendant permissions. The book is all the better for their efforts.

At Penguin, in addition to the aforementioned Moyers, Mia Council acted as editor and managing editor all in one. Copy editor Susan Johnson did an exemplary job whipping the prose into consistent shape. Randee Marullo oversaw the creation of the actual book, which then was escorted into public life by publicist extraordinaire Gail Brussel and marketing maven Danielle Plafsky. And thanks as well to Ann Godoff for blessing the project.

And to my nuclear family, Nicole, Griffin and Jasper, I hope this finished product at least explains part of what I have been doing the past few years; as important as it has been to me, it is nothing compared to each of you.

NOTES

A note on the notes: *The primary source materials for the book are the nearly 150 boxes of the Brown Brothers Harriman Collection that are now housed at the New-York Historical Society in New York City. These papers of Brown Brothers Harriman are referred to in the notes as BBH Papers. In addition to those archives, for the early- to mid-nineteenth-century portions of the book, I drew upon letters between Alexander Brown and his sons, and between the brothers, transcribed and printed in a corporate history by Frank Kent commissioned by Alex. Brown & Sons in 1925 and later updated in 1990. Other letters were transcribed and used by Edward Perkins in his meticulous study of Brown Brothers and their finance business in the nineteenth century,* Financing Anglo-American Trade. *Many of those are cited in the text, but for the sake of economy, not every letter is cited each time. In addition, at multiple points and again for the sake of economy, there are excerpts from speeches by public figures that are identified by time and place in the text but not then cited in the notes.*

CHAPTER 1: COMING TO AMERICA

1. John Crosby Brown, *A Hundred Years of Merchant Banking: A History of Brown Brothers and Company* (New York: privately printed, 1909), 4; J. C. Beckett, *Belfast: The Making of a City, 1800–1914* (Belfast: Appletree Press, 1983).

2. John Mayfield, *The New Nation 1800–1845* (New York: Hill & Wang, 1982), chap. 1; Jill Lepore, *These Truths: A History of the United States* (New York: Norton, 2018), chaps. 5, 6.

3. Robert Woods Sayre, *Modernity and Its Other: The Encounter with North American Indians in the Eighteenth Century* (Lincoln: University of Nebraska Press, 2017), 90.

4. Graeme Milne, *Trade and Traders in mid-Victorian Liverpool* (Liverpool: Liverpool University Press, 2000).

5. Sharon Ann Murphy, *Other People's Money: How Banking Worked in the Early American Republic* (Baltimore: Johns Hopkins University Press, 2017).

6. Quoted in Crosby Brown, *A Hundred Years of Merchant Banking*, 13. Also, Fritz Redlich, "Bank Money in the United States during the First Half of the Nineteenth Century," *Southern Economic Journal* (January 1944); Charles Morris, *Money, Greed*

and Risk: Why Financial Crises and Crashes Happen (New York: Times Business, 1999); Murray Rothbard, *A History of Money and Banking in the United States* (Auburn, AL: Ludwig von Mises Institute, 2002); Niall Ferguson, *The Ascent of Money: A Financial History of the World* (New York: Penguin, 2009).

7. Quotes from Alexander in Crosby Brown, *A Hundred Years of Merchant Banking*, 11, 68, as well as Aytoun Ellis, *Heir of Adventure: The Story of Brown Shipley & Co, Merchant Bankers* (London: Brown Shipley, 1960), 26–27.

8. Alex Brown to John Brown, December 21, 1812, in Crosby Brown, *A Hundred Years of Merchant Banking*, 33–34; William Brown letter on privateering quoted in Frank R. Kent, *The Story of Alex. Brown & Sons, 1800–1990* (Baltimore: J. W. Boardman & Co., 1990), 47.

9. Quoted in Kent, *The Story of Alex. Brown & Sons*, 49–50.

10. Walter Borneman, *1812: The War That Forged a Nation* (New York: HarperCollins, 2004); Donald Hickey, "An American Perspective on the War of 1812," PBS.org (http://www.pbs.org/wned/war-of-1812/essays/american-perspective/); Norman Gelb, "Francis Scott Key: The Reluctant Patriot," *Smithsonian Magazine* (September 2004); Alan Taylor, *The Civil War of 1812* (New York: Knopf, 2010).

11. Ellis, *Heir of Adventure*, 23.

12. Circular reprinted in John Kouwenhoven, *Partners in Banking: An Historical Portrait of a Great Private Bank, Brown Brothers Harriman & Co. 1818–1968* (Garden City, NY: Doubleday, 1968), 31.

13. Edwin Burrows and Mike Wallace, *Gotham: A History of New York City to 1898* (New York: Oxford University Press, 1998).

CHAPTER 2: THE B&O

1. Peter Bernstein, *Wedding the Waters: The Erie Canal and the Making of a Great Nation* (New York: Norton, 2005).

2. Philip Thomas quoted in James D. Dilts, *The Great Road: The Building of the Baltimore & Ohio, the Nation's First Railroad, 1828–1853* (Stanford: Stanford University Press, 1993), 35. Also see John Lauritz Larson, *Internal Improvement: National Public Works and the Promise of Popular Government in the Early United States* (Chapel Hill: University of North Carolina Press, 2001); John Steele Gordon, *An Empire of Wealth* (New York: HarperCollins, 2004); Daniel Walker Howe, *What Hath God Wrought: The Transformation of America, 1815–1848* (New York: Oxford University Press, 2007), chap. 7.

3. *The Early Correspondence of Alex. Brown & Sons with Regard to the Building of the Baltimore & Ohio Railroad* (Baltimore: Alex. Brown & Sons, 1927); John F. Stover, *History of the Baltimore and Ohio Railroad* (West Lafayette, IN: Purdue University Press, 1987), chap. 1.

4. Quoted in Kouwenhoven, *Partners in Banking*, 43, and in Kent, *The Story of Alex. Brown & Sons*, 64–65. The letter was signed "A. Brown & Sons," suggesting that it spoke not just for Alexander but for James and the other brothers as well.

5. Ellis, *Heir of Adventure,* passim.

6. J. R. Killick, "Brown, Sir William, first baronet," *Oxford Dictionary of National Biography* (London: Oxford University Press, 2009).

7. Kent, *The Story of Alex. Brown & Sons,* 83ff.

8. Sarah Gordon, *Passage to Union: How the Railroads Transformed American Life, 1829–1929* (Chicago: Ivan Dee, 1997), 26–30.

9. Letter of February 24, 1827, in *Early Correspondence,* 4; article in the *Niles' Weekly Register* quoted in Stover, *History of the Baltimore and Ohio Railroad,* 18.

10. Berkshire paper quoted in Dilts, *The Great Road,* 47. Alex Brown to William Brown, May 28, 1828, in *Early Correspondence,* 7. Also, Milton Reizenstein, *The Economic History of the Baltimore & Ohio Railroad* (Baltimore: The Johns Hopkins Press, 1897).

11. Description of the July 4 festivities draws from Dilts, *The Great Road,* 7–12; Albro Martin, *Railroads Triumphant: The Growth, Rejections & Rebirth of a Vital American Force* (New York: Oxford University Press, 1992), 3–7; lyrics from Seth Rockman, *Scraping By: Wage Labor, Slavery and Survival in Early Baltimore* (Baltimore: Johns Hopkins University Press, 2009), 16.

12. Letter of Alex Brown to William, January 29, 1829, in *Early Correspondence,* 8.

13. Tom Thumb race from Kent, *The Story of Alex. Brown & Sons,* 88–91.

14. Crosby Brown, *A Hundred Years of Merchant Banking,* 25.

15. Quoted in Ellis, *Heir of Adventure,* 52.

16. Quoted in Kouwenhoven, *Partners in Banking,* 71.

CHAPTER 3: EVERYBODY IS SPECULATING

1. Michel Chevalier writing in 1834 quoted in William Goetzmann, *Money Changes Everything* (Princeton: Princeton University Press, 2016), 398.

2. Jessica M. Lepler, *The Many Panics of 1837* (Cambridge, UK: Cambridge University Press, 2013), 8; Douglas Irwin, "Historical Aspects of U.S. Trade Policy," http://www .nber.org/reporter/summer06/irwin.html.

3. Stanley D. Chapman, *The Rise of Merchant Banking* (New York: Routledge, 1984).

4. The best study of the Rothschilds by far is the two-volume work by Niall Ferguson, *The House of Rothschild* (New York: Penguin Books, 1999).

5. Cotton production figures from Kathryn Susan Boodry, "The Common Thread: Slavery, Cotton and Atlantic Finance from the Louisiana Purchase to Reconstruction," unpublished doctoral dissertation (Harvard University, 2013), 40.

6. Quoted in Killick, "Sir William Brown, first baronet," 4; trade figures are from *Annual Report of the Secretary of the Treasury on the State of the Finances* (Washington, DC: United States Treasury Department, 1851).

7. Description from *The London Evening Express,* May 6, 1831, about the life of William Brown, in BBH Papers, Box 5. Also see J. R. Killick, "The Cotton Operation of

Alexander Brown and Sons in the Deep South, 1820–1860," *The Journal of Southern History* (May 1977), 169–94; Milne, *Trade and Traders in mid-Victorian Liverpool*.

8. Quoted in Charles Sellers, *The Market Revolution: Jacksonian America, 1815–1846* (New York: Oxford University Press, 1991), 333. Also, Bray Hammond, *Banks and Politics in America: From Revolution to the Civil War* (Princeton: Princeton University Press, 1957).

9. Many still argue along with Jackson that the bank was indeed an agent of the moneyed class and their efforts to control power and prosperity. David Graeber, *Debt: The First 5,000 Years* (Brooklyn: Melville House, 2014). On the advantages of early banking, see Richard Sylla, "Comparing the UK and US Financial Systems, 1790–1830," in Jeremy Attack and Larry Neal, eds., *The Origin and Development of Financial Markets and Institutions* (Cambridge, UK: Cambridge University Press, 2009).

10. Andrew Jackson, Farewell Address, March 4, 1837, at https://millercenter.org/the -presidency/presidential-speeches/march-4-1837-farewell-address.

11. Theophilus Fisk quoted in Arthur Schlesinger, *The Age of Jackson* (Boston: Little, Brown, 1953), 122.

12. Sven Beckert, *Empire of Cotton: A Global History* (New York: Knopf, 2014).

13. Quoted in Lepler, *The Many Panics of 1837*, 112.

14. Letter of Shipley, May 14, 1837, and letter of William Brown, May 29, 1837, in BBH Papers, Box 2.

15. Quoted in Ellis, *Heir of Adventure*, 47.

16. Lepler, *The Many Panics of 1837*, 204–6.

17. Kent, *The Story of Alex. Brown & Sons*, 112ff. Also, see the centenary history of the Philadelphia house in *Experiences of a Century 1818–1918* (Philadelphia: Brown Brothers and Company, 1919); Edward Perkins, "Financing Antebellum Importers: The Role of Brown Brothers and Co. in Baltimore," *The Business History Review* (Winter 1971), 421–51. George to William, November 1837, in Crosby Brown, *A Hundred Years of Merchant Banking*, 47.

18. Sellers, *The Market Revolution*, 362 and passim.

CHAPTER 4: DREAMS OF THE *ARCTIC*

1. Stephen Fox, *Transatlantic: Samuel Cunard, Isambard Brunel, and the Great Atlantic Steamship* (New York: HarperCollins, 2003), 128ff.; David Shaw, *The Sea Shall Embrace Them: The Tragic Story of the Steamship Artic* (New York: Free Press, 2002); "The Steamships of the Collins Line," *Scientific American*, April 1858.

2. William M. Fowler Jr., *Steam Titans: Cunard, Collins, and the Epic Battle for Commerce on the North Atlantic* (New York: Bloomsbury USA, 2017), 60ff.

3. Quoted in Ralph Whitney, "The Unlucky Collins Line," *American Heritage*, February 1957.

4. Killick, "The Cotton Operations of Alexander Brown and Sons in the Deep South," 169–94.

5. Philip Foner, *Business and Slavery: The New York Merchants and the Irrepressible Conflict* (Chapel Hill: University of North Carolina Press, 1941); Eric Foner, *Gateway to Freedom: The Hidden History of America's Fugitive Slaves* (New York: Norton, 2015), 129; Kathryn Susan Boodry, "The Common Thread; Slavery, Cotton and Atlantic Finance from the Louisiana Purchase to Reconstruction," unpublished doctoral dissertation (Harvard University, 2013), passim. Killick, "The Cotton Operations of Alexander Brown and Sons in the Deep South."

6. Quoted in Daniel Allen Butler, *The Age of Cunard: A Transatlantic History* (Annapolis: Lighthouse Press, 2003), 73.

7. Edward Perkins, *Financing Anglo-American Trade: The House of Brown 1800–1880* (Cambridge: Harvard University Press, 1975), 49. Also, Robert Greenhalgh Albion, *The Rise of the New York Port 1815–1860* (Hamden, CT: Archon Books, 1961).

8. William Brown letter, October 18, 1847, quoted in Killick, "Sir William Brown, first baronet"; Mark Collet and Francis Hamilton to William Brown, April 1853, quoted in Perkins, *Financing Anglo-American Trade*, 52. Brown's and Liverpool's attitudes toward defensive securities in Fowler, *Steam Titans*, 151, as well as Perkins.

9. Multiple letters quoted in Edward Sloan, "Collins versus Cunard: The Realities of a North Atlantic Steamship Rivalry, 1850–1858," *International Journal of Maritime History* (June 1992), 83–100.

10. Sloan, "Collins versus Cunard," 96. Also, Francis Hyde, *Cunard and the North Atlantic, 1840–1973* (New York: Macmillan, 1975), 30ff.

11. Fowler, *Steam Titans*, 194–96; Kouwenhoven, *Partners in Banking*, 96.

12. Quoted in Alexander Crosby Brown, *Women and Children Last: The Loss of the Steamship Arctic* (New York: G. P. Putnam & Sons, 1961), 169.

13. Crosby Brown, *Women and Children Last*, 159–61.

14. From Charles Nott's diary, in Crosby Brown, *Women and Children Last*, 209.

15. T. J. Stiles, *The First Tycoon: The Epic Life of Cornelius Vanderbilt* (New York: Random House, 2009), 256–64.

16. Fowler, *Steam Titans*, 264–67. *Harper's* article in BBH Papers, Box 40.

17. Debby Applegate, *The Most Famous Man in America: The Biography of Henry Ward Beecher* (New York: Doubleday, 2006).

18. Quoted in Crosby Brown, *Women and Children Last*, 187.

19. Augusta Moore, *Notes from Plymouth Pulpit: A Collection of Memorable Passages from the Discourses of Henry Ward Beecher* (New York: Derby & Jackson, 1859), 189–90.

20. Henry Ward Beecher, *The Sermons of Henry Ward Beecher* (New York: J. B. Ford and Company, 1873), 323.

CHAPTER 5: A VERY CIVIL WAR

1. Clifton Hood, *The Pursuit of Wealth: A History of New York City's Upper Class and the Making of a Metropolis* (New York: Columbia University Press, 2017), 100ff.; Sven Beckert, *The Monied Metropolis: New York City and the Consolidation of the American Bourgeoisie, 1850–1896* (Cambridge, UK: Cambridge University Press, 2001); Edwin Burrows and Mike Wallace, *Gotham: A History of New York City* (New York: Oxford University Press, 2000), 37–41.

2. Quoted in Crosby Brown, *A Hundred Years of Merchant Banking*, 232.

3. John Steele Gordon, *A Thread Across the Ocean: The Heroic Story of the Transatlantic Cable* (New York: Walker, 2002).

4. BBH Papers, Box 39, Folder 23.

5. Stewart Brown letter to James Brown, quoted in Perkins, *Financing Anglo-American Trade*, 55.

6. Burrows and Wallace, *Gotham*, 843.

7. Ellis, *Heir of Adventure*, 68.

8. Crosby Brown, *A Hundred Years of Merchant Banking*, 218.

9. Edward Perkins, "Tourists and Bankers: Travelers' Credits and the Rise of American Tourism, 1840-1900," *Business and Economic History*, vol. 8, 16–28.

10. *Harper's Weekly*, September 12, 1857, in BBH Papers, Box 7. Charles Kindleberger, *Manias, Panics and Crashes: A History of Financial Crises* (New York: Macmillan, 1996); Edward Chancellor, *Devil Take the Hindmost: A History of Financial Speculation* (New York: Farrar, Strauss & Giroux, 1999); Jonathan Sperber, *Karl Marx: A Nineteenth-Century Life* (New York: Liveright, 2013), 320ff.

11. Kent, *The Story of Alex. Brown & Sons*, 134–36.

12. Crosby Brown, *A Hundred Years of Merchant Banking*.

13. Amanda Foreman, *A World on Fire: Britain's Crucial Role in the American Civil War* (New York: Random House, 2011), chaps. 8–9; James McPherson, *Battle Cry of Freedom* (New York: Oxford University Press, 1988); Kouwenhoven, *Partners in Banking*, 127; BBH Papers, Box 9; Browns, letters about Seward quoted in Kouwenhoven, 127.

14. Wesley C. Mitchell, "The Suspension of Specie Payments, December 1861," *Journal of Political Economy* (June 1899), 289–326.

15. McPherson, *Battle Cry of Freedom*, 445–450; Wesley Clair Mitchell, *A History of the Greenbacks* (Chicago: University of Chicago, 1903).

16. Steven Hahn, *A Nation Without Borders: The United States and Its World in an Age of Civil Wars, 1830-1910* (New York: Penguin, 2016), 262–65.

17. Stewart Brown letter to James Muncaster Brown, April 25, 1865, in BBH Papers, Box 10.

18. Crosby Brown letters in Perkins, "Tourists and Bankers," 71.

CHAPTER 6: A NICE SENSE OF COMMERCIAL HONOR

1. Richard White, *The Republic for Which It Stands: The United States During the Gilded Age and Reconstruction, 1865–1896* (New York: Oxford University Press, 2017), 195.

2. Kouwenhoven, *Partners in Banking*, 132; Burrows and Wallace, *Gotham*, 1000–12. Also see Seymour Mandlebaum, *Boss Tweed's New York* (New York: John Wiley, 1965).

3. Matthew Josephson, *The Robber Barons* (New York: Harcourt, Brace, 1934), 140ff.; Burrows and Wallace, *Gotham*, 910–18.

4. Ron Chernow, *Grant* (New York: Penguin, 2017), 672ff.

5. Henry Adams quoted in H. W. Brands, *American Colossus: The Triumph of Capitalism* (New York: Random House, 2010), 42.

6. Perkins, "Tourists and Bankers," 75ff.

7. Justin Kaplan, *When the Astors Owned New York: Blue Bloods and Grand Hotels in a Gilded Age* (New York: Penguin, 2006).

8. Morris, *Money, Greed and Risk: Why Financial Crises and Crashes Happen*, 50ff.

9. Felix Martin, *Money: The Unauthorized Biography* (New York: Knopf, 2013), 165ff.

10. Josephson, *The Robber Barons*, 172; Morton Keller, *Affairs of State: Public Life in Late Nineteenth Century America* (Cambridge: Harvard University Press, 1977), 175ff.

11. James Garfield, "The Currency Conflict," *Atlantic Monthly* (February 1876).

12. Crosby Brown, *A Hundred Years of Merchant Banking*, 295.

13. Robert Handy, *A History of Union Theological Seminary in New York* (New York: Columbia University Press, 1987); BBH Papers, Box 40.

14. Kouwenhoven, *Partners in Banking*, 169.

15. BBH Papers, Box 53.

16. Kouwenhoven, *Partners in Banking*, 173.

17. John Crosby Brown to Amy Brown, May 15, 1888, in BBH Papers, Box 14, and to Thatcher Brown, October 6, 1896, in BBH Papers, Box 15.

18. Michael Kazin, *A Godly Hero: The Life of William Jennings Bryan* (New York: Knopf, 2006); Richard Hofstadter, *The Age of Reform* (New York: Vintage, 1960).

19. John Crosby Brown to Thatcher Brown, June 28, 1903, in BBH Papers, Box 15.

CHAPTER 7: NOTHING IS IMPOSSIBLE

1. For a good account of the film and its history, see Alex von Tunzelmann, "Butch Cassidy and the Sundance Kid: Surprise—It's Not Total Horse Pucky," *Guardian*, July 11, 2013, https://www.theguardian.com/film/filmblog/2013/jul/11/butch-cassidy-sundance-kid -reel-history.

2. Richard White, *Railroaded: The Transcontinentals and the Making of Modern America* (New York: Norton, 2011), 24.

3. Josephson, *The Robber Barons*, 221.

4. Maury Klein, *The Life and Legend of E. H. Harriman* (Chapel Hill: University of North Carolina Press, 2000); George Kennan, *E. H. Harriman: A Biography* (New York: Houghton Mifflin, 1922), 12.

5. Jean Strouse, *Morgan: American Financier* (New York: Random House, 1999), 420.

6. Kennan, *E. H. Harriman*, 124–25.

7. Caesar quote in Klein, *The Life and Legend of E. H. Harriman*, Kindle location 1581; Roland Harriman, *I Reminisce* (New York: Doubleday, 1975), 3.

8. Harriman, *I Reminisce*, 134ff.

9. Klein, *The Life and Legend of E. H. Harriman*, chap. 9.

10. Quoted in Klein, *The Life and Legend of E. H. Harriman*.

11. Donald Worster, *A Passion for Nature: The Life of John Muir* (New York: Oxford University Press, 2008), 362. Also see Douglas Brinkley, *The Wilderness Warrior: Theodore Roosevelt and the Crusade for America* (New York: HarperCollins, 2009); Douglas Brinkley, *The Quiet World: Saving Alaska's Wilderness Kingdom* (New York: HarperCollins, 2011).

12. David Nasaw, *Andrew Carnegie* (New York: Penguin Books, 2006).

13. BBH Papers, Box 35.

14. John Muir, *Edward Henry Harriman* (New York: Doubleday, 1911), 35–36; quoted in Kennan, *E. H. Harriman*, 195.

15. Quoted in Albro Martin, *Railroads Triumphant: The Growth, Rejection and Rebirth of a Vital American Force* (New York: Oxford University Press, 1992), 307.

16. Larry Haeg, *Harriman vs. Hill: Wall Street's Great Railroad War* (Minneapolis: University of Minnesota Press, 2013); Christian Wolmar, *The Great Railroad Revolution: The History of Trains in America* (New York: Public Affairs, 2012).

17. Quoted in Haeg, *Harriman vs. Hill*, 209. Also, "Jacob Schiff and the Northern Pacific Corner," *American Heritage* (July/August 1989).

18. Haeg, *Harriman vs. Hill*, 220ff.

19. Klein, *The Life and Legend of E .H. Harriman*, Kindle location 3545.

20. Haeg, *Harriman vs. Hill*, 256–66. Also, Edmund Morris, *Theodore Rex* (New York: Random House, 2001), 316.

21. The correspondence is reprinted in Klein, *The Life and Legend of E. H. Harriman*, Kindle location 5455, passim.

22. Quoted in Kouwenhoven, *Partners in Banking*, 186.

23. *New York Times*, September 10, 1909.

CHAPTER 8: THE REPUBLIC OF BROWN BROTHERS

1. Quoted in Walter LaFeber, *Inevitable Revolutions: The United States and Central America* (New York: Norton, 1983), 80. Also, Smedley Butler, *War Is a Racket* (New York: Round Table Press, 1935).

2. Thatcher Brown to John Crosby Brown, January 5, 1906, and July 11, 1906, BBH Papers, Box 15, Folder 25.

3. Robert Abercrombie Lovett Oral History, June 1981, in Robert Lovett Papers, Yale University Manuscript Division, Box 33.

4. Quoted in Howard Beale, *Theodore Roosevelt and the Rise of America to World Power* (Baltimore: John Hopkins University Press, 1956), 70. For the classic critique of American imperialism, see William Appleman Williams, *The Tragedy of American Diplomacy* (New York: Norton, 1959, 1988); a more nuanced view is Akira Iriye, *The Cambridge History of American Foreign Relations, vol. III* (Cambridge, UK: Cambridge University Press, 1995).

5. President Taft's message to Congress, December 3, 1912, https://millercenter.org/the-presidency/presidential-speeches/december-3-1912-fourth-annual-message.

6. Knox's message to the Senate, January 26, 1911, quoted in Emily Rosenberg, *Financial Missionaries to the World: The Politics and Culture of Dollar Diplomacy, 1900–1930* (Cambridge: Harvard University Press, 1999), 63. Also, Lester Langley, *The Banana Wars: United States Intervention in the Caribbean, 1898–1934* (Lexington: University Press of Kentucky, 1985); Peter James Hudson, *Bankers and Empire: How Wall Street Colonized the Caribbean* (Chicago: University of Chicago Press, 2017).

7. Ron Chernow, *The House of Morgan: An American Banking Dynasty and the Rise of Modern Finance* (New York: Grove Press, 1990).

8. *The World's Work* (February 1908), in BBH Papers, Box 17.

9. Thomas Walker and Christine Wade, *Nicaragua: Living in the Shadow of the Eagle* (Nashville: Westview Press, 2011); John Coatsworth, *Central America and the United States: The Clients and the Colossus* (New York: Twayne Publishers, 1994), chaps. 1–2.

10. Brown Brothers to Knox, February 2, 1911, quoted in Scott Nearing and Joseph Freeman, *Dollar Diplomacy: A Study in American Imperialism* (New York: Viking, 1975), 155.

11. "Message of the President of the United States, June 8, 1911," in U.S. Department of State, *Foreign Relations of the United States: 1912* (Washington, DC, 1919), 1073.

12. Harold Norman Denny, *Dollars for Bullets: The Story of American Rule in Nicaragua* (New York: Dial Press, 1929), 141–44; Michel Gobat, *Confronting the American Dream: Nicaragua under U.S. Imperial Rule* (Durham, NC: Duke University Press, 2005), 85ff.

13. Quoted in *Congressional Record—Senate* (August 21, 1912), 11431.

14. BBH Papers, Box 17; "Form Nicaragua Bank Here," *New York Times,* January 12, 1912. Also, Dana Munro, *Intervention and Dollar Diplomacy in the Caribbean, 1900–1921* (Princeton: Princeton University Press, 1964).

15. "Nicaragua's Monetary Reform," *Wall Street Journal,* April 29, 1912.

16. Roscoe Hill, *Fiscal Intervention in Nicaragua* (New York: P. Maisel, 1933), 6–9. Brown Brothers and Company and J. W. Seligman and Company to the Secretary of State, February 21, 1912, in *Foreign Relations of the United States,* 1096–98.

17. Denny, *Dollars for Bullets,* 109–12.

18. Bernard C. Nalty, *The United States Marines in Nicaragua* (Washington, DC: Historical Branch, U.S. Marine Corps, 1958); LaFeber, *Inevitable Revolutions*, 50; "2,000 Marines to Guard Americans," *Washington Post*, August 29, 1912; U.S. Department of State, *Foreign Relations of the United States: 1912*, 1033ff.

19. The American Minister to the Secretary of State, February 12, 1913, and the Secretary of State to the American Minister, February 4, 1913, *FRUS 1913*, 1035–36.

20. BBH Papers, Box 17, Folder 6.

21. John Kenneth Turner, "Nicaragua," *The Nation*, May 31, 1922. For corporatism, and its many definitions, see Frederick Pike, "Corporatism and Latin America–United States Relations," *The Review of Politics* (January 1974).

CHAPTER 9: SAVING MONEY

1. BBH Papers, Box 19; Liaquat Ahamed, *Lords of Finance: The Bankers Who Broke the World* (New York: Penguin, 2009); Kouwenhoven, *Partners in Banking*, 191.

2. Roger Lowenstein, *America's Bank: The Epic Struggle to Create the Federal Reserve* (New York: Penguin, 2015); Allan Meltzer, *A History of the Federal Reserve 1913–1951*, vol. 1 (Chicago: University of Chicago Press, 2003).

3. Lowenstein, *America's Bank*, 38–39; Ron Chernow, *The Warburgs* (New York: Random House, 1993), 130–40.

4. Quoted in Scott Nelson Reynolds, *A Nation of Deadbeats: An Uncommon History of America's Financial Disasters* (New York: Knopf, 2012), 211.

5. BBH Papers, Boxes 18–19.

6. Quoted in John Brooks, *Once in Golconda: A True Drama of Wall Street, 1920–1938* (New York: John Wiley, 1969), 3.

7. C. J. Bullock, "The United States as a Creditor Nation," *The Review of Economics and Statistics* (November 1932); Barry Eichengreen, *Golden Fetters: The Gold Standard and the Great Depression, 1919–1939* (New York: Oxford University Press, 1996); Adam Tooze, *The Deluge: The Great War, America and the Remaking of the Global Order, 1916–1931* (New York: Viking, 2014).

8. BBH Papers, Box 18.

9. Kouwenhoven, *Partners in Banking*, 191; BBH Papers, Box 36; Thatcher Brown, unpublished memoir, BBH Papers, Box 130.

10. Henry Schloss, *The Bank for International Settlements: An Experiment in Central Bank Cooperation* (Amsterdam: North-Holland Publishing Company, 1958).

11. BBH Papers, Box 36; Hugh Rockoff, "Until It's Over, Over There: The U.S. Economy in World War I," NBER Working Paper 10580 (June 2004); Stephen Broadberry and Mark Harrison, eds., *The Economics of World War I* (Cambridge, UK: Cambridge University Press, 2009).

12. Quoted in William Leuchtenburg, *The Perils of Prosperity, 1914–1932* (Chicago: University of Chicago Press, 1958), 30.

13. BBH Papers, Box 36; Ellis, *Heir of Adventure*, chap. 13.

CHAPTER 10: THE TAPPED

1. "Tap Day May Ring the Knell of Senior Societies," *New York Times,* April 27, 1913; Judith Ann Schiff, "How Secret Societies Got That Way," *Yale Alumni Magazine,* September 2004; David Alan Richards, *Skulls and Keys: The Hidden History of Yale's Secret Societies* (New York: Pegasus, 2017); Lovett Oral History, June 1981, Lovett Papers.

2. Rudy Abramson, *Spanning the Century: The Life of W. Averell Harriman, 1891–1986* (New York: William Morrow, 1992), 104.

3. Quoted in Walter Isaacson and Evan Thomas, *The Wise Men: Six Friends and the World They Made* (New York: Simon & Schuster, 1986), 43.

4. Isaacson and Thomas, *The Wise Men*, 45–50; Jerome Karabel, *The Chosen: The Hidden History of Admission and Exclusion at Harvard, Yale and Princeton* (New York: Houghton Mifflin, 2005), 26ff.

5. Quoted in Brooks Mather Kelley, *Yale: A History* (New Haven: Yale University Press, 1999), 308.

6. Quoted in Karabel, *The Chosen*, 41–44.

7. Quoted in Karabel, *The Chosen*, 32.

8. Karabel, *The Chosen*, 55.

9. Harriman, *I Reminisce*, 27ff.

10. Lovett Oral History, June 1981, Lovett Papers.

11. John Bainbridge and Margaret Case Harriman, "The Thirteenth Labor of Hercules: Profiles, Robert Lovett," *The New Yorker*, November 6, 1943.

12. Isaacson and Thomas, *The Wise Men*, 108–9; details of the prom in Marc Wortman, *The Millionaires' Unit: The Aristocratic Flyboys Who Fought the Great War and Invented American Air Power* (New York: Public Affairs, 2006), 74–77.

13. Lovett profile, *The New Yorker,* November 13, 1943.

14. John Seaman, *Brown Brothers Harriman: Two-Hundred Years of Partnership* (New York: Brown Brothers Harriman, 2019), 129.

CHAPTER 11: THE BUSINESS OF AMERICA

1. Woodrow Wilson, St. Louis speech of September 5, 1919, *Addresses of President Wilson* (Washington, DC: Government Printing Office, 1919), 28–33.

2. Quoted in Lepore, *These Truths*, 406.

3. Julia Ott, *When Wall Street Met Main Street: The Quest for Investors' Democracy* (Cambridge: Harvard University Press, 2011), chap. 6.

4. Robert Sobel, "Coolidge and American Business," 1988, at https://www.coolidgefound ation.org/resources/essays-papers-addresses-35/; David Greenberg, *Coolidge* (New York: Times Books, 2006); Amity Shlaes, *Coolidge* (New York: HarperCollins, 2013).

5. Speeches of Harding, https://millercenter.org/president/harding. Also, Daniel Okrent, *The Guarded Gate* (New York: Scribner, 2019).

6. Abramson, *Spanning the Century*, 125–30; Lars School, "The Harriman-Hamburg-American Line Agreement of June 1920," in Lewis Fischer, ed., *From Wheelhouse to Counting House: Essays in Maritime Business History* (St. John's, NF: International Maritime Economic History Association, 2019).

7. Quoted in Abramson, *Spanning the Century*, 130–31.

8. Steve Fraser, *Every Man a Speculator: A History of Wall Street in American Life* (New York: HarperCollins, 2005), chap. 11.

9. E. J. Kahn, "Plenipotentiary," *The New Yorker,* May 10, 1952.

10. Harriman Oral History Interview, 1971, digital copy available through the Truman Library at https://www.trumanlibrary.gov/library/oral-histories/harriman.

11. John Oller, *White Shoe: How a New Breed of Wall Street Lawyers Changed Big Business and the American Century* (New York: Dutton, 2019).

12. Quoted in Abramson, *Spanning the Century*, 197.

13. BBH Papers, Box 92.

14. BBH Papers, Box 98.

15. Notes, menu and speeches from the party in BBH Papers, Box 20.

16. Letters in BBH Papers, Box 66.

17. BBH Papers, Box 73.

18. Quoted in Leuchtenburg, *The Perils of Prosperity*, 202.

19. Quoted in Seaman, *Brown Brothers Harriman*, 156.

CHAPTER 12: FROM THE ASHES

1. Ahamed, *Lords of Finance*, 318ff.; Peter Temin, *Lessons from the Great Depression* (Cambridge: MIT Press, 1991); Leland Crabbe, "The International Gold Standard and U.S. Monetary Policy from World War I to the New Deal," *Federal Reserve Bulletin* (June 1989); David Kennedy, *Freedom from Fear: The American People in Depression and War, 1929–1945* (New York: Oxford University Press, 1999), 43ff.; Barry Eichengreen, *Hall of Mirrors: The Great Depression, the Great Recession and the Uses—and Misuses—of History* (New York: Oxford University Press, 2015).

2. Seaman, *Brown Brothers Harriman*, 156.

3. Kennedy, *Freedom from Fear*, 45ff.

4. Kenneth Whyte, *Herbert Hoover: An Extraordinary Life in Extraordinary Times* (New York: Knopf, 2017), 410ff.; Zachary Karabell, *The Leading Indicators* (New York: Simon & Schuster, 2014); Herbert Hoover, *The Memoirs of Herbert Hoover: The Great Depression* (New York: Macmillan, 1952), 32–33.

5. Gary Richardson, "Banking Panics of 1930–1931," Federal Reserve History, November 2013, at https://www.federalreservehistory.org/essays/banking_panics_1930_31.

6. Harriman, *I Reminisce,* 73ff.; Kouwenhoven, *Partners in Banking,* 16–17.

7. Kouwenhoven, *Partners in Banking,* 16.

8. Thatcher Brown, unpublished and untitled memoir, BBH Papers, Box 130; Lovett Oral History.

9. "Big Banking Houses Decide on Merger," *New York Times,* December 12, 1930, 1.

10. BBH Papers, Box 21.

11. Prescott Bush Oral History, Columbia University Oral History Collection, July 1966, 11; camping quotation and Roland views from Harriman, *I Reminisce.*

12. Ahamed, *Lords of Finance,* 404ff.

13. Abramson, *Spanning the Century,* 207–8, from Harriman private papers. Also, Prescott Bush Oral History, 19–20.

14. For the best kaleidoscopic look, see Studs Terkel, *Hard Times: An Oral History of the Great Depression* (New York: Pantheon Books, 1970).

15. Frank Freidel, *Franklin Roosevelt: A Rendezvous with Destiny* (Boston: Little, Brown, 1990); Jean Edward Smith, *FDR* (New York: Random House, 2007); H. W. Brands, *Traitor to His Class: The Privileged Life and Radical Presidency of Franklin Delano Roosevelt* (New York: Doubleday, 2008).

16. Brook, *Once in Golconda,* 149.

17. R. Christopher Whalen, *Inflated: How Money and Debt Built the American Dream* (New York: Wiley, 2011), 200ff.

18. Matthew Fink, *The Unlikely Reformer: Carter Glass and Financial Regulation* (Fairfax, VA: George Mason University Press, 2019).

19. Howard Preston, "The Banking Act of 1933," *The American Economic Review* 23, no. 4 (December 1933), 585–607; Julia Maues, "Banking Act of 1933," Federal Reserve History, November 2013, at https://www.federalreservehistory.org/essays/glass_steagall_act; Nomi Prins, "The Bankers Behind FDR and the Glass-Steagall Act," *Fortune,* March 19, 2014; Michael Hiltzik, *The New Deal: A Modern History* (New York: Free Press, 2011), 92–94.

20. Randall Kroszer and Raghuram Rajan, "Is the Glass-Steagall Act Justified?," *The American Economic Review* (September 1994), 810–832; on Joseph Kennedy and FDR, see Michael Beschloss, *Kennedy and Roosevelt* (New York: Norton, 1980).

21. Prescott Bush Oral History, 22.

22. Lovett to Averell Harriman, December 12, 1933, BBH Papers, Box 73.

23. BBH Papers, Box 45; Prescott Bush Oral History, 12.

24. Vincent Carosso, "Washington and Wall Street: The New Deal and Investment Bankers, 1933–1940," *The Business History Review* 44 (Winter 1970), 425–45. Also, Carosso, *Investment Banking in America: A History* (Cambridge: Harvard University Press, 1970).

CHAPTER 13: "WE WERE VERY HARD WORKERS"

1. Abramson, *Spanning the Century*, 210–13.

2. Abramson, *Spanning the Century*, 218–19; Wolmar, *The Great Railroad Revolution*, 310–15.

3. Harriman, *I Reminisce*, 138–39; Richard Neuberger, "Snow Sport in Far West," *New York Times,* December 13, 1936.

4. Prescott Bush Oral History, 44.

5. Mickey Herskowitz, *Duty, Honor, Country: The Life and Legacy of Prescott Bush* (Nashville: Routledge Hill Press, 2003), chap. 3.

6. Jacob Weisberg, *The Bush Tragedy* (New York: Random House, 2008), chap. 1; Kitty Kelly, *The Family: The Real Story of the Bush Dynasty* (New York: Doubleday, 2004); Prescott Bush Oral History, passim.

7. Sally Bedell Smith, *In All His Glory: The Life of William S. Paley* (New York: Simon & Schuster, 1990).

8. Prescott Bush Oral History, passim.

9. BBH Papers, Box 23.

10. Prescott Bush Oral History, 16.

11. Kouwenhoven, *Partners in Banking*, 198–99.

12. "Scattered Wealth," BBH Papers, Box 46. Also, Peter Schweizer and Rochelle Schweizer, *The Bushes: Portrait of a Dynasty* (New York: Doubleday, 2004), 49–54.

13. "Shattered Health," BBH Papers, Box 46.

14. MacLeish and Campbell correspondence, BBH Papers, Box 62. Also, various correspondence between MacLeish and Lovett in Robert Lovett Papers, Yale University Manuscripts Division, Box 20.

15. Edward Sorel, "The Literati: Mr. and Mrs. Dorothy Parker's Arrival in Hollywood," *New York Times*, September 7, 2018.

CHAPTER 14: A CALL TO SERVICE

1. Edward Lockett, "Leave It to Lovett," *Collier's,* June 20, 1951.

2. "The Thirteenth Labor of Hercules: Part I and Part II," *The New Yorker,* November 6 and 13, 1943; "Secretary Lovett: Just the Man to Keep Things Going," *Newsweek,* September 24, 1951; "Undersecretary of State Lovett: First the World, Then the Cobwebs," *Time,* March 29, 1948.

3. Lovett to Roland Harriman, September 25, 1939, in Lovett Papers, Box 12.

4. Lovett to Harriman, July 26, 1940, in BBH Papers, Box 73, Folder 11.

5. Lovett Oral History, 111.

6. Isaacson and Thomas, *The Wise Men*, 180ff.; Lovett letter to Major MacIsaac, July 27, 1970, Lovett Papers, Box 20.

7. Kai Bird, *The Chairman: John J. McCloy and the Making of the American Establishment* (New York: Simon & Schuster, 1992).

8. Address by Robert Lovett at the University Club, October 2, 1941, in Lovett Papers, Box 31.

9. Lovett address, Mutual Broadcasting System, June 14, 1941, Lovett Papers, Box 31.

10. Lynne Olson, *Citizens of London: The Americans Who Stood with Britain in Its Darkest, Finest Hour* (New York: Random House, 2010); Abramson, *Spanning the Century*, 288ff.; John Daniel Langer, "The Harriman-Beaverbrook Mission and the Debate over Unconditional Aid for the Soviet Union, 1941," *Journal of Contemporary History* (July 1979), 463–82.

11. "The Thirteen Labor of Hercules," *The New Yorker*, November 13, 1943.

12. David M. Jordan, *Robert A. Lovett and the Development of American Air Power* (Jefferson, NC: McFarland, 2019).

13. Quoted in Lockett, "Leave It to Lovett."

14. Benn Steil, *The Battle of Bretton Woods: John Maynard Keynes, Harry Dexter White and the Making of a New World Order* (Princeton, NJ: Princeton University Press, 2013); Robert Divine, *Second Chance: The Triumph of Internationalism in America During World War II* (New York: Atheneum, 1967).

15. Gates McGarrah, "The First Six Months of the Bank for International Settlements," *Proceedings of the Academy of Political Science* (January 1931), 25–36; history of the BIS at https://www.bis.org/about/history_2ww2.htm.

16. Robert J. Donovan, *Conflict & Crisis: The Presidency of Harry S. Truman, 1945–1948* (Columbia, MO: University of Missouri Press, 1977), 42.

CHAPTER 15: THE WISE MEN

1. Lovett Memo, June 20, 1946, in Lovett Papers, Box 31.

2. On Kennan's life, see John Lewis Gaddis, *George Kennan: An American Life* (New York: Penguin Press, 2011). Also Gaddis, *Strategies of Containment: A Critical Appraisal of Postwar American National Security Policy* (New York: Oxford University Press, 1982); Melvyn Leffler, *A Preponderance of Power: National Security, the Truman Administration, and the Cold War* (Palo Alto, CA: Stanford University Press, 1992); Walter LaFeber, *America, Russia and the Cold War 1945–1992* (New York: McGraw Hill, 1993); Frank Costigliola, *Lost Alliances: How Personal Politics Helped Start the Cold War* (Princeton, NJ: Princeton University Press, 2012).

3. Daniel Kurtz-Phelan, *The China Mission: George Marshall's Unfinished War, 1945–1947* (New York: Norton, 2018); David Roll, *George Marshall: Defender of the Republic* (New York: Penguin, 2019); "Undersecretary of State Lovett," *Time*, March 29, 1948.

4. Robert Lovett Oral History Interview, July 7, 1971, Truman Library, Independence, MO, and https://www.trumanlibrary.gov/library/oral-histories/lovett; Isaacson and Thomas, *The Wise Men*, 417.

5. Dean Acheson, *Present at the Creation* (New York: Norton, 1969).

6. Benn Steil, *The Marshall Plan: Dawn of the Cold War* (New York: Simon & Schuster, 2018), 147ff.; Diane Kuntz, "The Marshall Plan Reconsidered: A Complex of Motives,"

Foreign Affairs, May–June 1997, 162–70; Benjamin Fordham, "Economic Interests, Party, and Ideology in Early Cold War Era U.S. Foreign Policy," *International Organization* (Spring 1998), 358–96; Greg Behrman, *The Most Noble Adventure: The Marshall Plan and the Time When America Helped Save Europe* (New York: Free Press, 2007); Michael J. Hogan, *The Marshall Plan* (Cambridge, UK: Cambridge University Press, 1987).

7. "An Evening with Averell Harriman," *Bulletin of the American Academy of Arts and Sciences* (January 1972), 2–18; Lovett on IBM machines in Lovett Oral History, Truman Library.

8. Lovett Oral History Interview, Truman Library.

9. Lawrence Kaplan, *NATO 1948: The Birth of the Transatlantic Alliance* (New York: Rowman & Littlefield, 2007); Jordan, *Robert Lovett and the Development of American Air Power*, 169–73.

10. Douglas Irwin, *Clashing Over Commerce: A History of US Trade Policy* (Chicago: University of Chicago Press, 2017), 470ff.; Joanne Gowa and Soo Yeon Kim, "An Exclusive Country Club: The Effects of the GATT on Trade, 1950–94," *World Politics* (July 2005), 453–78.

11. Thomas Zeiler, *Free Trade, Free World: The Advent of GATT* (Chapel Hill: University of North Carolina Press, 1999), 110ff.; Francine McKenzie, "GATT and the Cold War Accession Debates, Institutional Development, and the Western Alliance, 1947–1959," *Journal of Cold War Studies* (Summer 2008), 78–109; Lovett Oral History Interview with Winthrop Brown, May 25, 1973, Harry Truman Library, https://www.truman library.gov/library/oral-histories/brownwg.

12. Gaddis, *Strategies of Containment*, 108–10.

13. Lovett diner party remarks, February 20, 1950, in Lovett Papers, Box 32.

14. Beatrice Heuser, "NSC 68 and the Soviet Threat: A New Perspective on Western Threat Perception and Policy Making," *Review of International Studies* (January 1991), 17–40; Ernest May, *American Cold War Strategy: Interpreting NSC 68* (New York: St. Martin's Press, 1993).

CHAPTER 16: IN THE VALLEY

1. Duncan Norton-Taylor, "How Top Executives Live," *Fortune*, July 1955.

2. "The Fifty Niner" and firm publications in BBH Papers, Box 23.

3. Paul Heffernan, "Old Wall St. Firm Flies New Flag," *New York Times*, May 11, 1958.

4. Herskowitz, *Duty, Honor, Country*, 92; Kelly, *The Family*, passim.

5. Kelly, *The Family*, 197; Weisberg, chap. 1; Herskowitz, *Duty, Honor, Country*, chap. 9; Bush Oral History; "Alfalfa Club Names Bush," *New York Times*, January 18, 1959.

6. David Halberstam, *The Fifties* (New York: Villard Books, 1993), chap. 35.

7. E. Digby Baltzell, "Rich Men in Politics," *The Nation*, May 31, 1958.

8. Robert Lovett Oral History conducted for the John F. Kennedy Library, July 20, 1964, Part 1.

9. Robert Lovett Oral History for the Kennedy Library, August 17, 1964, Part 2.

10. Prescott Bush Oral History, 34; assorted Roosa files, BBH Papers, Box 76.

11. Henry Fairlie, "Evolution of a Term," *The New Yorker,* October 19, 1968; Arthur Schlesinger, *A Thousand Days: John F. Kennedy in the White House* (New York: Houghton, 1965), quoted in Isaacson and Thomas, *The Wise Men,* 29 and 676ff.

12. Thomas Lamont to Lovett, June 10, 1966, in Lovett Papers, Box 16; Todd Gitlin, *The Sixties: Years of Hope, Days of Rage* (New York: Bantam Books, 1987); Godfrey Hodgson, *America in Our Time: From World War II to Nixon—What Happened and Why* (New York: Doubleday, 1976).

13. John Brooks, "The Gentlemanly Junket," *The New Yorker,* April 26, 1969; assorted material, BBH Papers, Box 29.

14. "Brown Brothers Sesquicentennial: Roosa Multi-Nation Marshall Plan for Developing Nations," *Weekly Bond Buyer,* September 23, 1968.

15. BBH Papers, Box 29.

16. *Weekly Bond Buyer,* September 23, 1968; "Bankers Say U.S. Dollar Is Still as Good as Gold," *Newsday,* September 17, 1968.

17. Charlotte Curtis, "Brown Brothers Harriman, of All People, Give a Party," *New York Times,* October 10, 1968.

18. H. Erich Heinemann, "Brown Brothers, at Age 150, Grows with Care," *New York Times,* September 15, 1968.

CHAPTER 17: WHEN IS ENOUGH ENOUGH?

1. Connie Bruck, *The Predator's Ball: The Inside Story of Drexel Burnham and the Rise of the Junk Bond Raiders* (New York: Penguin, 1988), 26ff.; Terry Robards, "Firestone Tire to Buy 25% of Drexel," *New York Times,* December 4, 1970.

2. For a nice summary of these developments, see https://history.state.gov/milestones /1969-1976/nixon-shock. Also, James Ledbetter, *One Nation Under Gold: How One Precious Metal Has Dominated the American Imagination for Four Centuries* (New York: Liveright, 2017); Mervyn King, *The End of Alchemy: Money, Banking and the Future of the Global Economy* (New York: Norton, 2018), 70ff.

3. Eric Weiner, *What Goes Up: The Uncensored History of Modern Wall Street* (New York: Little, Brown, 2005), 210ff.

4. Jesse Kornbluth, *Highly Confident: The Crime and Punishment of Michael Milken* (New York: William Morrow, 1992). Full disclosure: I was an unpaid nonresident fellow at the Milken Institute in the 2000s and know Milken passingly.

5. Leslie Wayne, "Going Public on Wall Street," *New York Times,* January 27, 1986.

6. Conversation with the author.

INDEX